COMPARING FAITHFULLY

COMPARATIVE THEOLOGY: THINKING ACROSS TRADITIONS

Loye Ashton and John Thatamanil, *Series Editors*

This series invites books that engage in constructive comparative theological reflection that draws from the resources of more than one religious tradition. It offers a venue for constructive thinkers, from a variety of religious traditions (or thinkers belonging to more than one), who seek to advance theology understood as "deep learning" across religious traditions.

COMPARING FAITHFULLY

Insights for Systematic
Theological Reflection

MICHELLE VOSS ROBERTS, EDITOR

Fordham University Press NEW YORK 2016

Copyright © 2016 Fordham University Press

All rights reserved. No part of this publication may be reproduced, stored in a retrieval system, or transmitted in any form or by any means—electronic, mechanical, photocopy, recording, or any other—except for brief quotations in printed reviews, without the prior permission of the publisher.

"A Case of You": Words and Music by JONI MITCHELL. Copyright © 1971 (Renewed) CRAZY CROW MUSIC. All Rights Administered by SONY/ATV MUSIC PUBLISHING, 8 Music Square West, Nashville, TN 37203. Exclusive Print Rights Administered by ALFRED MUSIC. All Rights Reserved. Used By Permission of ALFRED MUSIC.

Excerpts from *Longing and Letting Go* by Hillgardner, Holly (2016). By permission of Oxford University Press, USA.

Fordham University Press has no responsibility for the persistence or accuracy of URLs for external or third-party Internet websites referred to in this publication and does not guarantee that any content on such websites is, or will remain, accurate or appropriate.

Fordham University Press also publishes its books in a variety of electronic formats. Some content that appears in print may not be available in electronic books.

Visit us online at www.fordhampress.com.

Library of Congress Cataloging-in-Publication Data

Names: Voss Roberts, Michelle, editor.
Title: Comparing faithfully : insights for systematic theological reflection / Michelle Voss Roberts, editor.
Description: First edition. | New York, NY : Fordham University Press, 2016. | Series: Comparative theology: thinking across traditions | Includes bibliographical references and index.
Identifiers: LCCN 2016016997 | ISBN 9780823274666 (cloth : alk. paper) | ISBN 9780823274673 (pbk. : alk. paper)
Subjects: LCSH: Christianity and other religions. | Theology.
Classification: LCC BR127 .C587 2016 | DDC 261.2—dc23
LC record available at https://lccn.loc.gov/2016016997

Printed in the United States of America

18 17 16   5 4 3 2 1

First edition

CONTENTS

Introduction: A Place for Comparative Theology in Christian Systematic Reflection 1
MICHELLE VOSS ROBERTS

I Divinity

1   The Dance of Emptiness: A Constructive Comparative Theology of the Social Trinity 23
JON PAUL SYDNOR

2   Flower and Song: A Comparative Study on Teotlizing in Aztec Theology and Karl Rahner's View of Divine Self-Disclosure 46
ELAINE PADILLA

3   Comparative Theology and the Postmodern God of "Perhaps": A Response to Sydnor and Padilla 66
KRISTIN BEISE KIBLINGER

II Theodicy

4   Developing Christian Theodicy in Conversation with Navid Kermani 89
KLAUS VON STOSCH

5   Like a Dog's Curly Tail: Finding Perfection in a World of Imperfection: A Hindu Theodicy in the Tradition of Sri Ramakrishna 107
JEFFERY D. LONG

6   "Only Goodness Matters": Reflections on Theodicy with Klaus von Stosch and Jeffery Long 126
WENDY FARLEY

III Humanity

7 Longing and Letting Go: Lessons in Being Human from Hadewijch and Mirabai 149
HOLLY HILLGARDNER

8 Women's Virtue, Church Leadership, and the Problem of Gender Complementarity 171
TRACY SAYUKI TIEMEIER

9 Longing and Gender: A Response to Holly Hillgardner and Tracy Sayuki Tiemeier 185
AMIR HUSSAIN

IV Christology

10 What Child Is This? Jesus, Lord Lao, and Divine Identity 195
BEDE BENJAMIN BIDLACK

11 Who Is the Suffering Servant? A Comparative Theological Reading of Isaiah 53 after the Shoah 216
MARIANNE MOYAERT

12 Response: Christology in Comparative Perspective 238
HUGH NICHOLSON

V Soteriology

13 The Way(s) of Salvation: The Function of the Law in John Calvin and Abu Hamid al-Ghazali 255
JOSHUA RALSTON

14 Sleeper, Awake: Considering the Soteriological Promise of Popular Spiritual Gurus 274
SHARON V. BETCHER

15 Salvation in the After-Living: Reflections on Salvation with Joshua Ralston and Sharon Betcher 296
SHELLY RAMBO

List of Contributors 317

Index 321

COMPARING FAITHFULLY

Introduction: A Place for Comparative Theology in Christian Systematic Reflection

Michelle Voss Roberts

The North American religious context is changing. If, in recent generations, the dominant Protestant Christianity came to terms first with Catholicism and then again with Judaism and Islam as fellow "Abrahamic" faiths, today the pluralism within public, intellectual, and family life is even more evident. Many Christians are curious about this reality and open to learning about it. They are encountering religious diversity and evaluating their beliefs and practices in light of it.

Each generation of theologians must respond to its context by rearticulating the central insights of the faith. Christian thinkers have always made reference to the cultures and schools of thought that surround them, but there seems to be something momentous about this place and time. Diana Butler Bass believes that Christianity is in the midst of a deep transformation of the sort that happens, at most, every few hundred years. Just as Francis of Assisi tapped into the spirit of his age to bring about a shift in Christianity toward spirituality, simplicity, and preaching, leaders today are rising to respond to popular distaste for rigid institutional exclusions and a growing hunger for spiritual depth.[1] For movements such as the Interfaith Youth Core, the world's religious traditions seem to make better partners than competitors in this transformation.

Christian theological educators have responded to this growing interest in interreligious understanding, dialogue, and cooperation in a variety of ways. They have become aware that religious leaders are often asked questions about the rituals, beliefs, and sanctity of religious neighbors for which superficial knowledge of these traditions is insufficient. They have begun to draw on the important literature that has emerged related to the most effective methods for teaching and learning about other faiths.[2] Some seminary curricula require a course in another religious tradition; other theological schools are considering how to integrate what is learned in such courses into a larger program of preparing students for ministries with persons of diverse faith backgrounds.[3]

In Christian systematic theology, the theology of religious pluralism (or theology of religions) has emerged as a doctrine alongside other loci of Christian inquiry. Because each doctrine impacts the others, theologians are beginning to consider the systematic implications of religious pluralism for the full range of Christian doctrine.[4] Similar reflection is taking place in other religious communities. The contributors to this volume consider how to do this important theological work in their own traditions and offer examples of doctrinal reflection in light of the diversity of religious insights.

Comparative theology is one development in which the form of theology is beginning to embody the ecumenical spirit of this moment. This emerging field is defined by James Fredericks as "the branch of systematic theology which seeks to interpret the Christian tradition conscientiously in conversation with the texts and symbols of non-Christian religions."[5] Leading thinkers in this discipline employ a method of close, careful reading of religious texts in order to return to one's own tradition with new lenses, new categories, and new questions. Sensitivity to particularities replaces sweeping generalizations about religions. The scope is deep rather than broad: The theologian often chooses from among the internal diversity of a tradition to study a single thinker, text, or practice. The faith commitments of the theologian enter into a dialogue with the chosen exemplar, and the theologian then returns to particular texts and thinkers in her own tradition in light of this learning. The back-and-forth motion of comparison is prolonged and its effects subtle.

This discipline has the potential to enrich systematic theology and, by extension, theological education, at its foundations. Toward this purpose, and as a resource for pastors and theology students, *Comparing Faithfully: Insights for Systematic Theological Reflection* reconsiders five central areas of Christian doctrinal reflection in light of focused interreligious readings.

Why Not?

A volume like this one has been slow in coming. Its premise is simple: Christian theology occurs in a multi-religious world, and serious study of Christian theology should be mindful of this context. David Tracy wagered in his 1988 Dondyne Lectures that "we are fast approaching the day when it will not be possible to attempt a Christian systematic theology except in serious conversation with the other great ways."[6] Although it might take another generation or two to develop this systematic theology, he thought, interreligious dialogue must impact Christian self-understanding.[7] More than twenty-five years after this call, the number of theologians who seriously engage traditions other than their own has grown significantly. Nevertheless, there are strong reasons that this volume has not yet been written.

One of the biggest obstacles to constructive comparative theology is erected by Christians who hold an exclusivist view of non-Christian religions and maintain that traditions that do not profess the central and salvific role of Jesus Christ contain nothing but error or, at very least, do not contain enough truth or grace to mediate salvation. Other reservations come from those who say that religions *cannot* be compared. For them, religions are like languages: Their differing grammars and vocabulary make them incommensurable. Comparing Christianity and Islam is like comparing apples to automobiles. Still others say that religions *should not* be compared, especially by Christians in the West, in light of the colonialist, imperialist, and capitalist consumption of the resources of the global East and South for the past four centuries.[8] Comparison has also been attacked as an arbitrary and sloppy method—more like magic than science—that substitutes the scholar's imaginative perceptions of similarity for useful theory.[9]

Comparative theologians respond to these reservations in various ways. Some articulate inclusive views of religious truth; some sidestep final evaluations of other traditions entirely. Some argue that human beings can understand one another across cultures through shared rational, affective, or embodied capacities. Others employ methods of comparison that highlight power dynamics and are accountable to insiders of the traditions they study. Still others contribute greater clarity about the limits and objectives of comparison.

Perhaps the most important reasons that a volume of constructive essays in comparative theology has not yet appeared, however, come from within comparative theology itself. When Francis X. Clooney carved out a space for comparative reading between his theological training and his intensive study of Hindu traditions in the 1990s, his stated goals for comparative theology were modest, and its practices circumscribed. Few people, he recognized, would be able to acquire language training, have time to read another tradition's texts intensively, and be vulnerable to transformation through such a process. At that time, religious communities for whom comparative reading could be a central practice did not exist. It was also important, he counseled, not to rush to new statements of theological truth. Instead, comparativists should patiently continue in the process of reading and rereading the texts, an activity that is irreducible to any insights a reader might glean.[10]

The field has shifted in some ways. Today, because students of theology in North America live and breathe in the context of religious diversity, they are already forming their identities in relation to it. Initially, comparative work seemed a solitary and unusual endeavor, but as it has endured, communities have emerged around it. Scholarly gatherings, such as the Society for Hindu-Christian Studies, have become venues for collaboration as well as appreciative audiences for the fruits of comparison.[11] The practice of scriptural reasoning, in which practitioners of different traditions meet to study common scriptural texts, has also become a vibrant academic and spiritual pursuit.[12]

Comparative theologians have diversified and refined their methods of engagement, but the premise remains the same: Deep understanding of another religious tradition can fruitfully inform the understanding of one's own faith. Clooney now argues persuasively that comparative theological learning can be an "ordinary part of theological education."[13] Students can employ the same basic skills that they use elsewhere in theological study—reading primary texts, analyzing, comparing, and synthesizing—to learn about other traditions. There are more resources for engaging this process than ever before.

Predecessors in Constructive Comparison

This volume follows a number of pioneers in comparative modes of theologizing. Some of these predecessors arrive at comparison through work in theologies of religious pluralism. Theologians on this trajectory have moved from thinking theologically *about* religious others to thinking *with* them. In the *Faith Meets Faith* series from Orbis Books, for example, prominent theologians such as Leonard Swidler, John Hick, Paul Knitter, Aloysius Pieris, and Harold Coward consider, often with reference to the teachings and practices of other traditions, how Christians should assess traditions other than their own. The question of whether and how other traditions participate in God's revelatory and reconciling work is paramount. James Fredericks nudges this series in a comparative direction. Building on his argument that such meta-questions can get in the way of actual engagement with others,[14] he brackets them in favor of the search for greater understanding of religious neighbors. Rather than seeking to resolve the issue of Buddhism's truth or place in the Christian scheme of salvation, he asks, "How can Christians become more skillful in learning from Buddhists?"[15]

In this first trajectory toward the development of comparative theology, considerations of the general theological status of religious pluralism have given way to the more modest and engaged inquiry into the specifics of another religious tradition. This development illustrates the emergence of related but distinct fields: *dialogue* as gathering in person to discuss topics from different faith perspectives; *theology of religious pluralism* as the assessment of the truth or efficacy of other religions; and *comparative theology* as a prolonged study of another tradition, in which the process of understanding is primary and any conclusions secondary and provisional.

A second trajectory that informs this volume moves in the opposite direction, from the in-depth knowledge of religious traditions typical of the academic field of *comparative religion* toward normative, constructive theology. Forerunners in this trajectory tend to write in a creative, unfettered, and global manner. Raimon Panikkar, for example, offers comprehensive visions of reality out of his formation by Christianity, Hinduism, and Buddhism. He calls this work "intrareligious dialogue," a dialogue that occurs *within* an individual in whom multiple faith traditions meet.[16] Anglican theologian Keith Ward enlists perspectives from four religious traditions as well as modern scientific materialism to advance a systematic theological agenda. In a four-volume project on revelation, creation, human nature, and community, he aims to survey textual and living representatives of these traditions, to "convey authoritatively" what they believe, and then to "develop a Christian view which is sensitive and responsive to the concerns which the other traditions express."[17] These two theologians' contributions precede the current focus on close textual reading, yet their efforts to articulate a *constructive* theological method anticipate those of this volume.

These two trajectories—from Christian theological reflection on other religions toward disciplined comparison, and from knowledge of other traditions toward constructive theological reflection—converge in comparative theology. From both directions, theologians are searching for a way to hold religious commitments together with an appreciation of religious diversity.

The convergence of these concerns is also the site of a stringent critique: In both trajectories, Christian theology apparently holds the trump card. While this may be the unavoidable effect of situatedness of thought (everybody is somewhere), it also mirrors an uncomfortable legacy of Christian hegemony in academic studies of religion.

The Problem of Hegemony

Hugh Nicholson's genealogy of comparative theology shows a history in which Christian theologians unwittingly re-inscribe biases and exclusions toward other religions in the very attempt to overcome them. Nineteenth-century liberal theologians, for example, classify other faiths in a scheme of salvation through a distinction between "world religions," those that achieve a universal scope by transcending their particular cultures, and "natural religions," which do not. These writings then take back with one hand what they have given with the other, when they "proceed to challenge the universalistic claims of [the others], concluding rather predictably that Christianity alone merits the title of 'world religion,' that it is, in other words, the one religion which, by virtue of its inherent qualities, meets the religious needs of all humanity."[18] Nicholson finds a pattern of similar binary oppositions woven through the development of comparative theology and suggests that the binary of "theology of religions" and "comparative theology" is the latest iteration, with the latter again claiming the way forward beyond Christianity's exclusive past.[19] Comparative theology has thus emerged in the North American academy in the crucible of tensions between commitment to the truth of one tradition and openness to the truths of others.

In response to the problems of Christian and scholarly hegemony, diverse orientations and goals have surfaced among scholars who wish to continue their comparative efforts. Two influential scholars who have shaped North American approaches to comparison, though through different methods and toward different ends, are Francis X. Clooney and Robert Cummings Neville.

As noted previously, Clooney's comparative theology attempts to avoid the hegemonic exercise of power by choosing not to make constructive doctrinal claims on the basis of comparison. Clooney insists that whatever truths are to be found through comparative reading are in the process of reading itself, and that the process of immersion in religious texts of another tradition cannot be short-circuited. Furthermore, the very notion of "a tradition" must be broken down into the distinct points of view of its sub-schools, its influential thinkers, and even particular texts and their commentaries. The scholar therefore speaks not of "the Hindu tradition" or "the Christian tradition" but of particular lineages of reading and practice. In Clooney's recent books, he describes the nature of the transformation that occurs through comparison in affective rather than intellectual, propositional, or doctrinal terms. The comparative reader emerges not with a new set of truths but with an increasing *awareness* of one's particular religious commitments, alongside equally attractive and intense commitments held by others. A comparative theology thus becomes "dramatically charged and unsettled writing, irreducible to any tidy conclusions about the world or anything in it."[20]

By contrast to Clooney's focused, particular, and cautious process of reading, Neville's comparative theological work takes a broadly philosophical approach. Over the course of four academic years (1995–1999), he convened the Comparative Religious Ideas Project with scholars of six major world religions. The resulting volumes survey these traditions' perspectives on *Religious Truth*, *The Human Condition*, and *Ultimate Realities*. The contributors identify major themes within each topic for the religion they study, and Neville concludes each volume with reflections upon what can be learned about these topics through comparing these positions. The project's purpose is to test "the plausibility and relative importance" of the "vague categories" that frame the comparisons.[21] For example, the group's yearlong study of the human condition resulted in a further refinement of this category into cosmological, personal, and social dimensions, each with further subthemes.[22] While some might charge that the data of diverse traditions resist categorization, and that the imposition of categories constitutes an act of hegemony, Neville and his coeditor Wesley Wildman argue that because scholars inevitably bring categories to bear on new data, it is better to be explicit about these categories and revise them accordingly.[23]

A tension between orientations is visible within the Comparative Religious Ideas Project, pointing to wider debates among comparativists. The project brought together "generalists," who hoped to reach consensus on the conclusions of the group's comparisons, and "specialists" like Clooney and Paula Fredricksen (a scholar of early Christianity), who "resisted characterizations of their traditions as a whole, or even large chunks of their traditions" and restricted their claims to particular texts or historical periods.[24] The 2014 conference on "Methods and Criteria in Comparative Theology" in Paderborn, Germany, invited North American comparativists to consider still other approaches. The comparative theology program at the University of Paderborn, directed by Klaus von Stosch, tends to take dogmatic theological questions as the starting point for comparison. These scholars grant a large role to philosophy in justifying the work of comparison. They also place great emphasis on interpersonal collaboration, as the Muslims and Christians in the department each advance their constructive theologies through conversation with one another.[25]

The instructive point of this survey is not to set up new methodological absolutes, but to frame the range of organizing frameworks out of which this volume emerges. Some scholars retain a characteristically modern optimism in their attempts to discern theological truth in the presence of religious others. Others, beginning with a postmodern recognition of the situated and culturally contingent nature of knowledge, limit both their claims to have mastered another tradition and their judgments upon it. Each of these contemporary orientations, however, exhibits awareness of the needs to avoid generalizations and cultural stereotypes, to understand traditions in terms recognizable to practitioners, and to acknowledge the location and norms of the comparativist.[26]

The Approach of This Volume

Collectively, the intellectual genealogies of the contributors to this volume owe much to the approaches just described.[27] Like the Comparative Religious Ideas Project, this group of scholars has chosen categories for reflection across traditions with the intent of refining them, but the individual chapters have much in common with Clooney's methodology in that they focus on particular texts or thinkers rather than represent traditions as a whole. Taking an approach that is both particular and provisional, the essays do not purport to draw conclusions from a comprehensive survey of traditions.

The volume's destination differs from its predecessors as well. It aims at the transformation of neither the comparative reader alone, nor the academic study of religion, but the contemporary practice of theology. "How," Clooney asks in *Theology after Vedanta*, "does one get beyond reading, in order to know and state persuasively one's views about the world that exists outside texts?" Every reader emerges from the text into a larger world of meaning. The contributors of this collection aim to take up Clooney's question, as he cautions, "only in a properly consequent fashion, as truly after comparison, and not merely as the restatement of an earlier position."[28] Even though none of the contributors claims to have exhausted his or her studies, each finds it useful to pause and reflect on the categories, questions, and thinkers encountered thus far. More than a disinterested academic exercise, comparison can inform the meaning making of religious thinkers. This work therefore contributes to a growing body of constructive theology arising out of multiple traditions.[29] It risks normative theological reflection, but in a manner that is creatively unsettled in the company of other comparative possibilities.

Our title, *Comparing Faithfully*, highlights our intent to be faithful to multiple constituencies. As theologians, we undertake this work in the spirit of the Anselmian definition of theology as "faith seeking understanding." A theologian begins her quest shaped by a community or tradition—or sometimes more than one—kindled by the desire to connect its foundations to every aspect of life. Committed to these guiding principles, the comparative theologian also aims to be faithful to religious neighbors in the sense that a portrait aims to give a faithful rendering of its subject. Descriptions of another tradition should give an accurate and truthful portrayal that is recognizable to its members. Although the relation between these commitments can be complex (leading some, perhaps, to consider this project only comparatively faithful!), both are integral to the success of this constructive work.

The format of this volume is dialogical: Multivocality is the centerpiece of its approach. Each section of the book considers a major theological topic from several comparative angles. The sections start with two comparative essays, each of which engages in careful reading of two thinkers or texts. Each pair of comparative essays then receives a response by a third theologian. Because comparative work must be accountable to diverse communities, the respondents play several roles. They might verify or falsify the representations of traditions presented, but as theologians, they also reflect upon the constructive possibilities raised in the essays. It is perhaps easy to appreciate a single instance of comparison, but what should one make of radically different comparisons, on a single issue, placed side by side? This format is not intended to capsulize a set of doctrinal conclusions. Instead, it invites readers into a disciplined manner of thinking theologically in relation to the religious diversity that surrounds them. Although these offerings are the products of the authors' own transformations, which will not necessarily be replicated within the reader, they nevertheless invite a communal dimension to this work insofar as others will join this work as part of their own theological training.

Beyond this general shared destination, the authors in this volume hold varying definitions of comparative theology and therefore represent varying methodological possibilities. The variety of approaches to comparison taken here reflects the dynamism of the discipline. The volume includes Christian reflections on engagement with Hindu, Buddhist, Jewish, Muslim, Jain, and Confucian traditions; but it also stretches comparative theology beyond so-called "world religions" to consider a Mesoamerican indigenous tradition (Padilla) and a contemporary "spiritual but not religious" teacher (Betcher). In addition to essays that consider major, canonical thinkers in religious traditions (Sydnor, Bidlack, Ralston), several consider voices from the margins of these traditions (Hillgardner, Tiemeier) and twentieth-century voices worthy of greater attention (von Stosch, Long, Moyaert).

The contributors take various stances within these traditions. While some do comparative work for the sake of particular communities (primarily Christian denominations), others situate themselves somewhat marginally in relation to a religious tradition; still others, viewing religious identity as fluid and multiple, would be unwilling to claim the audience of their contribution as one community over another. Each, however, vigorously engages in the "faith seeking understanding" that marks theological activity as such.

The volume is further enriched by reflections from outside the Christian tradition. Contributions by Jeffery Long, a Hindu theologian, and Amir Hussain, a Muslim theologian, introduce the reader to the fruits of the discipline of comparison that are emerging outside Christianity. Their essays model solid methods of constructive comparative theology in the manner in which they read, represent, appreciate, critique, and constructively engage Christianity. Readers will also benefit from the content of their proposals. As Long has noted, for some traditions, it simply makes good sense to do constructive theology through comparison: In his neo-Vedanta lineage, "the sharing and attempted co-ordination of our various pieces of the puzzle . . . in order to expand and deepen our own understanding" is what theology is all about.[30] Rita Sherma has similarly remarked, "the 'Other' is not just an object of study, but also a subject from whom I can learn"; their ideas might be possible "for [my] own worldview."[31] Theology expands when it engages a wider community.

Although most of the authors pose Christian questions to texts from other traditions, and the topical schematic follows a pattern engrained within Christian systematic theology, the contributions of Long and Hussain show that theological questions can (and should!) come from both directions. Occasionally, Christians read texts in comparative work that pose these questions themselves, as when Islamic texts address Christian ideas, but today theologians can engage colleagues of various faiths in close proximity. These colleagues can hold Christians accountable in their representations of their traditions. New conversation partners also introduce options that may not otherwise come to mind, as when Amir Hussain asks readers to consider aesthetic dimensions of Islam as a "third" alongside the Christian and Indic traditions in the essays to which he responds. The contributors have discovered, both in person and in ongoing correspondence, that doing theology in the presence of others both destabilizes theological practice and holds it accountable. The book is better for it.

How to Use This Book

Religious diversity can be daunting. The sheer number of religious traditions, each of which has its own special gestures and vocabulary, is enough to make religious recluses of everyone, yet the demands of neighborliness beckon beyond superficial familiarity. The good news is that any student of theology who can read can also engage in comparative study.[32] This volume provides several points of entry: 1) as a way into Christian systematic theology; 2) as a way to test theological categories; 3) as a series of proposals for doctrinal reflection; and 4) as an invitation to the reader to take up the activity of comparative reading.

AS A WAY INTO CHRISTIAN SYSTEMATIC THEOLOGY

Many theology curricula engage religious diversity only marginally, as context for the study of particular historical moments or doctrinal developments within Christianity, or as a separate elective that is not integrated with the rest of the curriculum. This situation must change if theological education is to reflect the world in which students live and minister.

The essays in this volume offer a way to integrate religious diversity into the introductory study of theology. One or more of the essays in each section could be used as a "comparative moment" as students study particular doctrinal themes. When seminary students consider the traditional loci of God, evil, the human person, Christ, and salvation alongside the theological reflection of religious neighbors, they may see aspects of those teachings anew.

A reader sensitive to the history of Christian triumphalism may further use these essays as models of how to engage the pluralistic context with a spirit of mutual appreciation and respect. The process of understanding another religious point of view is at least as important as any resulting insights or changes in doctrine. Theology remains the process of "faith seeking understanding," but with the recognition that the search for understanding includes diverse conversations.

AS A WAY TO TEST CATEGORIES

The titles of the book's five sections reflect traditional Christian ways of thinking about systematic theology. Clearly, divinity, theodicy, the human being, Christology, and soteriology do not frame the intellectual reflection of every religious tradition. "Divinity," for example, is not a prominent category for many Buddhists, and "Christology" is far more specific a category than "divine embodiment," which would apply to a greater number of traditions. The five categories also do not cover the entire field. Other Christian doctrines such as creation, sin, church, and eschatology, as well as focal categories from other traditions such as "covenant" in Jewish theology would make excellent topics for comparative study.

This group of theologians ultimately settled on these five traditional Christian categories for the pragmatic purpose of opening interreligious comparison to a broader audience by demonstrating its usefulness for theological study. These topics offer an entry point for Christian systematic theologians, who might otherwise be tempted to neglect these conversations, as well as for new students, who come to Christian theology out of a religiously diverse world.

Although the five sections are recognizable as relatively stable loci in Christian doctrine, the essays ask the reader to test them against alternative ways of imagining them. The headings proposed for each section neither confirm particular doctrinal positions nor solidify new ones. The work of naming is provisional, ongoing, and dependent on the comparisons at hand. The arc of conversation certainly could have led this group to narrow or broaden its categories. The reader is therefore encouraged to examine these choices: Do the categories seem arbitrary? Are they responsive to the data? Do the confessional commitments of the authors obscure other possibilities? Do they reify similarity where difference should predominate, or vice versa?[33] From the relatively stable starting point of traditional loci, then, comparative conversation may transform how readers frame their own theological inquiry.

AS VALID THEOLOGICAL OPTIONS

All theology, like all attempts to understand religious others, must be an ongoing and unfinished labor. In this spirit, these essays forge ahead with initial outlines of what some of the classical loci might look like after sustained dialogue with particular traditions. The result of this collaborative work is not a single system, but a sampling of nodes of conversation that have formed around particular theological concepts, flowered in the authors' imaginations, and begun to bear the fruit of insight.

The lack of a single center is intentional: This volume embodies the fact that the great "system" of Christian theology has always been less centered than some would like to believe. It is, and it always has been, an unruly and rhizomatic venture. Hybrid varieties of Christian theology have flourished across time and place, in varying historical circumstances, with different conversation partners, and through the personal idiosyncrasies of various theologians. Comparison is nothing new to the theological endeavor. These essays therefore offer not only Christian doctrinal possibilities, but also examples of a theological method that readers may already employ to greater or lesser degrees. They invite Christian theologians to become explicit, intellectually rigorous, and unashamed about the impact of interreligious conversation on their thinking.

The third essay in each section, which responds to two comparative pieces, models for the reader how a theologian might reflect more widely on the options presented. The reader should also take up the role of respondent and observe patterns that emerge *across* sections. For example, many of the contributors emphasize the significance of the present world for the doctrines at hand by stressing divine immanence, lived wisdom, and a concern for the earth. Systematically, then, these essays reflect a shift away from transcendent or otherworldly approaches to theological loci. Because each doctrine holds implications for others, readers may also notice, for example, how considerations of evil and of the human being point back to nature of God considered in the first section, or what the scriptural titles applied to Jesus in the Christology section imply about salvation, which is treated in the final part.

AS ENCOURAGEMENT TO DO IT YOURSELF

This volume invites readers to extend ordinary methods of theological study—reading, considering historical perspectives, entering imaginatively into a world other than one's own, and assimilating information—to a wider set of conversation partners. Religious diversity does not belong to a remote corner of theological praxis. The challenges and possibilities cannot be exhausted in occasional public dialogues or in-house debates about religious pluralism,[34] but they must be brought into the center of theological reflection itself.

Every aspect of every tradition, and its significance for constructive Christian theology, cannot be represented in one volume. This volume's limitations are invitations for others to take up its work. Ideally, students who read this book will embrace a practice of comparative reading. They will follow their interests, choose a text from another tradition, take time to read it, understand its terms and context, and discover how it is used and understood within that tradition. Additional depth and rigor can be attained by studying the text's original language, but the wealth of scriptural and theological texts available in translation make this practice a much wider possibility. Returning to the thinkers, beliefs, and practices of the traditions that formed them, diligent students will notice resonances and tensions between what they read and what they bring with them to the texts. Sustained practice of this back-and-forth pattern will offer new questions and categories for reflection and subtly transform not only the reader, but the practice of theology as well.

The particularity of this process is one of the gifts of comparison. The individual reader and the distinct texts and practices studied will interact in unpredictable ways. As readers of this volume take up comparison as a practice, their work will produce further examples that deepen and complicate the portraits sketched here. Within Christian theology, numerous traditional loci remain to be discussed, as well as new loci emerging in the field (such as empire and economy, to name only two). Other hermeneutical perspectives (ordained, monastic, queer, psychoanalytic, ethnographic) promise to enrich the conversation as it unfolds. Theologians of different traditions and theologians who identify with multiple traditions will diversify the conversation as well. All such contributions are to be desired.

Overview

These modes of constructive engagement can be observed in the following essays, as each author takes up the task of comparison to consider possibilities within the doctrines of his or her tradition.

Throughout this work, the process of comparison opens new points of entry into familiar topics. Part I, "Divinity," places Trinitarian notions of divinity alongside Buddhist notions of emptiness (Sydnor) and Mesoamerican articulations of divine immanence and multiplicity (Padilla), with the result that any title seems inadequate for the dynamism and diversity of experience named with this category-beyond-categories. In Part II, "Theodicy," interreligious reflection directs the conversation to favor pastoral, pragmatic responses that are nevertheless clear about their tensions and limits (von Stosch, Long). When Part III, "Humanity," turns to theological anthropology, something remarkable happens: In contrast to its androcentric framing in much of the theological tradition, women's experiences infuse the character of human existence with embodiment, social relations (Tiemeier), and desire (Hillgardner). The comparative norm of focusing on particular voices and texts allows these perspectives to emerge because the authors refuse to speak about humanity as a generic, somehow disembodied whole. Part IV, "Christology," makes familiar titles of Christ strange by placing the names of divine saviors in their polemical contexts (Bidlack) with, in the case of the "suffering servant," a radically destabilizing effect (Moyaert). Part V, "Soteriology," retrieves dimensions of salvation that have been neglected after substitutionary atonement and postmortem destiny became the focus for Christian theologians. Beyond the calculus of crucifixion, the essays rehabilitate a role for law as a salvific path (Ralston) and tend to the urgent needs for pain relief that drive the spiritual search for many (Betcher). Comparison prompts the reader to re-envision each of these topics in light of encounters with other faith traditions.

The response essays interact with these diverse comparative projects as valid options for constructive theology. Kristin Kiblinger's answer to the shimmering play of divine immanence, transcendence, multiplicity, and apophasis in Part I calls upon John Caputo's notion of "weak theism" to imagine a shape for belief in the face of diversity. Wendy Farley's response to Part II observes that differences between traditions mirror differences within them. For her, the comparisons bring into relief tensions that beset Christian and Muslim theologians alike: How can the deep, formative insights of theodical thinking resist the temptation toward violence? Amir Hussain's reply to Part III delves into the aesthetic dimensions of the two comparative essays on theological anthropology and adds additional resonance to the songs they discuss through comparisons with Islamic mysticism. Hugh Nicholson's response to the Christology essays in Part IV highlights the role of polemic in the formation of doctrine. Recognizing its inevitability, he encourages Christians to take responsibility for the injuries of the past and to engage in contrast without denigrating religious others. As Shelly Rambo reflects on the essays in Part V, she observes the shifting location of salvation within the landscape of Christian systematic theology. Because the comparative reflections in this section of the book direct us to think about salvation as a life of transformation rather than postmortem ends, they have introduced additional doctrinal topics of reflection: pneumatology and eschatology. Rambo does not let comparativists off the hook regarding endings, but creatively reworks eschatology "as the arena of Christian thought that guides and instructs its students in how to live in the midst of uncertainty about endings."

This kind of systematic thinking will be enriched by noticing how the enlarged theological conversation prevents easy alliances and generalizations. As Amir Hussain notes in his essay, the addition of a third (or fourth, or fifth) interlocutor can unsettle binary thinking; it can also unsettle agreement. For example, while social trinitarian thinking may work well for Sydnor's comparison, it would be less congenial for most Jewish or Muslim interlocutors. Similarly, the two Christology essays sit uneasily next to one another: Bidlack's comparison between divine children works remarkably well, whereas Moyaert's comparison makes Christian use of the suffering servant motif almost untenable. Each of these junctures marks the nature of theology, "faith seeking understanding," as situated, expansive, and perpetually incomplete.

Onward

Much has been made among comparativists of John Dunne's metaphor of "passing over" into another tradition and "passing back" into one's own. Catherine Cornille describes the importance of the return journey: "Interreligious dialogue ... is not complete without a return to the tradition from which one entered it, now offering the fruits of the dialogue to that original tradition as a whole, by way of a process of discernment that transcends individual judgment."[35] This return expresses the commitment of the theologian to his or her tradition, but Cornille emphasizes that the religious tradition must also demonstrate commitment *to those who engage in dialogue* by being receptive to their new insights.[36] Openness to growth and change are the marks of a vibrant community that will inspire continued commitment amid experiences of religious difference. Without such openness, communities are in danger of the idolatry that equates particular, local articulations of theological truth with the truth itself.

Although the authors of this volume differ with regard to criteria for discernment of truth, they agree that their home traditions should not look the other way when its scholars engage in interreligious understanding. This book is offered in the hope that faith traditions will not simply tolerate the individual transformation of its theologians, but that the traditions might similarly be transformed. The places from which the student leaves, to which she travels, and to which he returns, are always changing. May the reader undertake the journey with a spirit of both adventure and fidelity.

Acknowledgments

This collaborative work is the outcome of "The Promise of Religious Pluralism" conference at Wake Forest University School of Divinity in the spring of 2014. The generous support of the Provost's office, the Humanities Institute, the Departments of Religion and Philosophy, and the School of Divinity at Wake Forest University made this gathering possible. Dean Franco and Michaelle Browers offered valuable interdisciplinary responses from the fields of literature and politics. Aaron Langenfeld, Jay Ford, Nelly van Doorn-Harder, and Neal Walls also contributed to the collegiality of the conversation. The students of Michelle Voss Roberts's comparative theology seminar challenged the group with their responses to the essays, and Lindsey Mullen kept the conference running smoothly. Laurie Kenyon prepared the index. Special thanks are due to Eric Newman and the editorial team at Fordham University Press for their expert guidance and support. With gratitude and anticipation, this group of scholars looks forward to widening the circle of conversation with the publication of these essays.

Notes

1. Diana Butler Bass, "Christianity after Religion," Steelman Lecture presented at Wake Forest University School of Divinity, Winston-Salem, North Carolina, January 22, 2013.
2. See, for example, Norma H. Thompson, ed., *Religious Pluralism and Education* (Birmingham: Religious Education Press, 1988); Judith A. Berling, *Understanding Other Religious Worlds: A Guide for Interreligious Education* (Maryknoll, N.Y.: Orbis, 2004); and Mara Brecht and Reid Locklin, eds., *Comparative Theology in the Millennial Classroom: Hybrid Identities, Negotiated Boundaries* (New York: Routledge, 2016).
3. The Association of Theological Schools recently sponsored a project in Christian Hospitality and Pastoral Practices in a Multifaith Society "to support schools in their work to prepare graduates to serve faithfully and effectively in contexts involving people of differing faith traditions." Stephen R. Graham, "Editor's Introduction," *Theological Education* 47, no. 2 (2013): iii. The results of these studies appear in *Theological Education* 47, no. 1 (2012) and no. 2 (2013).
4. Kristin Johnston Largen's *Finding God among Our Neighbors: An Interfaith Systematic Theology* (Minneapolis: Fortress, 2013) is a good example.
5. James Fredericks, "A Universal Religious Experience? Comparative Theology as an Alternative to a Theology of Religions," *Horizons* 22, no. 1 (1995): 68
6. David Tracy, *Dialogue with the Other: The Inter-religious Dialogue* (Louvain: Peeters, 1990), xi.
7. Tracy, *Dialogue with the Other*, 97–100.
8. For a survey of these issues, see Paul Hedges, *Controversies in Interreligious Dialogue and the Theology of Religions* (London: SCM Press, 2010).
9. Cf. Jonathan Z. Smith, "Epilogue: The 'End' of Comparison: Redescription and Rectification," in *A Magic Still Dwells: Comparative Religion in the Postmodern Age*, ed. Kimberley C. Patton and Benjamin C. Ray (Berkeley: University of California Press, 2000), 237–42.
10. Francis X. Clooney, *Theology after Vedanta: An Experiment in Comparative Theology* (Albany, N.Y.: SUNY Press, 1993), 187–88. Cf. Francis X. Clooney, SJ, *Beyond Compare: St. Francis de Sales and Sri Vedanta Desika on Loving Surrender to God* (Washington: Georgetown University Press, 2008), 208–10.
11. Francis X. Clooney, "On the Scholar's Contribution to the Contemplative Work of Hindu-Christian Studies," *Journal of Hindu-Christian Studies* 27 (2014): 10.
12. See, for example, David F. Ford and C. C. Pecknold, eds., *The Promise of Scriptural Reasoning* (Malden, Mass.: Blackwell, 2006).

13. Francis X. Clooney, "Comparative Theological Learning as an Ordinary Part of Theological Education," *Teaching Theology and Religion* 16, no. 4 (2013): 324.
14. See James L. Fredericks, *Faith among Faiths: Christian Theology and Non-Christian Religions* (Mahwah N.J.: Paulist, 1999).
15. James L. Fredericks, *Buddhists and Christians: Through Comparative Theology to Solidarity* (Maryknoll, N.Y.: Orbis, 2004), 95.
16. Raimon Panikkar, *The Intrareligious Dialogue*, rev. ed. (New York: Paulist, 1999). John Keenan borrows the term "intrareligious dialogue" to describe his interpretations of Christ and the Trinity through engagement with Mahayana Buddhism. John P. Keenan, *The Meaning of Christ: A Mahayana Theology* (Maryknoll, N.Y.: Orbis, 1989), 1, 222.
17. Keith Ward, *Religion and Human Nature* (Oxford: Clarendon, 1998), 8.
18. Hugh Nicholson, "The New Comparative Theology and the Problem of Theological Hegemonism," in *The New Comparative Theology: Interreligious Insights from the Next Generation*, ed. Francis X. Clooney (New York: T&T Clark, 2010), 50–51.
19. Nicholson, "The New Comparative Theology and the Problem of Theological Hegemonism," 53.
20. Francis X. Clooney, *His Hiding Place Is Darkness: A Hindu-Catholic Theopoetics of Divine Absence* (Stanford: Stanford University Press, 2014), 30.
21. Robert Cummings Neville, "Preface," in *The Human Condition*, ed. Robert Cummings Neville (Albany, N.Y.: SUNY Press, 2001), xx.
22. Robert Cummings Neville with Wesley J. Wildman, "Comparative Hypotheses: Cosmological Categories for the Human Condition," in *The Human Condition*, ed. Robert Cummings Neville (Albany, N.Y.: SUNY Press, 2001), 182.
23. Wesley J. Wildman and Robert Cummings Neville, "How Our Approach to Comparison Relates to Others," in *Ultimate Realities: A Volume in the Comparative Religious Ideas Project*, ed. Robert Cummings Neville (Albany, N.Y.: SUNY Press, 2001), 213–15.
24. Wesley J. Wildman, "Appendix A: On the Process of the Project During the Second Year," in *Ultimate Realities: A Volume in the Comparative Religious Ideas Project*, ed. Robert Cummings Neville (Albany, N.Y.: SUNY Press, 2001), 263.
25. The essays from this conference are forthcoming in *How to Do Comparative Theology: European and American Perspectives in Dialogue*, ed. Francis X. Clooney and Klaus von Stosch (New York: Fordham University Press, 2016).
26. Nicholson, "The New Comparative Theology and the Problem of Theological Hegemonism," 58–59.
27. Some contributors to this volume are the protégées of Fredericks, Clooney, or Neville. Others have participated in the Comparative Theology Group they helped to form in the American Academy of Religion (AAR), or in the Luce/AAR Summer Seminars in Theologies of Religious Pluralism and Comparative Theology that convened under the leadership of John J. Thatamanil in 2009–13.
28. Clooney, *Theology after Vedanta*, 187.
29. See, for example, John J. Thatamanil, *The Immanent Divine: God, Creation, and the Human Predicament* (Minneapolis: Fortress, 2006); Paul F. Knitter, *Without Buddha I Could Not Be a Christian* (Oxford: One World, 2009); Jon Paul Sydnor, *Ramanuja*

and *Schleiermacher: Toward a Constructive Comparative Theology* (Eugene, Ore.: Pickwick Publications, 2011); Michelle Voss Roberts, *Dualities: A Theology of Difference* (Louisville: Westminster John Knox, 2010); Michelle Voss Roberts, *Tastes of the Divine: Hindu and Christian Theologies of Emotion* (New York: Fordham University Press, 2014); Hyo-Dong Lee, *Spirit, Qi, and the Multitude: A Comparative Theology for the Democracy of Creation* (New York: Fordham University Press, 2014).

30. Jeffery D. Long, "(Tentatively) Putting the Pieces Together: Comparative Theology in the Tradition of Sri Ramakrishna," in Francis X. Clooney, ed., *The New Comparative Theology: Interreligious Insights from the Next Generation* (London: T&T Clark, 2010), 167.

31. Rita D. Sherma, "Introduction: The Hermeneutics of Intersubjectivity," in *Woman and Goddess in Hinduism*, ed. Tracy Pintchman and Rita D. Sherma (New York: Palgrave Macmillan, 2011), 2.

32. Clooney, "Comparative Theological Learning as an Ordinary Part of Theological Education," 325.

33. Cf. Wildman and Neville, "How Our Approach to Comparison Relates to Others," 218–30.

34. Clooney, "Comparative Theological Learning as an Ordinary Part of Theological Education," 326–27.

35. Catherine Cornille, *The Im-Possibility of Interreligious Dialogue* (New York: Herder & Herder, 2008), 78.

36. Cornille, *The Im-Possibility of Interreligious Dialogue*, 82.

PART I
Divinity

1 The Dance of Emptiness

A CONSTRUCTIVE COMPARATIVE THEOLOGY OF THE SOCIAL TRINITY

Jon Paul Sydnor

Human beings respond to difference, especially religious difference, in varying ways. Some people are repulsed by religious difference and attempt to insulate themselves from it. Others are fascinated by difference and see it as an opportunity to learn more about "the other"—the one who is different from us, the one who is not "the same"—and about themselves. For these people, otherness provides an opportunity to compare, which is a powerful means of insight. For example, democracy is understood in relation to dictatorship, freedom is understood in relation to slavery, and prosperity is understood in relation to poverty. So, too, the "religious other" presents an opportunity to compare and contrast our beliefs, practices, and moods with different beliefs, practices, and moods, and to reform ourselves in the light of difference.[1]

This type of comparative practice makes us aware of hidden aspects of ourselves. Our environments instill in us many of our habitual thoughts, feelings, and actions, religious and otherwise. Having unconsciously acquired them, we are rarely aware of them. They have been bequeathed to us by our culture, absorbed unknowingly from childhood to adulthood. Because these beliefs and behaviors are often unchosen, they are unfree. We are determined (unfree) whenever our thoughts or actions are instinctive rather than conscious. If we desire freedom, then we must become aware of who we are. We must bring to consciousness that which now lies hidden. Then we can analyze our beliefs and actions and revise them in accordance with consciously chosen values. This process will never be complete, but the more we do it the more free we become.

Fortunately, we can become more aware of our self, our values, our worldview, our family dynamics, and our cultural inheritance through comparison. Indeed, one of the most powerful ways of shedding light on our deepest self is to compare it with a deep self who is "other" to us, different from us. Comparison is the interrogation of the familiar—the obvious, the assumed—by the unfamiliar. Through comparison, otherness sheds light on oneself. The other's difference provides a contrast to our subconscious beliefs, raising them into consciousness, depriving them of their obviousness, and subjecting them to the vitalizing scrutiny of doubt.

Comparative theology is a new academic discipline that thinks across religious boundaries. For example, this discipline encourages Christians to study Buddhist doctrine, or vice versa. Comparative theology grants us greater awareness of our own faith by encountering a different faith. Once we have encountered this other faith, we have multiple options. We can leave ours the way it was, thankful for the increased awareness. We can revise our faith according to the challenge presented by the other. Or we can borrow aspects of the other faith and incorporate them into our own. We can even attempt to synthesize the two faiths into one, although this is rather difficult. Conversion is the final option, and it must be a real option for comparative theology to be effective. Comparative theology seeks to transform theology, and transformation demands risk.[2]

In order to gain a place at the table of theological method, comparative theology must become constructive, pastoral theology. In other words, it must produce new (constructive) theology—theology that goes beyond the history of theology or interpretations of theology—and this theology must be helpful to the church—to priests, pastors, and parishioners alike.

Commitment

When discussing Buddhism and Christianity, questions of salvation and the means of salvation soon arise. Buddhism has been characterized as offering a saving knowledge. This characterization was always inadequate, unfaithful to the Buddha's own teachings as well as to the vast geographic and historical scope of the tradition. As a result of Christianity's struggles with Gnosticism in the first centuries of the church's existence, it has developed an allergy to saving knowledge. Salvation is by grace, through faith, in Christ. At times, the allergy to saving knowledge expresses itself as an allergy to any spiritual insight.

Nevertheless, as a Christian, I have found my study of Buddhist doctrine to be spiritually helpful, even transformative. I remain Christian, irresistibly drawn to the grace of Jesus Christ. He is my prophet, rabbi, hero, friend, guru, healer, and savior. For me, divinity shines through him in a peculiarly powerful manner. Yet, the Buddha deepens my experience of Christ, and Buddhism broadens my practice of Christianity. I am now a Christian transformed by encounters with the Buddha and Buddhists and Buddhist practices. Comparison has broadened and deepened my faith.

NAGARJUNA'S DOCTRINE OF EMPTINESS

This essay compares the Protestant theologian Jürgen Moltmann's doctrine of the social Trinity with the Mahayana Buddhist writer Nagarjuna's doctrine of emptiness. It utilizes Nagarjuna's doctrine to develop Moltmann's social Trinity—not to synthesize the two into one, but to borrow from Nagarjuna to amplify Moltmann.

The Buddhist doctrine of emptiness (sunyata) develops from two preceding concepts ascribed to the Buddha himself—no-self (anatman) and dependent co-origination (pratitya-samutpada).[3] The Buddha sought to overcome the suffering associated with sickness, old age, and death. Like many other spiritual seekers in his age, he practiced a renunciant lifestyle through which he sought to transcend the material circumstances, which, for most of us, determine our happiness or unhappiness. One aspect of this endeavor was an interior search for his self (atman), his eternal, unchanging, indestructible interior being.[4] After six years of austerities, he had not found permanent transcendence or a permanent self, and he concluded that his cravings were one important cause of his suffering. In response, he preached the doctrine of anatman, or no-self, in order to free his followers from their own craving for self.

Then, in the interpretation of Nagarjuna, the Buddha extended this concept of no-self to all of reality. Just as humans have no eternal, unchanging self that can provide permanent happiness, so all existents lack an eternal, unchanging substance that can provide permanent happiness. Release from suffering cannot come through discovering the permanent self and residing there, or from discovering permanent happiness in any feeling, object, or thought. Release from suffering can only come through giving up all craving for permanence.[5]

The Buddha's doctrine of no-self is closely related to his doctrine of dependent co-origination (pratitya-samutpada).[6] This doctrine asserts that everything—all feelings, objects, thoughts—arises causally by means of all other feelings, objects, and thoughts. Everything is causing everything else and being caused by everything else, all the time, in one churning nexus of intercausality within which cause and effect are inseparable.[7] Here there is no permanence, solidity, or stasis. There is only insubstantial motion, a dynamic, shifting web of synergies in which the one thing that can provide bliss is the paradoxical realization that there is no thing that can provide bliss.[8]

Around 100 BCE, the Mahayana Buddhist Perfection of Wisdom (Prajna Paramita) literature began to appear. This literature furthered reflection on no-self and dependent co-origination by introducing the doctrine of emptiness (sunyata). Nagarjuna probably lived in the second century CE, two or three centuries after the Perfection of Wisdom first began to appear. He pushes the doctrine of emptiness to its radical limit. In his most famous work, the *Fundamental Verses of the Middle Way (Mulamadhyamakakarika)*, he utilizes logical analysis to establish the radical impermanence, interrelatedness, and hence emptiness of all things. In so doing, he explicitly rejects the two extremes of eternalism and nihilism. That is, he denies that there is a substantive, eternal self that can achieve a substantive, eternal state of bliss.[9] At the same time, he denies that there is nothing, that all is illusion, and that everything is unreal. Between these two poles he seeks the way of the "middle," an English word etymologically related to the Sanskrit term "madhya" in Nagarjuna's *Mulamadhyamakakarika*.[10]

Nagarjuna seeks to expound the Perfection of Wisdom so thoroughly as to free practitioners from any potential for cognitive, emotional, or physical clinging. He does so by asserting that everything—all selves, all beings, all feelings, all concepts, all gods, all matter—is empty of self-sufficiency (svabhava).[11] Svabhava can be translated as own-being, self-existence, self-sustenance, independence, enduring solidity, inherent nature, abiding essence, or isolated substance. Because no one, no thought, and no thing has own-being (svabhava), everything is empty.[12] And because everything is empty, everything is non-dual—samsara (the unending flux into which we are repeatedly reincarnated) and nirvana (release from the endless cycle of dissatisfaction) are ultimately indistinguishable, ignorance and truth are ultimately indistinguishable, and even craving and emptiness are ultimately indistinguishable. There are no distinctions, hence nothing to grasp after, hence nothing to suffer. Freedom is here already; it only requires recognition.[13]

Unfortunately, instead of realizing this pre-existing freedom, we thirst for abiding satisfaction from every thing, and we project the potential to provide abiding satisfaction onto every thing. But in truth, every thing is empty of the capacity to provide abiding satisfaction, so our pursuit is fruitless.[14] Our demand of static fullness from dynamic emptiness causes our turmoil. Only the recognition of emptiness as the nature of reality, and the experiential realization of that recognition, can free us from our suffering.[15]

MOLTMANN'S DOCTRINE OF THE SOCIAL TRINITY

The Christian doctrine of the social Trinity is enormously complicated, misunderstood, and controversial. An investigation of the social Trinitarian theology of Jürgen Moltmann will focus this conversation. Moltmann is a German Protestant theologian active in the twentieth and twenty-first century. His social Trinitarian theology is most thoroughly expressed in *The Trinity and the Kingdom of God*.[16]

The first hints of the Trinity already appear in the letters of Paul, only two or three decades after the life of Christ. In Paul's letters, greetings and farewells repeatedly invoke the Trinitarian formula of Father God, Jesus Christ, and Holy Spirit: "May the grace of our Lord Jesus Christ, the love of God, and the communion of the Holy Spirit be with you now and always" (2 Cor. 13.13, cf. 1 Cor. 12.4–6, Eph. 4.4–6). Most New Testament scholars believe that Paul was drawing on pre-existing Christian liturgical formulations. At this point, "Christianity" was still a Jewish sect, firmly monotheistic, yet already referring to its experience of salvation triadically.[17] Over the next four centuries, this Jewish sect would become a new religion. At the same time, it would try to understand why its religious life offered salvation through three persons experienced as one God.

Eventually, the larger Church, in a series of ecumenical councils, decided that the Father, Son, and Holy Spirit were all divine, all one God. The formula of three-in-one resonated with Christians' experience of the divine, although mathematicians and logicians found the doctrine wanting. Over the centuries, various theologians offered explanations for how God could be both three and one. One such explanation is the social Trinity.

The antiquity of the concept is disputed, but many scholars find intimations of it in the Greek fathers who conceptualized the three aspects of the divine as discrete persons and suggested that the best human analogy to the divine relations is the family.[18] In the West, Trinitarian thought took a different turn as Augustine found the image of the Trinity primarily in the individual.[19] Although he provided multiple analogies to the Trinity, one of the most influential is the psychological analogy for the Trinity, in which the memory, understanding, and will combine as three to make one self.[20] Contemporary social Trinitarian theologians shy away from this individualistic conception, fearing that if the individual images God, then community becomes accidental to salvation.

Instead, contemporary social Trinitarians such as Moltmann find the image of the interpersonal God within interpersonal human relationships. Individuals alone do not express the image of God; individuals in relation do. We fulfill our divine image by entering into community with others, forming one from many.[21] To be made in the image of God is to be made for deep relationship, and fulfillment of that call is theosis, or divinization.[22] God is three persons united by love into one divinity.[23] Humans, being made in the image of God, are called to overcome their separation from one another by uniting in love.[24]

POTENTIAL FOR COMPARISON

Preliminarily, one may note that the doctrines of emptiness and social Trinity both place a high value on interconnection. The doctrine of the social Trinity states that God is absolutely relational. The doctrine of emptiness states that reality is absolutely relational. Both doctrines stress that human beings lack self-sufficiency. And, in some interpretations, both doctrines stress that material reality (the world, matter) is also absolutely relational. Stated another way, in emptiness all existents are empty of independence; they need one another in order to be or, more accurately, in order to become. In the social Trinity, the three persons are empty of independence; they, too, need one another in order to be or, more accurately, in order to become.[25]

Nevertheless, this comparison is problematic. Nagarjuna's exposition of emptiness and Moltmann's exposition of the social Trinity arose in vastly different times for vastly different reasons. For Nagarjuna, emptiness served as a doctrinal medicine. He prescribed it in order to free people from the illusion that reality possesses a fullness that would everlastingly quench their thirst. "Emptiness" refers to all that is—material reality, our individuality, other people, even the gods. None of these things can extinguish the fire of desire. Moltmann's doctrine of the social Trinity was meant to invigorate an ancient Christian doctrine that had fallen into neglect over the past millennium. Continuing the Trinitarian explorations of Karl Barth, Karl Rahner, and others, he attempts to interpret the social Trinity as a fundamental ontology of relation with ethical consequences for individuals, communities, and even nations. Hence, the origin and function of our two concepts are distinct. Nevertheless, as we shall see, each can serve as a foil to the other, enriching the other by its presence.

Because, as a Christian, I am unqualified to further develop the doctrine of emptiness, this essay will now consider how Nagarjuna's concept might further develop the Christian doctrine of the social Trinity.

Absolute Relationality

Both concepts can be considered under the category of "absolute relationality." Such a grouping would be dangerous if taken to insinuate that they are the same doctrine or two different ways of articulating the same doctrine. But emptiness and social Trinity are characterized by difference as much as by similarity. Even when compared, each must be considered in itself; the uniqueness of each concept cannot be lost. Indeed, this difference is the fertile soil of comparative theology. Were they the same, then they could not challenge, inform, or buttress one another. Interreligious thought needs difference; sameness is intellectually sterile.

Conceptualizing Nagarjuna's "sunyata" (emptiness) as absolute relationality is both accurate and helpful. The term "emptiness" is problematic in English, in which emptiness is negative, usually suggesting the absence of some good such as meaning, purpose, or joy. To feel "empty" is to feel sad and depressed. But for Nagarjuna, "emptiness" is a positive term denoting infinite potential. Reality is empty of finality, limitation, and constraint. For that reason, some translators avoid the literal translation of "sunyata" as "emptiness" and turn instead to terms such as freedom, indeterminacy, the inexhaustible, and openness. (All of these terms, which are really metaphors, will play a role here.) Positively, we may imagine empty space, the sky, or the heavens as limitless realms of movement for birds in flight.[26] Or we may imagine an empty room that invites us to dance. Regardless of the metaphor, emptiness is a radically positive evaluation of reality: "Everything is possible for someone for whom emptiness is possible. Nothing is possible for someone for whom emptiness is impossible," writes Nagarjuna.[27]

The "absolute" in "absolute relationality" is not an exaggeration. So intent was Nagarjuna on denying permanence to any feeling, thought, or existent that some scholars have translated his concept of "sunyata" as "nothingness" or even "absolute nothingness."[28] However, Nagarjuna's point was not that nothing exists. Nagarjuna's point was that all things exist in relation to all other things—not some other things, not the nearest things, but all other things. Our becoming encompasses the entire universe, while the becoming of the entire universe finds expression in our own becoming. Reality is entirely kinetic.[29]

The consequences of this universal, absolute interdependence are manifold. For one, emptiness rejects monism, the assertion that everything is one homogeneous thing and that all difference and distinction are illusion. For Nagarjuna, difference is real, but each instant of difference is perfectly related to all other instants. Additionally, absolute interdependence rejects dualism. Buddhism does have sets of concepts that can be (mis)interpreted as opposed—samsara and nirvana, suffering and release, ignorance and wisdom, the demon Mara and the blessed Buddha. But these conceptual opposites must not be reified into ontological, conflicting opposites. We must not suppose that samsara, suffering, ignorance, and Mara are an interdependent whole united against the opposite interdependent whole of nirvana, release, wisdom, and Buddha.[30] For Nagarjuna, all of reality is one, universal, interdependent, dependently co-originating whole. Some concepts may help us to realize this experience, but the realization of this experience will annihilate both those concepts and any opposition they seemingly exhibited.[31] In the end, reality is empty of opposition, empty of metaphysical polarities, and empty of any conceptual essence. Indeed, it is even empty of emptiness.[32]

This radical ontology of relation applies to everything—feelings are impermanent and dynamic, thoughts are impermanent and dynamic, gods are impermanent and dynamic. Even the smallest units of existence, "dharmas" or psychophysical atoms, are insubstantial, impermanent, and dynamic.[33]

To what extent could this radical ontology of relation apply to the personal relationships ascribed to the social Trinity? Nagarjuna's doctrine of emptiness is a cognitive antidote intended to relieve people of their clinging by asserting that there is nothing solid enough or still enough to cling to. Moltmann's social Trinity explicates the fundamental Christian assertion that God is love. Because humankind is made in the image of God, Moltmann's theology has profound implications for his anthropology. The motives, emphases, and contexts of Nagarjuna and Moltmann diverge. Because of this divergence, no ladder-like, mechanical comparison can occur. The process will be much more intuitive than that, necessarily engaging cognitive processes such as synthesis and creativity. In this case, Nagarjuna will serve to agitate settled thinking, subvert unquestioned assumptions, interrogate lazy generalizations, and challenge subconscious evasions. Then, Nagarjuna will lend concepts and vocabulary to patch the weak spots and fill the holes.

Difference within the Social Trinity

One striking aspect of Nagarjuna's doctrine of emptiness is its inclusion of difference within a radically relational reality. Emptiness excludes nothing and includes everything. Properly understood, every thing in emptiness is constituted by the entirety of all other things in emptiness, and every thing in emptiness is resident within the entirety of the universe. We, all of us, are the universe, both through expression and impression.

As noted previously, Moltmann's doctrine of the social Trinity asserts that God is three persons united by love.[34] Love must have an object, because all love demands a beloved. Hence, all love is love *of*. There is no pure love, no love itself, without an external toward which that love can be directed. Love twisted back upon itself disappears into a black hole of egoism, collapsed under its own solipsistic weight. For there to be love there must be relationship, and for there to be relationship there must be an other. Most importantly, there must be difference.

So, when John asserts that "God is love" (1 John 4.8), he simultaneously and necessarily asserts that God is relational. Indeed, if he asserts that God in Godself is love, then he asserts that God in Godself is relational—internally relational, inherently relational, at least more than one.

Yet if God is more than one, then how can we balance this biblical assertion with the earlier, foundational monotheism that Christianity inherited from Judaism? "Hear, O Israel: The Lord our God, the Lord is

One" (Deut. 6.4). Here God is referred to with the proper name of Yahweh, which intensifies the assertion of singularity as well as the problematic of conceptualizing God as many. For the author of Deuteronomy 6.4, the Hebrews' beloved Shema, God is not only one deity but one personality, a unified personality deserving of a proper name—Yahweh.

Christianity has inherited the paradoxical assertion that God is one and many, singular and plural, an entity and a plurality. This inheritance presents Christianity with its greatest challenge and its greatest opportunity: the opportunity to worship, think, act, and feel as many who are becoming one, as many persons unified as one personality.

ANALOGY OF RELATIONS

Analogies for the Trinity draw on human experience to understand the means by which the divine can be three and one.[35] Although critics assert that this move privatizes theology and fragments the communal experience of the church,[36] Moltmann anticipates such criticisms and attempts to obviate them by thoroughly grounding his relational analogy in the Bible, thereby associating it with the long history of Judeo-Christian revelation rather than his own progressive agenda. The Bible itself utilizes analogies from human experience to confer knowledge of God: It speaks of God as a rock, shepherd, mother hen, potter, king, and father. The following analogical forays presume that the use of analogy to understand God is as legitimate as the Bible's. Analogy does not project human reality onto God.[37] Instead, it interprets our reception of God in this-worldly terms. Revelation flows from God to us, but our expression of that revelation must always be poetic.

Mary and Doug

Mary and Doug were two parishioners in my former church. Mary had been married to Doug for 60 years. They had an extremely loving relationship, one of those rare marriages that is near-perfect—same values, same desires, almost no arguments, great sex life, four children, unfailingly kind to one another, cheerful and supportive in each other's company, always praising each other. Then, Doug got sick and, after a three-month battle, died. Mary was devastated.

I was having lunch with Mary a few months later. When I asked her about life without Doug, she smiled gently and said that she felt like "half a person." She no longer felt complete. She wasn't whole once separated from Doug. Her self was lacking.

Mary's statement was both tragic and fascinating. She was saying that the two of them had become one, so that when one of the two was lost, the one who was left only felt like a half. They had a Trinitarian relationship, in a sense. Of course, they were not three; they were two. But their twoness produced oneness so that they were neither two nor one, but two in one, just as the three persons of the Trinity become three in one, through love.

Crucially, this union was predicated upon their difference, not their sameness. Mary and Doug did not fall in love or continually deepen their love because they saw themselves in the other. They loved one another because they saw someone different in the other. They were attracted to one another's uniqueness, not sameness. Certainly, they shared values, ideals, and goals that made their marriage work. But neither saw the other as an extension or reflection of the self. They saw each other as free selves, deeply united.

Mary and Doug's relationship achieved nonduality—they were neither one nor two—because neither sought to protect any aspect of her self or his self from the other. Using Nagarjuna's language, they embraced their sunyata, which might here be translated as openness.[38] Conversely, they denied their svabhava, which we can here translate as own being. Svabhava, applied to this situation, becomes a protected area of the self, a withdrawn portion of the soul, an invulnerable hardness in the psyche that shallows our relationships. Nagarjuna asserts that it does not exist in truth, but that craving for it conjures its illusion. And that illusion causes self-assertion, self-obsession, and ultimately self-suffering.

The Christian Soul and Buddhist No-Self

When the Buddha asserted the doctrine of anatman, or no-self, he rejected the existence of any pure, isolated, monadic self. But he was not asserting that each person is a nothingness. Instead, he asserted the existence of a dynamic, changing, impermanent, thoroughly related self. In other words, he did not assert that the self does not exist, but that all selves exist, together. We are not one self, but many selves, as one—one web, one nexus, one interconnected, interrelated, pulsing becoming.

This doctrine of absolute relationality, as derived from the Buddhist concept of no self, certainly challenges Christian concepts of God as an unchanging substance. It may seem to be in conflict with the traditional Christian belief in the soul, if the soul is seen as an unchanging substance. Indeed, Nagarjuna developed his doctrine of emptiness at least in part in order to oppose the belief of certain Buddhist schools (the Sarvastivadins) in a pudgala, a transmigrating personality that carries one's karma from one life to the next. If we have a pudgala, Nagarjuna worried, then we might be concerned to care for it, attend to it—we might even become attached to it. The doctrine of emptiness offers freedom from such attachment.

This particular context of Nagarjuna's innovation presents complications to Christian theologians, such as myself, who wish to apply it to Christian concepts such as the Trinity and, by way of extension, the soul. Because human beings are made in the image of God, our concept of God is relevant to our concept of humanity, and vice versa. To complicate the effort further, "the soul" itself is an enormously abstract concept with multiple permutations. Over the centuries, theologians have argued that:

1. The soul is good and the body is bad, and the soul needs to be freed from the body. (This Gnostic claim is contrary to standard Christian theology.)
2. The soul resides in the body and goes to heaven when the body dies.
3. The soul and body are one, unified entity. Neither is separable from the other.
4. Any discussion of the soul inevitably devalues the body, so all soul-talk should be avoided.[39]

Given the preceding list, any discussion of the soul in the Christian tradition can be controversial. Still, because most Christians do believe they have souls, and because Christian soul-talk is linked to Christian God-talk, we must discuss this doctrine in relation to the Buddhist doctrine of anatman, no-self or no-soul.

If Christians take the Buddhist doctrine of no-self and Nagarjuna's intensified doctrine of emptiness seriously, then must we forego belief in the soul? I argue that we do not, and that arguments to the contrary are based on a misunderstanding of the human soul. This misunderstanding is caused by the belief that the soul is, in some way, an independent, self-existing, substance. According to this view there is a part of us, the soul, or at least a part of that soul, which is not related to the universe.

We see the soul as a discrete substance that grants us individuality, that carries our sin and forgiveness, and that bears our eternal destiny. The soul, thus conceived, cannot be "empty" because it is so full of portent and individualized consequence.

Moreover, one might object, according to traditional doctrine this soul is also an expression of God since that is the part of the human being that is made in the image of God. Since God is unchanging (according to traditional theology), the soul must be unchanging. Therefore, it must be inert and static. It may be sustained by God, but it has no necessary relationship to other souls, its own body, the external universe, or time. Hence, it cannot be deeply relational. If God is an eternal, unchanging substance, then God must be characterized by fixated, unchanging subjectivity, and we as the image of God must also be ultimately characterized by fixated, unchanging subjectivity. Relationality is but an accidental property of this monad.[40] Conceived thus, the Christian doctrine of the soul resists conversation with an anatmavadin (no-soul-teacher) such as Nagarjuna.

The Relational Soul

Fortunately, the soul need not be conceptualized as monadic, inert, and unchanging. Instead, we can conceptualize it as our locus of relationality. That is, the soul is not a substance so much as a place through which we interact with the world, from which our individual difference arises, within which we find our greatest potential, and toward which other souls yearn, just as we yearn toward them. As such, the soul images a single person of the Trinity who is open and vulnerable to the other two persons of the Trinity. Hence, it becomes the portal through which we establish sacred relations with other souls.

As our locus of relationality, the soul is as vital as it is related. The more isolated the soul is, the more dead it is. The more related the soul is, the more alive it is. The relatedness of the soul draws us into divine life, which is itself fundamentally relational. God is not being itself or the ground of being. God is relationality itself, and if there is a ground of relationality, it is relationality again.[41] Thus, if human beings are made in the image of the social Trinitarian God, then fixated subjectivity is a harmful craving that must, for therapeutic reasons, yield to dynamic intersubjectivity.[42]

The Vulnerable Soul

A deeply related soul is an emotionally vulnerable soul. My own advocacy of relationality and vulnerability rightfully opens me to socioeconomic criticisms of privilege. My own vulnerability is much less dangerous than the vulnerability experienced by developing world workers, abused women, and political dissidents. I am safer than they are, as are the people that I love. Tragedies rarely happen in my world. So, it might be arrogant to prescribe vulnerability from my safe suburban home. In order to address this legitimate concern, I turn to the assistance of Toni Morrison.

Toni Morrison's *Beloved* grants a literary example of human openness under conditions of horrific suffering. In that novel, two former slaves disagree about the extent to which a human being should love in a racist, violent world. The maternal character, Sethe, is willing to risk love, while her lover Paul D recoils from such vulnerability:

> Risky, thought Paul D, very risky. For a used-to-be-slave woman to love anything that much was dangerous, especially if it was her children she had settled on to love. The best thing, he knew, was to love just a little bit, so when they broke its back, or shoved it in a croaker sack, well, maybe you'd have a little love left over for the next one.[43]

Paul D, understandably, wants to protect himself from the vagaries of an unreliable world and the cruelties of white slavers. The invulnerability that he pursues leaves him protected from loss, even the horrible losses experienced by blacks in mid-nineteenth-century America.

But Sethe disagrees. She understands that invulnerability, svabhava, is a dead zone. As inert substance it is safe but joyless, protected but remote, guarded but indifferent. It expects vitality of itself but only feels its lifelessness.

Yet, according to Sethe, this absolutely relational conception of human existence does not annihilate the self. Instead, it opens up the self to the other from whom it receives and to whom it gives love. The true self wants to live and give life, and it does so by giving and receiving love. The extent to which it can give and receive love is the extent to which it is alive.

Crucially, such self-donation is not self-annihilation. Self-donation is predicated upon differentiation between self and other, so that even perfect self-donation resists any disappearance into monism, or the identity of self and other.⁴⁴ Self and other can be perfectly unified, but they cannot be identified, or else all self-donation and other-reception would cease. Consummation resists absorption. The self finds its true self to be a boundlessly interrelated self, an infinitely open self that finds its being by becoming love.⁴⁵

Chord

Nagarjuna's concept of sunyata has also been translated as interdependence because all things exist only in, through, and with all other things.⁴⁶ This interdependence is total. There is no aspect, part, or portion of any thing that is not absolutely interdependent with all other things. The universe is a shimmering web of connected synergies in which a change in one produces a change in all. There is no thing that is not influenced by all things, and all things are influenced by every thing.

By way of analogy, the Trinity is three persons who "interanimate" one another.⁴⁷ Joy Ann McDougall's term "interanimation" is an excellent term for the social Trinity and, ideally, for human communal becoming. To the Latins, the animus was that part of the person that lent it vitality, energy, and life. The animus was associated with spirit and courage. So, to "interanimate" one another is to grant one another more vitality, energy, spirit, and courage. We have more life in relation than we can alone, and the deeper the relations the greater the life.

Nevertheless, the eternal threeness and oneness of the Trinity remain, at first glance, mathematically and logically problematic. From an objectivist or materialist perspective, it is impossible to be three in one or one in three. Rocks can't do it and, according to some rigorist forms of human cognition, if rocks can't do it then humans can't do it—not to mention God.

But it is possible to be three and one or one and three in human experience. Earlier in this chapter, the relationship of Mary and Doug demonstrated two in one and one in two. Another profound instance of interanimation is a musical chord. Imagine a C chord played on a piano. The three notes of C, E, and G make up the chord. They are three different notes that together constitute one thing. We can experience them separately as three or, more richly, together as one.

The beauty of this harmony, its experiential power, is predicated upon the tones' difference. The symphonic abundance of the C chord is not experienced *despite* the tonal differences between C, E, and G; it is experienced *because of* their differences. The three different tones interpenetrate each other to create a triunity.

Crucially for the concept of interanimation, to change one tone is to change the experience of each tone. Classically, lowering the E to an E flat converts the C major chord into a C minor chord, with a new mood of drama or sadness. The C and G, which had once contributed to an almost trite, happy mood, now sound dour. (Indeed, the German musical term for "minor" is "dur," the cognate of "dour.") Their interpenetration is so absolute that changing one changes them all, experientially. Hence, no tone is self-defined. Every tone is other-defined and other-defining, becoming more in the presence of the others and granting those others their own amplification.

The Dance of Emptiness

Nagarjuna's sunyata has also been translated as "freedom" and "indeterminacy" rather than "emptiness." The released self, the self that has realized its lack of own being, is an absolutely free and undetermined self. If we are controlled by external realities, that is a result of ascribing permanent solidity to them and to our selves. The illusion of permanent solidity, coupled with a craving for certain arrangements of the self and the world, causes self-assertion over against a resistant reality.[48] We try to get the world into an order that we like and keep it in that order, but the world does not cooperate. We become frustrated and try to force cooperation, but any pleasing success we achieve quickly falls apart. When an imagined solidity tries to coerce another imagined solidity into a permanently pleasing configuration, only turmoil can follow. In this situation dissatisfaction will be permanent.

However, if we realize our emptiness, then we will realize our freedom and indeterminacy. Because there is nothing solid or permanent anywhere or anytime, there can be no coercion, frustration, or disappointment. Whatever the situation is, that situation will soon be gone, so we need not fret over our situational emotions.[49] We can act skillfully within a situation, always knowing that those actions will soon be gone, and our future actions will be free.[50] Emptiness is a dynamic, unceasing movement into which we are invited. It presents ever new opportunities for new experiences and new actions.

Perhaps "dance" would be an excellent translation of "sunyata." In comparison, Moltmann applies the Greek term "perichoresis" to the three persons of the Trinity.[51] Although the etymology of the word is debated, it can be interpreted as "dancing around" or "dancing with." Moltmann does not explicitly embrace this translation, although the metaphor of dance almost perfectly dovetails with his explication of perichoresis. Other social Trinitarians, such as Catherine Mowry LaCugna, explicitly embrace this extraordinarily apt metaphor.[52]

The three persons of the Trinity dance. When a skilled couple dances, the observer cannot detect who is leading. There is no compulsion. Their movements appear spontaneously generated or, to use Buddhist language, dependently co-originated. Each defers to the other to produce perfectly synchronized action, action so spontaneous that it bodies forth freedom.[53] So it is with the Trinity. They dance freely, spontaneously, always in relation to one another but never determined by one another, co-originating one another in joyful mutuality, in perichoresis.[54]

Perichoresis is a beautiful term to describe the divine synergies of the social Trinity as well as, we might imagine, the experience of emptiness. Dance creates beauty out of motion, thereby creating grace out of time. Dance renders impermanence playful. The unique motions of the dancers unite to form the one harmony of the dance, so that the sum is greater than the parts. Interactions are (or appear to be) spontaneous, the product of trust, attentiveness, and communion.

We, being made in the image of God, are made to dance, both with God and with each other. In other words, our being is invited into God's dance and God's dance is invited into our being. Just as importantly, we are called to share God's dance with one another, to relate to one another freely and joyfully and equally, spontaneously effecting one another in a ballet of love.[55]

The energy of this love feels inexhaustible. Without the hindrance of obstinate self-assertion, energy multiplies itself logarithmically. An unexpected quantity of joy arises. But all of this can only occur if we first empty ourselves of svabhava, of "self-nature," of an unchanging essence.[56] And this emptying cannot be partial. It must be total, without remainder.

Once the dance of emptiness begins, there is no coercion and no oppression. Indeed, there is no law. True, each dancer enters into the dance autonomously, freely, "self-lawed." But once the dance begins, all law disappears along with all constraint and compulsion. Autonomy is not lost, but it is surpassed as the dancer's movements become interdependent with her partner's, and vice versa. But this interdependence does not make her motions heteronomous, or "other-lawed," because the partners co-originate each other's dance simultaneously, fluidly. Even from a theistic perspective, the dancers cannot be called theonomous, "God-lawed," because theonomy suggests the continued constraint of law, even divine law. But dance is antinomian, "against law." It embodies joyful freedom in community.[57] It expresses mutuality. It proves that two can dance together more gracefully, freely, joyfully, and spontaneously than one can dance alone. Through love, all law disappears and the music takes over, expressed through dance.

Law prevents self-assertive human society from degenerating into violence. Dance raises human society into beauty.

Freedom For

Such a concept of human social nature redefines freedom. Freedom is no longer characterized by autonomy, or freedom *from*. Autonomy frees us from external coercion, but this is only a preliminary step on the way to ideal sociality. The next step, which is dependent on but supersedes autonomy, is mutuality. Autonomy grants us freedom from the coercive other but leaves us in fragmented isolation. The isolation produced by autonomy must become the mutuality produced by interdependence. Freedom *from* best expresses itself as freedom *for*. The end of subjection allows the beginning of community.[58]

Including Difference

With reference to Doug and Mary, the C chord, and dance, we infer that the social Trinity is love unifying difference.[59] As such, the Trinity is a great symbol of hope. Only love can *unify* difference. Power can repress the frictions of difference to create a forcibly peaceful plurality. But true unity is only achieved when difference voluntarily unites into a differentiated unity.[60] According to emptiness and the social Trinity, human reification of difference is morally wrong because it is ontologically askew. Nationalism denies the possibility of communion with the other. Sexism asserts the inferiority of the female and her subservience to the male. Racism asserts the perpetual externality of difference. Heterosexism denies homosexuals' need for emotional intimacy. Co-religionism asserts tribal self-sufficiency.[61] All worldviews that valorize sameness and control create an artificial chasm between human and human, between culture and culture. Into this chasm we then fall, at the bottom finding a swamp of disgust and fear.

For the Trinity to be true, the Trinity must be open, and not just slightly open, but infinitely open. Indeed, this infinite openness is symbolized by the third person of the Trinity, precisely as the *third* person of the Trinity.[62] There is love of self and love of other. Just as importantly, there is the joy one experiences in the love of other for other, a third-party joy. Buddhists call this *mudita*, or sympathetic joy. This joy is a particularly selfless joy, since the self is not loved or loving, but perceiving love. It is also a particularly pure joy because it cannot be tainted by selfishness.

The necessity of the third person of the Trinity struck me one day while driving my two young sons to school. They were in the back seat playing with each other, tickling each other, laughing, giggling, playing, singing. I listened to them, occasionally glanced in the mirror to watch them, and was flooded with joy at their love for each other. I then became aware of the peculiar power and ecstatic movement of my third-party, sympathetic joy. I experienced it as a willing self-emptying, a movement toward the other two. I did not wish to disrupt their relationship or even join their relationship at that moment. I simply wanted to revel in it—in my perception of it, as third party—more fully.

The third person of the Trinity symbolizes openness to the love of an other for an other. However, the third person of the Trinity symbolizes more than just openness to two others. The third person symbolizes the infinite openness of the sacred to all that is, to the interdependence of all reality. We revel in all relatedness, not just our particular relatedness. We celebrate universal interdependence, not just those upon whom we are dependent or who are dependent on us. The third person of the Trinity, as *third* person, is the symbolic window through which the light of infinite relatedness flows.

MECHANICAL AND ORGANIC COMPARISON

This paper began by presenting the doctrines of emptiness and social Trinity separately, as two different concepts from two different traditions. They shared some promising similarities while offering fruitful differences. As the comparison began, the two doctrines remained discrete as we mechanically moved back and forth between the two, searching for cross-fertilization. But as the comparison proceeded, they gradually became less discrete and the comparison less mechanical. By the end of the essay, beginning with the section entitled "the dance of emptiness," the two doctrines resonated, suggesting the possibility of an integrated worldview. The totality of each was not synthesized into a new totality, à la Hegel. Instead, the comparison of their particulars produced a new particularity. So, the essay provides an experience of discrete, mechanical comparison at the beginning and concrete, organic comparison at the end.

Which works better? Specifically, which mode of comparison produces constructive theology that is more helpful to the church? The answer to this question should engender much debate, not only about comparative theology but also about interreligious relations generally. If comparative theology fuses religious concepts, then it might foster an interreligious syncresis in which all religions are indistinguishable within one world religion. But if we insist upon artificially maintaining doctrinal boundaries between the religions, then the pastoral promise of comparative theology may be lost.

We may apply our comparison of emptiness and social Trinity to this dilemma. The insistence on preserving religious distinction may reflect a fearful clinging to religious svabhava, or own being. As such, it will necessarily result in self-assertion and compromise the promise of interreligious relationality. Religions that conceptualize themselves as self-sufficient will see no need for other religions. But religions that see themselves as sunyata—open, free, dynamic, and unafraid—will seek out dialogue. This dialogue will necessitate risk because transformation necessitates risk, and faith is the daring quest for transformation.

So, comparative theology risks conversion to the other. But, from the perspective of emptiness and social Trinity, this is not the most probable outcome. It is also not the most frequent outcome historically. The most frequent outcome is a transforming self within differentiated community. In other words, Christianity interdependent with Buddhism does not become ChristoBuddhism. It remains Christianity, but a Christianity that is constantly renewing by means of Buddhism's challenge and stimulation. Christianity will be reformed, and always reforming.[63]

Within this framework all doctrine is impermanent. As soon as we state our current beliefs, we are called to outgrow them. This theological kinesis expresses theosis, the divine call to human divinization. For finite humans in deep relationship with the infinite God, change is vocation and stasis is sloth. The proposition "Jesus of Nazareth is the Son of God" might always hold true for the faith. Still, its interpretation by the church as a whole, and each individual within, must always deepen, as the church and its members accept the grace of God more thoroughly and reflect upon that grace intellectually. Other religions spur us to such deepening. In Christian terms, they serve as media of divine grace. Like the three persons of the Trinity, the religions may co-originate their best selves, calling one another into a blessed community of difference united by love. Then, at last, we may dance with one another and with our dancing God.

Notes

1. I would like to express my extraordinary gratitude to Joy Ann McDougall and, posthumously, Frederick J. Streng, for their assistance in understanding and comparing Moltmann and Nagarjuna, respectively. They have both achieved a penetrating understanding of their subjects, to which I am indebted. Any interpretive errors in this essay will be my own, not theirs.
2. David Tracy, *Dialogue with the Other: The Inter-Religious Dialogue* (Grand Rapids: Eerdmans, 1991), 73.
3. Ewing Chinn, "Nagarjuna's Fundamental Doctrine of Pratityasamutpada," *Philosophy East and West* 51, no. 1 (January 2001): 64.
4. I am not following the usual practice of italicizing "foreign" words here. Such italicization would endorse a foreign/native dualism in an essay that rejects all such dualisms.
5. Mark Siderits and Shoryu Katsura, *Nagarjuna's Middle Way: Mulamadhyamakakarika* (Boston: Wisdom Publications, 2013), 168–69.
6. Frederick J. Streng, *Emptiness: A Study in Religious Meaning* (New York: Abingdon Press, 1967), 58–59.
7. Jan Westerhoff, *Nagarjuna's Madhyamaka: A Philosophical Introduction* (New York: Oxford University Press, 2009), 27–28.
8. The term "synergies" was proposed by Theodor Stcherbatsky in *Buddhist Logic*, as quoted in Streng, *Emptiness*, 53.
9. Nagarjuna, *Mulamadhyamakakarika*, Chapter 4. References give chapters instead of page numbers. The chapters are very short and consistently numbered from the Sanskrit version of the text.
10. Kenneth K. Inada, *Nagarjuna: A Translation of His Mulamadhyamakakarika with an Introductory Essay* (Delhi: Sri Satguru Publications, 1993).
11. Siderits and Shoryu, *Nagarjuna's Middle Way*, 81–82.
12. Nagarjuna, *Mulamadhyamakakarika*, Chapter 15.
13. Streng, *Emptiness*, 159–60.
14. Westerhoff, *Nagarjuna's Madhyamaka*, 101.
15. Rupert Gethin, *The Foundations of Buddhism* (Oxford: Oxford University Press, 1998), 237–44.

16. Jürgen Moltmann, *The Trinity and the Kingdom of God* (San Francisco: Harper and Row Publishers, 1980).
17. Moltmann, *Trinity and Kingdom*, 178.
18. Joy Ann McDougall, *Pilgrimage of Love: Moltmann on the Trinity and the Christian Life* (Oxford: Oxford University Press, 2005), 118.
19. McDougall, *Pilgrimage of Love*, 104–5.
20. McDougall, *Pilgrimage of Love*, 104–5.
21. McDougall, *Pilgrimage of Love*, 116–17.
22. Moltmann, *Trinity and Kingdom*, 215–16.
23. Moltmann, *Trinity and Kingdom*, 95–96.
24. McDougall, *Pilgrimage of Love*, 116.
25. Michael von Bruck, "Buddhist Shunyata and the Christian Trinity," in *Buddhist Emptiness and Christian Trinity*, ed. Roger Corless and Paul Knitter (New York: Paulist Press, 1990), 49–59.
26. Hans Waldenfels, *Absolute Nothingness: The Foundations of Buddhist-Christian Dialogue* (Mahwah, N.J.: Paulist Press, 1980), 65.
27. Nagarjuna, *Vigrahavyavartani: Averting the Arguments*, in *Emptiness: A Study in Religious Meaning*, trans. Frederick J. Streng (New York: Abingdon Press, 1967), stanza 70: 227.
28. See, for example, Waldenfels, *Absolute Nothingness*.
29. Streng, *Emptiness*, 36–38.
30. Nagarjuna, *Mulamadhyamakakarika*, Chapter 22.
31. Siderits and Shoryu, *Nagarjuna's Middle Way*, 302–3.
32. Nagarjuna, *Mulamadhyamakakarika*, Chapter 27.
33. Nagarjuna, *Mulamadhyamakakarika*, Chapter 1.
34. Moltmann, *Trinity and Kingdom*, 58–59.
35. McDougall, *Pilgrimage of Love*, 102.
36. Eric O. Springsted, "Theology and Spirituality; or, Why Theology Is Not Critical Reflection on Religious Experience," in *Spirituality and Theology: Essays in Honor of Diogenes Allen*, ed. Eric O. Springsted (Louisville: Westminster John Knox Press, 1998), 53–59. For more on these methodological issues, see McDougall, *Pilgrimage of Love*, 9.
37. Paula M. Cooey, "Emptiness, Otherness, and Identity: A Feminist Perspective," *Journal of Feminist Studies in Religion* 6, no. 2 (Fall 1990): 17–19.
38. See, for example, Nancy McGagney, *Nagarjuna and the Philosophy of Openness* (Lanham, Md.: Rowman and Littlefield Publishers, 1997).
39. Geddes MacGregor, "Soul: Christian Concepts," in *Encyclopedia of Religion*, ed. Lindsay Jones, 2nd ed., vol. 12 (Detroit: Macmillan Reference USA, 2005), 8561–66, Gale Virtual Reference Library, March 19, 2013.
40. Christopher Ives, *Zen Awakening and Society* (Honolulu: University of Hawaii Press, 1992), 46.
41. McDougall, *Pilgrimage of Love*, 80.
42. See McDougall, *Pilgrimage of Love*, 97.
43. Toni Morrison, *Beloved* (New York: Penguin, 1998), 45.
44. Moltmann, *Trinity and Kingdom*, 57–58.

45. Joy Ann McDougall, "The Return of Trinitarian Praxis? Moltmann on the Trinity and the Christian Life," *The Journal of Religion* 83, no. 2 (2003): 187.
46. John D. Dunne, "Nagarjuna," *Encyclopedia of Religion*, ed. Lindsay Jones, 2nd ed., vol. 9 (Detroit: Macmillan Reference USA, 2005), 6392.
47. McDougall, *Pilgrimage of Love*, 97. See John Donne's "The Ecstasy" for an earlier use of the term "interanimate," lines 40–45.
48. Streng, *Emptiness*, 87–88.
49. Nagarjuna, *Mulamadhyamakakarika*, Chapter 19.
50. Nagarjuna, *Mulamadhyamakakarika*, Chapter 17.
51. Moltmann, *Trinity and Kingdom*, 174–76.
52. Catherine Mowry LaCugna, *God for Us: The Trinity and Christian Life* (San Francisco: HarperCollins, 1991), 270–78.
53. Jürgen Moltmann, "God Is Unselfish Love," in *The Emptying God: A Buddhist-Jewish-Christian Conversation*, ed. John B. Cobb, Jr. and Christopher Ives (Maryknoll, N.Y.: Orbis, 1994), 123–24. Again, Moltmann refers to the metaphor of spontaneity, not the metaphor of dance.
54. Here, we stray from Moltmann, who continues to insist on the monarch Father as origin of history of salvation, including the Son and the Spirit. See Moltmann, *Trinity and Kingdom*, 177–78.
55. LaCugna, *God for Us*, 299.
56. Mark Siderits, "On the Soteriological Significance of Emptiness," *Contemporary Buddhism* 4, no. 1 (2003): 9–10.
57. Richard Bauckham, "Jürgen Moltmann and the Question of Pluralism," in *The Trinity in a Pluralistic Age: Theological Essays on Culture and Religion*, ed. Kevin J. Vanhoozer (Grand Rapids, Mich.: Eerdmans, 1997), 158.
58. McDougall, *Pilgrimage of Love*, 188.
59. Robert Magliola, *Derrida on the Mend* (Indiana: Purdue University Press, 1984), 135–36.
60. Moltmann, *Trinity and Kingdom*, 148–50.
61. McDougall, *Pilgrimage of Love*, 138.
62. McDougall, *Pilgrimage of Love*, 86.
63. Jürgen Moltmann, "Is 'Pluralistic Theology' Useful for the Dialogue of World Religions?" in *Christian Uniqueness Reconsidered: The Myth of a Pluralistic Theology of Religions*, ed. Gavin D'Costa (Maryknoll, N.Y.: Orbis, 1990), 153. Moltmann experienced this intensification of self-understanding and other-understanding during open Christian-Marxist dialogue.

2 Flower and Song

A COMPARATIVE STUDY ON TEOTLIZING IN AZTEC THEOLOGY AND KARL RAHNER'S VIEW OF DIVINE SELF-DISCLOSURE

Elaine Padilla

> *I believe in one God . . . Maker of heaven and earth, and of all things visible and invisible.*
>
> —NICENE CREED

Introduction

Each Sunday, many Christians find themselves faithfully reciting the above words of belief embedded in the Nicene Creed. As if what is being stated is a self-evident truth, this phrase is echoed almost unquestioningly all over the globe. Yet the expansiveness of the statement, which includes an ambiguous interplay between things visible and invisible, placed as a poetic chiasm paralleling that of heaven and earth, might haunt us. Whereas one might find comfort in things divinely made being heavenly, would not their tangible manifestation in time and space offer an occasion to wonder about such divine makings? If we take this credal statement as a faithful Christian expression of divine creativity, if we witness its visible manifestations in concrete reality in the present time, and if we profess it in light of the horrors and violence plaguing our streets, then do not probing questions on things invisible sneak into our contemplative souls?

In seeking answers, this chapter assumes, and uses as point of departure, a model of divine creativity by which the cosmos continuously emanates from *within* God. This model is akin to the theology of Karl Rahner, for whom the cosmos is God's self-disclosure arising from the infinite expanse that encompasses everything.[1] Yet I offer a caveat, for the chapter also adopts the Aztec understanding that *teotl* (interrelated unity) can act as the container holding the whole of life (heavens, earth, navel, and region of the dead) that generates and conceives everything.[2] Because in this model the highest regions above (heavens) and the lowest below (the dead) interrelate within the divine container, the divine maker is viewed as giving rise to a *mixed* divine-cosmic creation. In this account, *the divine matrix of creativity is the process of begetting and becoming a fragile space.*

In taking an analogical turn to the visible to offer a pathway into that which is invisible, this comparative essay argues for a tangible form of divine space, which in drawing from the *Florentine Codex* becomes represented by darkness or the Aztec figure of Tezcatlipoca. The process of creation out of darkness—out of the darkness of Tezcatlipoca, or out of the depths of God—will here be called "teotlizing." Via teotlizing, primordial space begets itself and becomes tangible as cosmos. It entails two simultaneous motions in this comparative work: the movement toward differentiation of all things in the divine unity, upon which Rahner expounds (based on his understanding of self-disclosure), and the Aztec *nepantla*, or interweaving, the movement by which all differences are brought together into a fragile unity (the mystery expressed as "flower and song"). In summary, this chapter draws from Rahner's motion of differentiation and the Aztec's interweaving motion to explain the processes by which the divine matrix or primordial space begets and becomes itself. In doing so, the chapter explicitly highlights the role that the principle of freedom, as found in Rahner, can play in manifestations of destruction alongside creation, as found in Aztec theology.

Perhaps in beckoning the reader to peer at the fragile tangibility of "flower and song," one can affirm that the world is a sacred mystery of divine-cosmic quality. Even as one dwells amidst destructive forces, one might catch a glimpse of a red rose like that of the song by Jerry Leiber and Phil Spector, "Spanish Harlem," which can be perceived only when "the moon is on the run" and "all the stars are gleaming," and that grows through the cracks of the streets made out of concrete in Spanish Harlem. Though never seeing the sunlight, the Creator's processes of begetting and becoming cosmos, teotlizing, indeed can glow beautifully under the moon and stars.

A Christian Speaking Nahuatl?

> The mere fact that this word ["God"] exists is worth thinking about. When we speak about the word "God" this way, we do not only mean of course the German word. Whether we say *Gott* or "God" or the Latin *deus* or the Semitic *El* or the old Mexican *teotl*, that makes no difference here. It would, however, be an extremely obscure and difficult question to ask how we could know that the same thing or the same person is meant by these different words, because in each of these cases we cannot simply point to a common experience of what is meant independently of the word itself.[3]

When thinking of comparing texts containing Aztec theological thought with a Christian thinker whose views are fairly classical, I wondered who could be a most suitable dialogue partner to embark on such a journey. I transported myself to my early years when theology was new to me, and Karl Rahner immediately came to mind. He was the first theologian whose model of the God-cosmos relationship provided me with the linguistic framework with which to begin conceptualizing a cosmology that was imbued with gestures of love. Since meeting Rahner, I have progressed into process theologies, such as those of Catherine Keller and Joseph A. Bracken, whose indelible traces permeate this essay, to articulate the porous boundaries between God and world. Yet I continue to remember those first steps taken alongside Rahner, when my incarnational theology had merely begun to take shape. This chapter pays him homage, while nudging him toward those unsafe locations where my musings now nomadically dwell.

This essay prods Rahner by expanding his thoughts on "the old Mexican *teotl*," which he merely began to signify in the epigram that opens this section. To me, it was quite surprising to encounter *teotl* in his chapter on "Man in the Presence of Absolute Mystery," which is the focal text in this essay. Furthermore, that Rahner does not argue on behalf of "a common experience," but instead understands the particularity and weightiness that various terms within religious traditions carry, adds to the richness of this dialogue. This comparison becomes all the more fruitful because Rahner had an inkling of *teotl* as a term commensurate with, but not identical to, what he conceptualizes as "God." What would our account of the divine-cosmic processes look like after having developed taste buds for "the old Mexican *teotl*"? How might we incorporate these novel features into theologies like those of Rahner on God's tangible self-disclosure in creation?

Hence another impulse drives this essay. For a long time, I have been seeking to recover the philosophical thought in indigenous religions. It might be a matter of a remote ancestral memory, or of a determination to emancipate indigenous voices from the silence to which they have been confined, or simply of an ancient desire beckoning me. Among these religions, Aztec beliefs continuously draw me while paradoxically eluding me. Perhaps the same is true for many others with kindred interests; after all, Caribbean and Latin American indigenous views have been relatively absent from the scholarship of comparative theological work. Delving into Aztec theology on the creative processes of *teotl* through the *Florentine Codex* and some Aztec poetry will be but one step in response to this passion.

Admittedly, I bring Aztec theology into this field of comparative theology with some trepidation. The task of drawing insight from a marginalized voice such as that of the Aztecs can carry risks. On the one hand, this comparative piece opens space for the Aztec voice to enter the discourse of "world religions." Accordingly, it can interrupt categories such as "low religions," "primitive religions," or "little traditions" often assigned to so-called peripheral traditions.[4] In this chapter, Aztec theology not only stands on equal footing with others but also voices the perspective of forgotten memories, illustrating the multiple vantage points of the Latin American religious landscape.[5]

On the other hand, by bringing Aztec religious views into this field of study, this chapter risks alloying those Aztec views with occidental and modern forms of thinking and language—a risk that the Second Latin American Encounter Workshop in 1993 had already considered with regards to theology. The risk is amplified by the manner in which the refined theology of Aztec religious phenomena—temples, plastic arts, codices, priests, and ceremonies—was often privileged by later interpreters, at the expense of the common and quotidian forms of religiosity. One must also account for how these sources were passed on through the interpretative lenses of Spanish colonial times, and hence bear the traces of conquest. Occidental and modern footprints are palpable in the version of the *Florentine Codex* employed in this chapter, as it is an English translation of a manuscript compiled originally in Spanish by Sagahún, a Franciscan friar, for the evangelization and indoctrination of the colonial New Spain.[6]

Recognizing these risks, I pondered how to avoid reinscribing a hegemonic discourse when comparing two views that might be judged from the start as holding opposite locations on the spectrum of colonization and neo-colonization. In other words, in drawing Rahner's work on differentiation in unity nearer to the Aztec belief on teotlizing (the sacred mystery becoming tangible) present in *The Florentine Codex*, can one avoid falling into the trap of missionizing forms of comparison? How can one move beyond a utilitarian attitude toward the discovery of new worlds without engaging in multiform reenactments of conquest? Indeed, conceptualizing the process of divine creativity by means of comparison is no easy feat. While Aztec and Rahnerian theologies are equally philosophical, they come from centuries and worlds apart. Aztec texts date back to pre-conquest and conquest times in Mesoamerica, while Rahner is from the twentieth century. Even though both contexts are highly developed culturally, religiously, and socially, the fact that these views would locate themselves on opposing ends of the colonial spectrum cannot be easily overlooked.

From the onset, I hope that the anti-colonizing impetus of this study is evident in how I use the term "God" analogically by substituting it with Rahner's notion of "infinite" or "all-encompassing" reality. Rahner's terminology conveys a sense of incomprehensibility or non-objectification of the divine, even as it resonates with the sense of "God" as Creator that can arise from the world of experience. Akin to a divine matrix, this notion can hold a semblance to *teotl* without violating either view. By not taming or enlightening the dark components of Aztec *teotlizing* with principles from Rahner's transcendentalism, however, this chapter forestalls a pecking order of ascendancy from Aztec theology toward Christianity. Refusing to ease the tensions and apparent inconsistencies existent in the Aztec view on transcendence, which is symbolized by darkness, it thus seeks to avoid replicating the misguided nineteenth-century comparative efforts that were later perpetuated in Rahner's own concept of "anonymous Christianity."[7]

In order to respectfully and faithfully locate my own theological and philosophical reading within this eruptive opening, I partly follow in the footsteps of scholars who interpret *The Florentine Codex* and Aztec poetry from a Latin American perspective. Much of their work has been based on a common stock of "ethnohistories and dictionaries of early Spanish and mestizo chroniclers," "Aztec and other Conquest-era indigenous pictorial histories, ritual calendars, maps, and tribute records," "archeological evidence," and ancient and present correlations in the fields of ethnography, philosophy, and religion.[8]

In gleaning from these ancient sources and recent interpretations, the theology comparatively constructed in this chapter resembles a patchwork. Relying heavily on the fields of religious studies and philosophy, the Aztec theology I extract from them weaves exegetical work and speculative thought with practice. In the process, these textual worlds, both of the Aztecs through the *Florentine Codex* and poetry, and of Rahner's writings, refuse to be inhabited or conquered. The Aztec world encountered in these texts harbors an excess that cannot be contained.[9] So it can also be with the writings of Rahner, whose linguistic codes can take years to decipher and still continue to be deep wells of new meaning. Something ungraspable always remains in both text-worlds.

Lastly, this essay transforms both self and texts. I expose myself to these writings, as with Paul Ricoeur, with the intent of "receiving" from them "an enlarged self."[10] I risk struggle, disruption, and upsetting my orthodoxy. Here lies the usefulness of theology after comparative work. One is drawn beyond the self and into these texts, allowing both self and texts co-creatively to metamorphose through the encounter. In the end, I draw from the principles of both streams—differentiation (in unity), teotlizing (the divine process of begetting and becoming), and *nepantla* (interweaving of differences)—to construct a view of the tangible and sacredly mysterious becoming of the divine matrix.

S/he That Teotlizes

Theologizing on *teotl* involves viewing natural processes as expressions of a sacred reality that creatively transfigures itself. Early Spanish clergymen, perplexed by what they encountered in the Aztec religious world, and already inclined to perceive it through the lens of Christian monotheism, categorized these sacred expressions as its opposite, polytheism. On the surface, they could observe that Aztec cult and ritual employed a proliferation of terms in naming natural phenomena. Macroprocesses, with their various microprocesses, were personalized as "goddesses" and "gods," making the conquest's theological interpretations propitious. The "primordial creative origins," for instance, became clustered in a group of three: Ometéotl, Tezcatlipoca, and Xiuhtecuhtli.[11] This triad was identified by its "begetting" of other minor gods, the cosmos, and humans, and its guiding of their works (*FC*, II and III).

Recent scholarship, in challenging the early Spanish view of multiple deities or polytheism, points in the direction of an interrelated unity, principle, or being whose plural manifestations were equated with deities. Disguised as a thousand interrelated and interpenetrating gods and goddesses before Spanish eyes, this interrelated reality of sacred existence was named interchangeably *teotl* or Ometéotl.[12] For some scholars, the multiple gods and goddesses were simply the manifestations or children of the one singular deity. For others such as Miguel León-Portilla, Ometéotl was "the origin of all things and the mysterious nature of an invisible and intangible creator," existing beyond the heavens, by "self-invention," in perpetual creative activity.[13] This essay follows those scholars who identify *teotl* with a relational reality-in-process rather than a single and far removed deity.[14]

In the *Florentine Codex*, one reads of the various ways in which the term *teotl* was employed to describe multiple processes, events, and even types of individuals. The whole of existence, reality itself, was *teotl*, with all things arising from it. Such relationship was shown in how the Aztec amalgamated the term *teotl* even to common nouns. As Sagahún noted:

> This work will also be timely to inform the natives of the meaning of created things, that they not attribute divinity to them, because whatsoever creature they see as being eminent in good or evil they called *teotl*, which means god. So, they called the sun *teotl*, because of its beauty; likewise the ocean because of its grandeur, its fury; and so they called many of the animals by this name because of their frightening aspect and ferocity. From this it is inferred that this name, *teotl*, is taken as good and evil. And this is much better recognized when [the term] is in a compound: as in this name *teopilzintli*, a very handsome child; *teopiltontli*, a very mischievous or bad boy. Many other words are compounded in this same manner, from the meaning of which it can be conjectured that this word *teotl* means a thing consummate in good or in evil.[15]

Teotl is a primordial space of creativity that continuously *begets itself and becomes as the fragile cosmos*. This definition would be in partial agreement with James Maffie, in his understanding of Aztec-process metaphysics, for whom *teotl* is a reality of never ending processes "of recycling and transformation."[16]

Teotl's processes of continuous becoming fluctuate between two genders. Rather than a "Maker" implying a male figure who creates externally, *teotl* refers to a mutually transformative process arising from a genesis that is not quite male (Ometecuhtli) nor female (Omecihuatl), and to a form of intimate "creating" in the sense of begetting and becoming. Furthermore, because of its inter-relationality, *teotl* creates itself without being an intentional agent with a plan.[17] It is the space or whole that sets in motion within itself macro and microprocess that freely interact and give shape to one another and to the emergent cosmos. And because *teotl* denotes a process rather than a substantive entity, it is best understood for its gerundive meaning likewise borrowed from Maffie: teotlizing—which will be compared to the Christian concept of divine creativity from within God.

This divine transfiguring creativity, teotlizing, was signified as Tezcatlipoca. One of the three "primordial creative origins" (the other two being Ometéotl and Xiuhtecuhtli, as stated previously), Tezcatlipoca would beget the cosmos by darkness first giving birth to their sun, thus also, to all living things in need of light (*FC*, III:1; VII:2–9, 27). Tezcatlipoca—also known as Titlacauan, Yaotl, Moyocoyatzin, and Moquequeloa, among other names—was the overseer of the creation of the present age of the Aztecs, the fifth age, at the time of the arrival of the Spaniards.

Such teotlizing personified in Tezcatlipoca can be best described through the Aztec art of masking oneself, not in the sense of real (self) versus unreal (mask), rather as remaining "simultaneously complex, ultimately unknowable, ever-changing."[18] As a human shaman would take on the shape of a bird, being possessed by its powers through dancing, flapping her arms, encircling her feet, and whistling the flute, likewise the "primordial creative origins" or primordial space of creativity would continuously beget itself as cosmos, according to its manifold expressions, via Tezcatlipoca's shamanic power. Known as "the ultimate shape shifter," Tezcatlipoca became the divine figure symbolizing this ongoing process of "form-changing" of the primordial creativity.[19] As the elements of earth, wind, fire, and water would recombine themselves in multiple ways, they would render manifest plural or multifaceted cosmic expressions of existence. Hence, innumerous shapes would make teotlizing *partly* tangible, with much remaining to be known. The elements' physicality masks the sacred unity of their interrelated unity.

Personifying the darkness of primordial creativity that gave birth to the light, Tezcatlipoca was represented with dark attributes such as having black skin and being the night. Anticipating future views on cosmic dark matter and dark energy, with its bi-genderness and darksome body, s/he was depicted in paintings, drawings, or stone art as Citlalinicue, the "lady of the luminous starry skirt," and Tecolliquenqui, "lady of the black attire."[20] Among the creators of the stars, galaxies, and all the luminaries of the night, her black skin tones and ornamented attire are symbolic of the genesis and preservation of the whole cosmos. S/he is "the lord of the heavens and the earth" (*FC*, III:10) and the "Giver of Life," who creates itself and creates all things.

This dark night or sacred mystery typifies the space engendering and holding all things together, being described by Nezahualcóyotl, an Aztec ruler during pre-Colombian times, as the life-giving source always "intimate with You." This sense of "close vicinity" is most evident in the formula often used in Aztec prayers: "Master, our lord of the near, the nigh," "the presence of the near, the nigh" (*FC* [1970], I:5). Yet, as shamanic, the Tezcatlipocan intimacy would be equally obscured via the shape of her earthen frame, for as darkness she eclipses all contour, even herself. This principle is embedded in another prayer: "Behold thou wilt take unto thyself, wilt move unto thyself, wilt hide unto thyself thy wonder, thy glory" (*FC*, VI:42). The MSS *Cantares Mexicanos* likewise asks, "Where is the place of light / For He who gives life hides Himself?"[21] So pervasively and vital s/he was in all things that only at the side of "the lord of near, of the nigh" one could live on earth, even when unable to *fully* recognize her.

For some, like León-Portilla, this Tezcatlipocan opacity approximates some Christian understandings of transcendence. Tezcatlipoca, according to his understanding, points to the incommensurability of the divine intimate nearness, at times designated by the term Yoalliehécatl, literally meaning "night-and-wind": Tezcatlipoca thus signifies that which is "invisible like the night, intangible as the wind."[22] As "night-and-wind," the shamanic principle of teotlizing that makes things visible and tangible (light, sun) also holds the quality for taking on form and shape. As with the night's tendency to prevent full visibility into things, and of the wind not to disclose its points of origin and destiny, Tezcatlipoca's shamanic acts shroud as much as reveal the teotlizing intimacy that begets the light. Its quality of transcendence would be viewed as sacred mystery or the dark frame that manifests itself according to the cosmic orders in all their complexity.

Begetting and becoming are movements operating in unison: creating out of things perceived as invisible (that is, teotlizing according to the night), and giving them a quality of tangibility (in other words, teotlizing according to the sense experience of the wind). Hence the concept of teotlizing refers to the primordial space shaping itself as sacred mystery (Tezcatlipoca), who because of its darksome luminosity, can be perceived as if wearing multiple masks in phenomena also seemingly contrary to the heavenlies above the earth. In the *Florentine Codex*, sublime descriptions of "all-powerful," "invisible," and "untouchable one" (*FC*, VI:1) are coupled with manifold mundane and lowly metaphors. S/he is "in the plants, in the woods," the night birthing the dawn (*FC*, VI:48), and in the depths of the earth, its caverns, its protruding crags, its cliffs where they could slip and slide into the hereafter (*FC*, VI:10). From within the depths of frightful uncertainty, inhabitable, with "no standing, no place of exit," resembling a trap or snare, the voice of "the god of the near, of the nigh" could reverberate. Anyone could even encounter her presence in the navel of the world, the underworld (*FC*, VI:72).

The primordial creativity, multiply masquerading itself as the varied cosmic forms, with all its earthen opacity, continuously begetting and becoming cosmically, elicited awe and reverence in all that existed. Tezcatlipoca, the one who from the depths of her darkness gave birth to their sun, generated their fifth age, and saturated all things, meant that everything could potentially be the embodiment of her sacred darkness: provision and security as much as scarcity and terror (*FC*, VI). Her ubiquitous shadow could become rain and hail, causing growth in the land, and bringing abundance, sustenance, and health by means of ointments, and conversely it could cause all things to submerge under it, the waters to billow, swirl over, and drown travelers. Any sense of fear combined with awe (and perhaps indifference) that her shamanic mystery evoked was the result of its ineffable tangibility, its cosmicity of unspeakable yet also quotidian manifestations of the sacred.

Differentiating Unity

Rahner, analogically defining the term "God" as "holy mystery," arrives at a similar concept to the "old Mexican *teotl*," or what earlier has been named teotlizing. He uses the language of transcendence for the human capacity to identify an infinite horizon, which makes reflection possible and opens the self to "unlimited possibilities of encountering this or that particular thing."[23] As if taking a detour from describing God as the

Creator who is embedded in a created order capable of knowing God, Rahner refers to this horizon as the "absolute ground of every particular existent."[24] At this juncture, his view of God turns to the grounding reality, something like a divine matrix that discloses itself as "God" simultaneously as a "mediated immediacy as the one infinite reality and as the ineffable mystery."[25] What resembles Aztec theology is that this grounding reality mediates itself while maintaining the quality of ineffability.

As if employing process terminology, Rahner speaks of this mysterious mediation as self-disclosure. Creation *from* God would then mean that the all-encompassing reality, the unity of the whole that cannot be comprehended in its totality, mediates itself, and in making itself partly intelligible, it differentiates all things, including itself, within that infinite reality.[26] The process of creative self-disclosure first implies a generative ground continuously refusing to enclose itself. Nearing the shamanic teotlizing in Aztec theology, but by explicit means of differentiation, this infinite reality can disclose itself as cosmos without ceasing to be infinite. Likewise, the process of self-disclosure taking on the shape of ineffable mystery, while it can be given the name "God" (due to its weightiness), gives rise to all that is, including any concept we might hold of "God" with its various derivations like "Spirit." This understanding of geneses brings into greater intimate relationship Rahner's notion of "God" communicating Godself *essentially* through the symbol of the Trinity,[27] with his more cosmic gestures toward the ineffable as "appearances of God in our world and in time and space."[28]

The grounding matrix disclosing itself as Spirit, for instance, in a manner similar to the Aztec theological concept of the Tezcatlipocan "night-and-wind," in being mediated through "an actual categorical object," can be sensually experienced "in the midst of everyday life."[29] While difficult to define linguistically, the Spirit extends throughout the entire cosmos. Quite tangibly, the Spirit diffuses itself through it as "the light of a sun that we do not see as such," yet one can experience it visibly and corporeally. Like the darkened skin and starry skirt of Tezcatlipoca, the Spirit also becomes visible in the "tiny lights" of the night shining forth. On this, the element of darkness of the Tezcatlipocan teotlizing might approximate the process by which the holy mystery signifies "the most radical, the most original, and in a certain sense the most self-evident reality."[30] And vice versa, the disclosure of the infinite reality can be compared to Maffie's views on teotlizing in that everything that exists constitutes an "all-inclusive and interrelated unity."[31]

Yet the Rahnerian impetus is unique in that the divine ground discloses itself as cosmos, that is, continuously creates it from within as such, by explicit means of emanating differences. In doing so, it disturbs any notion of *teotl* as a unified, in the sense of uniform or homogeneous, reality. For Rahner, all things become, in their difference, by unity "letting emanate."[32] Each existent is unique in the determination or specification of its own becoming or self-constitution. The generative matrix is not identical with that which arises from it. Inasmuch as things become subjects (each existent, including "God"), the *grounding* whole can be one; and vice versa, such *fullness* in its original unity (as in the many being differentiated) becomes the condition of things being alive in their uniqueness.[33] In this view of a generative emmanation from the divine matrix, differentiation is transcendence, but this transcendence is more like a *spatial breath* shared between God and creatures, and between all living things, than a chiasm that would keep them apart. Valuing divine and human otherness can evoke wonder, a passion for making a difference among humans, and a devotion to the world that cares for the non-human.

What are the implications of this transcendental movement of creativity by means of differentiation for the purposes of comparison with Aztec theology? In drawing from this complex and plural form of infinite disclosures, teotlizing, for instance, can make itself vulnerable to the possibility of there being an*other* whom one can truly encounter and love, for whom to care. For Rahner, the grounding freedom to emanate, begetting, would also entail knowing what each thing is in terms of its sacredness. Even if freedom can result in the negation of co-creation, freedom can equally harbor the potential for newness and creativity, the possibility of disrupting non-beneficial patterns of being human. It can provide occasions for making a difference, of another age emerging.

Still, something more expansively risky in the disclosure of the divine matrix is in need of recovery if one is to appropriate more fully the concept of teotlizing. Creation from God in the form of disclosure, as defined by Rahner—that is, begetting by means of differentiation—eventually splits "luminosity" from its creative darkness.[34] Truer disclosures mean that in the grounding reality "there is no darkness," only light.[35] Light, as in the platonic metaphor of the sun (*The Republic*, 514a–520a), symbolizes another reality, the divine reality that from the outside shines its rays through this dark and cavernous place. The rays of light shining in the darkness, and not the darkness itself, are then what loves, differentiates, knows, and creates. Transcendentally that luminous horizon draws all things toward it. Rahner's philosophical impasse can be reflected in his insistence on darkness signifying things too improper to be sublime. For instance, losing the actual tangibility of darkness, as in "night-and-wind," can turn to a transcendentalism that is "intangible" in the sense of otherworldy, endangering Christian recognitions of the mysterious sacredness in the ugliest of forms of earthen embodiment.

In dichotomizing the profound and ambiguous continuity between things invisible and visible implied even in the Creed, the spatiality of the nightly darkness, which likewise births and nurtures the existence of all that is, is relegated to a secondary plane. The privilege of luminosity diminishes the value of the materiality itself, in which and by which all things are continuously being created. Furthermore, even if there could be an *excess* to luminosity that hints at a form of darkness intrinsic to the Creator in Rahner's model, would not the divine disclosure come dangerously close to binding things visible to the logic of self-evidence because of an "intrinsic lucidity" residing in the maker?[36] Could luminosity not lead to the sort of limits that, clothed in piety, dangerously reduce the mystery's ineffability to the facile categories that Rahner himself sought to avoid? We might become capable of pointing with our fingers and stating, as he puts it: "there is God," turning the sublime into an idol. The intelligibility of light can facilitate the pointing to otherness, perhaps even the use of designations that even Rahner uses, such as meaninglessness, irrelevance, non-being, evil, or immorality, in reference to that which is ethnically, religiously, politically, and sentiently different. Only such instances that radiate their "luminosity of being" would then be attributed with being like God.

Instead, pulling Rahner's principle of disclosure by means of differentiation in the direction of the dark teotlizing of Aztec theology, with its unexpected shapes and fecund self-actualizations that can appear antithetical to classical Christian views, can aid Christian understandings of divine creativity becoming sacred mystery. Hence, in circling back to Aztec theology, as a way to metamorphose Rahner's understandings of the process of the self-disclosure of the grounding matrix, the sublime can take a turn toward the fragrance of beauty seeping through withering flowers, joyful notes harmonized in songs of lament. Genuine configurations of the "holy" in the form of the shamanic incarnations of Tezcatlipoca could then make room for the sacredness of *tlazolli* or "stuff out of place" (disorder, decomposition, displacement, disintegration, decay).³⁷ In that regard, the ambiguity of teotlizing the primordial creative beginnings might explicitly weave constructive elements into things destructive.

Dark Mystery

Teotlizing—in which darkness can be recognized as creative, sustaining, and sacred—could be for Christians a means by which relationships of seeming contrasts are brought together by the divine matrix. In bringing all things into relationship by means of the offer of freedom for all things to self-organize themselves, the divine matrix activates the space for disruption and creation according to their own aim and agency.³⁸ These relationships shape the universe into a fragile togetherness that continuously interrupts itself, as organisms interact with one another in surprising ways. Thus is the becoming of the divine matrix.

Nearing Aztec theology, a darkened matrix begets light and all things visible, cradling each day, bringing all things spatially into an interruptive relationship. This kind of becoming follows the weaving-like motion of *nepantla*, "the principal pattern in *teotl*'s ceaseless becoming and transforming,"³⁹ consisting of a "dynamic condition of being abundantly middle, betwixt and between, or centered."⁴⁰ In Rahner, likewise, God, as generative and differentiating ground, expands into the space of another.⁴¹ The divine matrix that differentiates all things, hence, would beget itself. It would become as cosmos through an ongoing motion, interweaving divinity with cosmic macroprocess and microprocesses, things in their interrelated difference comingling, disrupting one another, becoming simultaneously same and other (*nepantla*). Single threads, when interlaced, create patterns, possibilities, and change.

To draw again from both Aztec theology and Rahner, by the divine matrix interweaving things creative into destructive elements, tangibility would mean that the sacred mystery will shift shapes in terms of the "continuous cyclical struggle (*agon*) of paired opposites, polarities, or dualities" becoming betwixt.⁴² Things prior can become disrupted "in the course of creating something posterior."⁴³ Viewed positively, destructive enfleshments can engender constructive shamanic manifestations at points of in/betweenness. Yet the embodiment of things creative, their becoming tangible, can be opaque due to their interwoven form, and so difficult to identify as purely creative or entirely destructive. This motion can be both the means of sober realization of the world's innumerable conflicts and a hopeful expectation of what might be beneficial for the whole.

Indeed, the fifth age in which the Aztecs were living (the period of the Spanish conquest), with Tezcatlipoca as its overseer, was already defined by this type of fragile togetherness. Louise M. Burkhart explains that for the Aztecs this age was characterized by a sense of looming destruction and threat.[44] The *Florentine Codex* ambiguously describes this age as having been born out of "a time when there was still darkness" (*FC*, III:1), an interval of terror, of demons coming down and devouring humans, an age ushered in by the death of two gods, Nanauatzin and Tecuciztecatl, who threw themselves into the fire to become gods in the shape of the sun and the moon (*FC*, VII:2–9, 27). This fifth age, while superior to all previous ones, contains the seeds of both birth and its potential collapse. Its portents are gods dying and, later, innumerous bodies of young captives being slain, prickly maguey spines stained with their blood. Day and night, sun and moon, continued to rise by means of death.

Such ambiguous interplay between destruction and creation that the generative darkness of Tezcatlipoca represented was incomprehensible to the Spanish friars. "Epithets pertaining to the major indigenous deities, Tezcatlipoca in particular, were applied to the Christian God if they were compatible with his character,"[45] Burkhart explains. Though for the Aztecs, *teotl*'s interrelated unity gives rise to all things and, hence, multiple ways of using the term *teotl*, the friars reduced it to a category of "moral order," while anything opposite to it was *tlacatecolotl*—antistructure, sorcery, ghostly, immorality, and the demonic. Tezcatlipoca, because s/he was the overseer of the Aztecs' present age, eventually evolved in Spanish vernacular into a power opposite to *teotl*, a disruptive force rent asunder from its regenerative potential. Not so for the Aztecs, for whom Tezcatlipoca, particularly as wisdom, continued to be creator and knower of humans, the seer seeking to guide them into benign forms of communal living (*FC*, VI).

This complex web of interrelationships—shaped by processes of begetting and becoming (teotlizing), differentiation, and interwoven dualities (*nepantla*)—takes on the divine-cosmic form of sacred mystery as "flower and song."[46] The divine matrix becomes "flower and song" as destructive elements of struggle, with negative enfleshments such as the bloodshed and conquest of war, take a creative turn. "Flower and song" arises as care in the human community, a (com)passion for the enhancement of quality of life. For instance, the mystico-military rituals and practices of priestly and warrior classes become interrupted by the poetry of the Aztec sages (*tlamatinime*), who believed that words of wisdom would transfigure the divine foundation of the universe and its human structures. Participation in "flower and song" would contribute to the self-sustaining, enhancing, and regenerating impulses that would recreate it.[47] Hence the sacred mystery of "flower and song" that the divine matrix becomes, rather than "making" in the sense of a brute force or divine will being imposed upon the cosmos, or of shaping the cosmos according to a luminous or perfected image, begets and becomes as fragile togetherness.

A poem of the Aztec ruler Nezahualcóyotl beautifully portrays this teotlizing aspect of "flower and song":

> With flowers You write, O Giver of Life;
> with songs You give color,
> with songs You shade
> those who must live on earth.[48]

A fragile relationality displaying an earthly kind of mystery then means that a sacred harmony of opposites can become concrete in the endless fashioning and refashioning into "flower and song" of "the consummate cosmic artist-shaman," the darksome matrix.[49] In Christian terms, a Tezcatlipocan divine maker creates (or teotlizes itself) from within spatially (differentiating unity) through the divine motion of *nepantla* (interweaving polarities). Things invisible materialize into a fragile loveliness, like a flower, amidst violence. Ubiquitously, God can be in horror too, interweaving creation into destruction. The cosmos, in embodying such paradoxical beauty, becomes "flower and song," a complex poem of affirmations toward creation seeping through the cracks of multiple negations. It is the temporary incarnation of creation arising from the divine darkness, quite Tezcatlipocan, by means of a betwixting motion. The cosmos in its open-ended shape shifting into "flower and song" then holds the infinite attributes in a manner that is dynamically sacred, tangibly yet inexplicably, shamanic.

Thinking Further: Possibilities

This comparative exercise leads me to think that the divine matrix teotlizing itself tangibly, that is, creation from God in the sense of the generative ground begetting itself and darkly becoming as cosmos, can offer an interplay between things visible and invisible that does not allow for a plain view of the maker nor the "making" process. The outcomes of all things being brought into fragile unity, our "flower and song," might tempt us to designate every Tezcatlipocan darkness—that is, the sacred mystery of another—as demonic, resulting not only in exclusion and separation but the designations of morality and immorality. In Christianity, nonetheless, some conceptualizations of God as distant Creator, with their conquering effects against the vulnerable—reincarnations of colonialism—show how obscure the tangibility of this sacred mystery can be.

Christians might compare the shape of this primordial space of creativity, teotlizing itself according to "flower and song," to God as Creator. In this space, interwoven with possibilities for creativity amidst disorder, nothing might be lost! This is not to condone any form of abuse or violence.[50] On the contrary, horror threatens the survival of our epoch, and again, if pulled in the direction of something like the Creator God, can then denote a not-too-distant divine reality. And because "everything is interconnected in a web of sacredness," as Sylvia Marcos puts it, nothing and perhaps no one can be kept apart from this sublime incarnation.[51] Rather than self-evident, the invisible becoming visible might be darkly fragile, and like a flower growing through cracks in Spanish Harlem, barely recognizable.

This would be the call for humanity, perhaps, for making a difference, for enmeshment in the world. A robust understanding of the cosmos calls for an enormous responsibility on the part of human communities, particularly religious communities, to build collaboratively a place where the manifold, and at times competing, ecosystems can find a sustainable home. As with Rahner, "even the most spiritual acts still have extension in that corporeal nature, by which human beings, even as spiritual persons, are in touch with one another in a real material spatio-temporal unity."[52] In a fragile togetherness, new social structures that liberate humanity from inflicting human sacrifice—of those within and beyond our borders—can be constructed at the political, economic, social, religious, and cultural levels. Reversing the effects caused by the conquering of bodies, any body, including non-human bodies, can aid in letting the earth flourish more abundantly in all its diversity of life. This would be another way, perhaps more darkly so, to describe Rahner's view on the incarnation of the mystery as God's free epiphany. In the embrace of this earthen epiphany as "flower and song," may creativity continue to disrupt destructive impulses in our world!

Notes

1. Karl Rahner, "Man in the Presence of Absolute Mystery," in *Foundations of Christian Faith: An Introduction to the Idea of Christianity* (New York: Crossroad Publishing Company, 1986), 76–77.
2. Miguel León-Portilla, *Aztec Thought and Culture: A Study of the Ancient Nahuatl Mind* (Norman: University of Oklahoma Press, 1963), 93. I am aware that the term "Nahua theology" has been used by some to capture components of theological thinking prior to the Mexica like that of the Toltecs and what is called Aztec proper. See Orlando O. Espín, "Aztec Traditional Religion," in *An Introductory Dictionary of Theology and Religious Studies*, ed. Orlando O. Espin and James B. Nickoloff (Collegeville, Minnesota: Liturgical Press, 2007), 930. In this chapter, I prefer the term "Aztec theology," because it is more widely recognizable.
3. Rahner, "Man in the Presence of Absolute Mystery," 45.
4. Through a similar project, though dealing with another religious tradition, participants in the Conference on the Globalization of Yoruba Religious Culture held in 1999 similarly challenged the manner in which the term "world religions" has been employed to hold in contempt, render invisible, exclude, and consider some religions like Yoruba as minor contenders. See Jacob K. Olupona and Terry Rey, eds., Introduction to *Orisa Devotion as World Religion: The Globalization of Yoruba Religious Culture* (Madison: University of Wisconsin Press, 2008). An earlier yet important essay challenging the term "little traditions" is that of Robert J. Miller, "Button, Button . . . Great Tradition, Little Tradition, Whose Tradition?" *Anthropological Quarterly* 39, no. 1 (1966): 26–42.
5. See Raúl Fornet-Betancourt, *Transformación intercultural de la filosofía: Ejercicios teoréticos y prácticos de filosofía intercultural desde Latinoamerica en el context de la globalización* (Bilbao, Spain: Editorial Desclée de Brower, S.A., 2001), 23–52.
6. *Florentine Codex, Introduction & Indices*, ed. Fray Bernadino de Sagahún, and trans. from the Aztec, with notes and illustrations by Charles E. Dibble and Arthur J. O. Anderson (Santa Fe, N.M.: The School of American Research and The University of Utah, 1978), 45; see also 53. From this point, notations from the *Florentine Codex* appear on the text as *FC*. The year of publication varies according to the volume.
7. See Hugh Nicholson, "The Reunification of Theology and Comparison in the New Comparative Theology," *Journal of the American Academy of Religion* 77, no. 3 (2009): 609–46. For a definition of "anonymous Christianity," see Karl Rahner, *Karl Rahner in Dialogue: Conversations and Interviews 1965–1982*, ed. Paul Imhof and Hubert Biallowons (New York: Crossroad Publishing Company, 1986), 135.
8. James Maffie similarly describes his project, in which also he engages these thinkers, as a reconstruction in Aztec philosophy. See James Maffie, *Aztec Philosophy: Understanding a World in Motion* (Boulder: University Press of Colorado, 2014), 10–11.
9. For Jacques Derrida, a meaning in the written text remains always postponed or deferred (never future enough) because of the disruptive element of difference already embedded in the text. Jacques Derrida, "Différance," in *Margins of Philosophy*, trans. Alan Bass (Chicago: University of Chicago Press, 1982), 1–28.
10. Paul Ricoeur, *Hermeneutics & the Human Sciences* (Cambridge: Cambridge University Press, 1981), 143.

11. Maffie, *Aztec Philosophy*, 88.
12. See León-Portilla, *Aztec Thought and Culture*, 89; Hermann Beyer, "Das aztekische Götterbild Alexander von Humboldt's," in *Wissenschaftliche Festschrift zu Enthüllung des von Seiten S. M. Kaiser Wilhem II, dem Mexicanischen Volke zum Jubiläum, seiner Unabhängigkeit Gestifteten Humboldt-dekmals von* (Mexico City: Müller hnos., 1910), 116. For a summary of the scholarship on the subject of *teotl*, see Maffie, *Aztec Philosophy*, 80–86. While the perceived phenomena were named in distinct ways by the various tribal groups, migration facilitated an expansion in the knowledge of the cosmic and divine manifestations. Over time, names corresponding to the natural forces evolved in accordance with the language of each tribal group, as the functions these represented traveled from culture to culture and from one period of time to the next. Hence, many names can be attributed to the same divine quality.
13. León-Portilla, *Aztec Thought and Culture*, 99.
14. See Maffie, *Aztec Philosophy*, 85–86; and Eva Hunt, *Transformations of the Hummingbird: Cultural Roots of a Zinacantecan Mythical Poem* (Ithaca, N.Y.: Cornell University Press, 1977), 55.
15. Sagahún, *Florentine Codex, Introduction & Indices*, 87.
16. Maffie, *Aztec Philosophy*, 24.
17. Maffie, *Aztec Philosophy*, 22.
18. Maffie, *Aztec Philosophy*, 85.
19. Maffie, *Aztec Philosophy*, 38.
20. León-Portilla, *Aztec Thought and Culture*, 98; Miguel León-Portilla, ed., *Native Mesoamerican Spirituality: Aztec, Ucatec, Quiche-Maya and Other Sacred Traditions* (New York: Paulist Press, 1980), 246. For a more detailed feminist interpretation of the bi-genderness of deities and cosmos (termed duality in her work), see also Sylvia Marcos, *Taken from the Lips: Gender and Eros in Mesoamerican Religions* (Leiden and Boston: Brill Academic Publishers, 2006), 11–29.
21. Quoted in León-Portilla, *Aztec Thought and Culture*, 80.
22. León-Portilla, *Aztec Thought and Culture*, 92; see also the *Florentine Codex, Book 1: The Gods* (1970).
23. Rahner, "Man in the Presence of Absolute Mystery," 61.
24. Rahner, "Man in the Presence of Absolute Mystery," 82, 85.
25. Rahner, "Man in the Presence of Absolute Mystery," 82, 85.
26. Rahner, "Man in the Presence of Absolute Mystery," 81.
27. The world, with its immense complexity, is the expression of the triune love of unity being made present in its plurality. See Karl Rahner, "The Theology of the Symbol," *Theological Investigations, Vol. IV: More Recent Writings* (Baltimore: Helicon Press; London: Darton, Longman & Todd, 1966), 221–86. The Trinitarian aspect of the divine self-communication is beyond the purview of this essay.
28. Rahner, "Man in the Presence of Absolute Mystery," 86.
29. Karl Rahner, *Spirit in the Church* (New York: Crossroad Publishing Company, 1985), 14–15, 17.
30. Rahner, "Man in the Presence of Absolute Mystery," 63.
31. Maffie, *Aztec Philosophy*, 85–86.
32. Karl Rahner, *Spirit in the World* (New York: Continuum, 1994), 351, 353.

33. Rahner, "Man in the Presence of Absolute Mystery," 65–85.
34. Karl Rahner, *Hearer of the Word* (New York: Continuum, 1994), 22, 28–30.
35. Rahner, *Hearer of the Word*, 57.
36. Rahner, "Man in the Presence of Absolute Mystery," 82–83.
37. *Tlazolli* could relate to excessiveness, licentiousness, and even filth and excrement (Maffie, *Aztec Philosophy*, 97).
38. I am drawing in part from the meaning that William E. Connolly gives to the term "self-organization," which he defines as "a process" or "activity" of an organism "encountering a shock or disturbance" that can "periodically help to bring something new into the world." William E. Connolly, *The Fragility of Things: Self-Organizing Processes, Neoliberal Fantasies, and Democratic Activism* (Durham and London: Duke University Press, 2013), 8.
39. Maffie identifies three types of motions in Aztec metaphysics—*olin, malinalli*, and *nepantla*—of which *nepantla* is the most fundamental. *Olin* can be analogous to the "up-and-down, back-and forth, to-and-fro movement of bouncing balls and the life-sustaining Fifth-Sun" (Maffie, *Aztec Philosophy*, 187). *Malinalli* refers to the motion of twisting and being twisted related to the processes of "spinning, whirling, revolving, and gyrating," also symbolic of transformation within and across life-death cycles (Maffie, *Aztec Philosophy*, 263–66, 355).
40. Maffie, *Aztec Philosophy*, 355–56.
41. Rahner, *Spirit in the World*, 364–65.
42. Maffie, *Aztec Philosophy*, 137.
43. Maffie, *Aztec Philosophy*, 27.
44. See Louise M. Burkhart, *The Slippery Earth: Nahua-Christian Moral Dialogue in Sixteenth-Century Mexico* (Tucson: University of Arizona Press, 1989), 74–75; Agustín Yañez, *Mitos indígenas* (Mexico: Ediciones de la Universidad Nacional Autónoma, 1942), xvi.
45. Burkhart, *The Slippery Earth*, 39.
46. León-Portilla, *Aztec Thought and Culture*, 46; David Carrasco, *Religions of Mesoamerica: Cosmovision and Ceremonial Centers* (Long Grove, Ill.: Waveland Press, Inc., 1990), 79.
47. Maffie, *Aztec Philosophy*, 106.
48. See León-Portilla, ed., *Native Mesoamerican Spirituality*, 244.
49. Maffie, *Aztec Philosophy*, 38–40.
50. Rita Nakashima Brock, *Journeys by Heart: A Christology of Erotic Power* (New York: Crossroad Publishing Company, 1988).
51. Marcos, *Taken from the Lips*, 118.
52. Karl Rahner, "Personal and Sacramental Piety," *Theological Investigations, Vol. II: Man In the Church* (Baltimore: Helicon, 1963), 120.

3 Comparative Theology and the Postmodern God of "Perhaps"

A RESPONSE TO SYDNOR AND PADILLA

Kristin Beise Kiblinger

This essay responds to Elaine Padilla and Jon Paul Sydnor by considering their arguments in light of the view of God developed by John D. Caputo. Caputo's view of God was chosen because it represents new, promising directions for conceiving God in our times and has important implications for comparative theology.

To place Caputo's God in context in very broad strokes, in the first half of the twentieth century, talk of God and religion had fallen out of favor among many philosophers, but then God made a comeback in philosophy in the late twentieth century with the postmodern movement. However, as Christina M. Gschwandtner has argued, this retrieved God has been significantly reconceived.[1] God is "back," but postmodern theologians, especially those influenced by French thought, are now speaking of God very differently. Caputo's God will illustrate this difference, and comparative theologians, I suggest, should consider it.

While of course Caputo's theological moves have not met with universal support (there is never consensus on anything in theology), his work has been much discussed and widely lauded.[2] Furthermore, Caputo's thought has much in common with numerous prominent thinkers of our time, such as Jean-Luc Marion, Richard Kearney, and Merold Westphal, who share Caputo's phenomenological approach, his view of human boundary experiences as having a religious character, his defense of passion, and his turn away from "the limits of reason alone."[3] Because it is important that comparative theologians consider current trends and developments, I use Caputo as one exemplar in order to look at his view of God alongside the views of Sydnor and Padilla, at the same time exploring the ramifications of Caputo's thought for our religiously pluralistic situation.

Sydnor compares Jürgen Moltmann's social Trinity with the Buddhist Nagarjuna's exposition of emptiness because he thinks that Buddhist thought about relationality can offer new ways to understand God as Trinity as well as the nature of the soul, freedom, and Christian love. Padilla compares Karl Rahner's "grounding matrix" to Aztec theology's *teotl* so that each thought system might be strengthened with the help of ideas from the other, resulting in more attention to love within the Aztec theological system and more sensuality and consideration of darkness in Rahner's thought.

I observe points of agreement between Caputo and both comparative theologians with their common emphases on immanence (Padilla) and relationality (Sydnor), but Caputo's thought also challenges them both in significant ways. I suggest that Sydnor and Padilla could benefit from following Caputo in his rethinking of God, because Caputo's postmodern God of "perhaps" helps respond to problems that have plagued past theology, illuminates issues involving immanence and relationality, and helps to justify (and lay the necessary theoretical groundwork for) comparative theology.

Caputo's God

Caputo's system begins with an emphasis on the fact that we are all historically located, thinking in particular languages and within certain cultures, shaped by various background experiences, and so forth.[4] As finite beings, we are conditioned and have no way to stand outside of our conditioning. Therefore, Caputo stresses that we can possess no unconditioned Truth—i.e., no unmediated access to what is unconditioned. Any occurrence that somehow breaks through or overcomes the conditions and constraints of our world—let us call it a sacred or transcendent happening—in being known by us and taking place in space and time, thereby becomes conditioned and interpreted, pulled into worldly economies. Thus, structurally speaking, whatever experience of truth we *have* is conditioned, while what is transcendent or *un*conditioned, we do not, and cannot, have. The unconditioned always slips away or is deferred, ever to come but never present.

Relatedly, because we lack this direct access and also because all earthly languages are conditioned, there can be no final way for us to speak of or name the unconditioned.[5] Therefore, in choosing his terms, although Caputo often uses Christian language due to his inherited legacy, he also deliberately varies his language, sometimes speaking of God or the kingdom, other times of justice, the gift, a call, a ghost, and so forth. Explaining his approach to language, Caputo argues that words *call for* something that they cannot deliver. Illustrating this point with the example of the word "democracy," Caputo reminds us that no actual democracy ever lives up to what is called for by that term.[6] When it comes to theology and his words for the unconditioned, Caputo is after what is *called for* by the words and not wedded to this or that particular name. He insists on translatability and will not give any name final privilege—not even the name "God."

Despite this recognized limitation of language, nevertheless in Caputo's view it is not futile to try to talk about the unconditioned precisely because of this ability of names to call beyond themselves. Here, I will mostly use the name "God" because of the topic at hand within this section of the volume, but this approach to that name (that is, the fact of its translatability and revisability) must be kept in mind and will be important to the implications for comparative theology, as discussed later in this chapter.

In trying to get at what names harbor and call for, Caputo utilizes Jacques Derrida's deconstruction. Caputo sees constant deconstruction as essential because deconstruction is a hermeneutic principle that exposes conditionedness in the name of that which is not conditioned.[7] For example, we must continually deconstruct our laws in the name of justice because our conditioned laws can never fully contain or accomplish perfect, unconditioned justice.[8] Similarly, we must question our human theologies perpetually, as they can never adequately conceive God. Any denying or forgetting that fact by claiming to espouse hard-and-fast religious truths would be idolatrous, an arrogant overestimating of our ability and a misjudging of our position, forgetting our finitude and trying to promote ourselves over others by exempting ourselves from admitting the conditioning that is universal to all humans.

In fact, because we cannot directly (i.e., without mediating conditioning) *know* God, Caputo, when he references such notions as God, often adds "if there is such a thing" and reiterates that he speaks from faith, not knowledge. Caputo will not speak of the unconditioned, or God, as identifiable or definite but instead stretches language to try to express God's murkier status in our experience, resorting to imagery such as ghosts or whispers that he describes as haunting our thinking and ways of living with radically other possibilities. Relatedly, because the unconditioned always slips away and can never be present (because in becoming present it would become conditioned), we thus go astray in doing ontology, speaking of God as being (or Being). According to Caputo, however, we should not just give up our pursuit of the unconditioned altogether because we can make the "phenomenological turn" and do what he calls hauntology.[9] That is, we can analyze phenomenologically this experience of feeling spooked, restless, and drawn to the hope of something else.

Caputo describes this experience of being haunted as akin to a call. Although we cannot grasp God, we feel called by God. We feel called toward what exceeds and defies our earthly economies. Caputo is careful to qualify, however, that the phenomenology that he has in mind is not your average phenomenology but rather is special in that it is a "phenomenology of what is *not given*" or a phenomenology of anonymity.[10] In other words, although we may experience a call, as a result of our conditioned state, we cannot identify with certainty the caller or even determine whether there really is a caller. Is it God? We are not in a position to know.

The bright side, however, is that Caputo sees this situation of uncertainty as the very condition for the possibility of genuine faith. If, when we express commitment to God, we feel that we *know* God's existence and nature, it is a different matter because our so-called faith would then be safe and would take shape within an economy of eternal rewards. This would not be authentic faith as Caputo defines it.

To explain, Caputo considers the cases of the biblical figures Abraham and Mary.[11] Inexplicably, a distraught Abraham was told to sacrifice his beloved son. Mysteriously, Gabriel tells a baffled, unmarried Virgin Mary that she is to bear the messiah. In these moments, Abraham and Mary must feel utterly bewildered, dumbfounded, and terrified, not secure in any knowledge. It is these biblical figures' "yes," their decision and commitment *when things are incomprehensible and the future unclear* that is admirable and is what has made these figures paragons of faith. Their non-knowing is crucial, for if they were saying "yes" to something understandable and within our horizons rather than something exceeding our horizons, it would be just more of the same rather than the opening to something radically new and other (i.e., the sacred). Their non-knowing is what allows their affirmative choices to be unselfishly motivated, unconditional, a breaking through of worldly economies, and thus an opening into sacred time. In contrast, if instead things had been clear, Caputo quips about Abraham that then Abraham would not have been "the father of faith but of good investments and estate planning."[12] The stories would lose their force, Abraham and Mary no longer remarkable or mythic. In sum, these are not stories of knowledge of something groundable; they are stories of fallible passions and risk.

The uncertainty central to Caputo's way of viewing faith shifts responsibility to us. God's truth is not an object for us to receive or know but something we must create or do. The unconditioned is trying to come, and we must help it come, as do Abraham and Mary. Caputo says that justice, for example, does not exist, but it calls; it makes a demand upon us to *make* this world just.[13] If we could have a firm hold of the unconditioned, if it could be known and present and named, that would not create this same onus; it is only when and because God is enigmatic, ever deferred and "to come," that we feel the vanishing trace that stokes our desire.

Thus, our effort and passion are best summoned not by ontotheology or metaphysics but by a more humble, "weak" theology that confesses that direct knowledge of God is elusive. Correspondingly, our effort and passion are best drawn out not by the traditional God Almighty but rather by conceiving of God as "weak." Here we have yet another of Caputo's themes. By the "weakness of God," Caputo means that the name of God is the name of an event, not an entity: of a call, not a causality. God's mode is vocative, not nominative.[14] We glimpse God in moments when business-as-usual is interrupted, our economies overcome with an unexpected excess of love or generosity that defies logical explanation and motive, our normal systems suspended, as when there is somehow a welling up of hope in the face of hopelessness, forgiveness of the unforgivable, or unmerited grace. Caputo wants a theology of this *event*.

In this system, God calls but does not coerce or determine. Events take place by the whispers that disturb, spook, inspire, unsettle. Events are awakenings of love; they are not brute forces. Therefore, calls are subject to contingencies such as going unheeded or being misunderstood. God as a weak force has no enforcing army, Caputo says. (Indeed, it is because God is but a weak force that Auschwitzes have been possible.)[15] In short, Caputo does not choose between seeing God either as an omnipotent super-being or a total fiction, between God as either the ultimate real or completely unreal; here, rather, God is what is not yet real. God is a "flicker of hope."[16]

In Caputo's recent book, *The Insistence of God*, Caputo explains all this by saying that he does not believe in God's existence but in God's insistence, and that "this is an insistence whose existence *we* are expected to deliver."[17] Moreover, if calls are subject to contingencies and it is up to us to assist the insistence, then the "truth of God may or may not come true," which is why Caputo's book thematizing insistence is subtitled "a theology of perhaps" and why he says that "one must . . . always say 'perhaps' for God."[18] "Does God exist?" Caputo asks. Perhaps. "It remains to be seen."[19]

Conventional, strong theologians want something safe, something to give them security and assurance while, in contrast, Caputo straightforwardly faces risk. Caputo argues that just as the risk of non-knowing is the condition for Abraham's genuine faith, risk is always a necessary condition for any kind of real love, virtue, or religiosity; it is the necessary condition for, and what is involved in, the event. This means that Caputo's theology of "perhaps" should not be seen negatively as indecisiveness or fence-sitting; on the contrary, it is strongly affirmative—yet what it passionately affirms is an insistence, the event trying to come. We cannot know whether anyone is out there to ensure it will all turn out well in the end.

The "perhaps" is what keeps God an insistence rather than an entity or being. That is, again, Caputo turns away from ontotheology, or theology about the sacred as Being or as a being, in favor of the event. Importantly, at the same time, this is a turn away from the otherworldly or supernatural and to this world and, with that, a turn from reliance on an omnipotent God to our own initiative and responsibility.

CAPUTO'S HANDLING OF PADILLA'S AND SYDNOR'S THEMES

This turn from the otherworld to this world and from God's omnipotence to human responsibility is the aspect of Caputo's thought that most closely pertains to Padilla's theme of immanence. Caputo, too, thematizes immanence in that he opposes two-worlds theology in favor of sticking with the plane of this material world. Moreover, Caputo does so by emphasizing relationality and interdependence, which happen to be Sydnor's central themes and are also discussed by Padilla.

Caputo sees his theology as "disabling the classical distinction between transcendence and immanence," because he redescribes transcendence as a "modality *of* the world."[20] That is, in Caputo's theology, if

God does not exist unless we "assist the insistence," then there is a mutual intertwining and interdependence "of God to us and us to God" rather than a human world versus divine world dichotomy or unbridgeable gap.[21] This resonates with Padilla's discussion of God and the cosmos co-creating one another according to Rahner's model.

On the one hand, Caputo has at times indicated a withholding of judgment about whether there is anything otherworldly. He has written, for instance, that "whether over and beyond . . . the lived experience of the call . . . , there is some entitative cause calling, some entity or hyper-entity out there with a proper name, verifiable by a metaphysical argument or certifiable by a divine revelation, is no part of my hypothesis, one way or the other." He leaves "that question in the domain of undecidability."[22] Caputo wants to suspend the question of the caller, change the subject, and stick to the experience of the call.[23]

On the other hand, however, especially in his recent book *The Insistence of God*, Caputo does announce clearly that he wants to look for more "material, experiential, existential, embodied" ways of thinking about religion, a direction shared by much contemporary religious thought.[24] "The supernatural," Caputo says, "must make a graceful exit."[25] Although Caputo's talk about humans being called by something other may still give the initial impression of dual worlds, and although the agnostic undecidability may still leave open the possibility of an otherworld or otherworldly being, ultimately Caputo maintains that the positing of anything otherworldly is detrimental.

Quite simply, for Caputo, the name of "God" is the name for the "promise of the world."[26] In support of this, Caputo remarks that the "inbreaking power of the Sermon on the Mount," for example, "does not consist in being a supernatural revelation delivered by a heavenman come down from the sky, proffering some account of things that lies beyond the ken of humankind." Rather, the Sermon on the Mount's power consists in it being "a shocking re-envisioning of human life, of an unprecedented form of life."[27]

If assisting the insistence means saying yes to the promise of this worldly life, however, it also means confronting all the risk that life involves. Caputo sees life not as a teleological movement but as riddled with chance.[28] Living in faith as Caputo defines it means that the outcome cannot be certain.

It is a principle of the two-worlds theology that Caputo opposes that if something is not eternal, it has no value; but Caputo thinks that the opposite is true. "The only things that can be valued or treasured," Caputo writes, "are things that are mortal, finite, transient, and temporal, their very impermanence being the condition under which we hold them dear."[29]

According to Caputo, the problem with submitting life to a "why" beyond life is that it "turn(s) this life into the coin of the realm in an eternal economy. The body of Jesus becomes a ticket to the great beyond.... It would be impossible to be generous... because everyone would know that generosity has its payoff in long-term returns," and so forth. Instead, the only way unselfishly and unconditionally to love God and one another is if there is no sure otherworld and God is not pictured as the Great Guarantor.[30]

Thus, although this way of thinking is materialism, we should not therefore assume that it is nihilism. Caputo is not a nihilist because he is not trying to "rid the world of 'transcendence' but simply to redescribe" transcendence.[31] For Caputo, "to invoke the name of God is not to call upon some otherworldly agent... It is to be called upon by something embedded within the world, and so also embedded within ourselves."[32]

Two-worlds theology is bound up with the old problem of the "gap," or distance, between the religious seeker or subject and the religious object. Caputo solves this problem of reference (or correspondence) by problematizing the polarities of this-world-versus-an-otherworld and of subject-versus-object. God and humans, transcendence and immanence are interdependent. He often calls this "chiasmic intertwining." Like Sydnor here, Caputo strongly emphasizes relationality.

To illustrate, Caputo uses the example of sight: "Our power of vision, as well as the particular structure of the color spectrum available to sight, is a direct and precise effect of the astronomical composition of our sun, which has set the parameters of vision which we... have evolved. To ask whether what we see, as if it were inside our head, 'corresponds' to what is out there, 'outside our head,' is to ask a question not only without an answer but without a meaning.... We are the relation between our bodies and our world." Our sight exists and arises in dependence on and in relation to what is seen. "The problem of 'epistemological correspondence' that goes back to Descartes... is finally resolved by being dissolved.... We do not have to 'build a bridge' to the world. We are the bridge.... We are neither obliged nor able to construct a relationship to the world because the relation constructs us."[33]

Caputo disputes another related problem in similar fashion. Critics of postmodern thought charge that, instead of finding reality, according to postmodernists we merely construct reality. By seeing everything as constructed, opponents say, "we have relativized the world to our knowledge and locked ourselves inside our own representations, cut off from reality."[34] To combat these charges, Caputo uses the work of Bruno Latour, who argues that construction and reality (or subjectivity and objectivity) are correlated directly, not inversely.[35] Take the famous case of Louis Pasteur as an instance of how reality is revealed. By designing various experiments and "ingenious stagings," Pasteur, in a manner of speaking, "tricked" the yeast in lactic acid "into making an appearance." The facts are *contrived* by experiment or construction, yet nevertheless "the ferment is invented not by Pasteur but by the ferment." An experiment is an event, Caputo thinks. Discoverers, Latour reminds us, are not just discoverers but actors. According to Caputo, then, "the pertinent distinction is not between construction and reality, but between successful and unsuccessful constructions...When constructions succeed, the result is [new] accessed reality."[36]

Caputo's stress upon intertwining and interdependence relates back to why this is not nihilism, narcissism, or total secularization but still contains a religious dimension. Caputo, as I understand him, is not simply saying that we are all there is: "There is no big Other, but neither are there merely human agents. There are events that take us by surprise."[37] Caputo describes his theology as a theory of interpretation, "not Feuerbach."[38] "We construct, but we do not create *ex nihilo*."[39]

Some think that "if a human hand has intervened" such that there has been some construction, the truth is thereby "sullied" or suspect. To them, theology must be "made directly by God, as opposed to a discourse produced by us about God." And yet, Caputo points out that in religion as in science, without the human hand, new reality could not come into view. The more construction and mediation, Latour argues, the more discovery of new reality. Caputo shows us that conditioning, or construction, which is inevitable, should not be seen as an "obstacle to reality but [as] an angle of entry into the real." However, and this is also key, because conditions and contexts change, the angles of entry and views of reality are always revisable. We should not dogmatically cling to any current angle or view. Deconstruction must be an ongoing pursuit or doing of truth.[40]

What, then, are the implications of Caputo's theology for religious plurality and comparative theology?

COMPARATIVE THEOLOGY AND THE POSTMODERN GOD OF "PERHAPS"

Caputo proposes not only a "weak" God (i.e., God as event, not entity; as a call, not a causality), but along with that, a "weak" theological discourse. The theology here is weak because it confesses the limits of our epistemic situation and thus is humble about what it can yield. Caputo fully admits that his approach "issues in a thin theology, not a corpulent body of beliefs." It cannot "serve up" direct access to God.[41] This theology proceeds in faith, not knowledge. It will not do metaphysics, but only hermeneutics and phenomenology. The unconditioned cannot be purely grasped; thus, even the very existence and nature of the unconditioned are undecidable, giving this theology a provisional quality, a modesty, and also an openness. Because this theology recognizes its dependence on a particular context, it is subject to translation, revision, and recontextualization. Clearly, all of this aids and helps justify comparative engagement.

For Caputo, truth is not correspondence. And if truth is not correspondence, then there can be more than one true religious discourse, and the structure of an event may stir within multiple traditions.[42] For Caputo, religions are "ways of figuring the event, ways events take form."[43] There is no *singular* event or revelation but event*s* and revelation*s* (plural), and yet each is unique—true in a different situation, springing from different concerns.

In this view, confessional religions, like names, contain something that they cannot contain (i.e., the event); they promise something that they cannot deliver.[44] Therefore, we need to ask, Caputo says, "whether we need God" (our own theology's particular language) "to describe what we think is going on in the name of God."[45] In other words, no particular tradition's language can be allowed to "have a lock on the event" because of the deconstructibility of languages as opposed to the undeconstructibility of the event.[46]

This way of seeing religion and the name of "God" has repercussions for how we see the self and our home traditions. In this framework, selves and particular traditions, because they are conditioned, are less autonomous, more vulnerable, and thus more receptive. In fact, Caputo problematizes the self-versus-other dichotomy, because if non-knowing and doubt are structurally necessary for faith, then suddenly the distinction between believer and non-believer, self and religious other, begins to give way. In addition, if, when I read the other, I admit that my reading is conditioned, then I cannot know whether my reading has more to do with the other's religion or with my own. The differentiating line is impossible to draw.[47]

It is not that Caputo thinks that we must float free of any religious affiliation or location. On the contrary, we must admit the ways that we are shaped by our inherited traditions and continue to speak our languages; what else could we speak? However, Caputo recommends "faithful infidelity." That is, he suggests belonging to our communities but with "considerable unease," for he warns that we must keep deconstructing our theologies. "Untroubled belief is trouble," he insists.[48] Such a stance, I would argue, helps the comparative theologian both confess his or her commitment and at the same time justify the need to turn to the other, giving the other's perspective weight as a disturber and haunting specter that unsettles us and keeps us considering other possibilities, mindful of the fact of our conditioning.

Caputo's work also helps address prevalent worries about comparative theology found in the theoretical literature. There has been concern that comparative theology may distort the other by seeing the other's system through the home system's lens and that comparative theology is a self-interested use of the other (hence the talk of hegemony, colonialism, and so on). If we approach comparative theology from Caputo's framework, however, *of course* our reading of the other is conditioned. How could it not be? This is not a problem to overcome but just to acknowledge and proceed accordingly. Caputo's work suggests that the comparative theologian should not aspire to tell the unconditioned Truth about the meaning of the other's text; instead, she or he is seeking to prompt an event of *new* meaning and insight via the comparative juxtaposition. The worries about distorting the other amount to the old philosophical concern about correspondence. For Caputo, however, truth is not correspondence, and the subject-object dichotomy is dissolved when subject and object are seen as necessarily interrelated. A conditioned reading is no longer a problem but now becomes an "angle of entry."[49]

Not only does Caputo emphasize that our attempts to seek truth are conditioned, he insists as well that consequently what we are after (structurally and by definition) remains elusive. Again, rather than being a problem, that fact is precisely what fuels and necessitates more and more comparative reading. It is what protects revisability and instills humility and openness. The religious other's different possibilities, with all of the doubts and risks bound up with them, are part of what haunts and calls us, prompting deconstruction.

Another worry expressed in the theoretical literature has been about grafting the other onto the home system rather than respecting deep difference. Influenced by Emmanuel Levinas, Caputo wants the other to remain other, for the other cannot help us deconstruct and cannot haunt us unless it is a genuinely new and different possibility. This is why Caputo's deconstruction prioritizes difference, particulars, and singularities.[50] Caputo is not saying that all theological discourses are different ways of speaking of the same reality. Caputo thinks we could never claim such a thing, because to know that, we would have to have a meta-view, a vantage point outside of our conditioned systems, which he denies is possible. The theology of religions underlying the comparative theory here is agnostic. Because of our conditioning, we cannot know whether one system is at the top of a hierarchy of degrees of truth, or whether we are all equals. We cannot know whether we are all attempting to speak of the same unconditioned or separate unconditioneds, or whether there even is such a thing. It is undecidable. Where would we be standing? If we knew for sure where we stood vis-à-vis others, we could not have authentic faith, since, again, faith requires non-knowing and risk, not assurance. (Assurance would pull our faith into an economy of reward.)

A possible objection might be that Caputo's approach imposes a particular Western philosophical viewpoint and suggests seeing others through its categories. However, Caputo does not mean to set out yet another view but rather to suggest a way of holding our views. His view of faith suggests a how, not a what. Caputo admits that his own system is conditioned and thus is not exempt from deconstruction. Caputo's weak theology is merely, he says, an "interim theology" or "work in progress."[51] Far from being imperialistic himself, Caputo thinks that it is *not* admitting our conditionedness, not admitting God's elusiveness that leads to imperialism, dogmatism, divisions, self-righteousness, and religious violence. By reminding us of the fragility and conditioned character of our institutions and doctrines, Caputo thinks that his theology provides the makings of a new and improved politics, "a politics of 'perhaps,' of a certain democracy to come."[52] In short, Caputo is not trying to dominate the closure; he opposes closure and says the whole point of his deconstructive system is to keep things open.[53]

In her description of the new way that God has been reconceived in postmodern thought, Gschwandtner admits that the thinkers she analyzes, including Caputo, are concerned with a version of the Jewish or Christian God and that her own analysis is in a Christian register, but she also thinks that some of the arguments may well apply also to other religious cultures and may be able to do productive work there.[54] Caputo, too, invites "analogous versions of something like the event in other traditions."[55] I myself have taken up that invitation with respect to Yogacara Buddhism.[56] For all of the reasons described previously, then, the objection about imposing Western categories can be answered.

COMPARING SYDNOR AND PADILLA TO CAPUTO

As I read Padilla's and Sydnor's stimulating comparisons, I found points in common with Caputo that I wish to applaud but also significant contrasts that helpfully raise some issues for further consideration. For Caputo, because we are conditioned, God (the unconditioned) cannot be directly accessed or known. Padilla, too, speaks of God as unknown when she insists that God is sacred mystery. However, Caputo explains the reason for his assertion that God is unknown and draws out the entailments of our non-knowing more than Padilla does, and those entailments prove to be quite important.

Padilla also shares with Caputo a desire to embrace risk (as does Sydnor); however, here again Caputo seems to go further than they do. For Caputo, the starting point of stressing our conditioning ultimately leads to conceiving of God only weakly as insisting, not existing, and it leads to keeping our theology weak. Because God only insists and calls (rather than coercing or causing) and because our theology cannot deliver knowledge of God (but only the confession that God always slips away), there is always a "perhaps" affixed to the name of God, which supports the embracing of risk and ensures that the risk goes "all the way down." Padilla endorses risk when she writes that she risks upsetting her own orthodoxy, but from what she says in her paper, it is not clear how her process framework was ever substantially in question or "weakened." Padilla promotes risk again when speaking of Aztec theology as pushing Rahner toward something less safe (in the sense of pushing Rahner's theology to confront darkness). However, it seems to me that she speaks of God as a sacred process without adding the "perhaps," without letting the risk go as deep as it might. She wants to encompass the darkness (emblematic of risk) into the sacred, but can we know that the darkness is sacred or whether there even is a sacred, as Padilla assumes? Or can we only have a passionate faith that there is a sacred and that the sacred can encompass darkness and then take responsibility ourselves for bringing light to darkness?

Likewise, Sydnor says that comparative theology demands taking risks, that he advocates vulnerability, and that conversion has to be a real possibility, and yet it is not clear from what he actually does in his paper that the possibility of conversion is ever really on the table, as he uses the religious other to deepen and bolster his original commitment. Also, Sydnor assumes a kind of teleology or positive outcome when the goal of emptiness is assumed to be a joyful, harmonious dance. Therefore, from Caputo's perspective, Sydnor stops short of the *deepest* uncertainty and risk, and so, with Caputo, I might encourage Sydnor to be even bolder in this respect.

A sharper difference between Caputo and the other two thinkers is that both Padilla and Sydnor speak in various ways of God manifesting or being present. For Caputo, however, the unconditioned can never be present, for in appearing, it becomes conditioned. God can only call or haunt, not be present. On the other hand, despite this key difference, the three thinkers nevertheless all do develop theologies that encourage us to strive to instantiate God in the world. Reading Caputo alongside the two comparativists, however, can help us consider the question of whether an incarnate God or a deferred God best fuels that striving.

Yet another instructive contrast between Caputo and the other thinkers has to do with Caputo's concerns about ontotheology. In promoting Caputo's work, it should be clear that I affirm a post-metaphysical trend in contemporary theology that he exemplifies. He wants to proceed via phenomenology, to work from how we experience God rather than trying to describe what God is. Sydnor shows glimmers of a turn to phenomenology when he speaks of learning about God by arguing from human experience and of interpreting *our reception* of God. In fact, he says at one point that God is not being. However, Sydnor's theology is not consistently post-metaphysical. He repeatedly refers to the "ontology of relation" and to "kinetic ontology." Sydnor moves away from a substance ontology to an ontology according to which being is dynamic and relational. That is a step in the right direction but still works on the level of being. Caputo, in contrast, wants to focus on what pulls us beyond being to what is not yet real. A theology of the event refers not to being of any type but rather to an "aspiration." It refers to "something that groans to be born, something that cannot be constricted to either the ontic or ontological order at all." An event, Caputo says, "is not an ontico-ontological episode on the plane of being but a disturbance within the heart of being ... that makes being restless."[57] Furthermore, it is worth noting that some scholars speak of Nagarjuna's emptiness as a rejection of ontology, whereas Sydnor characterizes it as a certain kind of ontology.[58]

In the end, both Padilla and Sydnor are trying to describe God; they both draw God as a plurality unified by relationship and love, whereas Caputo questions whether we can directly know and thus describe God's nature (as opposed to merely describing our experience of God). Rather than trying to describe God, Caputo says that God-talk, or theology, should instead be about what we are called to do in the name of God. In her own way, Padilla, too, wishes to emphasize duty, saying that the more robustly sacred world resulting from her comparative theology calls for more human responsibility. However, that appeal to human duty seems less integral to her system. Caputo's weak theology of "God, perhaps," it seems to me, more naturally lends itself to the focus on human initiative, for only if God is "God, perhaps" is it really up to us. Thus, again, perhaps Caputo could be helpful here.

Caputo desires to discard the otherworldly and turn to this world, and it is yet another strength of Padilla's work that she shares Caputo's concern with this material world, with all its warts and darkness. As Caputo presents God and humanity as interdependent, similarly Padilla affirms process thought's porous boundaries between God and the world. Padilla's process thought, like Caputo, is challenging traditional two-world theologies. However, although Caputo likes much about process thought, ultimately process thinkers are still doing metaphysics, albeit a distinctive metaphysics. Process thinkers are trying to construct a general description of reality, while Caputo wants to stick to describing human experience (i.e., phenomenology). Although admittedly there is debate among process thinkers about how to understand the relation of God and world, process thought is largely associated with panentheism. Caputo writes that "panentheism says that God's existence is *in* ours and ours in God's. But in a theology of 'perhaps,' God does not exist; God insists, and it is our responsibility to bring about something that exists."[59]

CAPUTO'S USEFULNESS FOR COMPARATIVE THEORY

Two more key motifs shared by all three thinkers, in various ways, are the themes of impermanence and interrelatedness. Addressing the former first, with the concepts of *nepantla* and *teotlizing*, Padilla stresses movement, process, and change in much the same way that Sydnor highlights positively the impermanence and change entailed by emptiness and dependent origination. Along similar lines, Caputo eschews Christian fixation with the stable and eternal, arguing instead that "the only things that can be valued or treasured are things that are . . . transient, and temporal, their very impermanence being the condition under which we hold them dear."[60] Positively, in their respective ways, then, each theologian embraces impermanence, insisting that love must be love in the midst of impermanence, death, and change. Caputo adds, however, a crucial emphasis on the fact that our theology, too, must be ever-changing and that deconstruction of religion must be an ongoing process—an emphasis that is useful for comparative theory.

Regarding the shared theme of interrelatedness, Padilla speaks at length of the interrelatedness of light and dark and of the way that everything might be seen as connected in a web of sacredness. Like Caputo, she wants to see God and the world as intermeshed. In expounding emptiness, concepts of interdependence and lack of own-being (*svabhava*) are central to Sydnor's work as well. Thus, all three scholars helpfully problematize various oppositional dualities by recognizing interdependences. However, also explicitly applying this line of thinking, as Caputo does, to the interconnection of subject and object, doubt and faith, and self and religious other again can be especially fruitful for comparative theory.

The three thinkers share not only certain key themes but also methodological aspects. Padilla dwells on the importance of poetry and art. Sydnor speaks of music and dance helping us to experience God when logic and math might fail. In addition, Sydnor stresses organic, intuitive integration over a mechanical comparison. This aligns with Caputo's use of poetics and myth and deconstruction's embrace of experimental, creative play rather than rule-governed interpretation.

Despite all these commonalities, when I nevertheless still encourage Padilla and Sydnor to follow Caputo in paying more attention to our conditioning and its implications, I do not mean to suggest that Sydnor and Padilla pretend to be completely unconditioned. On the contrary, Sydnor acknowledges that he stands in the Christian tradition, and Padilla notes her commitment to feminist and process thought. Clearly, these backgrounds condition their theologies. However, when it comes to theory, Sydnor and Padilla could benefit from Caputo's argument that conditionedness should not be viewed as a bad thing that we have to try to minimize or overcome as though we could ever access the other purely. Padilla spends much time defending her use of the *Florentine Codex*, recognizing its problematic conditioning under missionaries and translators. She states her aim to treat the Aztec system and Rahner's as "equal partners," avoiding any "pecking order" or "anonymous Christianity" (which is ironic, given the fact that she is using Rahner). In these and other ways, both Padilla and Sydnor distance themselves from the boogeyman of "colonialism." Caputo, I contend, could help comparative theologians defend against these worries if comparativists would take to heart and reiterate his points that 1) rather than an impediment, conditioning can be an angle of entry that can precipitate an event of new insight; that 2) we can never reach an unconditioned meta-location, so the thing to worry about is not how to lessen our constructions but instead which constructions are the most productive; that 3) emphasizing conditioning and drawing out its ramifications contributes to a new, more democratic politics; and that 4) the fear about being subjective subsides somewhat when we problematize the subject-object duality.

Further remarking on Caputo's usefulness for comparative theory, when we admit and stress our conditionedness, that very recognition of our conditioning helps to explain why we are questioning our viewpoints and looking to revise by considering others' viewpoints in the first place. Padilla posits that there are weaknesses of each pole of her comparison and that each pole may assist in remedying the other. Rahner needs more sensuality and less safety, while Tezcatlipocan darkness needs more room for love. She wants to take from Rahner for the Aztecs the concept of differentiation of everything in unity in order to enable love, while she wants to take from the Aztecs for Rahner the possibility that the constructive and destructive, rather than being opposed, can be creatively intertwined; thus the possibility of embracing as sacred even "disorder, decomposition, displacement, disintegration, decay." Padilla volunteers and stipulates these weaknesses and the turn to the other, but the root causes of those inclinations to humbly admit shortcomings and to pursue revision remain undeveloped.

Likewise, Sydnor largely presupposes that the other has something to teach us and that we need to reform our own understandings. He simply says that these assumptions, and the stipulation of a self vulnerable to the other, are postulates of comparative theology. Yet, from his piece, it is not clear what drives those presuppositions. I recognize that it is not Padilla's or Sydnor's project to do comparative theory in these essays and that a comparative approach may not need to be justified in a volume where a comparative theological approach is already assumed. Nevertheless, when we read Sydnor and Padilla alongside Caputo we see that, with Caputo, it is the admission and underlining of conditionedness that helps create the humility, openness, and provisionality that enables deconstruction and reconstruction via comparison and that keeps us searching, unsatisfied with current theologies as God eludes us. In other words, the stress on conditioning can help comparativists explain why they inhabit their traditions but with considerable unease, with a "faithful infidelity," and thus look to the religious other.

Padilla sounds like Caputo when she writes that the materials that she examines harbor an excess and that some meaning remains ungrasped and deferred, but she does not develop her theory of language. Sydnor parallels Nagarjuna's emptiness and Moltman's social trinity, but his piece lacks a clear theory of language as well. Again, developing a theory of language is not their aim here, and article-length pieces cannot be expected to cover everything. Still, without some way of justifying comparative pairings with a helpful theory of religious language, such as the one Caputo has, one could argue that there is something peculiar about using a Buddhist tradition that argued *against* God to "enhance" and "amplify" one's view of the Christian God. Thus, in this way, too, Caputo's theory of language (not to mention his theory of truth) could help lay the groundwork for comparative work.

Conclusion

In conclusion, therefore, my response to Sydnor and Padilla is to see an interesting overlap of laudable themes, but in places to push them further in Caputo's direction. Overall, comparative theologians might consider embracing Caputo's new way to conceive of the divine because doing so helps to justify the comparative endeavor, speaks helpfully to issues in comparative theory, and keeps comparative theology up to date with some important recent currents in theology and philosophy.

However, despite my desire to nudge Sydnor and Padilla toward the "weak" God of "perhaps," ironically Sydnor and Padilla, in doing their theology comparatively and digging so wonderfully into the particulars of various traditions, in some ways exemplify the directives of Caputo's theological argument better than Caputo himself does. I say this because Caputo's argument strongly suggests the need to proceed comparatively—but Caputo himself, feeling that he lacks the expertise in other religions, largely neglects to do so.[61] Caputo has left that task to others. Learning from Caputo, then, let us take up that work.

Notes

1. Christina M. Gschwandtner, *Postmodern Apologetics? Arguments for God in Contemporary Philosophy* (New York: Fordham University Press, 2013), especially xvii–xix.
2. For example, his *Weakness of God: A Theology of the Event* won the 2007 American Academy of Religion Award for Excellence in the Study of Religion.
3. Gschwandtner, *Postmodern Apologetics*, 292–93.
4. This portrait of God à la Caputo draws especially on the following works by him: *The Insistence of God: A Theology of Perhaps* (Bloomington: Indiana University Press, 2013); *What Would Jesus Deconstruct? The Good News of Postmodernism for the Church* (Grand Rapids: Baker Academic, 2007); *The Weakness of God: A Theology of the Event* (Bloomington: Indiana University Press, 2006); "God and Anonymity: Prolegomena to an Ankhoral Religion," in *A Passion for the Impossible: John D. Caputo in Focus*, ed. Mark Dooley (Albany: SUNY Press, 2003), 1–20; *On Religion* (New York: Routledge, 2001); "Apostles of the Impossible: On God and the Gift in Derrida and Marion," in *God, the Gift, and Postmodernism*, ed. John D. Caputo and Michael J. Scanlon (Bloomington: Indiana University Press, 1999), 185–222; *The Prayers and Tears of Jacques Derrida: Religion Without Religion* (Bloomington: Indiana University Press, 1997). I also draw on my own "Comparative Theology as Repeating with a Difference," *Harvard Theological Review* 108, no. 1 (2015): 1–29; and "After Deconstruction? A 'Weak' Theology of Religions?" in *Twenty-First Century Theologies of Religions: Retrospection and New Frontiers*, ed. Shanthikumar Hettiarachchi, Elizabeth Harris, and Paul Hedges (Leiden and Boston: E. J. Brill, forthcoming).
5. Caputo's theology is not negative theology, however. The fact that the unconditioned is always "to come" gives Caputo's theology a prophetic or messianic element such that he describes his theology as more prophetic and eschatological than apophatic and mystical (*Prayers and Tears*, xxiv). Caputo criticizes negative theology for being a refined way of affirming that God exists or hyperexists, whereas Caputo does not want to settle the question of God's existence one way or the other (*Prayers and Tears*, 7, 13).
6. Caputo, *What Would Jesus Do*, 58–59.
7. Caputo, *What Would Jesus Do*, 35.
8. Caputo, *What Would Jesus Do*, 63.
9. Caputo, *Prayers and Tears*, 120.

10. Caputo, "Apostles of the Impossible," 206–8; "God and Anonymity," 2–6.
11. Caputo, "God and Anonymity," 14; *On Religion*, 6.
12. Caputo, "God and Anonymity," 14.
13. Caputo, *What Would Jesus Do*, 61.
14. Caputo, *Weakness of God*, 8, 97.
15. Caputo, *Weakness of God*, 88–94.
16. Caputo, *Weakness of God*, 123; *Insistence*, ix.
17. Caputo, *Insistence*, ix–x.
18. Caputo, *Insistence*, ix, 9.
19. Caputo, *Insistence*, 37.
20. Caputo, *Insistence*, 51.
21. Caputo, *Insistence*, 20.
22. Caputo, *Weakness of God*, 40.
23. Caputo, *Weakness of God*, 115.
24. Caputo, *Insistence*, 98.
25. Caputo, *Insistence*, 113.
26. Caputo, *Insistence*, 168.
27. Caputo, *Insistence*, 94.
28. Caputo, *Insistence*, 46, 146.
29. Caputo, *Insistence*, 226–27.
30. Caputo, *Insistence*, 241.
31. Caputo, *Insistence*, 172.
32. Caputo, *Insistence*, 248.
33. Caputo, *Insistence*, 176.
34. Caputo, *Insistence*, 199.
35. Caputo, *Insistence*, 201.
36. Caputo, *Insistence*, 202–3.
37. Caputo, *Insistence*, 145.
38. Ludwig Feuerbach was a German thinker who lived in the 1800s and is best known for his *The Essence of Christianity* (1841). As a theorist of religion, he saw God as a human projection of our species's ideal essence. In this sense, for him, the origin of God is humankind and religion is an alienated form of human self-consciousness (i.e., alienated insofar as the religious consciousness fails to recognize its own role in constructing the divine reality that it experiences).
39. Caputo, *Insistence*, 105, 205.
40. Caputo, *Insistence*, 206–8.
41. Caputo, *Weakness of God*, 7.
42. Caputo, *Weakness of God*, 116.
43. Caputo, *Insistence*, 95.
44. Caputo, *Insistence*, 85.
45. Caputo, *Insistence*, 102.
46. Caputo, *Weakness of God*, 267–68.
47. Caputo, *Prayers and Tears*, xxix.
48. Caputo, *Insistence*, 80–81.
49. Caputo, *Insistence*, 207.

50. Caputo, *Weakness of God*, 140.
51. Caputo, *Weakness of God*, 292.
52. Caputo, *Insistence*, 261.
53. John D. Caputo, e-mail message to author, August 20, 2011.
54. Gschwandtner, *Postmodern Apologetics*, xxiii.
55. Caputo, *Weakness of God*, 303 n. 22.
56. Kiblinger, "Comparative Theology as Repeating with a Difference."
57. Caputo, *Weakness of God*, 5.
58. For example, see Richard King, "Early Yogacara and Its Relationship with the Madhyamaka School," *Philosophy East & West* 44, no. 4 (1994): 659–83, especially 667–68; Dan Lusthaus, *Buddhist Phenomenology: A Philosophical Investigation of Yogacara Buddhism and the Ch'eng Wei-shih lun* (New York: RoutledgeCurzon, 2002), 6; and David Loy, "The Deconstruction of Buddhism," in *Derrida and Negative Theology*, ed. Harold Coward and Toby Foshay (Albany: SUNY Press, 1992), 227–53.
59. Caputo, *Insistence*, 49.
60. Caputo, *Insistence*, 226–27.
61. However, Caputo does have a chapter discussing Heidegger, Eckhart, and Buddhism in his early book, *The Mystical Element in Heidegger's Thought* (New York: Fordham University Press, 1986).

PART II
Theodicy

4 Developing Christian Theodicy in Conversation with Navid Kermani

Klaus von Stosch

In my understanding of theology, the meaning of religious convictions always depends on a particular language game, i.e. on a certain theological context.[1] Because, for example, the sentence "God is love" can point to different meanings depending on to whom and in what context it is said, one can understand it adequately only if one perceives it as embedded in a particular dialogue or language game. Therefore, comparative theology can never result in a universal theory about religions and truth.[2] Because the meanings of basic religious beliefs within particular traditions are diverse, comparative theology focuses on select details within particular solitary cases and contexts.[3]

Although comparative theology may be geared toward any number of problems, the selection should address lay questions about theological sense, salvation, and truth in addition to critical challenges by specialists. Otherwise, comparative theology would become a playground for detail-loving eccentrics, those who meticulously compare irrelevant subjects. Capricious comparisons of themes within religious traditions are not automatically comparative theology.

Therefore, it is important that, as a first step, comparative theologians draft problems meaningful for a range of religious and non-religious traditions. Of course, it is not expected that there will be a uniform canon of questions for all comparative theologies in the world. But at least at the point of concrete research, one should identify shared problems and assess examples with a view to their competence in addressing them.[4]

These methodological observations contribute to decisions about the methodology used in this article. The first decision is to choose the problem of theodicy, or the problem of evil, because it is one of the most frequently discussed subjects in Western theology, and most scholars agree that it has not yet been solved.[5] This chapter does not compare how Muslims and Christians in general deal with this problem. Such an attempt should be reserved for comparative religion and is not the task of comparative theology. Instead, I struggle with the problem itself and try to stabilize it; and I do this as a Christian who is learning from dialogue with a Muslim.

The second decision is to learn from a particular, contemporary Muslim thinker in this context: Navid Kermani. He is perhaps the most well-known Muslim scholar from Germany today, and some of his works have already been translated into English. Kermani was probably the first Muslim scholar who challenged my theology in such a way that I learned from him and his thinking not only about Islam, but also about Christianity. I have had many conversations with him and we have much in common, although his theological style and his ideas are very different from mine. This great sympathy has to do with some points that I share biographically with Kermani: We both love the best and most multicultural city in the world (Cologne) and its soccer club. For both of us soccer has been a bridge from a bourgeois family to working class people;[6] for both of us humanistic and social engagement is central for religion; and for both of us prayer arouses feelings of ambivalence and strangeness.[7] Thus, there are important similarities in our worldviews that might help me to understand his ideas, although they are articulated in the framework of another religion. However, I intend to present only *my* approach to his ideas in relation to my own approach to the problem of theodicy, without claiming to give a complete or neutral overview of his theological writings[8] or the theological problem of theodicy.

Free Will Defense within Christian Theology

Before starting with Kermani, let me briefly introduce my approach to the problem of evil within Christianity. The most important German scholar who has influenced my own thinking on the problem of evil is a Catholic theologian from Munich, Armin Kreiner.[9] Unfortunately, he is completely unknown in the English speaking world. For an English-speaking thinker who comes close to his ideas, one may refer to the theodicy of William Hasker.

Theologians and philosophers like Kreiner and Hasker teach that one must use the methods of free will theodicy and natural law theodicy if one wants to defend the rationality of a theistic belief in the face of the problem of evil. Natural law theodicy is based on the assumption that the "world has developed to its present state through a complex evolutionary process and enjoys a considerable amount of autonomy in its functioning."[10] It is unavoidable that the universe that produces human freedom as the outcome of the evolutionary process "contains a great deal of suffering and death."[11] The advantage of this kind of theodicy is that it accepts "that severe pain, suffering, and death really are evil" and possibly against God's good will.[12] This argument regarding natural evil points as well to a free will theodicy because the very same laws that produce this natural evil are the precondition of free will.

A libertarian view of free will theodicy tries to show that free will is the central value of humanity and can be defended as the price of pain and suffering.[13] What is very important in this approach is the fact that it resists "the temptation to claim that all suffering has ... beneficial results."[14] On the contrary, it insists that much suffering makes no sense and is against the good will of God (this kind of evil is sometimes called *gratuitous evil*).

In the approach of free will theodicy, evil is not willed by God but is the result of the risk that God accepts in order to create a world with persons who have free will: "And this means that God is a risk-taker; in expressing his love toward us, he opens himself up to the real possibility of failure and disappointment."[15] Thus, if people act against God's good will, it is beyond God's power to prevent them from doing evil; otherwise God would destroy the free will, which had been the very reason for creation.

William Hasker takes one further step. For him, the only reason why God does not prevent all gratuitous evil is that through such interventions God would destroy "our own motivation to prevent or alleviate such evils."[16] But is gratuitous evil too high a price for this motivation? Hasker tries to respond to this argument through the observation that rejection of the possibility of evil implies rejection of the existence of humanity. It is impossible to reject humanity if one values or accepts life: "If I am glad on the whole about my own existence, and that of persons close to me, then I cannot reproach God for the general character or the major events of the world's past history."[17] Hasker too quickly presupposes that people will be grateful for their existence, an assumption that the tradition of skepticism from Hume to Kant and Schopenhauer contests. Thus, I do not defend the necessity of accepting life, but I have argued elsewhere that it is rational to hope that people in their encounter with Christ in death will accept evil as the price of freedom and love.[18]

Although I think that my formulation is more convincing than Hasker's, I have to admit that it cannot meet the moral challenges raised in Fyodor Dostoevsky's famous novel *The Brothers Karamazov*. In this novel, Ivan Karamazov refuses the admission ticket to a postmortem process of reconciliation. As illustration for this refusal, Ivan chooses a newspaper report on a Russian general and rich landowner who wants to punish the eight-year-old son of one of his bondmen for hurting the foot of one of his dogs while playing. The punishment consists of setting all his greyhounds on him and tearing him to pieces.[19] Although this crime is beyond awful, Ivan admits that after death God might be able to help the boy, his mother, and himself to forgive the crime of the landowner. It is possible that God will help all to praise his glory and justice after death. But at the same time, Ivan insists:

> I don't want to cry aloud then. While there is still time, I hasten to protect myself, and so I renounce the higher harmony altogether. It's not worth the tears of that one tortured child who beat itself on the breast with its little fist and prayed in its stinking outhouse, with its unexpiated tears to "dear, kind God"![20]

For Ivan, an atonement for the suffering of children is not conceivable. Thus, he refuses to accept the harmony of heaven if it is built upon the suffering of so many innocent people:

> I don't want harmony. From love for humanity I don't want it. I would rather be left with the unavenged suffering.... And so I hasten to give back my entrance ticket, and if I am an honest man I am bound to give it back as soon as possible.[21]

Ivan refuses the idea of recompense after death because, though rational, it comes too late.[22] Thus, although the free will defense and natural law defense might succeed in defending the rationality of faith in God, it fails in defending its morality.

Current debates on the problem of theodicy have taken up this challenge to give a convincing response that preserves both the rationality and morality of faith. The following section shows how Navid Kermani responds to this challenge with the help of the Muslim tradition in a combination of practical and theoretical theodicy that can also inspire the Christian tradition.

The Terror of God

In *The Terror of God: Attar, Job, and the Metaphysical Revolt*, which is the most important work on the question of evil in his writings, Kermani does not present an argumentative defense of the rationality of faith but sticks to the tradition of practical or authentic theodicy.[23] He refers to Job's rebellion against God and quotes Kant's critique of all speculative theodicy. In this tradition, he criticizes all forms of doctrinal theodicy and pleads instead for complaint, lamentation, and even accusation against God because of evil. The main source for this line of thought in Islamic tradition is the "Book of Suffering" of the Persian mystical poet Attar (1145–1221), which "teaches that the paths taken by those who quarrel with God can lead straight through the heart of Muslim piety."[24]

This kind of theodicy insists on God's justice against the injustice of the world. In this approach, one does not defend the existence of God's justice but demands for God to show it. Thus, the idea is to oblige God to demonstrate divine justice and mercy. The theologian's task is not to defend God but to demand God's self-defense. Theology cannot affirm, but only demand and postulate. The protest against God's absent self-defense is part of both the task of theology and the practical fight against suffering. All of these ideas are well known as practical theodicy in Western thinking. But Kermani, one of the first Muslim theologians to consequently buy into this tradition of theodicy, gives an unusual shape to them.

Kermani's suggestion is so unusual for Muslim theology because Islamic tradition usually criticizes the idea of accusations against God. The qur'anic Job, for example, is not a rebel at all. He most resembles the silent sufferer and servant of the narration of the first two chapters of the biblical book of Job. Job's rebellion, which starts in the third chapter, does not occur in the Qur'an (cf. Q 21:83, 38:44). Kermani is totally aware of the fact that this is typical for the Qur'an: "The Qur'an does not permit any form of lamenting piety, let alone one that accuses God."[25] But instead of drawing conclusions about Islamic piety from this observation, Kermani explains that the Qur'an cannot open up space for lamentations or even accusations against God because the Qur'an is conceived as the speech act of God. This is the decisive difference between the self-understanding of the Bible and that of the Qur'an. Whereas the Bible can open up the floor for people's lamentations and complaints because it is written by humans with the help of the Holy

Spirit, the Qur'an is understood by most Muslims as God's direct speech. And because of this literary category, complaints and accusations against God simply do not make sense in the Qur'an: "The textual concept itself already precludes the possibility of humans complaining about God, as it is He who speaks in the first person in the Qur'an."[26] This observation does not, however, suggest the consequence that lamentations, complaints, and even accusations by humans are impossible within the Islamic tradition.

Kermani uses this insight to invite his fellow believers to look through the Muslim tradition and to rediscover the tradition of lamentation and complaint in it. The attitude of protest against suffering demanded by atheists is not, then, anti-theistic but must be adopted by believers. Moreover, believers are able to make sense of this protest because they have someone to address in their accusations. They can include complaints in their prayer and dialogue with God and integrate them into the theistic perspective. This, at least, is what the believers presented in Attar's writings do.

In Attar's book the most faithful believers are those who ask why God persecutes them and leads them into misery.[27] They insist that God take responsibility for creation and persist in asking God to change the destiny of the deprived. Even though they live in ardent desire for God and accept all the blows of fate, they do not stop asking God for help. Because of their solidarity with other oppressed people, they blame God for lack of compassion: "in their despair, they are more religious than the believers who praise God, but turn a blind eye to the real state of His creation."[28]

Kermani's method of practical theodicy via Islamic mysticism can help respond to the question of protest atheism quoted at the end of the last section. Kermani shows a possibility of affirming God in the mode of protest and resistance. If faith is articulated in the way of the faithful fools in Attar's writings, it is very close to what Kant called a *postulate*, "a theoretical proposition, not demonstrable as such, but which is an inseparable result of an unconditional a priori practical law."[29] Such faith helps to transform all talk of God into the mode of demanding, waiting, desiring, insisting, and postulating. In the Qur'an God can use the indicative mood to articulate divine mercy and love. But we are not able—or at least morally speaking not allowed—to respond to this love in faith and confidence without showing the oppressed face of the world to God. Therefore, all affirmative and theoretical talk about God has to be articulated in the mode of demand and hope.

Through this shift within speech about God, it becomes clear that faith does not ideologically justify the suffering of other people but is a way of remaining in solidarity with the oppressed. If a protest atheist like Ivan Karamazov does not accept the possibility of recompensation for the tortured child, then, by implication, he must also give up hope for *all* the dead and the oppressed. As only God's love is stronger than death, only belief in God can give hope and ultimate sense to solidarity with tortured and slaughtered people. Thus, the protest of Ivan does not destroy belief in God as long as this belief is articulated as a desire and outcry in solidarity with the oppressed and marginalized people.

From Kermani's perspective, belief in God can thus express protest against suffering rather than justify it ideologically. This reminds me of the expression of Fidèle, a good friend of mine from Rwanda, who lost his whole family in the genocide of 1994 and who adopted numerous orphans in order to help them start a better life. When asked, "How can you still believe in God after all the terror you had to witness in your life?" his response was: "How can I stay human after seeing all those slaughtered people—without faith in God?" God, for him, is his last hope for his own humanity and for a better future. At the same moment, he both accuses the terror of God and persists in asking God to change God's behavior. No defense or theodicy changes his desire for God, who alone can be the response to his agony.

But with all respect to Fidèle and to the pious mystics in the writings of Attar: Why should people continue to blame God and place their hope in God at the same time? Doesn't the attitude Kermani recommends lead to schizophrenia? The mystics in Attar's writings are also called fools. It does not seem to be very rational to argue in this way. So why should one continue to have confidence in God? Why not use protest as a means of getting rid of faith?

The Beauty of God

Kermani gives his response to the question of why Muslims still surrender their lives to God despite awareness of divine terror in his dissertation on God's beauty.[30] Kermani depicts God as *fascinans et tremendum*: divine terror cannot be seen without divine beauty and vice versa.[31] The beauty of God attracts people so much that they dedicate their lives to celebrating and responding to this beauty. This terrific beauty and majesty helps them to endure oppression and encourages them to demand that God fulfill the promises given by this very beauty and goodness.

When I first read it in Kermani's dissertation, I found the reconstruction of revelation in aesthetic terms very unexpected and challenging. Here, "aesthetic" has to be understood in the broad meaning of the word *aisthesis* in the writings of Baumgarten and Kant: it stands for all forms of sensual perception.[32] Thus, Kermani wants to show that the Qur'an is much more than a challenge to reason.

Kermani notes that the idea of the Qur'an's aesthetic peculiarity first occurred decades, perhaps even centuries, after the life of Muhammad. Since the tenth century at the latest, one of the most important elements of Muslim belief has been that nobody was ever able to create something as beautiful, good, thrilling, and fascinating as the Qur'an.[33] No other text in history boasts so many witnesses to its unique aesthetic dignity. Let me quote one example from the many reports Kermani cites in his book. It is the story of the conversion of the later caliph Umar:

> Originally one of the most dangerous opponents of the young Muslim congregation, Umar was a man of thirty or thirty-five who was endowed with enormous muscular strength and energy, loved gambling, wine, and poetry, and was considered both sentimental and short-tempered.... On the day of the events recounted, Umar had originally intended to kill the Prophet, but, just when he wanted to go to him, he learned that his sister Fatima and her husband Said ibn Zayd had embraced Islam. Enraged, he ran to their house. From the street in front of their door, he heard someone reciting the Qur'an to them. Umar stormed into the room. The reciter hid as quickly as he could, while Fatima took the pages of the Qur'an and hid them under her legs.
>
> "What was that murmuring I heard?" Umar shouted at her.
>
> "You didn't hear anything," said Fatima and her husband, trying to calm him.
>
> Umar shouted, "Yes, I did, by God, and I know that you are following Muhammad in his religion!"
>
> He wanted to attack his brother-in-law, but Fatima threw herself between them so that Umar unintentionally struck her a violent blow.
>
> "Yes, we have converted to Islam, and we believe in God and His Messenger—so do what you want," Fatima and Said cried.

Umar already regretted his behavior; and the blood on his sister's face moved his heart. In a gentle voice, he asked her for the scripture. After Fatima had made him promise to return the manuscript undamaged and had also persuaded him to perform an ablution, since an unclean person must not touch the Qur'an, she handed it to him. Umar began to recite the sura *Ta Ha* (No. 20). After just a few verses he stopped, and exclaimed,

"How magnificent, how beautiful these words are . . . !"

Once he had read to the end, he immediately went to Muhammad to profess Islam before him.[34]

In this story of conversion, the beauty of the Qur'an transforms Umar from an opponent of Muhammad to his follower, but the story does not exaggerate its beauty so much that all other aspects of his conversion disappear. His sister's courage and openness are witnesses to the Qur'an's beauty and, in light of the fact that he has hurt her, they move him so much that he takes the Qur'an seriously. Umar can be fascinated by its beauty only because of this sensitivity and attentiveness to the recitation of the Qur'an. Thus, his sister's personal testimony of faith contributes to his conversion; but the aesthetic uniqueness of the Qur'an, which attracts him so much that he does not want to give it up, is the deciding factor.

Kermani impresses upon the reader how intensely God's beauty attracts people through the recitation of the Qur'an—so much that they accept the terror of God as the shadow side of the light, which captivates their life and faith. Moreover, he points out that the "comprehensive shift in norms that the Qu'ran caused throughout an enormous geographical territory, encompassing in particular the use of language and the aesthetic norms, is incomparable. As Bernard Lewis once remarked, that norm shift is actually the wondrous thing about the Arab expansion."[35] For the Arabs, the Qur'an is "a linguistic heaven on earth"; it is the realization of humankind's dream of a perfect language.[36] One part of this kind of reasoning is not only "the Arabs' recognition of the Qur'an as a divine work by its stylistic perfection, but also the fact that the Arabs, the nation of poets par excellence, were the ones who were obliged to admit the poetic miracle: a people who appreciated the art of oratory above everything else, and who could only be persuaded by a miracle of words."[37]

Thus, in Kermani's approach, the Muslim understanding of revelation depends on a personal-dialogical relationship between God, Muhammad, and the people. God communicates in an aesthetic way because this is exactly the kind of revelation the people can understand. God, in this approach, does not want blind obedience but the appreciative perception that is the foundation of love. And this love is awakened by the beauty of God. Thus—still in the reconstruction of Kermani—religious perception is aesthetically mediated in Islam "by the hearing of a speech that is called beautiful and makes the listener shiver, gives him gooseflesh, ... an experience of beauty."[38] The way of perceiving God's message in Islam is an aesthetic way of listening.

Muhammad did not receive a written textbook from God but listened to the revelation through the recitation of the archangel Gabriel.[39] Until today the liturgical recitation of the Qur'an for Muslims is the direct speech of God and a confrontation with divine beauty. According to Kermani, "God speaks when the Qur'an is recited. Strictly speaking, we cannot read his word; we can only hear it."[40] Thus, hearing, not representing, touching, or tasting, resides at the center of liturgy in Islam: "The central ritual is listening to or reciting the divine oration, the *salat*, the ritual prayer performed three to five times daily."[41] Recitation of the word mediates a perceiving of the proximity of God. Thus, Christians can understand the recitation of the Qur'an as a kind of sacramental act.[42] One must look at such acts, and at the intensity of the relationship of surrender to God, in order to understand why Muslims love God in good times and bad.

For Kermani faith is no blind leap but is grounded in perceptions, and these perceptions are in turn grounded in the beauty and majesty of God, which can be perceived through the recitation of the Qur'an. Kermani allows that reason can be a way to believe in God. Signs and hints for believers are shot through all of history and creation. But to *perceive* God and receive God's love, one must employ the heart and senses. This *aisthesis* reaches to the life-changing beauty of God, which can fascinate people so much that they dedicate their life to God. However, because one can never perceive the beauty of God without its majesty and terror, there is no easy way to God. One must simultaneously affirm divine beauty and resist the disasters of this world.

Rebellion and Love

Kermani invites readers to neither unthinking obedience nor an irrational leap of faith. He calls for a faith grounded in religious experiences. Such experiences are highly ambivalent. Religion promotes a sensitivity for reality that makes it difficult to appreciate life's beauty without seeing its terror. That is why, for Kermani, the beauty and the terror of God cannot be separated from each other. To surrender a life to God in complete awareness of all this ambiguity is only possible through love. Only love for and surrender to God, only fascination and mystical interweavement with divine mystery, can motivate people to believe and to dedicate their life to God. Love can help a person to stay aware of the high ambiguity of reality without losing confidence in God. The peculiar aspect of Attar's attacks against God consists of the fact that he is in love with the person he is attacking: "Only someone who believes in the Highest can throw stones up to heaven.... Those whose love exceeds the conventional degree dare to demand the kind of God He Himself revealed to them."[43] Thus, it is precisely through rebellion that people's most intimate moment of belief becomes visible, and it becomes visible as something inseparably linked with love.[44]

For a deeper insight into Kermani's notion of love, one may look to his novels and other literary writings. Many of his novels, short stories, and plays deal with the love between God and humanity. Kermani insists that there is no purely spiritual love, for even mystical love relates to erotic love. He refers to a long tradition in Sufism and in Christian and Jewish mysticism, which understands the relationship between God and humanity as a relationship of lovers.

It is arresting how much Kermani focuses on erotic love in his description of the divine-human relationship. Whereas the modern Christian tradition speaks of a loving God without sexual implications, Kermani quotes many traditional texts with explicit erotic language to describe the relationship between God and God's people. The language of sexualized violence, which is so important in the Bible, and which at the same time is so much neglected and even ignored in modern theology, is especially important to him. He argues that violence and terror are not the absence or opposite of love—as free will theism seems to imply—but that they are inherent in love itself. Kermani shows God as a lover disappointed by failed attempts at courtship. Sometimes Kermani focuses so much on the violence and jealousy of God's affections that it becomes unbearable. To me, his book *Du sollst*, which tells ten short stories, each of which explains one of the ten commandments through a narrative of love and violence between a man and a woman, is the most difficult to bear.[45] In this text, God's jealousy becomes revolting, and the terror of this highly erotic love is unacceptable.

This dynamic becomes even more challenging in Kermani's dramatic productions, which leave the spectator feeling violated by his language and by God's penetrating approach to humanity. The dramas do not permit uninvolved bystanders. In showing how persistently God invites people into love, they show the dark sides of this love. This ambivalence is grounded in the unconditionality of divine love and the unconditionality of the response it demands from humans. Both the completeness of surrender and the divine desire to possess completely manifest in all their ambiguity.[46]

Kermani takes seriously the Christian rhetoric of God's essence as pure love and shows its dark side. As he investigates the enduring power of talk of God as love, he goes to its breaking point by reading it from its hidden and tacit elements. He neither solves the problem of theodicy, nor separates the good God from evil, nor tries to pacify his thinking. He struggles, he wants to debate, he shows desire—in a word: he confronts theology with life.

Although Kermani's theology is deeply rooted in life experiences, he does not simply affirm all aspects of religious experience. His critique of the mysticism of suffering in Shi'a Islam and Christianity, for example, has been highly debated in the German speaking academic world, because many Christians see it as an insulting criticism of the theology of the cross. He articulates these ideas in a short essay, *Why have you forsaken us?*, which was first published in the most important Swiss newspaper in 2009. This critique is an important clarification of some ideas of his book, which could otherwise be read as a mystical transfiguration of suffering.

In contrast to the common understanding of the Qur'an, Kermani does not doubt the historical fact of the crucifixion, but he criticizes the excessive glorification of suffering in some branches of Christianity, visible in movies like Mel Gibson's on the passion of Christ. Inspired by Guido Reni's altar-piece "Crucifixion" from 1637/38 in San Lorenzo in Lucina in Rome, he confronts this glorification of suffering with the following interpretation of the cross:

> And now I was sitting before the altar-piece of Guido Reni in the church San Lorenzo in Lucina and I was so much moved by this view—it was so much full of blessings—that I did not want to get up again. It was the first time that I thought: I—not only you—I could believe in the cross. . . . Jesus is not suffering in order to release God as Christian ideology wants

it, but Jesus is blaming God: Not, why have you forsaken me, but why have you forsaken us?[47]

Jesus is not portrayed as the greatest victim and the "supersufferer." Rather, his humanity and vulnerability invite Kermani to feel solidarity with him. Jesus does not replace[48] humans but empowers them for a relationship with God, with all its ambiguity, in which they will call for justice and recompense for the oppressed and marginalized. Facing Jesus, Kermani becomes aware of the fact that he is not alone in his history of suffering and that the cry of Golgotha is the cry of agony, rebellion, and complaint, not of victory and hope. Hence, he understands Jesus in the tradition of the practical-authentic theodicy he is defending.

Kermani's point of view clearly excludes certain Christian implications of the cross. Kermani is and stays Muslim, and this is why his attempt to appreciate the cross is so important. His ideas are remarkable because they combine an acknowledgement of basic Christian intuitions with a critique that is highly acceptable for many Christians. It is really a shame that most Christian theologians did not welcome Kermani's invitation to dialogue but even rejected it as an unacceptable gaffe.[49] For his critics, the most disturbing aspect of Kermani's intervention seems to be that he, as a Muslim, takes part in the discussion of the interpretation of the cross.[50] When I remember the fanatical reactions to the book on Jesus by Reza Aslan in the United States (although he does not write it as a Muslim), I am afraid that the reaction to Kermani's suggestion would not be much more encouraging in North America. However, comparative theology thrives amid such interventions, and one can learn a lot from Kermani's suggestions.

The Theological Take-Away for Theodicy

Several points can be gained from discussion with Kermani. First of all, Kermani shows that it makes no sense to separate practical from theoretical theodicy. Whereas Christian discussions feature two groups of theologians—those who defend an argumentative approach to the problem of evil like the free will defense and those who defend a practical-authentic theodicy in the tradition of Kant—Kermani provides arguments from both sides of the discussion. On the one hand, he seems to understand all theological statements in the mode of postulates and thus invites a practical-authentic theodicy in the tradition of the dialogues in the book of Job. On the other hand, he refers to aesthetic religious experiences as the foundation of a theology of revelation, reminiscent of a free will theodicy. Thus, he takes the most important part of the free will defense, which is the focus on the value of love, and he combines it with his practical theodicy.

Second, this combination is possible because Kermani stresses the majesty and ambiguity of God, who is always *tremendum et fascinans*, both terrible and fascinating. Through this operation, love itself becomes an ambiguous phenomenon. God, in this perspective, is not purely good and innocent, but confronts humanity with dark sides of God's essence, which seem to be a result of divine love. From discussions with Kermani, I know that, at the moment, he defends a mystical approach in the tradition of Ibn Arabi, combining Muslim thought with a mysticism that overcomes all duality.

I am not sure whether I can finally accept Kermani's approach to the problem of evil. For me, it is very important that God is purely good and that God's love is always just and redemptive. God's anger—in my interpretation—is always a call for love. To me, God's nature is unambiguous. In the context of the free will defense, I argue that the practical dimension of theodicy consists of postulating this God against the ambiguity of humankind. God's love is the aim of human protest against all humiliation of humankind. In response to Ivan, I insist that he should not give up the child killed by the greyhounds. From my perspective, the cry for escape and recovery for the child is a moral duty out of solidarity with the mother of the child. Thus, the origin of the word "God" is—as Johann Baptist Metz puts it—a cry of humankind, an expression of hope and solidarity with the oppressed, and an act of resistance against despair.[51] In this approach, free will and natural law theodicy can be defended against the protest of Ivan and of protest atheism through understanding every theological utterance as a postulate for justice and recovery. In this approach, everything depends on God's pure goodness, which is both the postulate of practical reason and the content of the defense of God in free will theodicy.

Nonetheless, I have to admit that God's mercy with criminals like Hitler stays a scandal for me, too. Thus, perhaps there is something like ambiguity in the love of God, exactly because of its pureness and unconditionality. How can one defend unconditional love if one faces its consequences on the battlefields of this world? I also have to admit that Kermani's idea of an ambiguous God supports a kind of reading of the

Bible that I sometimes try to avoid. It is true that the jealous love of the biblical God can be disturbing. Thus, Kermani forces me to a closer reading of the Bible and invites me to a different connection of practical and argumentative theodicy. In this connection, the terror of this world is also a part of the terror and mystery of God.

Although Karl Rahner and others in my own tradition have suggested similar ideas,[52] what is so interesting in Kermani's case, and what makes it so difficult to reject his approach, is his aesthetic mode of expression. It is very compelling that Kermani conveys important aspects of his theology in his novels, poems, and plays. Literature has the capacity to express an aesthetic approach to revelation and the problem of evil with greater clarity and persuasive force than academic theology ordinarily can.

The encounter with God as a solution to the problem of evil at the end of the book of Job (42:5) is so convincing because it is told in narrative form. When I had to explain the book of Job in a sermon, I myself used the means of a drama to perform the explanation. In a dramatic context, it is so much easier to see that the solution to the problem of evil is the presence of God rather than a theological theory. This makes understandable why, especially in the context of the problem of evil, the Muslim tradition insists on repeating the sentences of the Qur'an. Just as the recitation of Qur'an is nothing other than the presence of divine love in all its beauty and ambiguity, Kermani bears witness to this kind of response to the problem of evil in his own writings. In his novels and plays, he stresses the ambiguity of God, which is sometimes forgotten in theology, and through this he tries to reintroduce the terror and the beauty of God in theological discourse. Although I cannot follow him to the mystical, non-dual conclusion of this approach, my ongoing struggle with its implications is a good example of how fruitful the comparative approach can be for systematic reasoning.

Notes

1. See Klaus von Stosch, "Wittgensteinian Fideism?" in *The Contemplative Spirit: D. Z. Phillips on Religion and the Limits of Philosophy*, ed. Ingolf U. Dalferth and Hartmut von Sass (Tübingen: Mohr Siebeck, 2010), 115–34.
2. "Working by examples also has the advantage of making it clear that I am not attempting a general theory about theology and religion nor about Christianity and Hinduism in order to explain everything, all at once." Francis X. Clooney, *Hindu God, Christian God: How Reason Helps to Break Down the Boundaries between Religions* (Oxford: Oxford University Press, 2001), 14.

3. Clooney talks about a "careful consideration of some details of a few particular cases" and requires that every criticism of his statements be illustrated with examples (*Hindu God, Christian God*, 15). Clooney's criticism of Dupuis's strongly apriorically arranged criticism of religion is symptomatic (cf. *Hindu God, Christian God*, 23).
4. For further explanations, see Klaus von Stosch, "Comparative Theology as Challenge for the Theology of the 21st Century," in *Religious Inquiries* 1, no. 2 (2012): 5–26; and Klaus von Stosch, *Komparative Theologie als Wegweiser in der Welt der Religionen* (Paderborn: Ferdinand Schoningh, 2012), 193–215.
5. As an introduction to the problem of theodicy, see Klaus von Stosch, *Theodizee* (Paderborn: Ferdinand Schoningh, 2013).
6. Cf. Kermani's autobiographical portrayals in Navid Kermani, *Wer ist Wir? Deutschland und seine Muslime* (München: C. H. Beck, 2009), 133.
7. In one of his essays, Kermani describes prayer as an experience with something strange because German society is not accustomed to praying people. On the one hand, this leads to a great solidarity among those who pray; on the other hand, praying becomes something demonstrative that does not befit prayer (Navid Kermani, *Beten heute*, March 11, 2008). This act of displaying one's piety in public is criticized by Jesus (see Mt 6:5), and it is an aspect of public religiosity that has always been a source of suspicion for me.
8. If I wanted to examine all theological writings of Kermani, I would have to refer to his detailed discussion of Abu Zayd, *Offenbarung als Kommunikation: Das Konzept wahy in Nasr Hamid Abu Zayds Mafhum an-nass* (Frankfurt a.M.: Peter Lang, 1996); and Nasr Hamid Abu Zaid, *Ein Leben mit dem Islam. Aus dem Arabischen von Chérifa Magdi. Erzählt von Navid Kermani* (Freiburg: Herder/Spektrum, 1999), which, however, are not as relevant for the problem of evil.
9. Armin Kreiner, *Gott im Leid. Zur Stichhaltigkeit der Theodizee-Argumente* (Freiburg-Basel-Wien: Herder, 1997), 168.
10. William Hasker, *The Triumph of God Over Evil: Theodicy for a World of Suffering* (Downers Grove, Ill.: InterVarsity Press, 2008), 138.
11. Hasker, *The Triumph of God Over Evil*, 138.
12. Hasker, *The Triumph of God Over Evil*, 140.
13. Cf. Hasker, *The Triumph of God Over Evil*, 150 and 155; and Robert Kane, *The Significance of Free Will* (Oxford: Oxford University Press, 1996). The notion of "libertarian" is used here in the philosophical sense of believing in free will, not in a political sense.
14. Hasker, *The Triumph of God Over Evil*, 164.
15. William Hasker, "A Philosophical Perspective," in *The Openness of God: A Biblical Challenge to the Traditional Understanding Of God*, ed. Clark Pinnock et al. (Downers Grove, Ill.: InterVarsity Press, 1994), 151.
16. William Hasker, "An Adequate God," in *Searching for an Adequate God: A Dialogue Between Process and Free Will Theists*, ed. John B. Cobb and Clark H. Pinnock (Grand Rapids, Mich.: Eerdmans, 2000), 215–45, 237.
17. William Hasker, "On Regretting the Evils of This World," in *The Problem of Evil: Selected Readings*, ed. Michael L. Peterson (Notre Dame, Ind.: University of Notre Dame Press, 1992), 164.

18. See von Stosch, *Theodizee*.
19. Fyodor Mikhailovich Dostoevsky, *The Brothers Karamazov*, ed. William Benton (Chicago: *Encyclopedia Britannica*, 1952), 125.
20. Dostoevsky, *The Brothers Karamazov*, 126.
21. Dostoevsky, *The Brothers Karamazov*, 126.
22. Cf. Karl-Heinz Menke, "Der Gott, der jetzt schon Zukunft schenkt. Plädoyer für eine christologische Theodizee," in *Mit Gott streiten. Neue Zugänge zum Theodizee-Problem*, ed. Harald Wagner (Freiburg-Basel-Wien: Herder, 1998), 169.
23. Cf. Regina Ammicht-Quinn, *Von Lissabon bis Auschwitz: Zum Paradigmenwechsel in der Theodizeefrage* (Fribourg-Freiburg: Universitätsverlag, 1992), 43; and Johann Baptist Metz, "Theologie als Theodizee?" in *Theodizee—Gott vor Gericht?* ed. W. Oelmüller et al. (München: Wilhelm Fink Verlag, 1990), 103–18.
24. Navid Kermani, *The Terror of God: Attar, Job and the Metaphysical Revolt* (Cambridge: Polity Press, 2011), 163.
25. Kermani, *The Terror of God*, 129.
26. Kermani, *The Terror of God*, 129.
27. "He has made faith bitter for me today, what will He do to me tomorrow?" (Kermani, *The Terror of God*, 139); "In *The Book of Suffering* it is the fools, the crazy people, the idiots, who call out loudly what most believers hardly dare to think: that God has evil intentions. A fool is asked if he knows God. 'How could I not know him? He is the one who cast me into misery'" (141).
28. Kermani, *The Terror of God*, 167.
29. Immanuel Kant, *Kritik der praktischen Vernunft*, ed. K. Vorländer (Hamburg: Meiner, 1990), A 220.
30. Cf. Navid Kermani, *Gott ist schön: Das ästhetische Erleben des Koran* (München: C. H. Beck, 1999). In the references that follow, I follow the English version: Navid Kermani, *God Is Beautiful: The Aesthetic Experience of the Quran*, trans. Tony Crawford (Cambridge, UK: Polity Press, 2015).
31. Cf. Rudolf Otto, *Das Heilige* (München: C. H. Beck, 1917).
32. Cf. Navid Kermani, "Appelliert Gott an den Verstand? Eine Randbemerkung zum koranischen Begriff *aql* und seiner Paretschen Übersetzung," in *Encounters of Words and Texts: Intercultural Studies in Honor of Stefan Wild*, ed. Lutz Edzard and Christian Szyska (Hildesheim-Zürich-New York: Georg Olms, 1997), 43–66.
33. Cf. Kermani, *God Is Beautiful*, 7, 49.
34. Kermani, *God Is Beautiful*, 17.
35. Kermani, *God Is Beautiful*, 83.
36. Kermani, *God Is Beautiful*, 129.
37. Kermani, *God Is Beautiful*, 7.
38. Kermani, *God Is Beautiful*, 10.
39. Cf. Kermani, *God Is Beautiful*, 137.
40. Kermani, *God Is Beautiful*, 134.
41. Kermani, *God Is Beautiful*, 171.
42. Cf. Kermani, *God Is Beautiful*, 171–84.
43. Kermani, *The Terror of God*, 134, 167.
44. Cf. Kermani, *The Terror of God*, 165.

45. Navid Kermani, *Du sollst. Erzählungen* (Zürich: Ammann Verlag, 2005); cf. as a typical Muslim reaction, Hamideh Mohagheghi, "Der 'Islam' in Navid Kermanis literarischen Schriften," in *Islam in der deutschen und türkischen Literatur*, ed. Michael Hofmann and Klaus von Stosch (Paderborn: Schoningh, 2012), 259–66.
46. Cf. Friedrich Nietzsche, "Die Liebe zu Einem ist eine Barbarei: denn sie wird auf Unkosten aller Übrigen ausgeübt. Auch die Liebe zu Gott." "Jenseits von Gut und Böse," in *Friedrich Nietzsche Sämtliche Werke: Kritische Studienausgabe V.*, ed. Giorgio Colli and Mazzino Montinari (München: Deutscher Taschenbuch Verlag, 1993), 86.
47. Navid Kermani, "Bildansichten: Warum hast du uns verlassen?" in *Neue Züricher Zeitung*, March 14, 2009.
48. In German, the distinction between *Stellvertretung* and *Ersetzung* is decisive here; cf. Karl-Heinz Menke, *Stellvertretung. Schlüsselbegriff christlichen Lebens und theologische Grundkategorie* (Freiburg: Einsiedeln, 1991).
49. Cf. Jan Heiner Tück, "Religionskulturelle Grenzüberschreitung. Navid Kermani und das Kreuz. Nachtrag zu einer Kontroverse," in *IkaZ* 38 (2009), 220–33. In German he speaks of a "religionskulturelle Entgleisung."
50. See, for example, Tück, "Religionskulturelle Grenzüberschreitung," 225ff.
51. Cf. J. B. Metz, *Theologie als Theodizee?* 104.
52. Cf. Karl Rahner, "Warum läßt Gott uns leiden?" in *Schriften zur Theologie XIV* (Zürich: Einsiedeln, 1980), 450–66.

5 Like a Dog's Curly Tail: Finding Perfection in a World of Imperfection

A HINDU THEODICY IN THE TRADITION OF SRI RAMAKRISHNA

Jeffery D. Long

This chapter develops a theodicy in the Vedanta tradition of Sri Ramakrishna and Swami Vivekananda, building on the teachings of these two masters as found, in the case of Sri Ramakrishna, in the primary sources available on his life and teaching, and in the case of Swami Vivekananda, in the Swami's own *Complete Works*. This shall be a comparative project to the degree that it engages with the thought of two prominent Christian thinkers—John Hick and David Ray Griffin—as it unpacks the deep implications of Ramakrishna's and Vivekananda's teaching on the nature of suffering and evil: namely, that these phenomena exist in order to provide spiritual aspirants with needed obstacles to overcome in the process of spiritual purification on the path to God-realization.

In terms of the broader discourse of theological comparison, one interesting outcome of this exercise is that one finds that, despite the fact that John Hick and David Ray Griffin hail from the same religious tradition—Christianity—Hick at least appears at first glance to be in much closer agreement with Sri Ramakrishna and Swami Vivekananda on the topic of theodicy than any of the three are with Griffin's process theology.

For Hick, as for Sri Ramakrishna and Swami Vivekananda, the suffering of this world can be justified as a necessary prelude to the realization of a limitlessly better possibility. As Hick writes of the problems of suffering and evil:

> The only line of response that seems to me at all adequate to the full depth of the challenge sees our human existence on this planet as part

of a much longer process through which personal spiritual life is being gradually brought in its own freedom to perfection that will justify retrospectively the evils that have been part of its slow creation ... The insight that suffering constitutes the intrinsic cost of person-making is supported by the fact that in our apparently haphazardly painful world there are heights of love, compassion, self-giving for others which could not occur, because they would not be called for, in a world that was free of "the heart-ache and the thousand natural shocks that flesh is heir to."[1]

Hick here clearly echoes Vivekananda, who says, "The world is a grand moral gymnasium wherein we have all to take exercise so as to become stronger and stronger spiritually."[2]

While Griffin does not reject, and indeed affirms and argues for, the idea of suffering and evil as inevitable effects of free will, and for free will itself as a condition for a better, far richer world than would obtain in free will's absence, he does reject the idea that present suffering will *necessarily* lead to the better outcome affirmed by Sri Ramakrishna, Swami Vivekananda, and John Hick. He does, however, argue that there is good reason for two types of eschatological hope: "hope for a victory of good over evil on this planet" and "hope for a victory of good over evil beyond this life."[3] Vivekananda, interestingly, does not affirm the first of these hopes, but does affirm the second. Griffin's modification of necessity to hope arises from his critique of traditional theism, which makes God, to use his term, "indictable" for the suffering and evil in the world.[4] If God has placed evil and suffering in our path, even with the intent that we will eventually overcome it and be thereby improved, God thereby becomes morally culpable as the ultimate source of evil. According to Griffin, and process thought more generally, it is better to see God as omnibenevolent, but not omnipotent, than as omnipotent and therefore responsible for all evil.

This observation of the complex interrelations of the theologies of these four thinkers is in keeping with Francis X. Clooney's preference that comparative theologians focus upon specific texts and thinkers rather than on broad, and arguably superficial, comparisons of entire traditions, as a result of which "a Christian theodicy" would consist of X and "a Hindu theodicy" would consist of Y, without much, if any, regard for subtlety, nuance, or the internal diversity of traditions, either as ahistorical "systems," or as transformed in the work of specific thinkers throughout history. As should already be evident, the situation is far more complex than a simple lining up of abstract Christian and Hindu theodicies could possibly allow.

In terms of the constructive project itself, this essay will yield a modified form of the Sri Ramakrishna–Swami Vivekananda–John Hick theodicy, which sees suffering and evil as necessary components of the path to the realization of a limitlessly better future state, in light of David Ray Griffin's approach, which sees most suffering, and certainly all evil, as a thwarting of the will of a wholly good but non-omnipotent God. The integration of Griffin's seemingly discordant view on this topic not only refines and sharpens Vedantic theodicy in a way that might not otherwise have been possible—and thus underscores the value of the comparative enterprise for thinkers inhabiting various traditions—but it also draws attention to the important distinction within Vedanta between Brahman, the ground of all being, and Ishvara, the supreme being: a distinction often elided when both of these heavily laden Sanskrit terms are translated using the single English word "God."

Finally, I will simply note my peculiar situatedness both within this volume and within the enterprise of comparative theology as a whole. Unlike most comparative theologians, who operate from within a Christian worldview and set of commitments, my orientation is Vedantic. I am therefore not a Christian theologian looking into a Hindu tradition for insights to advance a Christian self-understanding; I am, rather, a Hindu theologian who is looking, in this case, into the work of two Christian thinkers for insights to advance my Vedantic understanding. This is, in one sense, a cause for celebration; for many Christian thinkers rightly lament the degree to which comparative theology remains a Christian-dominated exercise, and they are rightly concerned to ensure that comparative theology constitutes a break with, rather than a continuation of, a Christian hegemonic discourse.

At the same time, I am an unusual Hindu in that I was not born to this tradition but came to it later in life, and was raised and educated to be a Roman Catholic Christian (albeit a very stubbornly independent-minded one). In one sense, then, any comparative work that I do with Christian materials is not simply a "looking over," across a religious boundary, but also a "looking back," to the tradition of my youth and upbringing: the tradition in which I was formed (at least in this life). I think, therefore, that any celebration of my involvement with this enterprise as marking an opening up of comparative theology and a breaking of Christian hegemony is mitigated by the fact that many of my assumptions, as a practitioner of this discipline, were shaped by the very tradition from which it emerged. A critical reader, therefore—particularly a critical reader who was born and raised Hindu—could conceivably argue that, rather than being "authentically Hindu," this work of mine is really just a peculiar form of Christian theology. To "look back" in a positive way to one's native tradition, as someone who has joined a different one, may raise the risk that one's co-religionists will misunderstand this engagement, mistaking it for "looking back in longing," or as signaling a lack of commitment to the tradition of one's living practice. Such criticisms, however, seem to arise from insecurity, not from the work itself, which is pursued in the service of the Hindu tradition.

I have no further reflections to add on this fact for now, other than to point it out as a possible question for future engagement. Is there something peculiarly Christian, or at least peculiarly "Western," about the enterprise of comparative theology, and if so, should this trouble us, or might it be circumvented in some creative way?

Vedanta: A Very Brief Introduction

I presume that most readers will have at least some familiarity with Hindu traditions, and with Vedanta in particular, but it may be useful and also relevant to the main point of this essay to give some background to the discourse called "Vedanta" and what, precisely, I mean by it, as well as where this project stands in relation to that discourse.

Vedanta, a Sanskrit compound combining the terms *veda*, or "wisdom," and *anta*, which means "end, aim, or purpose," is an enquiry into the nature of Brahman, the divine source and ground of all being. Its earliest extant explicit articulation is in the *Upanishads*, a set of texts also known as the *Vedanta*, both because these texts form, literally, the "end of the *Veda*," being the latest stratum of Vedic literature to be composed, and also because the ideas that they express are believed, by their adherents, to constitute the highest end or aim toward which all earlier Vedic teaching and practice naturally lead.

Somewhat later than the *Upanishads*, the best known of which were composed in the first millennium before the Common Era, are the *Vedanta Sutras*, or *Brahma Sutras*, and the *Bhagavad Gita*, a dialogue drawn from the epic *Mahabharata*. These three sets of texts taken collectively—the *Upanishads*, the *Brahma Sutras*, and the *Bhagavad Gita*—form the *Prasthana Traya*, or "threefold foundation" of Vedanta as a formal system or school of philosophy, or *darshana*. Authoritative commentators who have expounded upon these three writings, such as Shankara, Ramanuja, Madhva, Nimbarka, and others, are known as *acharyas*: teachers who have established a system of Vedantic thought and practice. The traditional systems of Vedantic interpretation, such as the Advaita of Shankara, the Vishishtadvaita of Ramanuja, the Dvaita of Madhva, and the Bhedabheda of Nimbarka, are distinguished from one another by the hermeneutical principles that they utilize in the act of interpreting Vedantic writings. Shankara's non-dualism, or Advaita, thus focuses upon the non-duality between Brahman and the realm of phenomena, and sees Vedanta as pointing to the realization of this non-duality. Other systems, like those of Ramanuja and Madhva, focus on the relationship of *bhakti*, or devotion, between the individual soul, or *jiva*, and Ishvara or Bhagavan, the Supreme Lord. They see Vedanta as being primarily about cultivating this relationship.

In the modern period, Vedanta has become the dominant system for interpreting Hindu thought and practice, particularly among English-educated Hindus and other Hindus with extensive interaction with the west. The story of this rise of Vedanta is controversial and complex. At one end of the spectrum are authors who argue that this rise is due entirely to the agency of European interpreters of Hinduism who found in Vedanta, especially the Advaita Vedanta of Shankara, a very convenient medium for understanding what would otherwise be seen as a bewildering array of practices and schools of thought as forming a coherent unity. This trend was picked up, so the argument goes, by early modern Indian nationalists, such as Swami Vivekananda, to provide a conceptual foundation for Indian, or at least Hindu, national unity. At the other end of the spectrum are authors who argue that Vedanta, essentially as it is conceived today, has always been the unifying principle underlying the "eternal religion," or *Sanatana Dharma*, now known as Hinduism. Recent scholarship is beginning to show a way beyond these two extreme views through drawing attention to the ways in which medieval Vedantic commentators had already begun to integrate various schools of thought once seen as independent, or even in opposition to one another, into a unity recognizable, from today's perspective, as Hindu, long before this process was accelerated by European scholarship and the rise of Indian nationalism.[5]

By all accounts, both critical and laudatory, Swami Vivekananda is key to understanding how Vedanta has come to be articulated today as the central underlying and unifying philosophy of Hinduism. Vivekananda did not, of course, emerge from a vacuum, but was shaped, in his early years, by the thinking of the Brahmo Samaj—an organization of Hindu reformers inspired by the teachings of Ram Mohan Roy, who is widely seen as the father of modern Hinduism—but even more so by his spiritual master and mentor, the sage of Dakshineshwar, Sri Ramakrishna Paramahansa, who is regarded by his devotees as a divine incarnation and as the world teacher who established a new, global Vedanta for the modern era.

Ramakrishna, unlike the more traditional Vedantic acharyas, was not characterized by his mastery of texts so much as by his mystical virtuosity. A keen—and indeed, voracious—seeker for firsthand spiritual experience, Ramakrishna sought first to have a vision of the Goddess Kali, the Hindu Divine Mother and wife of Shiva, in whose temple he served as a priest for most of his life. Having attained this vision after long and torturous spiritual effort, he then proceeded to seek similar depths of experience by means of the variety of paths available to him: various forms of Hindu practice from across the whole spectrum of Vaishnava, Shaiva, and Shakta traditions, and encompassing such paths as *bhakti* and tantra, as well as Advaita Vedanta, and even including non-Hindu paths such as Christian and Islamic devotion.[6] Based upon his attainment of states of deep mystical communion—or in the case of his Advaitic practice, a state of complete non-duality between the subject and object of contemplation—Ramakrishna concluded that all paths lead to the same goal. *Yato mat, tato path*: All systems of belief and practice are valid paths to the infinite. This direct, experiential realization on the part of Ramakrishna is the basis of the affirmation, which is a central characteristic of modern Vedanta, of religious pluralism. All spiritual paths, practiced with intensity, converge in the realization of the divine ground of being.

The transformation of Ramakrishna's personality and character that were wrought by his powerful experiences of mystical illumination—the wisdom and compassion that he began to exhibit in his life and teaching—exerted an almost magnetic attraction on a wide swath of nineteenth-century Bengali society. This included young, middle class men who had been influenced by both Christianity and Western skepticism through the introduction of English education into India, and by the Brahmo Samaj and such reform-minded Hindu intellectuals as

Devendranath Tagore and Keshub Chunder Sen: young spiritual seekers such as Narendranath Datta, later to be known as Swami Vivekananda.

In Vivekananda's hands, the teaching of Ramakrishna—less a system of philosophy than a series of inspired, experientially based proclamations—was transformed into a new system of Vedanta, drawing upon the teachings of the ancient texts and the various commentarial traditions based upon them, but reinterpreted and reoriented in light of what Vivekananda learned at the feet of his master, and also as he traveled the length and breadth of India as a wandering *sannyasi*, or renouncer, and witnessed the suffering of his people under British oppression. Modern Vedanta, the Vedanta of Swami Vivekananda, is based not on faith in a supernaturally revealed set of texts, or even on authoritative commentarial traditions (though he did draw upon both), but on experience and reason: "My teaching is my own interpretation of our ancient books, in the light which my Master shed upon them. I claim no supernatural authority. Whatever in my teaching may appeal to the highest intelligence and be accepted by thinking men, the adoption of that will be my reward."[7]

Vedantic Theodicy

In delineating the approach to theodicy in the thought of Ramakrishna and Vivekananda, it will be useful first to distinguish between the two phenomena to which the question of theodicy is addressed: evil and suffering. In Christian theology, these two are sometimes conflated within the category of evil and then differentiated into moral evil and natural evil. Moral evil can be defined as the deliberate infliction of unnecessary suffering, or even more broadly as cooperation or complicity with such suffering, either as an active participant or as a willfully passive onlooker. Natural evil, on the other hand, is suffering that arises not out of any deliberate infliction on the part of a moral agent, but simply as an effect of living in a world of uncontrollable material forces (such as losing one's home in a natural disaster or being injured or killed in an automobile accident). Theodicy is addressed to both types of evil through the question of how a good God could permit the massive levels of suffering that actually occur, both through deliberate infliction through the misuse of free will and through what one could argue are design flaws in a cosmos in which things like tsunamis, tornados, and meteor strikes occur.

Moral evil is typically seen in Vedanta as an effect of primordial ignorance, or *avidya*. Unlike Abrahamic traditions, in which sin—moral evil—is generally taken as the basic problem of the human condition to be addressed, Vedanta, much like Buddhism, sees sin as the result of the deeper problem of ignorance. This does not mean that people simply are unaware or misinformed about what is expected of them morally, and once they are properly instructed, they cease engaging in immoral behavior. Indeed, it could be argued that an act is only properly evil if it is carried out in the full knowledge of its immoral—or in the case of Vedanta, *adharmic*—nature. Neither Vedantists nor Buddhists are so naïve as to deny that evil truly occurs—evil that consists of people deliberately doing wrong.

Avidya, rather, is a deeper ignorance of the true nature of existence, and specifically of the central insight of Vedanta—that all beings are fundamentally one, so that any suffering inflicted upon another is ultimately being inflicted upon God and upon oneself. In the words of Pravrajika Vrajaprana, "All fear and misery arise from our sense of separation from the great cosmic unity, the web of being that enfolds us. 'There is fear from the second,' says the *Brihadaranyaka Upanishad*. Duality, our sense of separation from the rest of creation, is always a misperception since it implies that something exists other than God. There can be no *other*."[8] Thus, from the perspective of Vedanta, when Jesus says, "Whatsoever you do to the least of my people you do unto me," what he says is literally true. The Golden Rule, found in various forms in many religions, enjoining us to treat others as we, ourselves, wish to be treated, is based upon a solid metaphysical foundation: the ultimate unity of existence. All beings are manifestations of Brahman: "You and I are little bits, little points, little channels, little expressions, all living inside of that infinite ocean of Existence, Knowledge, and Bliss."[9] This is the basis of Vedantic ethics.

The ultimate source of evil, and indeed of all suffering, is our sense of separation from the ground of our being. According to Vivekananda, "The Self is the essence of this universe, the essence of all souls; He is the essence of your own life, nay, 'Thou art That.' You are one with this universe. He who says he is different from others, even by a hair's breadth, immediately becomes miserable. Happiness belongs to him who knows this oneness, who knows he is one with this universe."[10] The Vedantic approach to theodicy thus becomes a practical one. The question changes from "How or why does God allow evil to occur?" to "How do we realize oneness so as to free ourselves from evil?"

One could, of course, raise the question of why we see ourselves as separate from our true nature and source to begin with. This would be the Vedantic equivalent of the question raised in the Christian tradition of why there is so much suffering and evil in the world. Why is there the sense of separation that gives rise to this suffering?

Not unlike thinkers in Buddhist traditions, Vedantic thinkers do not typically spend much time on this question, working instead from the pragmatic starting point that the deluded sense of separation does, indeed, exist, and is, indeed, the source of suffering, and that therefore, once this sense of separation is overcome, suffering will be overcome. It is not that the question is never raised at all, and possible answers posited. In the *Upanishads*, the question of the origin of a world of separate beings—and so of suffering—is addressed almost playfully, through anthropomorphisms, such as the story of Brahman being alone, and so feeling lonely, and so then dividing Itself into many in order to enjoy company. In later Vaishnava thought, one sees this image expanded into the idea of divine *lila* or play, according to which the creation of the world is the divine self-expression, the overflow of infinite joyful creativity in a burst of galaxies and planets and species and civilizations. At least a couple of contemporary Vedantic thinkers, both of whom have emerged from North American cultural backgrounds, have posed the issue in a somewhat Hegelian way, suggesting that, in order for Brahman fully to be what it is—infinite being, consciousness, and bliss—it must experience itself as infinitely many beings making the effort over the course of many lifetimes to realize infinite consciousness and bliss: to make concrete, as the lived realization of countless beings, what is already always the case in the abstract realm of eternity.[11] This is also a central teaching of Sri Aurobindo, whose Integral Yoga is in many ways in continuity with and builds upon Swami Vivekananda's Vedanta. Sri Aurobindo himself cites Vivekananda as a major influence upon his thought, and saw his own work as a continuation of Vivekananda's.

Again, however, even if one allows oneself to advance a metaphysical theory within the Vedantic framework, such as those just mentioned, these theories themselves propel one back into the realm of practice, for the whole point of the emergence of Brahman as this universe of finite selves pursuing infinite potential is for that infinite potential to achieve its concrete realization. We are here to become what we already are: centers of infinite being, consciousness, and bliss. The whole point of our falling asleep in the first place has been to wake up to this fact, to realize it not only as an abstract concept or even as an article of faith, but as the deepest and truest reality of our lived being.

So the question, again, is not "Why is there so much evil and suffering in the world?" but "What are we to do about it?"

Theodicy and Karma Yoga

In regard to the question of moral evil, then, the answer to the question "What are we to do about it?" is, while quite difficult and complex in practice, fairly straightforward from a Vedantic perspective: Cultivate an awareness of the living presence of Brahman within oneself and all others whom one meets. Overcome the *avidya* that is at the root of evil and evil will itself be overcome. In the words of the *Bhagavad Gita*, "One who sees me everywhere and sees everything in me will never be separated from me, nor will I be separated from him."[12] We are directed not to explain the evil that others do, but rather to uproot it from out of our own being. In the words of a popular Vedantic prayer, "May we not find fault with others, but try to find our own faults. May we not treat others as strangers, but learn to make the whole world our own. May we feel the whole world to be our own."[13]

But what of the suffering caused both by the misdeeds of others (moral evil) and by the vicissitudes of life in the material world (natural evil)? This question was raised a number of times to Sri Ramakrishna, particularly as social reform and poverty relief were central preoccupations of reform-minded Hindus in Bengal during his lifetime. Sri Ramakrishna once paid a visit to the famed philanthropist, Pundit Ishwar Chandra Vidyasagar, and had a dialogue with him in which he presented the core of what would later be developed by Swami Vivekananda into the philosophy of Karma Yoga. According to Ramakrishna, "Shuka and other sages cherished compassion in their minds to give people religious instruction, to teach them about God. You are distributing food and learning. That is good too. If these activities are done in a selfless spirit they lead to God. But most people work for fame or to acquire merit. Their activities are not selfless."[14] According to Vedanta, as with most Hindu schools of thought, as well as Buddhism, Jainism, and Sikhism, action infused with desire leads to corresponding results. The inevitable results of desire-infused action must be experienced by their doer. This, of course, leads to rebirth if, in a given lifetime, one has not yet experienced all of one's accumulated results. This law of action and reaction is generally known as *karma*, which itself simply means either "action" or "work." But to do action with no desire for a resulting reward, but selflessly, as service to suffering beings, is a path to liberation from rebirth: the Karma Yoga.

One can of course misuse one's freedom and do evil to others, bringing unjust, unneeded suffering into their lives. This, however, will result in "bad karma." By bringing harm to others, one brings harm to oneself, by the principle of the oneness of existence presented earlier. By doing good to others out of a desire for a reward, one will indeed receive that reward, either in the form of worldly recognition or other benefits to be experienced in the future. This, according to Ramakrishna, is actually why most people do good: "Most people work for fame or to acquire merit."[15] But by doing good with no thought for reward for oneself, but simply because it is good—out of the spontaneous compassion for others' suffering that one would also naturally feel for oneself—one performs an act that does not bring about a karmic result and indeed serves as a form of purification of false notions of self, of separation from other beings, from one's consciousness, through a lessening of the sense of egotism by living as a servant of others and through cultivating the habit of seeing others' suffering as no different from one's own.

Swami Vivekananda would build upon this theme—introduced into the Vedantic tradition as early as the *Bhagavad Gita*, whose third chapter is devoted to this topic—in dramatic and powerful ways, directing the monks of the Ramakrishna Order to devote themselves to the service to the poor, rather than being exclusively focused upon meditation and the study of scripture, the more traditional occupations of Hindu *sannyasis*. The organization that the monks direct, the Ramakrishna Mission, "is one of the largest Hindu institutions in the world. In just 2012–2013, they provided relief to half a million; welfare to 3.6 million old, sick and destitute people; medical services to 8 million through 15 hospitals, 125 dispensaries, 60 mobile medical units and 953 medical camps; spent US$40 million on education for 329,000 students; and financed development projects benefitting 4.3 million rural and tribal people."[16]

Vivekananda's teaching emphasizes the centrality of the attitude with which one engages in service to its efficacy as a spiritual practice. To believe that one actually does good to another, while appearing noble, is a form of spiritual arrogance. One must view oneself as a servant, not a magnanimous giver of charity, to practice the Karma Yoga. We do not help others out of a sense that we can thereby solve all of their problems, but in a spirit of gratitude, because they have given us an opportunity for spiritual advancement by serving them: "Our duty to others means helping others, doing good to the world. Why should we do good to the world? Apparently to help the world, but really to help ourselves . . . If we consider well, we find that the world does not require our help at all. This world was not made that you or I should come up and help it."[17]

Such statements can be shocking if removed from their spiritual context. When Swami Vivekananda says that, "This world was not made that you or I should come up and help it," he is not recommending quietism, nor discouraging or downplaying service. What he is doing, as spiritual masters of many traditions so often do, is making us shift our point of view in a radical way: It is *we* who need help. It is *we* who are in spiritual need. If we see another person suffering, we should be filled with gratitude. They are suffering for our sake, to allow us the opportunity to serve them, and to thereby help us spiritually. And indeed, if one reads the accounts of those who have dedicated themselves to serving those who suffer, or if we have had the privilege to pursue such service ourselves, what we find is not an attitude of superiority—"Look how great and benevolent I am, that I have done so much for these poor, suffering people!"—but rather an attitude of deep humility and gratitude for how much those who suffer have taught us about the real meaning and purpose of life: "Is it not blasphemy to say that the world needs our help? We cannot deny that there is much misery in it; to go out and help others is therefore the best thing we can do, although in the long run we shall find that helping others is only helping ourselves."[18]

To make the point even more sharply, and reorient us even more radically back toward the central teaching of Vedanta—that all is truly Brahman—Vivekananda even says, "This world is perfect. We may be perfectly sure that it will go on beautifully well without us, and we need not bother our heads wishing to help it."[19] It is not the world that is in need of repair—it is ourselves; but the act of repairing the world, pursued selflessly, is precisely how *we* will be repaired.

The seeming imperfection of the world can be likened to the exercise equipment in a gym. It is there so we can do the work that we need to do in order to realize our goal: "The world is a grand moral gymnasium wherein we have all to take exercise so as to become stronger and stronger spiritually."[20] To quote Swami Atmarupananda, "Life is problem-solving."[21] We may indeed solve specific problems, such as hunger, poverty, or sectarian conflict. But to expect the world to be free from problems, especially as a result of our own efforts, is not only cosmically arrogant, it is to expect the wrong thing from a world that is here for our spiritual advancement. The seeming imperfection of the world is part of its perfect design. In the words of Vivekananda, "This world is like a dog's curly tail, and people have been striving to straighten it out for hundreds of years; but when they let it go, it has curled up again. How could it be otherwise?"[22]

Does this way of thinking, though, not raise the danger that we will rationalize or in other ways minimize the sufferings of those whom we encounter? That we will say, "This is the inevitable result of the way the world is," or even worse, "It must be their karma that is causing them to suffer in this way," and then do nothing to relieve that suffering? The world is, after all, perfect! Such a response, however, misses the point that Vivekananda is making, for it seeks to avoid doing the moral workout that the world is offering to us. It is a response that arises from profound moral laziness and a false sense of separate "self" and "other" that is the very dichotomy that non-dual consciousness is intended to dispel. When we encounter the suffering of another, the right response is always, in every case, compassion—to see the suffering of the other as an opportunity to serve, rather than to judge or rationalize, and ultimately, to see the suffering of the other as our own, for according to Vedanta, there ultimately is no absolutely separable "self" or "other," if we fully grasp the implications of non-duality. To quote another authority of the modern Vedanta tradition, the Holy Mother Sarada Devi (the spouse and spiritual companion of Sri Ramakrishna), "If you seek peace, my child, never find faults of anyone. Always blame yourself. Learn to make the world your own. Nobody is a stranger. The whole world is your own."[23] Compassion is both rooted in and enables the realization of non-duality.

Bringing Vedantic Theodicy into Conversation with John Hick

John Hick, a prominent Christian philosopher of religion, is probably best known for his contributions to the discourse of religious pluralism, through his Pluralistic Hypothesis, according to which, much as in Vedanta, the world's religions are seen as varied human responses to a single transcendent reality. His contributions to the discourse of theodicy, however, are no less significant. And like his Pluralistic Hypothesis, Hick's theodicy is strikingly similar to, and may even be argued to bear the imprint of, modern Vedanta. At the same time, at least from a Vedantic perspective, Hick clearly operates from within the Christian tradition inasmuch as he poses the question of theodicy not so much from the point of view of practice as in terms of causes and origins: "Why does God permit the level of evil that actually occurs in the world?"

In developing his philosophy of religion, Hick first rejects materialism (which he terms "naturalism") as "bad news for the many."[24] The sheer magnitude of suffering that human beings have experienced throughout history—one recalls Thomas Hobbes's statement that most persons' lives have been "nasty, brutish, and short"—necessitates, if one is to affirm anything like a just universe, some promise of redemption beyond this life, some limitlessly better possibility in terms of which past and present suffering might be retroactively justified. One possibility is, of course, that the universe simply is unjust, as materialism affirms. Whatever its merits, this possibility would seem to radically undermine, at least for many, the foundations for any kind of guiding moral vision for society. It could even raise the question, on a personal level, of why one should keep on living from day to day in a world so miserable and bleak. It is, in any case, the opposite of what Hick calls the "cosmic optimism" that underlies the world's religions, an optimism that his theodicy seeks to unpack and articulate: "'Cosmic optimism' is not a term that figures in the distinctive vocabulary of any of the world faiths. It is however a generalization of their distinctive affirmations about the Transcendent in its relation to human beings."[25] In various ways, these faiths "teach that we can, whether suddenly or gradually, whether on earth or in heaven, whether in this life or through many lives, receive or achieve the salvific transformation into a new relationship to, or a newly discovered identity with, that ultimate reality."[26] For Hick, as for Vivekananda (and Ramakrishna), the suffering experienced in this world is part of the personal transformation process that leads us to our eventual right relationship, loving union, or realization of identity with the ultimately real.

David Ray Griffin's Critique

Turning now, however, to another Christian philosopher with a very different conception of the problem of evil, David Ray Griffin, we find a perspective that, at first glance, appears radically at odds with the vision shared by Hick and Vedanta of a world moving *inevitably* toward the realization of limitlessly better possibilities, which can justify the massive suffering of the present and the past.

Griffin's issue is not with the idea of suffering as transformative, and even necessary for certain kinds of transformation to occur. Indeed, he argues along with Hick that there are certain goods that can only be realized if they are freely chosen; and, of course, the possibility of evil arises necessarily from the fact of freedom itself. A good is only freely chosen if it might also not be chosen.

> *Any beings in any possible world capable of the kinds of values we can enjoy would also necessarily have the kind of freedom we have*, including the freedom to act contrary to the will of God ... In bringing about beings with the capacity for the accomplishments of a Jesus, a Gautama, a Hildegard, a Michelangelo, a Shakespeare, a Newton, a Mozart, a Madame Curie, or a Sojourner Truth, God necessarily brought about beings with the capacity for creating the evils of slavery, genocide, pollution, and the extermination of entire species for sport and profit.[27]

If the good, however, might *not* be chosen, then this throws a wrench into Hick's (and the Vedanta tradition's) cosmic optimism, at least if this optimism is read as *necessitating* the eventual transformation that will redeem the suffering of the world. If the good might, at any point, not be chosen, then the world's suffering might not be redeemed. Rather than experiencing spiritual transformation, we may simply suffer, eon after eon, with no end in sight.

Classical theistic thought, at least in the west (and to some extent in India as well), might address this by affirming that God will in some way ensure that the results of all of our choices will inevitably conspire to bring about the desired transformation. From Griffin's point of view, however, this involves at least two difficulties. First, although God may in fact manage to direct our choices and their results in such a way as to bring about the desired outcome—and Griffin does affirm this possibility, and sees it as a basis for hoping that the desired outcome will indeed occur—to see this as *inevitable* is to deny the freedom of the beings making up the world. Secondly, if the world has been in some sense set up or designed in advance with this inevitable outcome in mind, God becomes responsible, in a moral sense, for all of the evil and suffering that has occurred in the world. Griffin claims such a morally ambiguous God is not worthy of worship: "Can we completely admire the wisdom and goodness of a deity who would create our kind of world ... simply for the satisfaction of knowing that those souls who do become good do so freely?"[28]

Griffin's solution preserves divine omnibenevolence at the cost of divine omnipotence. God indeed aspires to the kind of cosmic transformation that Hick affirms as an eventual reality. But God's ability to bring this transformation about is limited by, and dependent upon, the free choices of the beings making up the cosmos. And this is not a matter of God "allowing" beings to be free in order to bring about this desired end; for if it could have been otherwise, we again run into the problem of divine moral culpability. In the process model of God that Griffin affirms, beings are free because it is in the very nature of things for them to be so. This is not by divine design, but a matter of logical necessity: "From the point of view of process theism, we need not debate that question [of divine culpability] because ... God could *not* have created beings like us in every way except guaranteed by God always to be and do good."[29]

Vedanta after Griffin

It is important to note that Griffin does not reject Hick's cosmic optimism. He tempers it, however, affirming it as a "hope" rather than as an inevitable outcome of a cosmic design that has rigged the game in advance.[30] There is every reason to hope that the benevolent, guiding hand of God will direct us all to choose the path of selfless service and transform ourselves, in harmony with the divine will, into the potentially divine beings that we are. But it is also possible that things will just keep rumbling along as they have throughout history, full of pain and anguish for countless living beings, for if the divine will could not be thwarted, our freedom would be an illusion.

Can this tempered process version of cosmic optimism be integrated into Vedanta? And are there advantages to the Vedanta tradition in such integration?

First, it is interesting to note that Griffin sees reason to hope not only for an eventual victory of good beyond this life, as both Hick and Vedanta do as well, but also for victory for the good on earth.[31] Griffin may actually be, in this sense, more optimistic than Swami Vivekananda, who affirms, as we have already seen, that "This world is like a dog's curly tail." In this sense, Vivekananda is in harmony not only with most Hindu traditions, but also with Buddhism and Jainism, in seeing the realm of *samsara*, the realm of rebirth, as inherently a place of trial and error, a place of learning that will never be perfect if by "perfect" we mean "problem free." Specific problems in the world may be solved, but it would not be much of a "grand moral gymnasium" without any workout equipment for the souls inhabiting it.

The idea of an eventual victory for good beyond this life that would not necessitate an omnipotent God is, however, quite plausible from a Vedantic framework. If one bears in mind that, in Vedanta, there is no absolute beginning or end of time, and that souls will continue to experience death and rebirth as long as they have not attained realization, the possibility emerges that some beings may, indeed, forever choose not to utilize their free will in a way conducive to their liberation—though, given infinite time, there is reason to hope that even the most stubborn souls will eventually realize their best interests lie in seeing themselves in the other and the other in themselves. Vedanta does not look toward an eschaton in which all beings will achieve liberation at the same time. It is a perpetual process, with neither beginning nor end. There is certainly a personal eschaton, in the form of liberation. This universe, however, this dog's curly tail, could be seen, to shift the metaphor, as something akin to a soul factory, in which living beings are constantly given opportunities for advancement. Sometimes living beings take up these opportunities, and sometimes they reject them. The universe, however, never gives up on these beings. It is a universe of infinite second chances.

The God who directs this process cannot be omnipotent, if the soul formation process is to be genuine. This insight draws the attention of the modern Vedantist to the traditional Hindu distinction between Brahman, the ultimate ground of all being, beyond categories such as personal and impersonal, and Ishvara, or Bhagavan: the supreme personal being who lovingly directs us toward our goal. Ishvara, like the process God, cannot interfere with our choices and is even limited by the constraints of karma. Even Krishna, who is God incarnate, is slain by the arrow of a deer hunter, his body being subject to the laws of material action. But given infinite time, there is plenty of reason to hope that the divine will can exert its influence on all beings, that all beings might eventually attain liberation, but that, beings being infinite in number, there will always be more souls working their way through the grand moral gymnasium of the material world, eventually to find their way home.

Notes

1. John Hick, *An Interpretation of Religion: Human Responses to the Transcendent* (New Haven: Yale University Press, 1989), 118, 120.
2. Swami Vivekananda, *Complete Works* (Kolkata: Advaita Ashrama, 1989), 1:80.
3. David Ray Griffin, *Reenchantment without Supernaturalism: A Process Philosophy of Religion* (Ithaca, N.Y.: Cornell University Press, 2001), 230.
4. Griffin, *Reenchantment without Supernaturalism*, 229.
5. The best recent summary of these issues is Andrew J. Nicholson, *Unifying Hinduism: Philosophy and Identity in Indian Intellectual History* (New York: Columbia University Press, 2010).
6. I am using the terminology of "Christian and Islamic devotion" to avoid the claim that one sometimes hears that Sri Ramakrishna literally practiced Christianity and Islam. It is not clear, as some critics have pointed out, that Sri Ramakrishna's Christian and Islamic *sadhanas*, or spiritual practices, would constitute full and proper affiliation to Christianity or to Islam as these would be recognized by most members of either tradition. But they were certainly "Christian" and "Islamic" in the broad sense that they were focused quite intensively upon the figures of Jesus and Muhammad, respectively; with both, Ramakrishna experienced a profound mystical communion at the culmination of each of these phases of his practice. These practices were more akin to the Hindu practice of focusing one's attentive devotion upon one's *ishtadevata*, or chosen deity, than to what one might call conventional Christian or Islamic practice, though they certainly do have parallels with the more intensively devotional and mystical practices of these two faiths, and Ramakrishna did have contact with actual, living Christian devotees and Islamic Sufi practitioners during these phases of his spiritual journey.
7. Vivekananda, *Complete Works*, 5:186.
8. Pravrajika Vrajaprana, *Vedanta: A Simple Introduction* (Hollywood, Calif.: Vedanta Press, 1999), 62.
9. Vivekananda, *Complete Works*, 1:374.
10. Vivekananda, *Complete Works*, 1:374.
11. Swami Atmavidyananda, "Vedantic Paradigms in Relation to Scientific Inquiry" (paper presented at the International Conference on Swami Vivekananda on the 150th Anniversary of His Birth, University of Southern California School of Religion, October 18–19, 2013) and Jeffery D. Long, *A Vision for Hinduism: Beyond Hindu Nationalism* (London: I. B. Tauris, 2007), 82–84.
12. *Bhagavad Gita* 6:30, my translation.
13. This prayer is regularly recited in Vedanta centers in North America. It is based on several popular sayings of the Holy Mother, Sarada Devi, wife and spiritual companion of Sri Ramakrishna and a major guiding light to the Vedanta movement since its inception.
14. Swami Nikhilananda, trans., *The Gospel of Sri Ramakrishna* (New York: Ramakrishna-Vivekananda Center, 1942), 101.
15. Nikhilananda, *The Gospel of Sri Ramakrishna*, 101.

16. "Ramakrishna Mission's Annual Report: Going Strong," Hindu Press International, February 17, 2014, http://www.hinduismtoday.com/blogs-news/hindu-press-international/ramakrishna-mission-s-annual-report—going-strong/13441.html.
17. Vivekananda, *Complete Works*, 1:75.
18. Vivekananda, *Complete Works*, 1:75.
19. Vivekananda, *Complete Works*, 1:76.
20. Vivekananda, *Complete Works*, 1:80.
21. Personal communication, February 1, 2014.
22. Vivekananda, *Complete Works*, 1:79.
23. Abhaya Dasgupta, *Saradadevi: Atmakatha* [Autobiographical Talks of Saradadevi] (Golpark, Calcutta: Ramakrishna Mission Institute of Culture, 1979), 122 [cited in Narasingha Sil, *Divine Dowager: The Life and Teachings of Saradamani the Holy Mother* (Selinsgrove, Pennsylvania: Susquehanna University Press, 2003), 121].
24. John Hick, *The Fifth Dimension: An Exploration of the Spiritual Realm* (Oxford: Oneworld Publications, 1999), 19–24.
25. Hick, *Fifth Dimension*, 57.
26. Hick, *Fifth Dimension*, 57.
27. Griffin, *Reenchantment without Supernaturalism*, 227, 229. Emphasis in the original.
28. Griffin, *Reenchantment without Supernaturalism*, 227.
29. Griffin, *Reenchantment without Supernaturalism*, 227.
30. Griffin, *Reenchantment without Supernaturalism*, 230.
31. Griffin, *Reenchantment without Supernaturalism*, 230.

6 "Only Goodness Matters"

REFLECTIONS ON THEODICY WITH KLAUS VON STOSCH AND JEFFERY LONG

Wendy Farley

Rory Block, the great blues singer, poses the question of evil in her wonderful song, "Faithless World."[1] In her characteristic way, she evokes the poignancy of suffering, leaving the question of meaning visceral and open. She identifies us as "travelers" in this place of "many wonders" and "tears." Her hard road has taught her that suffering is not punishment but rather a task given to the "enlightened," a "lesson to be learned," which each individual must learn for themselves. This "faithless world" is as, Jeffery Long puts it, a kind of moral gymnasium; it is a place of suffering against which we, as Kermani argues, are invited to protest. Rory Block's musical gifts invite us into the raw place where suffering remains mysterious and unhealed. It is a good place to begin a conversation with these fine scholars.

The essays by von Stosch and Long, and the rich cast of characters they bring to our attention, suggest something of the complexities entailed in the perennial realities of evil and suffering. They also indicate some of the irreconcilable ways in which humans have tried to arrive at some existentially satisfying way to inhabit this reality. The response to these papers will fall into three parts: a brief reflection on the project of comparison itself, an engagement with the particular arguments presented, and finally a few of my own reflections on theodicy in light of this exercise in dialogue and comparison.

Comparison as Comportment

Both von Stosch and Long indicate a turn away from the effort to construct grand theories of comparison. Departing also from a preoccupation with a unified or essential Christianity, Islam, or Hinduism, they focus on particular thinkers, particular texts, particular arguments. This focus on micro-narratives emphasizes the great complexity of religious traditions: traditions and individuals alike have a certain fluidity to them, they change over time, and are characterized by interior diversity. These features make attempts to compare large traditions in a formalistic way somewhat misleading. Though scholars can identify larger patterns across and within traditions, comparison is not primarily a question of Christians believing this and Muslims believing that but rather of entering into conversation with one another so that understanding continues to grow and deepen. This does not mean that there can be nothing useful that arises from more formal comparisons, but the fine-grained analysis provided by Long and von Stosch allows readers rich avenues of interpretation.

This deepening of understanding through dialogue is partly intellectual, but it is also a kind of ethical practice. The mood of generosity and openness is called for in dialogue. Meeting others with an open heart and an awareness of one's own limitations allows us to comport ourselves toward others in ways that are less governed by our anxieties or attachments. Von Stosch and Long offer good examples of the ethical as well as the intellectual virtues of comparison. They engage their texts with care, providing rigorous analysis of the arguments and worldviews of their interlocutors. But they also approach their dialogue partners with appreciation and generosity, even when they offer critical assessment. Readers may open to further understanding of the problem of evil, even as we participate in the living process by which thinking and understanding continues.

The Beauty of God and the Gift of Endless Second Chances

This comportment of openness and generosity is precisely what is threatened by the theme of this section: suffering and evil. In our perennial vulnerability to suffering, oppression, ignorance, and wrong-doing, it is difficult to maintain an open heart toward others, including religious others. Reflecting on the conversation among Klaus von Stosch, Navid Kermani, Jeffery Long, and his Vedantic and Christian interlocutors may give us more tools for interpreting this difficulty.

Von Stosch draws attention to a phenomenon familiar to Christianity: the apparent gap between the goodness of the Creator and the terror of human history. Von Stosch and Kermani agree that a response to this terror must not only be theoretical, but also practical. It must not only make belief in God rational but must be morally compelling as well. Von Stosch presents the "free will defense" as a useful theoretical construct, but his engagement with Kermani opens innovative ways of considering the relationship of God to human suffering.

Kermani's response to this is fascinating and profound, including three interlocking elements: protest against God, the beauty of God, and the intermingling of beauty and terror within the divine majesty. Kermani's first impulse (like von Stosch's) is solidarity with suffering. In the face of human suffering and oppression, the only possible religious response is protest. The difficulty of this emerges almost immediately, as Kermani, like many theists, is compelled to trace ultimate causality within creation to God. "Does evil befall a city, unless the Lord has done it?" (Amos 3:6). Certainly, responding to the suffering of others is a basic ethical impulse, but how does one do this when God is the ultimate cause of it? Kermani appeals to the Islamic mystic, Attar, to insist that even if evil is traced to the divine glory, we must protest and lament. Like Job, we must accuse God and, in doing so, draw God back to God's own self-revelation as compassionate love.

The idea of protest is rooted in scripture: the Psalms are full of protest and lament, and the book of Job centers around accusation. It is found in Jewish thinkers such as Elie Wiesel and David Blumenthal.[2] As von Stosch points out, the patron saint of protest theology is Dostoevsky's Ivan, who is in rebellion against a world in which children are mercilessly and pointlessly tortured. The moral goodness made possible by divine revelation requires us to protest against the horrors of creation and, in the name of God, rebel against God.

If God were only this terrorizing deity, protest should turn to rejection of faith altogether. Kermani emphasizes that it is possible to remain devoted because of the dazzling beauty of God. God wishes not blind obedience, but appreciation that is the root of love. Reciting the Qur'an is itself an aesthetic act. Because we are in love with the divine beauty, we are able to endure the divine terror.[3] Like Attar, the protesting faithful are in love with the person they attack. As von Stosch puts it in his essay,

> This *aisthesis* reaches to the life-changing beauty of God, which can fascinate people so much that they dedicate their life to God. However,

because one can never perceive the beauty of God without its majesty and terror, there is no easy way to God. One must simultaneously affirm divine beauty and resist the disasters of this world.

For Kermani, the resolution of this ambiguity between the terror and beauty of God is love: Love makes it possible to surrender to this reality "without losing confidence." Only love makes possible the intimacy that enables the faithful to love the one they attack: "Only someone who believes in the Highest can throw stones up to heaven. . . . Those whose love exceeds the conventional degree dare to demand the kind of God He Himself revealed to them."[4]

This intermingling of protest, beauty, and love brings to mind the dedication of couples who struggle through misunderstandings, fights, and conflict to preserve their love for one another. Rather than simply leave—either physically or emotionally—they stay at it, willing to struggle in order to tend the preciousness of their mutual devotion. These kinds of relationships can not only be successful marriages, but spiritual practices in which the struggle in the relationship brings out what is best in both partners. Lovers protest against those deficiencies that are unworthy of their beloved.

For Kermani, the metaphor of sexual intimacy does capture these connections between love, protest, and surrender. But he does not leave it there. He argues that terror and love are essentially interconnected in the divine being. Sexual violence becomes a metaphor for God's relationship to "his" lovers. Humanity is not only a lover devoted to deeper intimacy, but an abused wife who has no recourse but to adore the hand that brutalizes her. Kermani is presenting us with a picture of love in which terror and beauty, intimacy and violence are *essentially* interdependent. The response to theodicy is to protest, in solidarity with sufferers, and to surrender to the violence of our beautiful, personality disordered, lover.[5]

Von Stosch, for all his sympathy with Kermani's work, is himself troubled by his fiction, in which "God's jealousy becomes revolting, and the terror of this highly erotic love is unacceptable." Like von Stosch, I cannot accept the projection onto God of the too-human impulse to terrorize and violate intimate partners. But I would suggest we linger here for a few minutes, investigating the logic at work here.

There is a governing set of metaphors and narratives that shape many forms of western theism. This story concerns an absolutely powerful deity that has created the cosmos and entered into particularly intimate relationship with humanity (or at least that part of humanity that participates in one's own religion). God is both the divine sovereign governing events and also the source of ethical conduct, moral ideals, and intuitions of social justice and charity. God is all-powerful and all-good in the sense that a human sovereign would be. This produces the quandary: Why do evil, suffering, and injustice dominate human experience? Religions offer many different responses to this theoretical quandary and existential catastrophe. Because God is all-powerful, there must be some sense in which evil is traced to God himself. Theologians are then put in the position of justifying God's role in generating evil. The most common way of doing this is to blame humanity, both for particular evils and for the existence of evil itself—through a fall, for example. God created the world, and God punishes humanity for the evils that arise within it.

In much of Christianity, this requires a permanent division between those who are saved and those who are damned. The providential plan is a kind of never-ending Third Reich: Those who are rejected by the leader are burned and tormented. Those who retain allegiance to the leader are rewarded. In this way, the faults of humanity are reharmonized into a vision of divine righteousness: The saved reveal divine mercy, the damned reveal God's retributive justice.

Kermani does not follow this logic; rather than being governed by what Ricoeur calls the "myth of punishment," he draws on images of beauty and sexual desire. He identifies an interdependence between harmony and terror, loving submission and sexual violence. But Kermani incorporates into this duality the obligation to protest against it. God demands that we protest against the kind of being God is, in the name of God. As disturbed as I am by his apotheosis of sexual violence, it is a milder way to conceive of God's predilection for violence than the standard Christian eschatology. The fundamental relationship remains one of beauty and love, and God seems to wish to be called back to the angels of his better nature.

What remains to be investigated is why metaphors of domination should so structure the way we think about evil and suffering. Kermani is a rich and creative thinker, and we can be grateful to von Stosch for bringing more attention to his work. In particular, resuscitating an aesthetic understanding of divine reality is a welcome enrichment of our theological imagination. For Christians, it may lead us back to Pseudo-Dionysius and others for whom beauty is a "name" of God. Nonetheless, investigating the roots of our theological fascination with violence remains important. The conclusion to this essay will take up the question whether it might be desirable to protest not against God, but against religions' attribution to God of our own evil tendencies.

We enter a quite different conversation with Jeffery Long and Vedanta. With Ramakrishna and Vivekananda, we enter a world of contemplative practitioners who are consciously orienting their tradition toward dialogue with the modern world. Here the emphasis is less on a struggle to understand why there is suffering and evil but rather a dedication to practices aimed at overcoming it. The mood recalls the famous story of the Buddha: We are as people shot with an arrow and instead of endless demands to know who shot it, the kind of bow it was, and the reason for the violence, we should instead focus all of our energy on getting the arrow out. In this effort, Vedanta advises us to attend to our ignorance of our fundamental nature. Our ultimate nature is united with divine reality and through it with all beings. Our deepest suffering arises from our ignorance (*avidya*) of this truth. Vedanta offers methods to cultivate wisdom, that is, immediate awareness of divine reality.

Ramakrishna, the great modern interpreter of Vedanta, teaches a path of contemplative wisdom. Vivekananda, Ramakrishna's disciple, adds active practices of compassion to contemplative practice. The transformative power of compassionate action is not understood to arise from our benevolent attitude toward others, as if we are doing a great favor to someone. Neither is it understood as an activity that will fundamentally change the structure of our world. Evil and suffering will remain characteristics of the human experience. Compassionate practice represents a non-vicious circle through which the radical truth of inter-relationship is realized: When we act with compassion toward others, we become more aware of our connection to them; in realizing this connection, we are compelled to act with compassion. As we are more identified with divine reality, when we encounter suffering, we are compelled to act with compassion. We immediately perceive not only the beauty and holiness of others but also our intimacy with them. We respond compassionately not for some other end but because we must, just as we must pull our hand from a fire.

From this perspective, the suffering of the world is real but penultimate. A person on the path of liberation will use the suffering they encounter as an element of their spiritual practice. Thinking along these lines, we might imagine the encounter with someone harmful to us as the occasion not only to find appropriate ways to defend ourselves (or someone else) but also the occasion to engage the difficult work of connecting with compassion (perhaps fierce compassion) to someone whose connection to the divine source is deeply hidden. The full range of the greatness of the human spirit—courage, resourcefulness, peacefulness, mercy—are challenged and enhanced as they are practiced in difficult situations. From this perspective, we are spiritual athletes, practicing goodness, compassion, and wisdom not only in the calm of a meditation hall but in the rough and tumble of life in the world. Our spiritual capacities are not only meditated on, but enacted in every situation. At the same time, the capacity to act with courage and goodness in every situation requires that we become ever more deeply united with our divine source and identity. This union is what creates the deepest capacities for wisdom and compassion.

Whatever the ultimate explanation for humanity's alienation from divine reality, whatever reasons suffering arises, through spiritual practice, the world becomes a "moral gymnasium" that enables us to get at the root of suffering and be liberated from its causes. Though this task is rarely fully accomplished in any individual life, we can be confident that the universe holds us all until we are able to attain greater stability in awareness of ultimate reality. The universe is one of endless second chances. In this we see a cosmic optimism as well as a deep sense of compassion that does not give up on any person, however seemingly incorrigible. As Long puts it:

> The God who directs this process cannot be omnipotent, if the soul formation process is to be genuine. This insight draws the attention of the modern Vedantist to the traditional Hindu distinction between Brahman, the ultimate ground of all being, beyond categories such as personal and impersonal, and Ishvara, or Bhagavan: the supreme personal being who lovingly directs us toward our goal.... But given infinite time, there is plenty of reason to hope that the divine will can exert its influence on all beings, that all beings might eventually attain liberation.

In the conversation with Kermani, we found underlying assumptions similar to those of much orthodox Christianity. Here we find themes more familiar to contemplative strands within Christianity: divine goodness is completely reliable, and through spiritual practices of contemplation and compassion, human beings can enter into this goodness ever more fully. Long does not appeal to Christian contemplatives, but finds in John Hick and David Ray Griffin contemporary theologians whose ethical commitments make them seem to lean more toward certain Vedantic interpretations than Christian orthodoxy.

David Ray Griffin, like other process theologians, rejects the conflation between sovereignty and power characteristic of classical theism. As Long suggests, divinity cannot be omnipotent if there is genuine free will. Omnipotence also entangles us in hopeless ethical problems, as we have seen, because it makes it very difficult to avoid tracing evil back to divine providence. In process theology, human freedom—in fact the freedom of the cosmos—makes evil possible and even inevitable. Through participation in ethical, social, and political activities, we can hope for the transformation of history and strongly hope for an eschatological reconciliation. God is not master of our fate, but the ever-present, ever-alluring tug toward the good and the beautiful.

Long turns to Hick to surface other non-Augustinian strands of Christian theodicy. Hick identifies Irenaeus and Schleiermacher as representatives of a theodicy which assumes that human beings cannot be created in the fullness of spiritual maturity but must develop. Evil is a consequence of the gradual and painful task of spiritual maturation. Notwithstanding the appalling suffering in the world, it is possible to remain confident in God's utterly reliable love.[6] Suffering is neither punishment nor divine condemnation.[7] It is the occasion of growth and transformation. Hick's own conclusions reflect Irenaean sympathies. He draws on John Keats to argue that the world is a place of soul-making. Keats, writing two years before his early death, laments that Jesus's splendor was concealed by "men interested in the pious frauds of religion."[8] Keats surmises that suffering is inherent to all life; through it the divine spark is joined to the concreteness of personal existence. He suggests, "this system of Soul-making may have been the Parent to the more palpable schemes of redemption among Zoroastrians, Christians and 'Hindoos.'"[9] Keats, an early practitioner of interreligious dialogue, found the emphasis on spiritual formation consoling as his brother, and then he himself, succumbed to tuberculosis.

The theme of soul-formation in its Vedantic form construes evil to derive from ignorance of our divine nature.[10] This ignorance is itself a kind of suffering, and it causes us to act in ways that further promulgate suffering. In these senses, suffering is intrinsic to life in the world. But the world is not only a place of estrangement; as a "moral gymnasium," suffering is essential to our purification and return to our divine source. Ramakrishna emphasizes the role of teaching the path of liberation. His disciple, Vivekananda, combined these practices with what westerners might think of as more concrete alleviation of suffering. We work to relieve suffering, our own and that of others, by combining the path of liberation with compassionate service.

In the Vedantic and Christian versions of soul-making, certain problems that haunt the monarchial metaphor for God are avoided. Theologians are not put in the position of justifying the divine use of coercive and violent power; they are not forced to "call evil good and good evil" (Isa. 5:20) by attributing injustice or evil to God. Suffering is unfortunate and properly evokes compassion, but it is an essential element in the process of spiritual transformation. Grace Jantzen puts it more forcefully in describing the theodicy of Julian of Norwich: "The only way in which subsequent reward could compensate for suffering would be if the reward were intrinsic to the suffering and impossible without it."[11] The point here is not simply that suffering somehow is "good for us" or "makes us stronger." Rather, it is only through suffering that our spiritual greatness will be brought to fruition. Human beings are like great athletes who must arduously train to perfect their skill. Children put through this training without understanding why will find it meaningless and dehumanizing. But if one understands its point, then one's own suffering becomes the occasion for deep spiritual wrestling; suffering of others provokes practices of compassion. In both ways, the ego is stripped of its ignorance and craving, allowing compassion and wisdom to flow ever more freely.

Every theodicy, as practiced by imperfect human beings, will cast its own shadow. The balance between equanimity and philosophical acceptance can tip in the direction of indifference. Other people's suffering becomes quite easy to bear if it is cast onto an eternal horizon of second chances. This becomes even more problematic when it slides into a justification of structural injustice. Even with the luminous counter-examples of Gandhi or Vivekananda, religious defense of the inferior status of women or of Dalits (untouchables) shows that the collateral damage of theodicies can contribute to suffering rather than alleviate it.

In this conversation with Long and his Vedantic and Christian interlocutors, there are differences that will stand out to Christians: the question of endless time contrasting with eschatology; a hope that the arc of history is not only toward justice but toward universal liberation. Is evil ignorance or sin? Do we justify it or try to alleviate it? Would alleviation consist of a contemplative path, compassionate service, or the pursuit of the kingdom of God on earth? In these long conversations struggling with the crushing truth of suffering, all theodicies can too quickly slide into collaboration with the causes of suffering. And yet, they are also the great witnesses that the truth of suffering is not ultimate and that every human bears a capacity for spiritual greatness. A battered wife, a slave, or a Dalit can all know that beyond the hopelessness of their current situation, they participate in another reality and the truth of that identity will not be forever thwarted.

In comparing these various texts, we witness differences as well as common sympathies that occur both across and within traditions. Keats seems to have found more consolation in "Hindoo" thought than in Christianity's "pious frauds." Another Christian might find more resonance with Kermani: The veneration of controlling power animates the imagination of Augustine and Calvin, as well as much mainstream Christianity. By contrast, Hick and Griffin challenge the bifurcation of goodness and violence within the god-head. Though they do not share the Vedantic view of reincarnation, they share its hope in universal salvation. They resist the temptation to pit wrath and love or heaven and hell against one another to preserve an imperial model of divine power. In this they may find Vedantists more amenable to their deepest commitments than Calvinists.

We see in these various options for reflecting on evil and suffering that the religions of the world consider this problem in quite different and even incompatible ways. But we also see that these differences characterize different religious sensibilities that occur within as well as across traditions. The final section of this essay will revisit von Stosch's insistence that theodicy must be ethically as well as rationally satisfying. Because much of what we think about evil and suffering is rooted in the paradigms and metaphors through which we think about human freedom and the fundamental nature of ultimate reality, we will reflect further on the way our assumptions shape theodicy.

"Only Goodness Counts"

For several of our writers, freedom and free will are crucial elements of theodicy. Whether free will emerges naturally from the process of evolution, through God's creative act, or is gradually uncovered through contemplative practice, the existence and value of freedom provides a meaningful context for suffering and evil. Though they do not offer a simplistic "free will defense" in which any amount of suffering and destruction is "worth it" to preserve the ultimate value of choice, we may still pause and consider whether there are significant differences between free choice and freedom.

According to a natural law approach, a mode of existence has arisen in which it is characteristic to act not only instinctually but also through rationality, judgment, and choice. Through this way of operating, human-caused suffering and oppression also evolve. Predators may eat prey, but they do not condemn them to serfdom, prisons, or death camps. This tragic structure is simply part of the human phenomenon, and religions must address it as an element of our created being. In this version, it is not so much a question of free choice being "worth it" as it is simply a fact of our existence that requires us to reflect on ways in which divine power interacts with natural processes.

On the one hand, this approach addresses many difficult issues. It interprets suffering as a fact of human life without having directly to attribute to God our worst actions and motivations. It honors the necessity of personhood and agency for genuine spiritual life. On the other hand, there seems to be embedded in the very idea of free choice the logic of modern liberalism, and it is presumably not a coincidence that this way of conceiving of the problem of evil arises in the modern period. I confess, when I read the news about Boko Haram's kidnapping of school girls—or any other of the ten thousand atrocities that transpire every day—the operation of free choice does not appear as an obvious good.

But a different kind of problem lies in the imagination of choice as something that operates unconstrained by external forces. Christian theology in many of its traditional forms has tended not to rely on a free will defense in part because it is skeptical that human beings' actions are governed by genuine freedom.[12] Though this point is often made through quasi-mythological images of a mysterious past in which a fall deprived us of our natural capacity for good, the general point that our basic faculties are distorted before we begin using them seems apt. We humans are under the tyranny of oppressive and egocentric attachments and aversions. We are possessed by habitual passions: fear, envy, greed, anger, lust, jealousy and so on.[13] This distortion means that negative and destructive mental patterns are not simply passing emotions but fundamental dispositions that compel us to act in deluded or unethical ways. These distortions shape our fundamental way of seeing, interpreting, and responding to our world. Governed by the passion of anger, we encounter others primarily as a threat to our well-being. Governed by lust, we encounter others as objects reducible to our private pleasure and gratification. As Emmanuel Levinas suggests, "ethics is optics."[14] But because of a primordial distortion, we cannot "see" others as human or as bearers of the divine image.

Contemporary theologians add analyses of ways these delusions are embedded in social systems that themselves teach us what is real, who is human, or what action might be considered virtuous. It is not, for example, simply an ethical problem when a bad husband beats his wife; in a misogynistic subculture, it is almost impossible to "see" women as human. The leader of a Baltimore gang describes his moral universe, in which "woman naturally serves him, Consoling him, Cooking for him, Rearing their children... The New Man uses these three steps to discipline his wife: He verbally reprimands her. He refuses to sleep with her. He beats her lightly."[15] Climate change denial is likewise not simply a moral choice; it is a way of experiencing reality. Changing these views is not a question of acquiring more information or choosing differently, but of reconstructing one's perception of reality.[16]

Our ethical behaviors are constrained before we act by the construction of reality by social systems, our dispositions and habits, genetics, and whatever mysterious factors undermine our desires for the good. Prior to any choice, we are defrauded of the ability to experience the full depth of compassion, wonder, or joy. Our rationality is taken into the service of our delusions: much energy is spent in constructing not only individual meaning but social, economic, and political worlds that uphold our fears and desires. If our world is constructed according to racist ideologies and social structures, a genuine encounter with someone of another race as fully human will be very difficult. If a society constructs women as reducible to their capacity to gratify male fantasies of nurture and pleasure, neither women nor men will be able to freely experience the full range of human potential in its female forms. Free choice is constantly subject to forces that limit it or redirect it to actions that do not serve it.

This bondage and incapacity extends not only to systems of oppression but to experiences of ourselves as inferior, unworthy, paralyzed by fear, or crushed by anxiety. Teresa of Avila describes this "slough of cowardice, pusillanimity and fear" as a fundamental shape of sin. "'Dare I begin such and such a task?' . . . 'Can anyone as wretched as I engage in so lofty an exercise as prayer?' . . . Oh, God help me, daughters, how many souls the devil must have ruined this way!'"[17] She refers to this paralysis and lack of self-respect by the Spanish word *ratero*: "creeping, flying low, content with a low standard."[18] This infection of our deep sense of self is described by Levinas as the gentleness of internalized coercion so one no longer requires external compulsion; one is one's own prison guard: "the supreme violence is . . . [the] supreme gentleness."[19] We have become the low-creeping entity we were taught to be.

The illusion that we are the center of reality, the tyrannies of destructive emotional *habitus*, the construction of our root sense of reality by social illusions such as racism, consumption, or unworthiness, are all indications of ways in which our free choice is grossly limited. To a large extent, our free choice is like that of an alcoholic or drug addict. The structure of choice is present, but desire and reason have already been hijacked. If negative or violent actions arising from free choice are more expressions of bondage and servitude, then the role of free will in theodicy may need to be reconsidered and refined.

Religions of the world hold freedom in the highest honor. Freedom and liberation are among the central metaphors for spiritual attainment. The Gospel of John suggests that Jesus's invitation is toward a freedom that is yet to be experienced: "know the truth and the truth will set you free" (John 8:32). As we saw in Vedanta, this freedom is not something we possess but something to be attained—even through great difficulty and through the cycles of many lives. Freedom is not interpreted here as random choice but as the liberation from ignorance, craving, and the slavery of egocentrism. When liberated from these poisons, we become free to act as a truly humane person: with wisdom, compassion, and equanimity. This point is echoed by many contemplative authors within Christianity. The desert ascetics understood their practices as efforts to reduce and overthrow the passions, to achieve "apatheia," whose child is *agape*.[20] Thus, the state of freedom from negative emotional attachments and dispositions (*apatheia*) makes it possible to experience the deepest and most universal quality of non-egocentric love (*agape*).

If this freedom is something to be sought rather than something already possessed, we are forced back to prior questions: Whence the bondage? Whence the distortion of reason and emotion? Whence the incapacity for those actions—love, compassion, wonder, courage, peacefulness, joy, nurture—that make us genuinely happy and free?

Questions of theodicy hearken back to fundamental questions of theological anthropology. They also, as we have seen, force us to more disciplined reflections on the nature of divine reality. Notwithstanding the most sublime attention of the greatest of theologians and contemplatives to the apophatic, non-conceptual reality of the divine, theodicy nonetheless continues to import paradigms of divine power from human relationships: sovereigns and subjects, fathers and children, men and their lovers.[21] It is not accidental that these are all patriarchal relationships in which the inferior is relatively passive and dependent on the good will of the master. Theologians try to imagine benevolent forms of these relationships, but because the basic structure is one of domination, the images quickly degenerate into justifications of physical or emotional violence. Our authors are struggling against this very thing, but in Islam and Christianity, theodicy continues to be shaped by this paradigm.

The imagined world of these metaphors is one of ostensibly moral agents, one of which has limited free choice and one of which has supreme power. This is a tangled up image, implying a zero sum game between human and divine freedom and power. Is the use of dominating force against free will ethical? In the free will argument, it is unethical and therefore God withholds "his" power. Is the use of such force ethical when it comes to smiting—out of righteousness, predestination, or the anger of a betrayed lover? Solutions twist and turn against these rip-tides.

In many obvious senses, human beings are the cause of much suffering and evil. But as creator and sovereign, these basic structures and possibilities and perhaps the actions themselves must be traced to divine providence. Evil is produced by agents (human or divine) choosing actions or relationships that cause destruction or suffering. When this choice is by human beings, we condemn it as immoral but justify the general framework in which free choice is an ultimate good. When this choice is made by God, we praise it or protest against it or wait to understand it "by and by," but remain devoted to God's majesty regardless of the immorality of God's actions.

When free will and coercive power are construed as ultimate, the propensity for violence and domination are imported into the divine (and human) life as essential attributes. In doing this, we must first accept that power and coercion are identical. But human life witnesses to many counter-examples: Gandhi's non-violent *satyagraha*, forgiveness, compassion. Jean Valjean's entire life is liberated and transformed by a simple act of mercy in *Les Miserables*. Hopelessly entrenched racist laws were overthrown by a non-violent civil rights movement. Gregory of Nyssa assures us that it is Satan, not God, who deploys violent methods.[22]

We have available to us other models for divine power. Investigating these alternatives is all the more urgent because of the inherent conflict between dominating power and the nurture of freedom and personhood. Dominating power is, by its essential nature, unmoored from ethical reality. In identifying it with divine reality, we are forced to admire something that in ordinary human life we condemn as antithetical to transcendent good or genuine freedom. We are thus compelled to praise and revere God for practicing what, in human beings, are the most destructive and horrifying human impulses. It is not difficult to track this veneration of divine violence into a defense of human violence, sexual and otherwise. In Kermani, this becomes explicit in the veneration of sexual violence as a metaphor for divine power. But this veneration of divine violence is characteristic of much orthodox Christian theology as well, as we have seen. In this, comparative theology witnesses to a veneration of violence at the heart of more than one religious tradition.

There is a high price paid for this. Provoked into the position of worshiping violence, this kind of theology justifies human violence and can only further maim the human person and religion itself. This is the move that Levinas rejected in his critique of all theodicy that justified violence rather than responding with justice and compassion to its victims.[23] Another kind of spiritual violence is present in the monarchial/patriarchal image or paradigm itself. The basic shape of reality is one in which human beings must accept the role of children, subjects, or (abused) wives. In church history, this has entailed real children, subjects, wives, and slaves accepting their subordination as divinely intended while parents, rulers, husbands, and masters underwent a different kind of spiritual destruction in their acceptance of techniques of domination.

Is freedom identical with free choice? Is divine reality best conceived through metaphors of coercion, sovereignty, or control? I would argue that the underlying metaphor here of the divine as a supreme monarch is in tension with the sacredness of personhood as well as with attributes of goodness or love. The idea that human beings are created in the divine image implies we are structured by features of divine being. This is envisioned through the metaphor of personhood or agency. Does personhood—divine or human—consist in arbitrary choice? This seems a severely impoverished construal of personhood, which has effectively eviscerated ethical and spiritual qualities from religious life.

It is possible to disconnect personhood (divine or human) from ethical attributes and associate it with arbitrary choice and dominating power. But personhood is more typically associated with what is inherently good, ethical, and beautiful. Kermani appeals to the ultimacy of the ethical when he protects the right of humanity to protest against God. The ethical person has powers of love, mercy, compassion, joy, wonder. This is not simply a list of possible choices: vanilla, chocolate, love, hatred, compassion, cruelty. They are the powers of personhood as they are more fully realized, as they are liberated from the painful constraints of egocentrism and its addictions to pain-relieving strategies and delusions.

Our highest ethical attributes require personhood, therefore agency. This agency is not simply the random assertion of a deluded free choice. It is the freedom to act according to our deepest nature, in love, compassion, mutual joy, mercy. We use the metaphor of personhood for divine reality as a way of capturing this connection between our own spiritual perfections and our groundedness in the divine.

Here we re-enter the conversation with Vedanta. There are many irreconcilable differences between traditions that remain, but the shared recognition of a connection between the deepest good of the human being and our divine source may spark a spiritual friendship. Even protest against God is, paradoxically, rooted in the depth of divine goodness. It is the goodness and justice we have learned from God that compels us to demand these things from God. We do not see this spirit of protest in Vedanta, perhaps because it is not indebted to the monarchial metaphors that so constrain western theisms. Even so, Vivekananda's dedication to compassionate action implies a protest against concrete suffering. Rather than protesting divine power or even the samsaric nature of human experience, his unitive practices tap into a deep root that inspires his resistance to the empire of pain. Regardless of their variant theologies, we see in our authors impulses to respond to suffering with care and to imagine a dimension of reality in which evil is not ultimate.

As Socrates said, we cannot hope for wisdom on this matter, which is a thing only for the gods; but we can be animated by the desire for wisdom.[24] In this desire, we can attend to what best enables us to respond with a good heart—a courageous and wise heart—to the assaults on living beings. In the spirit of dialogue rather than definitive theories or answers, I offer my own conclusions.

Von Stosch rightly points out that the Voice from the whirlwind does not respond to Job's increasingly desperate demands with an explanation. The Voice defends Job's right to protest; the comforters' facile confidence in the equation between suffering and punishment is rejected: "My wrath is kindled against you and against your two friends; for you have not spoken of me what is right, as my servant Job has" (Job 42:7). But Job must be consoled by presence rather than answers. In this we see something of the beauty of Kermani's approach: Bewildered protest can bring us into intimacy with the divine in a way that correct answers may not.

But what if our protest is not directed against God's arbitrary power but rather against theologies that attribute violence and cruelty to God? Our theologies are, after all, constructions through which we try to orient heart and mind to ultimate reality. "Here below" we should expect that our constructions will reflect the logic of imperial power, fantasies of patriarchal pleasure, and confidence in the kingdom of might. We may justify them by finding a sentence from scripture here and there that supports our view—but surely we know how adept the devil is at this game? Perhaps we should, like many of the authors explored in these chapters, use the revelation of divine goodness to inspire our own goodness and to critique those elements within religion and theology that conspire with the dynamics of evil. The comparative project provides rich resources in this task.

We may remain baffled by the meaning of suffering, but I suspect we know a great deal about goodness. We know that a mother tenderly caring for her child is preferred to one beating her children up. We know that it is not Hitler and Auschwitz that represent our best ideals of power but Martin Luther King or Gandhi. According to root Christian symbols, we look, not to Caesar's wealth, military might, or legal codes but to a manger, a cross, and companionship with outcasts for the presence of the divine on earth. We know that holding onto hatred does not heal us, but seeking the fierce courage of a merciful heart can. Why would we navigate our way in this troubling world by attributing everything that is worst about us to God?

There are no answers to why we suffer. There is no theology that captures the depth of the divine life. But there is joy in compassionate responses to suffering. I believe that theology can help form this compassion in us or mutilate it. I also believe that the spiritual friends we find in our own tradition and in every tradition can encourage us in this task. I will conclude with Kermani's words. In the preface to *The Terror of God*, he acknowledges that he is not himself a deeply religious person but that he sees in the example of his family members that truly religious people are intrinsically good. He adds: "they hold a privileged place—for in the end, on the last day or before the final judgment, it is only goodness that counts, nothing else."[25] So let us aspire to be good and to imagine that ultimate reality, too, is good, even when evil tempts us to think otherwise.

Notes

1. Lyrics are available at http://www.kulturserver-nrw.de/home/the-long-road/releases-studio/discography/aint-i-a-woman.html.
2. See Elie Wiesel's play *The Trial of God*, trans. Marion Wiesel (New York: Schocken Books, 1979) and David R. Blumenthal's (somewhat troubling!) *Facing the Abusing God: A Theology of Protest* (Louisville: Westminster John Knox, 1993).
3. This theme is not alien to Christian theology. It is present, for example, in Augustine's *City of God*, explicitly in his use of aesthetic metaphors and the essential interdependence of light and dark in the creation of beauty and, by implication, creation of the world. It is present, implicitly, in his dramatic contrast between the goodness and mercy of God and God's predestination of angels and human beings and the divine ability to torment throughout endless time: both wrath and mercy, torment and grace are necessary to reveal God's majesty. John Hick's book *Evil and the God of Love* (New York: Macmillan, 1966) provides a rich and nuanced analysis of the aesthetic dimension of Augustine's theodicy.
4. Navid Kermani, *The Terror of God: Attar, Job and the Metaphysical Revolt* (Cambridge: Polity Press, 2011), 134, 167.
5. Rainer Maria Rilke suggests a different understanding of the relationship between beauty and terror in his "Duino Elegy," 1. He writes: "for beauty is nothing but the beginning of a terror, which we are barely able to endure and are awed because it serenely disdains to annihilate us"; but for him this connection is the intensity of beauty rather than its violence (Rainer Maria Rilke, *Duino Elegies: Bilingual Edition*, trans. Edward Snow [New York: North Point Press], 5). We are here more in the domain of John of the Cross, for whom love of God carries us into a dark night of the soul, where the soul's pain is only its resistance to open to the tenderness of divine love. There is here nothing in God that is violent, only the painfulness of transformation.
6. "The glory of God is the human being fully alive," as Irenaeus says; and this glory will not be thwarted by temporary set-backs. Julian of Norwich is another theologian who sees the sin and suffering of humanity as an inevitable aspect of a spiritual being in sensible form, loved by God for all of our faults, and ultimately led to union with the divine.

7. The list of Christian contemplatives who tacitly or explicitly operate outside the mythology of divine penalty and the identification suffering with punishment is long. This theme threads through much of Mechthild of Magdeburg's *Flowing Light of the Godhead*. Julian of Norwich's *Showings* is a more famous example of a reinterpretation of the meaning of sin and suffering. Gregory of Nyssa, John Scotus Eriugena, Friedrich Schleiermacher, and Paul Tillich are among many others who form a chain of Christian thought that represents a non-violent understanding of God's relationship to sin and suffering.
8. John Keats, in a letter to his siblings George and Georgiana Keats, Sunday, February 14—Monday, May 3, 1819, "The Vale of Soul-Making," http://www.mrbauld.com/keatsva.html. This lovely letter is well worth the few minutes it takes to read it.
9. Keats, "The Vale of Soul-Making."
10. We find this theme of lack of self-knowledge in many Christian contemplatives, including John of the Cross, Teresa of Avila, Julian of Norwich, Meister Eckhart, and others.
11. Grace Jantzen, *Julian of Norwich: Mystic and Theologian* (New York: Paulist Press, 1987), 186.
12. I am offering the kind of generalized analysis that I was critical of earlier in this chapter. Metaphors of tyranny are typical of early Christian writings, especially the idea of being enslaved to Satan (for example, Gregory of Nyssa's Great Catechism). Tyranny of the passions is characteristic of the theology and spiritual practice of the desert ascetics (for example, Evagrius Ponticus). The more theologically developed idea of the bondage of the will emerges with Augustine, especially during the Pelagian controversy. The insightfulness of this analysis is somewhat marred by coupling it with a mythology of eternal punishment, with the result that humanity is totally incapable of not sinning but totally guilty for it and deserving of eternal and horrific torment. Nicolas Berdyaev's writings on slavery and freedom, both in the literal sense of victims of totalitarian regimes and in the sense of constrained and bound spiritual capacities, are a more recent version of some of these arguments.
13. The characterization of negative mental states as "passions" occurs in the writings of the desert ammas and abbas. See, for example, Evagrius Ponticus, *Praktikos and Chapters on Prayer*, trans. John Eudes Bamberger (Collegeville, Minn.: Cistercian Publications Inc., 1972) or the sayings of the desert fathers. Roberta Bondi's *To Love as God Loves* (Minneapolis: Fortress Press, 1987) is a very nice introduction to this material.
14. Emmanuel Levinas, *Totality and Infinity: an Essay on Exteriority*, trans. Alphonso Lingis (Pittsburgh: Duquesne University Press, 1969), 29.
15. Quoted by Jeffry Toobin, "Letter from Baltimore: This is My Jail: Where gang members and their female guards set the rules," *The New Yorker*, April 14, 2014, 28.
16. On a more popular level, a recent airing of "On Being" was dedicated to Jonathan Haidt's presentation of his psychological studies that point to political differences (conservative versus liberal) as rooted in personality types rather than information or even ethical values. http://www.onbeing.org/program/jonathan-haidt-the-psychology-behind-morality/6341
17. Teresa of Avila, *Interior Castle*, trans. E. Allison Peers (New York: Image Books, 2004), 1.2, p. 9.

18. Teresa of Avila, *Interior Castle*, translator's note, 9.
19. Emmanuel Levinas, "Freedom and Command," in *Collected Philosophical Papers*, trans. Alphonso Lingus (Dordrecht: Kluwer Academic Publishers, 1993), 16.
20. Evagrius Ponticus, *Praktikos*, 14.
21. Sally McFague's *Metaphorical Theology: Models of God in Religious Language* (Minneapolis: Fortress Press, 1982) remains a masterful reflection on the damaging effects of translating metaphors for God, especially violent or patriarchal ones, into models of reality.
22. Chapter 21 in Gregory of Nyssa, "Great Catechism," *The Nicene and Post-Nicene Fathers*, Series 2, Vol. 5: *Gregory of Nyssa: Dogmatic Treatises, Etc.*, trans. and ed. Philip Schaff and Henry Wace (Grand Rapids, Mich.: Eerdmans, 1954), 492.
23. See also Levinas's brief but incisive critique of the exercise of theodicy: Emmanuel Levinas, "Useless Suffering," in *The Provocation of Levinas: Rethinking the Other*, ed. Robert Bernasconi and David Wood (London and New York: Routledge, 1988), 156–67.
24. Plato, *Phaedrus*, trans. R. Hackforth, *The Collected Dialogues of Plato Including the Letters*, ed. Edith Hamilton and Huntington Cairns, Bollingen Series LXXI (Princeton, N.J.: Princeton University Press, 1961), paragraph 278.d.
25. Kermani, *The Terror of God*, 2.

PART III
Humanity

7 Longing and Letting Go

LESSONS IN BEING HUMAN FROM HADEWIJCH AND MIRABAI

Holly Hillgardner

> *If anyone dares to fight love with longing,*
> *Wholly without heart and without mind*
> *And Love counters this longing with her longing*
> *That is the force by which we conquer Love*
>
> —HADEWIJCH[1]
>
> *And he has invited a standing, stubborn love.*
>
> —MIRABAI[2]

"Longing is the heart's bosom; we shall receive if we would stretch out our longing as far as we can," wrote Augustine, recognizing longing and its cultivation as a worthy goal.[3] At the same time, he viewed longing as having a direct purpose toward a clear end: "Our hearts are restless until they rest in thee, O God."[4] In other words, we desire fervently until we find ultimate repose in God. From this perspective, on the other side of longing the self rests—at peace, in wholeness, completed. What a consoling thought in a world where we often suffer and helplessly watch others suffer. Simply imagining the self at final rest from the turbulent vicissitudes of longing soothes the weary life traveler.

Despite the comforts of this view, such a vision of the self at ultimate rest runs some theological risks, most notably a devaluing of the longing inherent in being human. In contrast to a vision of the perfected self, saved from the difficulties of yearning by unity with God, this essay submits that the longing self persists, even in blessed communion with the divine. Put another way, the incompleteness and fragmentation exposed by a longing self may not connote a sinful state of alienation from God; instead, longing reflects the relational nature of the self. From the moment of our births, we find ourselves vulnerable, dependent, and constituted by our relationships with others, and deny it as we might, this remains our life-long state. The methods of comparative theology can be employed to construct an account of the role and the power of the longing self. In rethinking this longing self not as a problem to be solved, but rather as a site from which the complex relationality of self and other can be embraced, might we find alternative orientations for how we might live—longing, letting go, and loving together?

Hadewijch and Mirabai, the guides for this comparative theological experiment, each speak across the centuries and miles about selves that passionately embrace longing—not as a means to yearning's end but as a means to an embodied life in God and with others where longing is not extinguished. Their writings reveal glimpses of yearning women who come into communion with God, yet the flames of their desire still burn brightly. The persistence of the longing self has important implications for theological anthropology, the traditional term for the study of being human.

This essay first explores what Hadewijch, a thirteenth-century Christian woman, teaches about the power of longing as it relates to the self, specifically through her unique concept of "noble unfaith," which is a result of her unquenchable desire for God. Then another guide from the past enters the conversation. Mirabai, a sixteenth-century Hindu woman, suffuses her world with longing for God, known in her tradition as *viraha-bhakti*. Finally, revisiting Hadewijch's longing, this essay asks how our understanding deepens in light of our reading of Mirabai. When one reads Hadewijch's idea of the yearning self through the lens of Mirabai's *viraha-bhakti*, what new insights, patterns, and emphases emerge?

As the essays in this volume demonstrate, comparative theology avers that we can no longer think theologically in a mono-religious vacuum. From its inception as a Jewish sect emerging in a diverse Graeco-Roman context, Christianity's theological constructions have always been comparative. There has always been much to learn from other voices, books, and practices, and today, we continue to learn from those both on other shores and in our own neighborhoods, workplaces, and schools. In our interconnected, religiously-plural world, we risk insularity and its attendant dangers if we neglect to hear other voices. This essay, driven by the imperatives of comparative theology to continue interfaith conversations and work, dares to put two diverse thinkers from wildly different religious traditions in conversation. Yet the question remains, why pair *these* two women?

Certain intriguing resonances between Hadewijch and Mirabai inspired this pairing. When I first encountered these women, I became fascinated with their respective writings of full-bodied, sensuously imaged longing for divine love. Mirabai, for example, writes,

> Come to my bedroom,
> I've scattered fresh buds on the couch,
> Perfumed my body.[5]

Hadewijch, for her part, offers this description of lover and beloved coming together in rapturous communion: "But they abide in one another in fruition, mouth in mouth, heart in heart, body in body, and soul in soul."[6]

Further reading uncovered that, in addition to the heat of each woman's desire, each also concurrently practiced her own unconventional variant of religious asceticism. In addition, Mirabai's hagiography presents her as a rare female itinerant, who left her home and family to live simply and sing songs of divine love. Hadewijch was a leader in the early Beguine movement, one of the women who created a new way of uncloistered devoted service, a path that offered another option between the traditional options of marriage and the nunnery. I began to see in each woman's life and writings unique practices of "passionate non-attachment," ways of living that emcompassed energies of desire *and* renunciation.[7] Each woman differently inspired me to explore how these energies might be held together coherently. Reading them alongside one another, I asked my own pressing questions: "How can one find courage to love in this world of loss? How can one find the strength to nurture the tenuous relationships on which one's own precarious, vulnerable life depends? How does one ever let go of such integral and intense passions?" These concrete questions paved the way for the unfolding of this comparative theological journey into longing and letting go.

We focus on a number of Hadewijch's and Mirabai's writings, which I call "focus texts." These focus texts work to spotlight one theme found throughout much of their writing—*love-longing*. In different ways, Mirabai and Hadewijch highlight what might be called the "middle spaces of longing." It is in these middle spaces—where the erotic desire for union with God is mixed with the grief of the thwarting of that full union—where much of their writing is located. In the texts examined here, Hadewijch and Mirabai voice the difficulties of their separations from the divine presence: Both write in longing voices that are continually restless ... yearning ... reaching.

As we contemplate Mirabai's and Hadewijch's different practices of longing, I draw out how these practices, in unique ways, contain the seeds of non-attachment, that is, the letting go of the cravings, aversions, fears, and false identities that keep the self bound in an illusory self-possession that walls it off from others. From two very different traditions, then, Hadewijch and Mirabai show the intertwinings of non-attachment and desire; yet, in the longing seen in these women's writings neither desire nor non-attachment is subordinated. Both energies prove integral to each woman's diverse devotional practices. Mirabai and Hadewijch, in their own ways, find their practices of longing ushering them into realms of non-attachment. In other words, as each of their practices of longing takes them deeper into their interior lives, these embodied practices at the same time loosen their attachments to certainties about spiritual life itself. Caught up in the desire and grief of longing, each finds herself letting go of cherished understandings of her relationships with God and the world.

Longing, for each of them in different ways, stands at the heart of a radically relational theological anthropology, one in which energies of desire and renunciation—of passionate non-attachment—help widen the "I" into fruitful, mysteriously entangled relationships with God and the world. Longing, as it connects to theological anthropology, then, is an intense desire that can rupture the boundaries of the self to allow a recognition, if only a partial one, of how the "I" does not exist without its entanglements with others.[8] Reading Hadewijch's and Mirabai's texts of longing together provides resources for articulating a relational theological anthropology of passionate non-attachment.

Hadewijch and Love-Longing

> ... nevertheless this noble unfaith can neither feel nor trust Love, so much does unfaith enlarge desire.
>
> Hadewijch[9]

Hadewijch's themes of love-longing must first be located within her own context as a medieval writer who creatively combines the genres of

Christian bridal mysticism and secular courtly love. In this way, she creates an uncommon vocabulary and set of tropes that are on full display in her innovative concept of "Lady *Minne*," her term for divine Love. *Minne* provides a female-gendered term of fantastically flexible valence. After contextualizing Hadewijch as a thirteenth-century Beguine writer from lowland medieval Europe, we delve into a focus text that displays her unique concept of "noble unfaith," a term that names a specific kind of passionate non-attachment.

Scholarly consensus holds that Hadewijch was much influenced by the interpretive schema of bridal mysticism, or *Brautmystik*, which harnessed the eros in *Song of Songs* as an allegory for the relationship between God and the soul.[10] In this literary tradition, which drew theological sustenance from both the mysticism of the Church Fathers and the Pseudo-Dionysian apophatic tradition, an image of the female bride represents the human soul, who attains perfection through her union with the divine male Bridegroom.

As she worked with the resources of *Brautmystik*, Hadewijch contributed a transformative element, the predominantly secular genre of courtly love verse, or *fins amour*.[11] *Fins amour* highlights the courtly lover, or the knight-errant, who sings troubadour songs of unfulfilled desire and performs difficult deeds to win the love of a distant, noble beloved. Combining elements of *fins amour* and *Brautmystik*, Hadewijch came to write in a new genre, which Barbara Newman names *mystique courtoise*, or "courtly mysticism."[12]

Hadewijch's creative combination of genres allows her images of lover and beloved to take on complex, rich resonances. For example, in *mystique courtoise*, traditional *Brautmystik* themes of mystical absence become heightened with the addition of a haughtily distant beloved from the *fins amour* tradition. *Brautmystik* by itself is characterized by divine distance and absence, as seen most vividly in the image of the bride waiting for the arrival of her groom—an arrival that is nonetheless inevitable. Yet the mixing of elements of bridal mysticism with elements of courtly love poetry shifts the connotations of divine distance and absence toward uncertainty concerning the final outcome of this waiting. More specifically, the courtly love tradition insisted that desirous love from afar represented the ideal, and by maintaining a distance between the lover and beloved, it apotheosized a beloved who could not be finally and totally possessed. The lady love was thus ultimately unattainable, and the distance between the knight and the lady love only increased the knight's desire. The best kind of love, according to this schema, needed distance to stay alive. Coupled with the erotic longing of *Brautmystik*, which played on a not-yet-consummated coupling, the element of necessary distance in *fins amour* added complex connotations to Hadewijch's depiction of the relationship between God and the self. By adopting the tropes of courtly love and *Brautmystik*, Hadewijch's *mystique courtoise* holds space open between the lover and beloved, as it provides options other than a greedy grasping for possession of the other.

This dynamic plays out in verses that discuss Hadewijch's "noble unfaith." For example, in the following poem, Hadewijch first elaborates upon the superiority of desire as the means for her knightly "conquering" of Love:

> Love does not allow it [desire] to have any rest:
> Even if all the suffering were massed together
> That ever was, or is, or shall be,
> It could not conquer so much
> As desire of veritable Love can.

As the poem continues, she discusses the quality of restlessness that Love gives to desire:

> Desire snatched at suffering above all measure
> And at work that Love will grant it;
> So it is allotted perturbation and turbulent unrest.
> Love does not allow it to be at rest;

Next, "noble unfaith" is introduced as a form of such restless desire:

> It undergoes pressure from noble unfaith,
> Which is stronger and higher than fidelity:
> Fidelity, which one can record by reason,
> And express with the mind
> Often lets desire be satisfied—
> What unfaith can never put up with.

With further imagery of conquering, Hadewijch describes the work that "noble unfaith" does to inspire Love's "reach":

> Fidelity must often be absent
> So that unfaith can conquer;
> Noble unfaith cannot rest

So long as it does not conquer to the hilt;
It wishes to conquer all that Love is:
For that reason it cannot remain out of her reach.[13]

In this excerpt, part of a couplet poem that discusses Love's demands on the lover, Hadewijch discusses desire as a force that Love encourages to increase—mainly by not allowing it any rest. *Minne*, the lady love, translated Love here, demands a response to her love that includes "perturbation and turbulent unrest," difficult states that propel the knight of love to work harder for her sake in order to "conquer all that Love is."

Here, Hadewijch contrasts faith or fidelity (*trouwe*) with unfaith (*ontrouwe*).[14] Hadewijch declares that while fidelity problematically allows yearning to cease and desire to be satisfied, unfaith, on the other hand, will not abide "[letting] desire be satisfied." Because unfaith cannot abide the satisfaction and ceasing of desire, unfaith demands that faith must "be absent." Faith thus gets in the way of Hadewijch's remaining within Love's reach because faith already has the satisfaction it seeks. Faith must absent itself, so that unfaith can do its knightly work of conquering Love. In other words, by letting desire be prematurely satisfied before communing with Love, faith stands in the way of the lover's continual reaching for Love. In contrast, the longing of unfaith expands the lover's reach and allows her to come closer to Love. Faith is satisfied with less intimacy with Love, but through the gift of unfaith, Love bestows an "unquiet life" of longing to those who hunger for her in unfaith.[15]

Through *mystique courtoise*, Hadewijch inverts and destabilizes the virtue of faith by contrasting unfaith with this traditional virtue and then elevating unfaith over faith. Love provides this gift of unfaith as a catalyst that keeps desire flowing bi-directionally, even as this flow turns both "sweet and bitter" along the way.[16] Referencing the longing that the lover experiences, Hadewijch writes that Love responds in kind:

That longing swallows up all Love's gifts,
And she must continually press this mode of action.[17]

The conquering Hadewijch references—accomplished by longing—is thus mutual. Hadewijch writes of the dual conquest by the lover and by Love: "Love conquers him so that he may conquer her."[18] Unfaith continues to enlarge love; it, in Hadewijch's words, "spurs on, or indeed is, love's desire for Love."[19]

"Noble unfaith" grants Hadewijch permission to resist over-attachment to the outcomes of her faith—namely, the desire to possess, grasp, and consume Love. Thus unfaith can be the noblest of faith practices as it refuses to try to capture God, which allows longing to flourish ever more. "Noble unfaith" is faith that God will always be to some degree ungraspable and uncontainable. Unfaith resists the ways in which faith and belief too often are grounded in tangible proofs, desires accomplished, and possessions received; rather, it finds God in the very acts of longing for a God that can never be fully known.

Hadewijch thus loves a Love who incites both desirous longing and a letting go of everything, save her longing. In "noble unfaith," Hadewijch longs for Love so intensely that she lets go even of her faith in order to continue enlarging her desire for Love. In such a stunning example of passionate non-attachment, Hadewijch turns away in fervent eros and grief from her familiar modes of faith, reason, humility, and trust when they cannot deliver her into what she calls fruition (*ghebruken*). As "noble unfaith" enlarges her desire for Love, she and Love tumble together into a "fathomless unknowing." Attempting to describe this unfathomable abyss, Hadewijch can only utter, "Then the soul sees, and it sees nothing."[20] She writes of these dark, desirous spaces of unknowing:

> If I desire something,
> it is not known to me, because
> I find myself at all times imprisoned in fathomless unknowing.[21]

In this exploration of Hadewijch's concept of "noble unfaith," we discover that her persistent longing leads to the gift of unfaith, which is the greatest kind of faith for Hadewijch. From longing, unfaith is birthed, and from unfaith springs an apophatically resonant unknowing of herself, Love, and the bond between them. Hadewijch intimates that the self, stretched from longing, has its usual boundaries undone.

What more might be glimpsed about longing's vital role in widening the self? How can longing be sustained, especially in light of the suffering it may cause? How should the suffering concomitant with longing be viewed? How can desire and non-attachment be held together in the self? As we read Hadewijch's texts of passionate non-attachment, we have begun to explore these and other questions. We now ask, "What further insights about Hadewijch's practices of longing, specifically her curious practice of 'noble unfaith' and its implications for theological anthropology, can we glean by reading her alongside Mirabai?"

Mirabai and Love-Longing

> The colors of the dark One have penetrated Mira's body,
> all the other colors washed out.
>
> Mirabai[22]

This comparative exploration of the role of longing in constructing the self now oscillates, perhaps dizzyingly, from the lowlands of thirteenth-century Europe to sixteenth-century northern India. Legend has it that the passionate poet-princess Mirabai moved from a cloistered palace into the streets, where she ran off to join a community of fellow devotional singers in an itinerant life. Dispossessed of her home and family, she traveled out into the world singing and dancing for Krishna, whose name can be translated as both "one who attracts" and "to drag, to give pain."[23] Consonant with this etymology, Mirabai's songs portray her as a lover who grapples with desire for the seductive divine, as well as with the pain that accompanies this longing. This next section delves into Mirabai's excruciating, exquisite expressions of longing—what David Dean Shulman calls "delicious distress"[24]—that fuel both her erotic love relationship with Lord Krishna and a non-attachment to self, the divine, and the narrower world she once knew. The complex texture of her longing fits the genre of *viraha-bhakti*, whose central dynamic involves rising and ebbing moments of presence and absence between humanity and divinity.

In early academic *bhakti* studies, *bhakti* was often read narrowly as "devotion," an emotional, spontaneous phenomenon, drastically different from religious paths that emphasized the intellect, philosophical contemplation, or rituals. In their quest to define the field, some *bhakti* scholars missed many of the ways that Indian religious traditions overlap. *Bhakti*, it turns out, can be intellectual, intentional, and hospitable to both ritual and contemplation. Not simply an unbridled emotion that negates or ignores the intellect, *bhakti* is "participation" and "committed engagement," as Karen Pechilis aptly describes it. This committed engagement presupposes an active, multifaceted involvement with God, rather than the passive adoration signified by defining *bhakti* solely as "devotion."[25] *Bhakti* thus speaks to the integral participation of the author of the songs, of her listeners, and of the longed-for divinity in a shared love life.

The subcategory of *viraha-bhakti*, here delineated as "participation in love-longing," will be employed as an interpretive lens for Mirabai's songs. *Viraha-bhakti* is part of the wider category of Krishna *bhakti*, which, as Friedhelm Hardy explains, evolved as an "aesthetic-erotic-ecstatic mysticism of separation."[26] In Mirabai's *viraha-bhakti* tradition, tension exists between the desire for an experience of ultimate unity with God and the desire to experience the fruits of *viraha-bhakti*, the "bitter-sweetness of love-in-separation."[27] Participants experience a communal sense of both the difficulties of separation and the fulfilling bliss of presence-in-absence that longing reveals. *Viraha-bhakti* can be described as a mystical eroticism of separation, the primary dynamic of which involves the divinizing, oscillating movement between divine presence and absence.

In many of Mirabai's songs, themes of desire are mixed with those of renunciation, which creates vignettes of passionate non-attachment. For example, in the following excerpt, Mirabai speaks of complementary practices of fasting and lovemaking:

> The colors of the dark One have penetrated Mira's body;
>   all the other colors washed out.
> Making love with the Dark One and eating little, those are
>   my pearls and my carnelians.
> Meditation beads and the forehead streak, those are my
>   scarves and my rings.[28]

As longing suffuses her body like a dye, here we see Mirabai mixing metaphors of two paths of devotion, marriage and asceticism. The marks of a yogic life of renunciation, such as meditation beads and the forehead markings, get reconfigured as adornments that signify the devotion of a married woman. She also includes lovemaking with the practice of fasting in the same line. Does Mirabai display non-attachment even in the embodied embraces of mutual erotic longing, and desire even in its ascetic moments?

Viraha-bhakti helps construct a paradoxical coherence between these seemingly incompatible desirous and ascetic selves. Consider that erotic devotion may represent Krishna's and Mirabai's highest flow of communion, while yogic asceticism may represent their lowest ebb of communion, both of which are necessary to the fullness of the oscillations of *viraha-bhakti*. Rather than representing separate and exclusive choices, the lover and the yogi may represent locations that she passes through repeatedly on the winding path of *viraha-bhakti*. The oscillations of *viraha-bhakti*, mirroring the seemingly contradictory roles of *yogi* and lover, represent Mirabai's journey through different intensities of presence-in-absence.

Each part of the journey speaks to an intimacy between herself and the divine. She views herself as a partner to Krishna; she wants to "search through the world as a yogi does with you—yogi and yogini side by side."[29] Even as she suffers the pangs of separation, these pangs represent signs of the extant relationship between herself and God. *Viraha-bhakti* maintains that there is no place completely outside of divine presence and no place where full possession of the divine exists. Oscillating back and forth, she resides in the middle spaces between those poles, where she and God abide together in different intensities of communion-in-separation. In the way of life that is *viraha-bhakti*, Mirabai reverses the logic of what counts as spiritual victory: The *virahini* can find different levels of communion, even that experienced as presence-in-absence, but can never find ultimate, total communion. Attaining any sort of final end is not the focus; instead, *viraha-bhakti* celebrates the desire to live and long in the middle spaces of love-in-separation. Rather than serving as an intermediate step on the path to ultimate spiritual fulfillment, the yearning of *viraha-bhakti* constitutes mystical union itself as it exists in the flesh and blood of bodies on earth in the here and now. Put another way, *viraha-bhakti* is not the means to the goal of perfect union with the divine; rather, *viraha-bhakti is* in fact the goal itself. The path of longing delivers its own rewards. Because complete unity with the divine is not necessarily waiting at the end of the journey, a sole focus on endings or conclusions misses the middle spaces of longing that the *viraha-bhakti* path highlights.

Separation then serves not as a preliminary step on a path that ends in ultimate fulfillment, but as an integral part of the beginning, middle, and even end of the path itself. In *viraha-bhakti*, the devotee's yearning is thus viewed as a form of joy, a "delicious distress,"[30] and a deepening of the devotion she experiences bodily. Such a reading emphasizes that no matter how much she longs for Krishna, the middle spaces of love-longing remain her primary state.

Unlike some forms of Hinduism that tend to see the world as illusion, Mirabai is situated within a tradition that does not deny the reality of the world; it values embodied love of the divine in the world as one of its ultimate goals. In *viraha-bhakti*, there is a "deeply ingrained acceptance of man's [sic] empirical being—his emotions, senses, and desires—through the belief in the world as Krishna's place of 'work' and manifestation and as man's place of achieving his perfection through sharing in the work of Krishna."³¹ Mirabai's embracing of presence-in-absence and love-in-separation is integral to her *viraha-bhakti*, which promotes a "deep engagement in the life of the world, even, it could be argued, a basic acceptance of life, for all its horrors."³²

Despite Krishna's often inexplicable absences, which Mirabai experiences among life's horrors, an intimacy nonetheless marks the love between Mirabai and Krishna. In fact, it is *because* of his absences that her longing, the mark of their bond, may flourish. In other words, the very grief that Mirabai experiences is read within the *viraha-bhakti* schema as evidence of their mutual desirous devotion. Mirabai thus trusts in the oscillations of *viraha-bhakti*, despite its vagaries and uncertainties. A stubborn persistence characterizes her longing while she waits for Krishna. She concludes one song with these evocative lines:

> Me—
>   my love's in a distant land
>   and wet, I stubbornly stand at the door.
> For Hari is indelibly green,
>   Mira's Lord,
> And he has invited a standing,
>   stubborn love.³³

In her mode of persistent longing, she stands stubbornly at the door in the rain, soaked with anticipation and energized by love.

Comparisons and Conclusions: The Middle Spaces of Longing

Viraha-bhakti—through its language of mourning and grief, its themes of transformative devotion in the midst of charged absence, and its intense cultivation of longing—provides a fruitful lens to consider Hadewijch's longing, as it relates to the self's formation and spiritual destiny. Longing is the main mode of communion with the divine in Mirabai's songs, and when Hadewijch's writings are read alongside Mirabai's expressions of *viraha-bhakti*, the primacy of Hadewijch's mode of longing comes even more strongly to the forefront. For example, here Hadewijch's longing can be clearly seen as the powerful force through which she and Love effect their mutual conquering:

> If anyone dares to fight love with longing,
> Wholly without heart and without mind
> And Love counters this longing with her longing
> That is the force by which we conquer Love.[34]

Hadewijch's longing unleashes the longing of God to catalyze the coming-together of the self and God. At the moment when her desire for God comes into conflict with Hadewijch's limits as a human being who cannot grasp the totality of God, longing and letting go become her weapons. As she lets go of the idea that she can match the divine Love, she still longs with all her passionate energy to "conquer" Love anyway.[35]

As Hadewijch practices longing in the middle spaces of presence-in-absence, she writes that "the incompletion of this blissful fruition is yet the sweetest fruition."[36] In this stunning realization, she explicitly values the "sweetest" *incompletion* of the fruition between herself and Love. Fruition, for Hadewijch, might be understood as an experience of satisfaction that is never ultimately satisfying; that is, sweet longing remains.

Her realization of the sweetness of incompletion, read alongside *viraha-bhakti*, takes on even deeper resonances concerning the never-completed work of longing. *Viraha-bhakti*, as we have seen, employs a logic that does not equate incompletion with failure. Through Mirabai's practices of longing, she cultivates a grief that takes her deeper into communion with the divine, despite and even *because* of Krishna's absence. As such, *viraha-bhakti* recognizes presence-in-absence as a mark of a sustaining, desirous mutual relationship with the divine. Hadewijch's understanding of the incomplete yet satisfying relationship of longing between the lover and the beloved may similarly be said to echo and honor life's vicissitudes; that is, it does not set a mystical peace and satisfaction above the restlessness and grief of an embodied love. Through the grief and desire that longing entails, Hadewijch gains entry into the depths of a Love that does not privilege any completed state of blissful consciousness or totalizing union but celebrates a passionate, embodied longing in which indeed "the incompletion of this blissful fruition is yet the sweetest fruition."[37]

In the light of *viraha-bhakti*, Hadewijch may be read as embracing her embodiedness with its incumbent limits and bittersweet longings while also cultivating a vulnerability born from the uncertainties of longing.

When Mirabai practices *viraha-bhakti*, she leaves herself vulnerable to the desire and grief of her longing. "... Abandonment scorches my heart. / Only those who have felt the knife can measure the wound's deepness," she writes.[38] Hadewijch writes also of the wounds that Love creates in her:

> Those to whom Love grants her wounds,
> And shows how wide her knowledge is,
> Desire keeps them open and unbound
> And Love shines fiercely through.[39]

Viraha-bhakti provides a lens for thinking about these "unbound" wounds that do not fully heal. Hadewijch might be said to cultivate longing, as the *virahini*s do, by learning to lean into, if not fully accept, the inevitable griefs of separation. In *viraha-bhakti*, longing exists as the highest expression of the bond between the human and the divine, and this connection of longing exists as something to celebrate, as "these sorrows are apprehended as signs of the living relation between the two parties, hence of the rapturous connection which only separation makes possible."[40] Less blissful aspects of life, including the pain of longing, are to be embraced, valued, and integrated in a full life with God. Hadewijch, in her own way, comes to realize that experiential states of unity with the divine—wonderful as they may be—are not the sole goal of her spiritual life.

Read in light of *viraha-bhakti*, Hadewijch's longing, even as it results in burdensome physical and mental consequences, may be best viewed as an acceptance of bodily life. Not courting pain, she nonetheless accepts the grief and pain inherent in longing as a given for her earthly, embodied life. Despite the value *viraha-bhakti* places on grief, it remains a life-affirming stance. *Viraha-bhakti* celebrates the sometimes painful, sometimes joyful presence-in-absence that emerges when one discovers the object of desire cannot be possessed. Rather than trying to escape her longings, Hadewijch may be said to linger in these middle spaces between presence and absence, as she experiences a complex mixture of fruition and non-fruition with God.

Furthermore, Mirabai's focused longing does not result in a divine engulfing of the yearning self. In the longing of the *bhakti* poets, there exists a "degree of duality—there is a tension between the desire for the ultimate unitive experience and the desire to continue to experience the bitter-sweetness of love-in-separation."[41] In its varying oscillations of absence and presence, the cultivation of longing for the divine *is* the path of liberation for Mirabai; that is, *viraha-bhakti* serves as an integral part of Mirabai's spiritual liberation. A common *bhakti* saying is that the devotee does not want to *be* sugar, she wants to *taste* sugar. In other words, she does not long to be completely subsumed in the divine presence. She thus desires to relate to God as herself—not in a self-extinguishing union, but in a union that necessitates separation with its concomitant sense of longing. For Mirabai, liberation consists of this "tasting" as it exists in the presence-in-absence of *viraha-bhakti*. She issues the following invitation to her friend to "drink in" the divine:

> Come, my companion, look at his face,
> Drink in the beauty with thine eyes . . .
> On a glimpse of His visage I live.[42]

Even a Mirabai song that speaks of a "happy ending" of ultimate togetherness (and most songs do not) speaks of a qualified nondualism with difference intact. For example, in the following verse, Mirabai is not fully united with Krishna, even in the vision of their reunion:

> This coming and going will end,
> says Mira,
> with me clasping your feet
> forever.[43]

A kind of merging-in-differentiation is evident in Hadewijch, as well. In her own words, she and Love are "both one thing through each other, but at the same time remain two different selves—yes, and remain so forever."[44] In this way, she remains paradoxically "self-possessed," even as she is being dispossessed by desire.

This short study has not focused on what might be considered grand spiritual "successes" or moments of consummate communion between God and the self, but on presence-in-absence, longing, and the resulting vulnerabilities of interdependence. When one is focused only on moments of union, one misses the moments of in-betweenness where much of life takes place—the middle spaces of longing. But what difference does living in these middle spaces make?

By dwelling in the middle spaces, Mirabai and Hadewijch reverse the logic of what can be considered perfection or completion. In other words, linear progress toward a predefined goal is not what is valued; instead, attending to the spaces between union and separation becomes the focus. Indeed, a kind of messy and mundane beauty may be unexpectedly found in the unreachability of the other. In the recognition that neither the self nor the longed for beloved can be said to contain either permanence or immutability, conditions are created for both desire and non-attachment to flourish together. Reading Hadewijch alongside Mirabai's *viraha-bhakti* brings into view the middle spaces of longing, which can otherwise get obscured by Hadewijch's imagery of focused conquering. Instead of prioritizing the completion of mystical union, or total presence, Mirabai's middle spaces of longing value the spaces betwixt and between the poles of absence and presence. Such a focus on the middle spaces avoids any tendency to conceptualize "stages" of the spiritual life on a straight continuum that begins in separation and ends in union. The middle spaces thus suggest that the longing self does not become extinguished at an apex, but continues to practice yearning, as it stretches and widens its connectivity with the divine and others, without annihilation or diminishment.

Mirabai's and Hadewijch's primary spiritual practices each consist of cultivating attachment, rather than non-attachment. Neither wants to lessen or let go of attachments; instead, each nurtures their growth. Hadewijch yearns to the point of almost breaking from her maddening desire, but nurtures desire regardless. Celebrating her own attachment to the divine, Mirabai sings, "Strong had my attachment grown to the peacock crowned dancer."[45] In another song, she reiterates, "I have become attached to your face, beloved Mohan, I have become attached to your face."[46] She does not long to be rid of her attachment, no matter how difficult the accompanying grief.

Through the strength of their attachments, both women find their way into energies of non-attachment. That is to say, as each cultivates longing, non-attachment *happens* in the midst of their yearnings. In different yet resonant ways, desire and grief crack their selves wide open, and they each grieve their inabilities to fully grasp and understand the divine. As their increasing desire and the griefs born of separation threaten to overwhelm them, non-attachment may then be born. This occurs through a letting go of their respective comprehensions of the self, the divine, and, in Hadewijch's case, faith itself, which provides insight into Hadewijch's concept of "noble unfaith."

As energies of non-attachment emerge, however, they do not stamp out desire. Rather, non-attachment encourages desire to flourish further by sustaining an interval between the lover and the beloved. Both Mirabai's and Hadewijch's longing, in different ways, allows desire to flourish with something like a built-in release valve, which dispossesses desire from a grasping greed to consume the riches of the other. Thus, conscious and sustained lingering in the middle spaces of longing—their practices of longing—opens Mirabai and Hadewijch to possibilities for mutual, non-possessive relationships with the other, divine and otherwise. Through the preservation of a space between the lover and the beloved, non-attachment keeps desire alive, as desire needs the difference and space of separation in order to avoid a grasping, consuming concupiscence. The oscillations between desire and non-attachment thus nourish Hadewijch's and Mirabai's respective bonds of love-longing.

In this recycling of energies, non-attachment and desire are seen to be intimately connected, and neither is ultimately privileged. Non-attachment is not the highest goal, and neither is erotic communion. Neither Mirabai nor Hadewijch leap over desire to go straight to non-attachment, as if non-attachment is the ultimate goal. At the same time, neither eschews non-attachment to dwell endlessly in the fires of union with the divine. Both non-attachment and desire are necessary ends *and* means for the respective embodied communions that Hadewijch and Mirabai describe. Intertwined with each other, desire and non-attachment interact with one another in a recursive process, each fueling the other in a cyclical dynamic of longing and letting go.[47]

Mirabai's and Hadewijch's practices of longing do not stay in the "vertical" realms between one woman and her God without widening out into "horizontal," this-worldly spaces. Each woman's practices of longing offer clues for a way of living—a lived ethic—that encourages desire for the flourishing of the world, without that passion consuming the world, the other, or the self. Mirabai does not become indifferently detached from the world as she writes and sings songs of communal longing; instead, she leaves her scripted courtly life in order to face bravely into the wider, unknown world. She sings, "It's time to take my songs into the street."[48] *Viraha-bhakti* is thus not best understood as an insular narrowing of her world to a single point, but a comprehensive infusing of desire into her broadening world.

As one reads Hadewijch through the lens of *viraha-bhakti* and her own tradition's resources, the widening of her world, born of longing, also comes into focus. "Love makes me wander outside myself," Hadewijch declares.[49] Love does not send her deeply into a separative interiority, but dispossessing her of herself, sends her beyond herself.

Attempting to describe a moment of communion with the divine, Hadewijch writes, "[Infinity] has undone me / Wider than wide."[50] Here, we see the result of her longing: an undone, widening self. Hadewijch's communion with God involves her letting go of the boundaries of her self, as demarcations among the self, God, and others show themselves to be more porous than she previously knew. Hadewijch describes such an expanding sense of self as a fluid community in which God and "his friends, in mutual interpenetration, enjoy such blissful fruition, and are flowing into his goodness and flowing out again in all good."[51] Rather than staying bounded in the confines of the self-possessed "I," a widened Hadewijch finds herself connected with *other* longing selves. Longing in this key provides resources for a whole-hearted engagement that does not occlude the other. An ethic of passionate non-attachment shelters the life-giving multiplicity of the world and the flowering of desire. By lingering in the middle spaces of longing, Mirabai and Hadewijch cultivate the potential for mutual, non-possessive relationships between themselves and others.

Hadewijch and Mirabai both admit, however, that they long to grasp the totality of the other. Each yearns for the whole of the divine before she realizes, not without some grief, both the futility and undesirability of such goals. In such moments, longing can open up into non-attachment and potential mutuality, which then protects desire from its shadow side that nurtures egotistical myopia and truncates relationship. As longing dispossesses the self, rigid boundaries around identity become loosened. Where there is less attachment to a separative "I," a more commodious sense of relationality emerges, as well as more fluidity in the way identity gets named and imaged.

As we long and let go, we also encourage the world to flourish by letting go of our desire to control others. Otherwise, attempting to control the world, we cannot even enjoy the diversity and beauty of the world because we make of the other a tool for individual satisfaction or personal consumption. Encouraging the flourishing of the world, not just the flourishing of ourselves, can be understood as unleashing the powers of desire. Thus, a decentering of the self, or a non-attachment to the self, paves the way for further expressions of desire. Through non-attachment, without a preoccupation with centering the self, we recognize the value and beauty of diverse others. Here, an icy isolationism, one that requires self-possession and denies the fires of warmer connective energies that create and undo the self, emerges as a dangerous fiction.

Within both Hinduism and Christianity, non-attachment and desire are often presented as opposing forces, but Hadewijch and Mirabai each illuminate, from their respective traditions, the integral, tensile relationship between desire and non-attachment. Each woman shows that passionate love-longing necessitates certain kinds of renunciations, or non-attachments. Some paths within both Hinduism and Christianity teach that desire should be solely satisfied in God, held lightly, or even completely eradicated; however, Mirabai and Hadewijch do not desire to let go of desire. Some traditions within Christianity and Hinduism emphasize renunication in an attempt to ameliorate the very real dangers that desiring subjects are to both themselves and others. Hadewijch and Mirabai do not conform fully to this path either.

Mirabai's and Hadewijch's different yet related ways of knowing and seeing the world each point to passionate non-attachment: paths of attachment fueled by longing, yet sheltered from possession or consumption-based systems of desire by these very energies of longing. Their practices of longing and letting go embrace the complexities of life with its inevitable loves, griefs, and other entanglements. Desire, loosed from its egotistical impulses, can topple hegemonic powers and foster solidarities for justice, and letting go, coupled with desire for a more just world, allows us wider, more interconnected perspectives. Across the centuries and miles, Mirabai and Hadewijch invite us both to long and to let go.

Notes

1. Hadewijch, "Couplet Poem 1: The Nature of Love," in *Hadewijch: The Complete Works*, ed. and trans. Columba Hart (New York: Paulist Press, 1980), lines 17–20, 311.
2. Mirabai, "Pada 56," in "Mirabai and Her Contributions to the Bhakti Movement," trans. S. M. Pandey and Norman H. Zide, *History of Religions* 5.1 (1965): 68.
3. Augustine, "Tractate 40," trans. John W. Wittig, *The Fathers of the Church Book 88: A New Translation: St. Augustine Tractates on the Gospel of John 28–54* (Washington: Catholic University of America Press, 1993), 133.
4. Augustine, *Confessions*, trans. Henry Chadwick (New York: Oxford University Press, 1991), 1.1.1, 3.
5. Mirabai, "mhare dere ajyo," in *For Love of the Dark One: Songs of Mirabai*, trans. Andrew Schelling (Prescott, Ariz.: Hohm Press, 1998), 4.
6. Hadewijch, "Letter 9: He in Me and I in Him," in *Hadewijch*, trans. Hart, lines 4–12, 66.
7. Coining the term "passionate detachment" to describe a similar dynamic, Wendy Farley, through her crucial insight that eros contains energies of non-attachment that can

attenuate drives toward totalization, offers a key inspiration for this article. See Wendy Farley, *Eros for the Other: Retaining Truth in a Pluralistic World* (Louisville, Ky.: Westminster John Knox Press, 2005), 83.

8. This insight has been much influenced by Judith Butler's relational ontology, specifically articulated in Judith Butler, *Precarious Life: The Powers of Mourning and Violence* (London: Verso, 2004).
9. Hadewijch, "Letter 8: Two Fears about Love," in *Hadewijch*, trans. Hart, lines 41–42, 65.
10. In the ancient tradition of interpreting the Song of Songs, often traced back to Origen, Hadewijch was particularly influenced by the works of Bernard of Clairvaux and William of St. Thierry.
11. See Barbara Newman, *From Virile Woman to WomanChrist: Studies in Medieval Religion and Literature* (Philadelphia: University of Pennsylvania Press, 1995), 164, for a discussion of how *fins amour* and *Brautmystik* mutually shaped each other: Courtly love literature had been influenced by the Cistercian allegorical literature on the *Song of Songs*, as can be seen in *La Queste del saint Graal* and in Gottfried's *Tristan*, for example. Along with some of her fellow Beguines influenced by *fins amours*, Hadewijch provided a reciprocal influence on *Brautmystik*.
12. Describing the intersecting threads of this new genre, Newman explains, "Sacred and secular met in *mystique courtoise* when the aura of Caritas enveloped the originally profane figures of Amour and Minne, giving rise to the awesome Goddess of the beguines." Newman, *Virile Woman to WomanChrist*, 78.
13. Hadewijch, "Couplet Poem 10: No Feeling But Love," in *Hadewijch*, trans. Hart, lines 93–98, 337.
14. While the common translation of *ontrouwe* is "unfaith," an alternative translation is "infidelity." While I focus on "unfaith," the translation "infidelity" leads to intriguing implications regarding the actions of the lover of *Minne*.
15. Hadewijch, "Couplet Poem 10: Not Feeling But Love," in *Hadewijch*, trans. Hart, line 66, 337.
16. This reference comes from one of Hadewijch's "visions" that speaks of the power of noble of unfaith. Hadewijch, "Vision 8: The Six-Winged Countenance," in *Hadewijch*, trans. Hart, lines 179–82, 300.
17. Hadewijch, "Poems in Couplets 1: The Nature of Love," in *Hadewijch*, trans. Hart, lines 61–62, 213.
18. Hadewijch, "Poems in Stanzas 40: Love's Remoteness," in *Hadewijch*, trans. Hart, line 33, 244.
19. John Giles Milhaven, *Hadewijch and Her Sisters: Other Ways of Loving and Knowing*. (Albany, N.Y.: SUNY Press, 1993), 61.
20. Hadewijch, "Letter 28: Trinitarian Contemplation Caught in Words," in *Hadewijch*, trans. Hart, lines 129–30, 111.
21. Hadewijch, "*Mengeldict* 25 (Poems in Couplets)," in *The Measure of Mystic Thought: A Study of Hadewijch's Mengeldichten*, trans. Saskia Murk-Jansen (Goppingen: Kummerle Verlag, 1991), lines 1–3, 87. Murk-Jansen proposes that this text was written by a figure she names Hadewijch II.
22. Mirabai, "Why Mira Can't Go Back to Her Own House," in *Mirabai: Ecstatic Poems*, trans. Robert Bly and Jane Hirshfield (Boston: Beacon Press, 2004), 21.

23. In Monier-Williams's Sanskrit dictionary, *krs* has the meaning of plowing and by extension "to draw into one's power, become master of, overpower" and "to draw or tear out, . . . to pull to and fro, cause pain, torture, torment." M. Monier-Williams, *A Sanskrit-English Dictionary*, Reprint (Delhi: Motilal Banarsidass, 2005), 306.
24. David Dean Shulman, "Modes of Meaning and Experience: *viraha* and *vilaiyatal*," *Parabola* 11.3 (1986): 15.
25. Karen Pechilis, *The Embodiment of Bhakti* (London: Oxford University Press, 1999), 20–24.
26. Friedhelm Hardy, *Viraha-Bhakti: The Early History of Krishna Devotion in South India* (New Delhi: Oxford University Press, 1983), 573.
27. Deidre Green, "Living Between the World: Bhakti Poetry and the Carmelite Mystics," *The Yogi and the Mystic: Studies in Indian and Comparative Mysticism*, ed. Karel Werner (Richmond, U.K.: Curzon Press, 1994), 134.
28. Mirabai, "Why Mira Can't Go Back to Her Own House," in *Mirabai: Ecstatic Poems*, trans. Bly and Hirshfield, 21.
29. Mirabai, "Caturvedi's *Pada* 117," in *Songs of the Saints of India*, trans. John Stratton Hawley and Mark Juergensmeyer (New York: Oxford University Press, 2004), 139.
30. Shulman, "Modes of Meaning and Experience," 15.
31. Hardy, *Viraha-Bhakti*, 10.
32. Shulman, "Modes of Meaning and Experience," 12.
33. Mirabai, "Caturvedi's *Pada* 82," in *Songs of the Saints of India*, trans. Hawley and Juergensmeyer, 135.
34. Hadewijch, "Poems in Stanzas 38: Nothingness in Love," *Hadewijch*, trans. Hart, lines 53–56, 238.
35. Paul Mommaers, *Hadewijch: Writer—Beguine—Love Mystic*, with Elisabeth M. Dutton (Leuven, Belgium: Peeters, 2005), 114.
36. Hadewijch, "Letter 16: Loving God with His Own Love," in *Hadewijch*, trans. Hart, lines 16–17, 80.
37. Hadewijch, "Letter 16," lines 16–17, 80.
38. Mirabai, "Mira Is Mad with Love," in *Mirabai: Ecstatic Poems*, trans. Bly and Hirshfield, 38.
39. Hadewijch, "Poems in Stanzas 14," in "Some Aspects of Hadewijch's Poetic Form in the *Strofische Gedichten*," trans. Tanis M. Guest (The Hague: Matinus Nijhoff, 1975), 278.
40. Shulman, "Modes of Meaning and Experience," 11.
41. Green, "Living Between the World," 134.
42. Mirabai, "Caturvedi's *Pada* 16," in *The Devotional Poems of Mirabai*, trans. A. J. Alston (Delhi: Motilal Banarsidas, 1980), 39.
43. Mirabai, "karanam suni syam meri," *For Love of the Dark One*, trans. Schelling, 61.
44. Hadewijch, "Letter 9: He in Me and Me in Him," in *Hadewijch*, trans. Hart, lines 1–12, 66.
45. Mirabai, "Caturvedi's *Pada* 9," in "Poison to Nectar: The Life and Work of Mirabai," trans. Madhu Kishwar and Ruth Vanita, *Manushi* 50–52 (1989): 89.
46. Mirabai, "Caturvedi's *Pada* 18," in "Poison to Nectar: The Life and Work of Mirabai," trans. Madhu Kishwar and Ruth Vanita, *Manushi* 50–52 (1989): 70.

47. Gavin Flood's concept of the ascetic body helps elucidate how these practices of attachment can be seen as *askesis*. He writes, "The ascetic submits her life to a form that transforms it, to a training that changes a person's orientation from the fulfillment of desire to a narrative greater than the self." *The Ascetic Self: Subjectivity, Memory, and Tradition* (New York: Cambridge University Press, 2004), 2.
48. Mirabai, "barasam ri badariya savan ri," in *For Love of the Dark One: Songs of Mirabai*, trans. Andrew Schelling (Prescott, Ariz.: Hohm Press, 1998), 26.
49. Hadewijch, "Poems in Stanzas 6: Conquest of Love—At a Price," in *Hadewijch*, trans. Hart, line 49, 143.
50. Hadewijch, "*Mengeldict* 21," lines 21–22, in *The Measure of Mystic Thought*, trans. Murk-Jansen, 108.
51. Hadewijch, "Letter 12: The Jacob Letter," in *Hadewijch*, trans. Hart, lines 57–59, 71.

8 Women's Virtue, Church Leadership, and the Problem of Gender Complementarity

Tracy Sayuki Tiemeier

Recently, I was asked how a thinking woman could be Catholic. The question threw me—not because I had never been asked that before (indeed, I have been asked the question many times), but because it was a prominent Christian leader whose work focused on collaborating with Catholic communities who had asked the question. Although he knew many "thinking women" who were Catholic, he still did not understand how we could stay Catholic.

Of course, many have left the Catholic Church over concerns of sexual prejudice and violence. For these people, the Church has been abusive. And just as I would never encourage someone to stay in an abusive family, I would not encourage someone to stay in a church that physically, mentally, or spiritually abused them. While I do not characterize my own experiences with the Catholic Church as abusive, they have been admittedly ambiguous.

I grew up a mixed (*hapa*) Japanese-German American girl in St. Louis, Missouri. My Japanese American mother had converted to Roman Catholicism when she married my father, but many in my family remained Buddhist. As a result, I grew up in multiple religious and ethnic worlds. My grandmother taught me about her (Buddhist/Shinto) family altar, and showed me how to feed our ancestors and care for them. In return, our ancestors would care for us. The death of a favorite relative saddened me, but I was consoled by his presence truly felt in the stars and wind. This did not seem at all in contradiction with my Catholic experience. The Catholic world of Mary and the saints seemed just like my ancestors, offering comfort, protection, and friendship. I set up my own altar and offered toys and treats. Unlike the stereotype of the "tragic mulatto (mixed-race person)," who is a victim of both worlds, my mixed childhood was nourishing in many ways, full of bridges and connections between worlds.

At the same time, I was growing up in the Midwest in the 1980s—multiraciality and multireligiosity were not acceptable in my church or in broader St. Louis middle-class society. I never felt white enough or Catholic enough. I prayed desperately to the beautiful Mary statue at the church, asking to be made white and blonde like the classmates who were inevitably chosen to crown her during May Marian celebrations while I looked on from the sidelines. It did not help that I felt called to the priesthood. A brown girl with Buddhist inclinations? Unthinkable. Unacceptable. Impossible. Even so, I prayed fervently and dedicated myself to a Church that did not seem to want me.

And then, I was sexually assaulted. I did everything I thought I was supposed to. I fought back. I told the authorities. I told my parents. I was overpowered. The authorities ignored me. My father, a loving man, became enraged. He wanted the perpetrator to be found and held accountable. He wanted the authorities fired. He wanted the institution where the assault occurred shut down. He drilled me about the specifics: what the perpetrator did and what he looked like; the name of the authorities I told; the exact timeline that everything occurred. I was confused and afraid by my father's reaction more than anything else that had happened. It seemed to me that I had done something wrong. I downplayed the assault. I begged him not to pursue legal action. I was sure that I was somehow to blame. I prayed desperately at Mass to be shown a reason for what had happened, and I was sure I must have committed some terrible sin. The next time I was sexually assaulted, I told no one.

Catholic teachings on women, gender, and sexuality did not help me, as they demonstrate little knowledge of the actual experiences and dilemmas people encounter in the real world. And principles without compassionate engagement are cold comfort for people like myself. We see an obsession with controlling our sexuality without an acknowledgement of the complicated contexts in which we live our lives or the need to care for our overall wellbeing. We wonder how there can be such an interest in protecting our unborn children (something for which I am grateful), but an appalling lack of interest in protecting our children from the sexual abuse of priests (something that I abhor). The apparent hypocrisy makes some of us wonder whether the Roman Catholic Church is truly pro-life, or whether it is instead merely anti-abortion, anti-euthanasia, anti-gay, and yes, anti-woman.

And yet it was precisely through—and not despite—my Catholicity that I was able to heal. The sacramentality of Catholic faith and spirituality, the emphasis on the holiness of all of creation, was key for embracing my self, my body, and my sexuality. Rather than viewing myself, bodies, and other religions as marked by sin (though, of course, they all are), I sought to find God in all things, particularly in myself. The Catholic intellectual tradition was also a healing revelation to me, as it championed the rigorous investigation of reality in all its complexity, confident that the truth would lead us to a more just society and to God. I came to see the core of Catholic faith, then, as holistic and even liberating. How could a thinking woman be Catholic? For me, being Catholic *was* being a thinking woman.

Through practice and prayer, I discerned a different (non-ordained) way to serve the Church as a Catholic feminist comparative theologian. I would seek to understand gender and sexuality theologically, build gender justice in the Church and in the world, and draw on the wisdom of religious traditions other than Christianity. It would do Catholic Christian theology *my way*, a way that honored my multicultural, multireligious background. I would embrace a dynamic, faithful, and sometimes critical relationship with the Church and Roman Catholic tradition. I would see myself as a fully participating member of my faith family, a grown adult engaging her parents (the Catholic hierarchy). I would be respectful of my parents' wisdom and even deferential to it where appropriate. But my own experiences would also enrich that family, challenging its way of being if necessary. I would sometimes disagree with my parents and grow frustrated with them when they treated me as a child; but I would still engage them and participate in life with them. In a concrete and real way, this meant that I knew my own experiences would find something highly problematic with Catholic hierarchical understandings of gender and sexuality; and yet I would engage those theologies to understand them and try to re-envision them. And, if I could not, then I would try to pivot to other theologies that could help the Church rethink its doctrine.

The area of expertise I chose was theological anthropology, as theological anthropology was the area of Christian theology that explores gender and sexuality. Broadly speaking, theological anthropology is a field of theology that examines the complexities and meanings of human being in relation to the divine. From the dynamics of our creation in the image of God, to sin and grace, to the freedom of the will, to the problem of suffering, to the religious significance of race, sexuality, and gender, theological anthropology aims to draw from a range of religious, historical, cultural, and scientific sources to shed light on our humanity.

A comparative theological anthropology examines questions of human being in light of multiple religious traditions and their diverse ways of answering those questions. A comparative approach presumes that there are similar enough questions asked across religious traditions that comparison is possible. It also presumes that to situate theological anthropology comparatively is not just possible, but that it is meaningful—that examining the similarities and differences across traditions yields insights on human being that would not have otherwise been made. Theologies of gender and their relationship to anthropologies of religious leadership (who can lead and why) are examples of theological anthropologies that can be analyzed comparatively, as questions of the significance of gender in relation to religious roles cross traditions.

This essay will look more closely at these questions by focusing on Catholic papal teaching on women, Mary, and priestly ordination in light of South Indian (Tamil) understandings of women's virtue and ritual power. Although both traditions assume gender complementarity (the notion that gender differences lead to distinct but equally valuable social and religious roles), the Tamil context refuses to universalize one discourse of women's virtue. As we will see, it also undoes the very theology of women's virtue that it upholds. In the end, I argue against simply discarding wholesale Catholic hierarchical theology of gender, gender complementarity, or the religious significance of gender. Instead, the more fluid and complex Tamil approach suggests a more complex way of thinking about women and leadership that both affirms and subverts the significance of gender.

Mary as Virgin and Mother

Mary as Virgin and Mother has become central to Catholic teaching on the significance of women. The late Pope John Paul II saw that the *"two dimensions of the female vocation* [virginity and motherhood] *were united in* [Mary]."[1] He says,

> Motherhood involves a special communion with the mystery of life, as it develops in the woman's womb. The mother is filled with wonder at

this mystery of life, and "understands" with unique intuition what is happening inside her ... *women are more capable than men of paying attention to another person*, and ... *motherhood develops this predisposition even more* ... In this wider context, *virginity* has to be considered *also as a path for women*, a path on which they realize their womanhood in a way different from marriage ... Nevertheless, the renunciation of ... [physical] motherhood, a renunciation that can involve great sacrifice for a woman, makes possible a different kind of motherhood: [spiritual] motherhood.[2]

For the Pope, a woman's physical role as mother reveals and develops her spirituality and her personhood as nurturing self-gift. Although consecrated virginity (vowed religious life) is seen as a distinct path from physical motherhood, it is still an expression of womanhood as nurturing self-gift. The calling of physical and spiritual motherhood is connected to women's more receptive and nurturing nature. Mary's receptive openness to God is manifest from the beginning in her consent to Jesus's conception. Such receptivity is both biologically natural and spiritually essential. Men lead the Church, as Christ did, while women receive Christ and others in their homes and in the world though motherhood and religious sisterhood, as Mary did. Mary as Virgin Mother shows both women and men the value and depth of the receptive, self-giving reality of womanhood.

The complementarity of male and female, seen in the complementarity of Mary and Jesus, plays out across salvation history. Pope Emeritus Benedict XVI highlights this in a letter to bishops before he was elected Pope. Following a common theme in Christian thought, the gendered dynamic of salvation history is interpreted through bridal imagery, beginning with Adam (male) and Eve (female), moving to God (male) and Israel (female), and reaching completion/redemption in Jesus (male) and Mary (female).[3] Church life and leadership carries on this sacred, gendered dynamic. Men and women are distinct, but equal. "To look at Mary and imitate her does not mean, however, that the Church should adopt a passivity inspired by an outdated conception of femininity."[4] At the same time, all are called to Mary's faith: "The existence of Mary is an invitation to the Church to root her very being in listening and receiving the Word of God, because faith is not so much the search for God on the part of human beings, as the recognition by men and women that God comes to us; he visits us and speaks to us."[5] Mary reveals both distinct roles and "feminine values" that are important to all persons of faith.

Even as the Pope Emeritus does not want to subscribe to an outdated understanding of gender, one cannot help but wonder whether theological arguments based on gender complementarity as described are not somewhat arbitrary. If the feminine receptivity is something all persons can and should strive for, if Mary reveals something for both women *and* men, then why are roles in the Church rigidly defined according to gender? Is the theology of Mary and gender complementarity simply about those in power marginalizing and excluding women from power? Let us turn now to another religious anthropology of gender and women's roles to see if it can shed light on gender complementarity and its complex relationship to leadership.

The *Cilappatikaram*

The *Cilappatikaram* is a fifth-century South Indian Tamil epic that reflects the religious diversity of South India at the time. Although the *Cilappatikaram* depicts a variety of religious traditions and practices, it presents largely as Jain. The attributed composer is Jain, as are the central characters. Moreover, the pervasive concern with karma fits with Jain sensibilities, as karma is repeatedly invoked as the cause of events.

The overarching narrative of the *Cilappatikaram* centers on the power of a chaste wife. Praised for her chastity or virtue (*karpu*), Kaṇṇaki is absolutely devoted to her husband, Kovalan. She remains so even when he leaves her for a courtesan and impregnates her. When Kovalan finally returns to Kaṇṇaki penniless, she takes him back without question. She even offers her precious anklet as a way to replace the money her husband squandered on his lover. Kaṇṇaki accompanies her husband on a difficult and dangerous journey so they might sell her anklet. They meet a female Jain renunciant along the way, Kavunti, who advises and protects the couple. After Kovalan enters the city of Maturai to sell the anklet on his own, he is falsely accused of stealing the queen's anklet, which looks on the outside just like his wife's anklet. The king has Kovalan executed without an investigation, which would have exposed the accuser as the thief. A devoted wife even after her husband's death, Kaṇṇaki becomes enraged and stands in judgment of the king and his town, proving her husband's innocence by breaking open her anklet and revealing the unique jewels inside. The king dies from his guilt, and the queen dies in response. Kaṇṇaki, now a widow, is rendered powerful by her constant devotion to her husband. She rips off her left breast, circles the city three times, and curses the city. She summons Agni, the god of fire, and commands him to destroy the city, sparing only the children, the elderly, Brahmins (the learned priestly class), and all virtuous men and women. Hearing of the tragedy of the wife and her husband, Kavunti takes the Jain vow of ultimate renunciation and fasts unto death.[6] Kaṇṇaki wanders for fourteen days and then ascends to heaven with Kovalan. She is now the "goddess of chastity" and protectress of the Tamil people.

In the *Cilappatikaram*, Kaṇṇaki is described as an ideal woman. Married at twelve, Kaṇṇaki is beautiful, virtuous, and chaste. Kaṇṇaki adores her husband, Kovalan, and is famous for her homemaking. Their life is portrayed as happy and passionate. When Kovalan leaves her for the dancer, Matavi, Kaṇṇaki goes into mourning. As Kovalan sings to his lover, "Patience is the highest virtue of young women,"[7] Kaṇṇaki waits for her husband to return. And when he does, she welcomes him back without reproach, soothing him when he admits squandering his money with another woman.

Kaṇṇaki shows frustration only once, just before Kovalan leaves to sell her anklet. A delicate woman not fit for exhaustive travel, Kaṇṇaki goes through the wilderness with Kovalan to journey with him to Maturai. Feeling bad for what he has done, he wonders what she has done to deserve such pain. She retorts, "You have done things that good men/ Would have stayed clear of. As for me, I have lived/ A blameless life. Therefore, I got up and followed you."[8] If Kovalan is tempted to seek answers in past deeds, Kaṇṇaki emphasizes the virtue of her present actions.

To underscore her own chastity, Kaṇṇaki details the virtue of seven other women just before she delivers justice to the town of Maturai. These virtuous women are not just idealized models; they demonstrate power in their virtue. As the epic earlier says, "Don't you know/ The old saying that in a land where women/ Are virtuous, the rains never fail, prosperity/ Never declines, and the triumphs of the king/ Of this vast world never diminish?"[9] Kaṇṇaki places herself in the line of chaste women, claiming her own power and declaring, "If I too am truly a virtuous woman ... The force of my vengeance you will see."[10] Kaṇṇaki curses the town and wrenches off her breast, summoning Agni to destroy it. Like other chaste wives, Kaṇṇaki has very real power. Kaṇṇaki's absolute devotion to her husband above all else is active, discriminative (she decides who is punished), deadly, and liberative for her and her husband.

The *Cilappatikaram* balances the cosmic force of karma and past actions with the significance of one's current actions. The reason for Kovalan's fate is his failure to follow a vow of nonviolence in a previous life and the unjust killing of another man. And Kaṇṇaki is told that she is being held accountable for failing to keep her husband's vow in a previous life. Yet, even as she recognizes that she is a "slave . . . of cruel karma," she insists that she is by "nature . . . innocent."[11] Indeed, Kaṇṇaki is never blamed—and even more, she is consistently praised for her virtue. When Kaṇṇaki ascends to heaven with Kovalan, the text underscores that even the gods worship a woman who devotes herself to her husband above all else. Kaṇṇaki is not devoted to any god or goddess. It is her single-minded devotion to Kovalan that makes her virtuous, ritually powerful, and worthy of adoration.

The *Cilappatikaram* provides a contrasting example of devotion to one's husband in the character of the queen of Maturai. When the king dies from shame upon realizing his guilt of executing an innocent man, his queen dies after crying, "There is no refuge for a woman who has lost her husband."[12] Both women are widowed, without their object of devotion. But they follow very different paths. Which example of devotion better demonstrates the ideal of female virtue? The *Cilappatikaram* takes up the question directly, but the answer is equivocal.

> May the joys of heaven wait upon the queen
> Who gave up her life before she felt the pain
> Of surviving her husband. And may the goddess
> Of chastity who has come to our good land be honored.[13]

Both women are devoted and virtuous. But is one better than the other? Arti Dhand argues that the *Cilappatikaram* is claiming that Kaṇṇaki is the most virtuous, thereby offering a unique vision of female chastity. For Dhand, Kaṇṇaki's dynamic power reconfigures the standard of wifely devotion from a more passive model to a more active one, where the wife chooses *not* to commit suicide and works on his behalf, even after his death.[14] For this, Kaṇṇaki becomes "the goddess of chastity," worthy herself of worship by humans and gods alike.

Even if this is true, the queen is still righteous and makes no less of an active choice than Kaṇṇaki. Indeed, the *Cilappatikaram* suggests that her spontaneous death may be a way for the queen to indict her husband:

"Perhaps she wanted to tell you ... / Of the terrible injustice done to her / By the mighty [king]."[15] This intriguing suggestion means that the queen was not following her husband to death because life without her husband was meaningless, but that it was a way for her to demonstrate that the king not only failed in his duties as king (made clear in his own death), *but also failed as a husband*. Thus, a married woman may have a strong code of virtue that requires absolute devotion to her husband. But it does not preclude chastising her husband and holding him responsible for his very real duty as a husband. Thus, even as we may be inclined to find the queen's suicide disturbing, we may also see that she perhaps did not give into fate so passively.[16] She, too, can be an agent of virtue.

Beyond multiple ways of modeling wifely virtue, the *Cilappatikaram* provides in the person of Kavunti an entirely different model of virtue predicated on the renunciation of gendered life. Her ascetical practices (which would have included fasting, celibacy, and other physical austerities) are renowned, and she is and "first among the pure at heart."[17] While Kaṇṇaki is powerful through devotion to her husband, Kavunti is powerful through her ascetical practices. When an immoral couple cruelly teases Kaṇṇaki and Kovalan of being married siblings, Kavunti curses them by the power of her penance and transforms them into jackals. Both Kaṇṇaki and Kavunti have real power through their bodies, though they follow very different spiritual paths.

Kavunti acts as a spiritual advisor to Kovalan and Kaṇṇaki, explaining the cosmic, karmic context for their woes: "In this world / Those who regard women and food / As their sole pleasure bring untold suffering / On themselves. Wise men have renounced / Both."[18] Indeed, so inexorable and intertwined is karma, death or renunciation awaits many of the characters of the *Cilappatikaram*.[19] Thus, in an epic concerned to detail the importance of kingly righteousness, wifely chastity (for her, her husband, and ultimately for the whole Tamil people), and even husbandly virtue, it also portrays the tragic pull of karma and preserves the value of renouncing the very virtues celebrated. Kavunti is therefore an essential character for the epic, teaching and representing another way in the world. Through her, it is clear that women can be virtuous in renouncing their wifely role.

From a modern Western perspective, it is perhaps difficult to see the *Cilappatikaram* as anything but problematic. The women of the *Cilappatikaram* certainly have largely tragic endings. Even Kaṇṇaki can be seen as losing out; by becoming a national Tamil goddess, she is mythologized and pedestalized out of the complexities of her humanity. It is important, however, to notice that not just the female characters find tragedy: Many of the characters, male and female, end up dying or renouncing the world. Such is the way of karma, which is an essential theological teaching of the epic. Moreover, it is essential not to miss the subtle dynamics as female characters subvert male and societal expectations. For while Kaṇṇaki and the queen exemplify devotion to husbands, and are limited by circumstances beyond their control, they practice virtue in different and divergent ways that are both powerful (even over men and in judgment of them). Finally, Kavunti's life of renunciation is an explicit rejection of gender complementarity and gendered virtue—also powerful and bodily, and beyond male control.

Complementarity as Both Problem and Possibility: Gendered Power, Bodily Power

Recently, Pope Francis has said that Mary is an "icon of womanhood . . . As mother of all, she [Mary] is a sign of hope for peoples suffering the birth pangs of justice. She is the missionary who draws near to us and accompanies us throughout life, opening our hearts to faith by her maternal love."[20] Here, Mary and motherhood are seen as active openness to others; and evangelization through the lens of femininity is of solidarity and accompaniment. As the "star of the new evangelization,"[21] Mary becomes a model for the Church and for all persons.

Interestingly, the Mary traditionally associated with evangelization is Mary Magdalene. Although the only real New Testament information about Mary Magdalene is that Jesus exorcised seven demons from her (Luke 8.2 and Mark 16.9), the Western Christian tradition has conflated her with the penitent sinner who anointed Jesus's feet with oil (Luke 7.36–39) and frequently portrayed her as a reformed prostitute. But Mary Magdalene has also been called the "apostle to the apostles" or the "first evangelist" for being the first to witness the resurrected Jesus and to tell the other disciples of his resurrection (Mark 16.9–10, John 20.14–18).

In reading the evangelical Mission of the Church through the lens of Virgin Mother Mary, and not Mary Magdalene, Pope Francis shifts the "feminine" character of the "new evangelization" to what he considers the "motherly" activities of solidarity and accompaniment. In doing so, the Pope articulates the most activist papal understanding of Mary and motherhood. But while he shifts out of the receptive understanding of motherhood to an active understanding, he cannot yet let go of a representational (iconic) understanding of Christ's (male) body and the priest's (male) body. He has clearly stated that there can be no reconsideration of women's ordination. In affirming that male-exclusive ordination is a closed question, he points to complementarity: The all-male priesthood is a sign of Christ the (male) Spouse.[22] Thus, even as the new Pope has given many people around the globe hope that the Roman Catholic Church will focus its energies on social justice and shift its sexual teachings, gender complementarity seems to be here to stay.

The *Cilappatikaram* both praises and problematizes women's gendered power, endorses and subverts gender complementarity. On the one hand, Kaṇṇaki and other chaste wives have real bodily power. By devoting themselves to their husbands above all else (even the gods), their bodies are made powerful. This power through conformity to religio-social roles could be said to be the same in Catholic magisterial (authoritative) discourses on Mary and women. Women have distinct, but essential and powerful, roles. Just as the wives of the *Cilappatikaram* are central, Mary reveals how essential women are for the Church and for salvation history.

But there is an important difference. Even as Kaṇṇaki is playing her role as wife, she is not the only exemplar. The *Cilappatikaram* recognizes that there is more than one way to be a wife. Indeed, the wives of the *Cilappatikaram* make different choices and live out their devotion to their husbands in different ways. In this sense, the *Cilappatikaram* provides more than one picture of women's virtue, even as the role of wife is upheld. Mary's portrayal as *the* ideal woman, then, presents a more reductive view of women's virtue. And even Pope Francis's more activist view of the Virgin Mary can be seen as reducing women's power to one discourse of femininity. His move to integrate the Magdalene tradition, a tradition that has long been seen as offering a strong non-virginal, non-motherly alternative and demonstration of women's activity in the Church, is problematic in this sense.

Second, Kaṇṇaki's actions reveal real *ritual* power. When she rips off her breast, circles the city, and summons Agni, she follows a ritual for judging the city and avenging Kovalan's unjust death. It is precisely through the gendered body that women are rendered ritually powerful. What might this mean for women's ordination and leadership in the Church? It is possible that Kaṇṇaki's ritual power suggests distinct women's rituals, but not necessarily access to priestly ordination.

However, as Sarah Coakley notes, the priest acts in the Eucharist both *in persona Christi* (in the person of Christ) and *in persona Ecclesiae* (in the person of the Church), fluidly crossing boundaries in our bridal symbolism of Christ and Church, Male and Female.[23] While she highlights here the fluidity of human gender and the proto-erotic nature of the Eucharist, where desire is more fundamental than human gender, Kaṇṇaki could suggest something else. Gendered bodily practices are themselves powerful, and the exclusion of women (or men) in the complex drama of the Eucharist is problematic. Both men and women may be actually necessary for symbolizing the mystery of salvation.

Finally, even as gender complementarity is bodily and ritually powerful, Kavunti's renunciation of householder life, her ascetical practices, and her fasting unto death undoes gender through bodily and ritual practices predicated on the renunciation of wifely virtue and womanhood. Kavunti's renunciation of gender complementarity is therefore also an undoing of heteronormativity (male-female complementarity as normative for society, religion, and families).

In Catholic magisterial teaching, consecrated virginity (for men and women) is seen as distinct from, but continuous with, natural, biological roles—spiritual fatherhood and motherhood instead of physical fatherhood and motherhood. This is not the case in the *Cilappatikaram*: The rejection of gendered practices is itself powerful. Here again there are lessons for theological anthropology. Ritual power can be bodily, and yet explicitly reject gendered practices of complementarity.

Moreover, Kavunti's path can help Christians to rethink Mary as Virgin and Mother. Rather than Mary being the "icon of womanhood" who unifies "two dimensions of the female vocation," Mary could be the one who confirms the significance of gender (in her motherhood) and *undoes it at the same time* (in her virginity). This interpretation would emphasize the contradictory nature of Mary in Catholic thought, not because Mary is the pure ideal no woman could live up to but because Mary embodies precisely what people can achieve through their messy, complicated, and sometimes contradictory lives.

The lesson here, then, would be that gendered practices are indeed powerful, but not absolutely so. Indeed, they could be seen as problematic without ritual and bodily practices that also undo gender. In this regard, women again could be seen as ritually powerful (and therefore fit for ordination)—but not because they are women, but because they, like men, have the capacity to undo their own gender through their ritually powerful bodily practices. If this is the case, all persons are ritually powerful, able to affirm and undo their gender and sexuality through their bodily practices.

This brief comparison between the women of the *Cilappatikaram* and Catholic papal understanding of Mary and women's ordination cannot solve the many issues involved in the Christian theological understanding of women, gender, and leadership in the Church. And I certainly do not think that this comparison will be convincing to the Catholic magisterium or others who support the exclusion of women from the priesthood for anthropological, biblical, or traditional reasons. However, what this comparison can show to Catholics and non-Catholics alike is that gender complementarity does not always have to be rigid, inflexible, and fundamentally sexist or heterosexist. In the desire to construct just theologies, the temptation to argue that there is absolutely no religious significance to bodies, gender, and sexuality is strong. But this move devalues embodiment and disembodies spiritual belief and practice. Instead, Christian theologies of bodiliness can both hold onto and subvert gender, embracing multiplicity (or even contradiction) in their discourses on women, gender, and sexuality without enforcing a rigid, inflexible complementarity. More complex theologies can then allow for more nuanced approaches to religious leadership that value bodies without being reductive or exclusive.

Notes

1. John Paul II, *Mulieris Dignitatem* (Vatican: August 15, 1998), 17, http://www.vatican.va/holy_father/john_paul_ii/apost_letters/documents/hf_jp-ii_apl_15081988_mulieris-dignitatem_en.html, emphasis in the original.
2. John Paul II, *Mulieris Dignitatem*, 18, 20–21, emphasis in the original.
3. Joseph Ratzinger, "Letter to the Bishops of the Catholic Church on the Collaboration of Men and Women" (Vatican: May, 31, 2004), http://www.vatican.va/roman_curia/congregations/cfaith/documents/rc_con_cfaith_doc_20040731_collaboration_en.html.
4. Ratzinger, "Letter to the Bishops," 16.
5. Ratzinger, "Letter to the Bishops," 15.
6. The Jain ritual of fasting to death, *sallekhana*, is a rare but highly regarded practice of purging negative karma for select persons who meet strict requirements, such as no further obligations in life. See Christopher Key Chapple, *Nonviolence to Animals, Earth, and Self in Asian Traditions* (Albany: SUNY Press, 1993).
7. Rajagopal Parthasarathy, trans., *The Tale of an Anklet: The Cilappatikaram of Ilanko Atikal* (New York: Columbia University Press, 1993), 66.

8. Parthasarathy, *Tale of an Anklet*, 163.
9. Parthasarathy, *Tale of an Anklet*, 156.
10. Parthasarathy, *Tale of an Anklet*, 193.
11. Parthasarathy, *Tale of an Anklet*, 191.
12. Parthasarathy, *Tale of an Anklet*, 189–90.
13. Parthasarathy, *Tale of an Anklet*, 223.
14. Arti Dhand, "*Karpu*: the Ideal of Feminine Chastity in the *Cilappatikaram*," Arc 23 (1995): 107–20, 115–16.
15. Parthasarathy, *Tale of an Anklet*, 222.
16. In the ambiguous confluence of wifely virtue, active power, and self-destruction, both Kaṇṇaki and the queen can be related to the misunderstood and rare Indian practice of *sati* (widow burning). In theory, a wife is rendered powerful by home rituals and devotion to her husband and family. During her husband's life, she can bless her home and family; after his death, she can liberate herself and her husband through the *sati* ("good" or "pure" woman) ritual, which involves no human intervention or external fire (burning occurs through the internal and fiery power of virtue). The widow also judges the broader community through blessings and/or curses, before and after her death. Kaṇṇaki herself does not self-immolate, but she does have fiery power that ultimately liberates herself and her husband, and it divinizes her as a goddess over the Tamil people. The queen's suicide is less dramatic and powerful, but it is not merely a passive death due to a lack of purpose after her husband's death. She exposes the king's lack of husbandly virtue and passes judgment on him. Her virtue therefore also has power. Thus, as both Kaṇṇaki and the queen show, wives and widows are (or ought to be) far from passive and powerless victims. Of course, such a display of bodily power comes at the cost of one's self; and the theology is certainly vulnerable to exploitation. Nevertheless, the power is real and cannot be ignored, even as it is ambiguous and multivalent. For a more complex discussion of *sati*, see John Stratton Hawley, ed., *Sati, the Blessing and the Curse: The Burning of Wives in India* (Oxford: Oxford University Press, 1994).
17. Parthasarathy, *Tale of an Anklet*, 130.
18. Parthasarathy, *Tale of an Anklet*, 141.
19. Matari (a character who takes care of Kaṇṇaki) kills herself by jumping into a fire when she hears of Kaṇṇaki and Kovalan's fate. Kavunti fasts unto death. Kovalan's father gives away all his possessions and enters a monastery. Kovalan's mother dies after her husband enters the monastery. Kaṇṇaki's father becomes an ascetic. Kaṇṇaki's mother dies after her husband takes vows. Kovalan's lover, Matavi, and their daughter, Manimekalai, join a Buddhist nunnery.
20. Francis, *Evangelii Gaudium* (Vatican: November 24, 2013), 285–86, http://www.vatican.va/holy_father/francesco/apost_exhortations/documents/papa-francesco_esortazione-ap_20131124_evangelii-gaudium_en.html#II.%E2%80%82Mary,_mother_of_evangelization.
21. Francis, *Evangelii Gaudium*, 288.
22. Francis, *Evangelii Gaudium*, 104.
23. Sarah Coakley, "'In Persona Christi': Gender, Priesthood and the Nuptial Metaphor," *Svensk Teologisk Kvartalskrift* 82 (2006): 145–54.

9 Longing and Gender

A RESPONSE TO HOLLY HILLGARDNER AND TRACY SAYUKI TIEMEIER

Amir Hussain

> *And the love that loves the love that loves the love that loves the love that loves to love the love that loves to love the love . . .*
>
> —VAN MORRISON, "MADAME GEORGE"

As a believing Muslim, I begin with thanks. In the Qur'an, the word for unbelief, *kufr*, is almost always linked with the word for thanks, *shukr*. The implication is clear: The one who does not believe is the one who is not thankful. Thanks to Holly Hillgardner and Tracy Sayuki Tiemeier for their contributions to this volume. It was a privilege to read them, and an honor to be asked by Michelle Voss Roberts to respond to them when they were first presented at the conference she hosted at Wake Forest University in March 2014.

The chapters are superb, which counterintuitively makes the task of the respondent all the more difficult. One cannot simply point to flaws in the arguments, or provide information that the authors have neglected to include. Again, I reiterate, the chapters are superb. Therefore, for a response, I want to make some connections between the Christian and Indic traditions that Professors Hillgardner and Tiemeier have so aptly discussed with the Islamic traditions that are the primary focus of my work. I do this because in my own courses on comparative theology, I find that introducing students to a third tradition often moves them beyond simple binaries or the either/or dichotomies from which they get only superficial or surface-level understanding. (Either that or a decade of teaching in a Catholic university has begun to introduce some sort of "Trinitarian hegemony" into my life as a Muslim scholar of Islam.)

I need also add that it was a delight to read two chapters that were both so well-*written*, composed with an eye to the fact that they would be read as literary products, and not simply to convey information. So much scholarly writing, unfortunately, while being scholarly, is not often also elegant and well-written. Reading the chapters, both of which focus on love, brought to mind the following lines of poetry: "Part of you pours out of me / in these lines from time to time." Those are from a Canadian artist, painter-turned-singer Joni Mitchell, from her 1971 song "A Case of You."[1] I steal from Joni as often as I can, and I remind my students that they should not cut and paste from Wikipedia, but instead turn to the work of great artists. I could write for a thousand years and not come up with something as beautiful as one of Joni's lines.

Tracy Sayuki Tiemeier looks at gender complementary in Catholicism and a Tamil text, the *Cilappatikaram*. In her discussion of Mary, there are many comparisons that could be made about Mary in the Islamic tradition. As is well-known, the Qur'an mentions Mary and Jesus, as well as other figures from the New Testament, such as John the Baptist and Zechariah. What is less well-known is that Mary is mentioned more by name in the Qur'an (34 times) than she is in the New Testament (19 times), and that she is, in fact, the only woman mentioned by name in the Qur'an. The nineteenth chapter of the Qur'an is the Chapter of Mary (*Surah Maryam*), where the story of the virgin birth is mentioned. The Chapter of Mary contains a moving Muslim description of Jesus, who is described by God as "a sign unto people and a mercy from Us [God]" (Qur'an 19:21).

The Qur'an speaks about the fact that Mary was criticized by some in her community, who could not accept the virgin birth. Mary asks the infant Jesus to speak on his own behalf, and he does so:

> Mary pointed to the child then; but they said, "How shall we speak to one who is still in the cradle, a little child?" Jesus said, "Lo, I am God's servant; God has given me the book and made me a prophet. God has made me blessed, wherever I may be; and God has enjoined me to pray and to give alms so long as I live, and likewise to cherish my mother; God has not made me arrogant or unprosperous. Peace be upon me the day I was born, and the day I die, and the day I am raised up alive." (Qur'an 19:30–35)

Tiemeier mentions the importance of Mary for the thought of Pope John Paul II, and I have often wondered if the blessed saint became interested in interfaith dialogue with Muslims because he recognized a billion people who also held Mary in the highest regard.[2] This also helps Pope Francis in the new evangelization with Mary that Tiemeier describes. And in full confession (another expression I have begun to use easily after a decade at a Catholic university), it was Mary who brought me into the study of theology. I was studying the poetry of William Blake as an undergraduate at the University of Toronto. Jerry Bentley, the renowned Blake scholar who was our professor, showed the class an image of Blake's "Great Red Dragon and the Woman Clothed with the Sun" that is at the Brooklyn Museum. He then mentioned, almost as an aside, that this story came from the twelfth chapter of the Book of Revelation. Not having heard of this book before, I put up my hand and asked Professor Bentley what it was. He began to recite: "And there appeared a great wonder in heaven; a woman clothed with the sun, and the moon under her feet, and upon her head a crown of twelve stars ...," when I interrupted him to repeat my question, which indicated the depth of my ignorance. "What's the Book of Revelation?" I asked again. And Professor Bentley kindly explained its place in the New Testament. I went home that night and began to read the New Testament, not from the opening Gospel of Matthew, but from Revelation 12. It was, in hindsight, a great hook, as the great red dragon waiting to devour the child delivered by the woman, and the subsequent war in heaven, piqued my interest in biblical literature in a way that Matthew's opening genealogy did not. And years later, when I moved to Los Angeles, I would encounter the woman clothed with the sun again, as Revelation 12 is also the textual referent for the Virgin of Guadalupe.

Jesus, who Tiemeier describes in his complementarity to Mary, is also an important figure for Muslims. He is mentioned in fifteen chapters and ninety-three verses of the Qur'an. Eleven times in the Qur'an, Jesus is referred to as "Messiah." But this simply means "the anointed one," a direct parallel with the usage in Hebrew. Although "Messiah" is translated into Greek as "Christ," and assumes divine significance, it is important to point out the differences between Christian and Muslim usages of that term. The Qur'an expresses the Muslim understanding of Jesus in the following verse: "The Messiah, Jesus son of Mary, was only the messenger of God, and God's word that God committed to Mary, and a spirit from God" (Qur'an 4:169).

Another significant difference is that the ascetic traditions that Tiemeier describes in both Catholicism and the lives of Kannaki and

Kavunti are atypical in Islam. While the Qur'an gives high regard to Christian monks and priests for their monasticism in one verse (Qur'an 5:82), married life and not monasticism is seen as the rule for religious leaders, both male and female. What transformed early moments of ascetic piety in Islam was the all-consuming love of the divine exemplified by an early woman mystic named Rabi'a al-'Adawiyah of Basra (c. 713–801). Born into a poor family, Rabi'a was orphaned and sold into slavery as a child, but her master was so impressed with her piety that he set her free. She lived the rest of her life in mystical contemplation, loving God with no motive other than love itself.

Mystics from various religious traditions have used the language of erotic love to express their love for God. Rabi'a was perhaps the first to introduce this language into Islamic mysticism. She loved God with two loves, the love of passion and a spiritual love worthy of God alone. One of the most beloved stories about Rabi'a has her roaming the streets of Basra carrying a bucket of water and a flaming torch, ready to put out the fires of Hell and set fire to the gardens of Paradise so that people will worship God for the sake of Love alone.

The Sufi tradition provided one of the few outlets for women to be recognized as leaders. Because the Sufis believed the Divine to be without gender, the gender of the worshipper did not matter. After Rabi'a, women could be Sufi leaders for both men and women together, even though they were prohibited from being imams for mixed gender congregations (women, however, were trained to be imams for groups of other women). In addition, the shrines of Sufi saints, whether male or female, are often cared for by women. As places where women have some measure of control, they tend to attract more women than men, inverting the usual gender breakdown of attendance at mosques.

The complementarity between men and women, as created pairs, is of course also to be found in Islam. But while the Qur'an often speaks of creation in pairs, and talks about the creation of men and women, one of its most interesting pairs is human and *jinn* (described, for example, in Qur'an 55, *Surah al-Rahman*). While humans are created out of clay, the Qur'an tells us that *jinn* (compare our English word "genie") are created out of smokeless fire. Iblis (compare with the Latin *diabolus*) is the most famous of the *jinn*, one who leads human beings away from God. So in many ways, the Qur'anic tension is not between men and women, but between humans (both male and female) and *jinn*.

In the story of Iblis, one finds Muslim understandings of what it means to be human. One cannot properly speak of a "theological anthropology" in Islam because Muslims deny the incarnation. However, one can certainly talk about what it means to be human. Theodicy is connected to this: We do not suffer because of God; we suffer because of the damage that we human beings do. In the Qur'an, as in the Bible, human beings are among the last of the things that God creates. The Qur'an tells us that "your Lord said to the angels, 'Indeed, I will put a vicegerent [*khalifa*] upon the earth.' They said: 'Will You place upon [the earth] one who causes corruption therein and sheds blood, while we declare Your praise and sanctify You?' God said, 'Indeed, I know that which you do not know'" (Qur'an 2:30). The angels know that we will "cause corruption in the earth and shed blood," and unfortunately, this is what we have done in our history and our present as human beings. But we are put here as the *khalifa*, the representative of God on earth, which carries with it a great responsibility to act appropriately.

Turning to Holly Hillgardner's chapter, while there is no bridal imagery in Islam between God and the *ummah* (community of believers), there is a tradition of courtly love that enters the European Christian tradition via Islam. The late María Rosa Menocal published a groundbreaking book in 1987 about that penetration, *The Arabic Role in Medieval Literary History*. In that book, she talked about a derivation for the English word "troubadour" (in Provençal *trobar*) from the Arabic word *taraba*, meaning "to sing": "'*Taraba*' meant 'to sing' and sing poetry; *tarab* meant 'song,' and in the spoken Arabic of the Iberian peninsula it would have come to be pronounced *trob*; the formation of the Romance verb through addition of the *-ar* suffix would have been standard."[3]

So the tradition of troubadours, playing guitar and singing love poetry, which is a hallmark of medieval European society, has deep roots in the Islamic world. In the contemporary world, one of the best modern troubadours is Richard Thompson, a British convert to Islam who has lived in Los Angeles for decades.[4] That challenges the easy assumption of a simple dichotomy between "Islam" and "the West," when we consider that one of the best guitar players in the world is a Muslim. In all seriousness, for me Richard Thompson playing the Fender Stratocaster guitar is one of the proofs for the existence of God. Of spirituality in music, Richard has said in an interview on his web page: "Music is spiritual stuff, and even musicians who clearly worship money, or fame, or ego, cannot help but express a better part of themselves sometimes when performing, so great is the gift of music, and so connected to our higher selves. What we believe informs everything we do, and music is no exception."

Hillgardner's discussion of love brought to mind one of my beloved teachers. I had the extraordinary privilege of being mentored by Wilfred Cantwell Smith, and I always turn to his work. He was the one who taught me that the Arabic word belief is connected to love.

Things change.

That is his first paragraph in the chapter "The English Word 'Believe,'" in his book *Faith and Belief*.[5] Then in the third paragraph, he writes, "Languages, too, have histories. Words change their meanings with the centuries, some more than others." And then he writes in the third paragraph and fourth paragraphs:

> Let us begin with etymology.
>
> Literally, and originally, "to believe" means "to hold dear": virtually, to love. This fact—and it is a hard, brute, fact—provides the underlying force and substance of our thesis here. Let it be emphasized, and reiterated. Let it be remembered, throughout the remainder of this chapter and even, if one be allowed so to plead, throughout the remainder of each reader's life. Literally and originally, "to believe" means "to hold dear."[6]

I also appreciated Hillgardner's thoughts on oscillations in her chapter. Sometimes when people write about love, and they are really talking about infatuation or puppy love, I want to ask them a simple question, "Have you ever been in love?" In Hillgardner's writing, it is clear that she has, and that she understands the complexities involved. I think in music, not in prose, and so I began my response with a meditation on the complexities of love from one of our great singers, Van Morrison.[7] And in thinking of Hillgardner's thoughts on "turbulent unrest," a song by Blue Rodeo, "Rain Down on Me," comes to mind.[8] The story is told from the male point of view, and there's such a depth of feeling in Jim Cuddy's voice when he sings the bridge, something that must be heard (like the Qur'an) to be fully appreciated:

> Oh now she talks to strangers
> who bring her flowers for her hair

but every night you count on me
to get you out the door
Oh then you smile and watch me lose control . . .

These two brilliant chapters on being human capture some of this complexity of love lost and love found, and of our relationship to God, the source of love.

Notes

Chapter epigraph courtesy of Van Morrison.

1. Joni Mitchell, "A Case of You," on *Blue*, Reprise, 1971, 4:20. For those unfamiliar with the song, there is a marvelous YouTube clip of Joni performing the song in 1974 on the dulcimer, the same instrument she used on the original recording of the magisterial record *Blue* on which the song first appeared: http://www.youtube.com/watch?v=IAsXMlkwXgs.
2. See Hosn Abboud's book on Mary in Islam, *Mary in the Qur'an: A Literary Reading* (London: Routledge, 2013).
3. María Rosa Menocal, *The Arabic Role in Medieval Literary History: A Forgotten Heritage* (Philadelphia: University of Pennsylvania Press, 2004 [1987]), xi.
4. For more information, see his web page, http://www.richardthompson-music.com/.
5. Wilfred Cantwell Smith, *Faith and Belief: The Difference between Them* (Princeton: Princeton University Press, 1979), 105.
6. Smith, *Faith and Belief*, 105.
7. For a discussion of what I mean by the "complexities" in this song, see the magisterial review by the late Lester Bangs on *Astral Weeks*, the record that contained "Madame George": https://personal.cis.strath.ac.uk/murray.wood/astral.html.
8. Blue Rodeo, "Rain Down on Me," on *Lost Together*, Risque Disque, 1992, YouTube video, 4:50, from the official music video, posted by "Blue Rodeo," February 11, 2012, http://www.youtube.com/watch?v=yoy8tUVwoUs. Lines from the song are used here courtesy of Blue Rodeo.

PART IV
Christology

10 What Child Is This?

JESUS, LORD LAO, AND DIVINE IDENTITY

Bede Benjamin Bidlack

In those days, in the reign of Tanjia of Yin with the year star in gengshen, *in the month . . . the Highest Venerable Lord came down from the eternal realm of the Dao. He harnessed a cloud of three energies and strode on the essence of the sun. Following the rays of the nine luminaries, he entered into the mouth of the Jade Maiden of Mystery and Wonder. Taking refuge in her womb, he became a man.*

In the year gengshen, *on the fifteenth day of the second month, he was born in Bo. Nine dragons sprinkled water over him to rinse and wash his body, then they transformed into nine springs.*

At that time, the Venerable Lord had white hair. He was able to walk upon birth. A lotus flower sprouted under each step he took. After nine steps, he pointed to heaven with his left hand, to the earth with his right hand and announced to the people: "In heaven above, on the earth below, I alone am venerable. I shall reveal the highest law of the Dao. I shall save all things moving and growing, the entire host of living beings. I shall wander across the ten directions and reach to the dark prisons of the underworld. I shall lead all those not yet saved and all those lost in error to certain salvation."[1]

Comparative theology begins with reading across religious boundaries until the reader finds a doctrine—or a practice, trope, or work of art—that resonates with his or her own faith. Close study disturbs the theologian's categories and presuppositions. Usually, such a disturbance results in the expansion of a category, its rediscovery, or simply the growth of the reader. Such is the supposed path of the theological explorer.

In a process of exploration, however, unexpected turns are bound to occur. One such possibility is that reading across religious boundaries brings the reader to foreign territory that appears so familiar that it is uncomfortable on the basis of that similarity. What happens when similarity evokes in the reader not a sense of common humanity gazing at a single Ultimate Reality, but a sense of competition? Such a challenge to doctrinal loyalties can impel the reader to make a hurried retreat to the comfort of the faith from which the project began.

The preceding tale is the birth narrative of the Highest Venerable Lord, or Lord Lao, in the *Huahu jing* (*The Scripture of the Conversion of the Barbarians*), a sixth-century Daoist text. As a result of the extraordinary events of Lord Lao's birth, and the pronouncement of his intention to save all beings, Lord Lao's birth narrative strikes the Christian memory of Jesus's birth. The Christian, however, takes the birth of Christ as a unique event and a pivotal moment in a single, divine plan of salvation. In this case, the comparative theologian must trust the method of comparative theology, which insists on reading closely across religious boundaries so as to examine carefully the texts in question. Only by having the courage to face the similarities head-on can the theologian save Christmas.

This paper examines the birth narrative of Lord Lao in the *Huahu jing* and the birth narrative of Jesus Christ in Luke. Rather than challenge the uniqueness of Jesus Christ, a close reading of these parallel stories results in a reconsideration of divine embodiment and its meaning for salvation history.[2]

Historical Background of the Texts

HUAHU JING

In 386 CE, the Toba, a Hunnish people, conquered northern China to establish the Wei Dynasty (386–535). They were small in number and unable to rule a large kingdom by themselves. Typical of colonialism, the Toba utilized the native Chinese to officiate over their new lands. Thinking it unwise to empower Confucian bureaucrats, who swore an oath to the Chinese emperor, the Toba looked to the educated class of the other religions, Buddhism and Daoism, to run the country. In order to help the rulers choose a religion, the Toba organized court debates between the Buddhists and Daoists. The first was in 520. To prove the superiority of Daoism over Buddhism, the Daoist representatives looked to the *Huahu jing*.

The Daoist tradition viewed the world as constantly falling out of harmony with Ultimate Reality, the Dao. It taught that in order to return the world to its natural state of peace and prosperity, Lord Lao descended into the world on a regular basis to provide guidance to rulers and to transmit sacred scriptures.[3] The *Daode jing* encapsulates this combination of practical wisdom and sacred scripture. This text is commonly understood as having been authored by the sagely philosopher Laozi, but in the Later Han Dynasty (25–220 CE), he went through a metamorphosis. By the second century, Daoists came to worship him as Lord Lao, the embodiment of the Dao.[4]

Lord Lao comes down when the ways of humankind sufficiently wander from the Dao, fall into grave error, and need instruction to get back into harmony with the Dao. He appears to the ruler, or to a person such as Zhang Daoling, who later becomes a religious leader as a result of the divine vision. Thanks to his instruction, the world can move from a state of chaos and suffering to one of prosperity, growth, and happiness.

Birth stories accompany some accounts of Lord Lao's descent. Daoists took the revelation of Lord Lao's birth to be historical, but the version under examination here is intentionally polemical in character.[5] In Toba court debates, both Buddhists and Daoists were competing for royal favor and the suppression of the other religion.[6] The Daoists looked for support to the *Huahu jing*, first compiled around 300 CE, but having since gone through several versions.

The version from which the preceding birth narrative of Lord Lao comes is from the early eighth century. It is divided into three categories: Lord Lao's hagiography, demonological and theoretical issues, and scholastic discussions on good government. Lord Lao is seen as the creator of the universe, a supporter of rulers, the source of scriptures, and the personification of the Dao.[7] The rest of the story, in the Yuan period version of the *Huahu jing* (dated 1281), escalates the polemical character of the text: Lord Lao and his companion, the border guard Yin Xi, journey to the west; there is an exchange of banquets with the barbarian kings; Lord Lao and Yin Xi undergo ordeals; after emerging from the ordeals, they punish the barbarians for their unbelief; they try to civilize the barbarians with Buddhist precepts; and Lord Lao leaves to convert other lands, while Yin Xi remains as the Buddha.[8] Daoism, the text argues, precedes Buddhism, is the source of Buddhism, and is superior to Buddhism. Lord Lao was born in 1311 BCE, but Buddha did not appear until 1029 BCE.[9] He lived and taught before the Buddha, and travelled to the west where Buddhism was born; thus he is the superior source of Buddhism.

The template for this story comes from Sima Qian's *Shiji* (*Record of the Historian*), a seminal work of the second century that provides a picture of ancient China. The *Shiji* identifies him, not as Lord Lao, but as a Zhou Dynasty (1050–265 BCE) historian who leaves court life after tiring of its corruption. Traveling westward, he approaches the last pass before exiting China forever. Yin Xi discerns the old man to be a sage. He begs the old man to leave his wisdom behind before venturing further. Five thousand characters later, the sage finishes his *Daode jing*, leaves it for posterity, and then disappears through the western pass.

Chronological primacy was at issue in the debates of the sixth-century Toba court: Whoever came first—Lord Lao or Buddha—must be the superior source of the religion. Building from sources like the story of the *Shiji*, the *Huahu jing* explains how Lord Lao finds his way to India and how he—or Yin Xi in some versions—becomes the Buddha.[10]

The interaction with Buddhism in the court debates and elsewhere resulted in a free exchange between Buddhism and Daoism. The Buddhist influence on Daoism cannot be overstated. For example, Lord Lao appears with the seventy-two signs and eighty-one auspicious marks on his body. These can be traced to the thirty-two signs and eighty marks of the Buddha. The numbers are simply adjusted to fit Daoist numerology.[11] The birth narrative, too, shows close links to the stories of Buddha's birth. By adopting the birth story and other elements of Buddhism, Daoism claims itself as a universal religion and Lord Lao as the seat of all creation and the source of all teachings.[12]

LUKE

Commonly accepted as being a two-part work, Luke-Acts is the largest portion of the New Testament. With its narrative style, Luke presents itself as a work of history that will assure a persecuted church of its divine, Jewish origin and of the reliability of its message. One of its sources is the Gospel of Mark, which is typically dated around 65–70 CE. Luke, therefore, appears after that, but it is unclear when.[13] A confident date is 85 CE plus or minus five to ten years.[14] Since the prologue discounts Luke as an eyewitness of the events he reports (Luke 1:1–4), and if one accepts the gospel's composition to be late in the first century, one can discern his purpose for writing the account: so his reader(s) Theophilus can trust in the truth of the teachings the author records (Luke 1:4). The need for reassurance resulted from the delay of the second coming of Christ and the persecution of the church. Though ostensibly writing for only one patron, Luke's account is an open letter and accessible to members of the community (communities) living around Greece.

Luke wants to assure the church that the Christian tradition is rooted in the second of three periods of salvation history. The first is the Period of Israel (creation to the appearance of John in Luke 1:5–31), followed by the Period of Jesus (from his baptism, through his public ministry, to his ascension), and then the Period of the Church under Stress (from the ascension to the *parousia*). Luke is writing during the third period for the purpose of raising the confidence of a suffering church in the presence and guidance of the Holy Spirit until the second coming.[15] The narrative style and logical order of Luke-Acts help communicate the message that God has not changed the divine plan with the coming of Christ, but has fulfilled it. The people of Israel were longing for a messiah; Luke says that Jesus of Nazareth fulfills that longing.[16]

A COMPARISON OF BIRTH NARRATIVES

What follows is a passage from the third version of the *Huahu jing* (early eighth century), compared side-by-side with passages from the second chapter of Luke.

Luke	*Huahu jing*
In the sixth month, the angel Gabriel was sent from God to a town of Galilee called Nazareth, to a virgin betrothed to a man named Joseph, of the house of David, and the virgin's name was Mary. (1:26–27)	In those days, in the reign of Tanjia of Yin with the year star in *gengshen*, in the month [. . .], the Highest Venerable Lord came down from the eternal realm of the Dao. He harnessed a cloud of three energies and strode on the essence of the sun. Following the rays of the nine luminaries, he entered into the mouth of the Jade Maiden of Mystery and Wonder. Taking refuge in her womb, he became a man.
In those days a decree went out from Caesar Augustus that the whole world should be enrolled. This was the first enrollment, when Quirinius was governor of Syria. (2:1–2)	

While they were there, the time came for her to have her child, and she gave birth to her firstborn son. She wrapped him in swaddling clothes and laid him in a manger, because there was no room for them in the inn. Now there were shepherds in that region living in the fields and keeping the night watch over their flock. The angel of the Lord appeared to them and the glory of the Lord shone around them, and they were struck with great fear. (6–9)

The angel said to them, "Do not be afraid; for behold, I proclaim to you good news of great joy that will be for all the people. (10)

For today in the city of David a savior has been born for you who is Messiah and Lord. (11)

And this will be a sign for you: you will find an infant wrapped in swaddling clothes and lying in a manger." And suddenly there was a multitude of the heavenly host with the angel, praising God . . . (12–13)[17]

After three days they found him in the temple, sitting in the midst of the teachers, listening to them and asking them questions and all who heard him were astounded at his understanding and his answers. (2:46–47)

In the year *gengshen*, on the fifteenth day of the second month, he was born in Bo. Nine dragons sprinkled water over him to rinse and wash his body then they transformed into nine springs.

At that time, the Venerable Lord had white hair. He was able to walk upon birth. A lotus flower sprouted under each step he took. After nine steps, he pointed to heaven with his left hand, to the earth with his right hand and announced to the people: "In heaven above, on the earth below, I alone am venerable. I shall reveal the highest law of the Dao. I shall save all things moving and growing, the entire host of living beings. I shall wander across the ten directions and reach to the dark prisons of the underworld. I shall lead all those not yet saved and all those lost in error to certain salvation."[18] (tr. Kohn 1993, 72)

The Birth of Lord Lao

The birth of Lord Lao is situated in history, even to the date and location, as is Jesus's birth in Luke (Luke 2:1ff). This date has become the standard date for the birth of Lord Lao, but it had changed over the centuries to meet needs of the time. For example, Lord Lao, the Zhou historian, is reported in the *Shiji* to be fleeing the corrupt Zhou Dynasty. The corruption reached a height when the Zhou king You fled east in 771 BCE, and so Lord Lao's westward emigration was linked to this low point of the Zhou Dynasty. However, if he is to be the source of Buddhism, his date of birth must be pushed further back. In contrast, his birthplace at Bozhou, first mentioned in the *Shiji*, has been constant.[19]

While the annunciation of Jesus to Mary is a subdued conversation with an angel, Lord Lao's conception is told with a spectacle of light and energies. He ends up, like Jesus, in a virgin's womb, where he becomes man. Other accounts of his birth have him emerging from the left side of the maiden, such as the left armpit or the hip. These birthing stories show a Chinese preference for the left, the side of *yang*.[20]

Dragons accompany his birth, which not only serve to represent nature—as do the presumed animals in Jesus's stable—but also angels, insofar as they are beings that travel as messengers between heaven and earth.[21] On the one hand, as representative of nature, the dragons signal the immanence of the Dao as it pulses through the entire cosmos. Classical texts, such as the *Daode jing* and the *Zhuangzi*, begin a tradition of viewing the mysterious Dao as something that cannot be grasped but only intuited. And the best place to intuit the Dao is in nature. For example, the symbolism in the *Daode jing* makes heavy use of agrarian images to describe the Dao and how people are to live in it. The result is a theology that presents the Dao as encompassing all of the cosmos and, like nature, as constantly changing. On the other hand, the dragons as emissaries between humankind and Heaven preserve the transcendence of the Dao. Lord Lao is coming to earth in the first place because it is in disharmony with the Dao and is drifting ever further from It.

At birth, Lord Lao has a hoary head. In a culture that values youthful vigor and long life, presenting a deity in this way may seem strange. He could, for instance, be born with a full head of black hair and a beard, and the author would clearly have distinguished the child. Indeed, Daoist iconography presents all gods and goddesses with jet-black hair, except Lord Lao. The tradition comes from his name, Lao, which literally means "old."[22] Other appellations attributed to Lord Lao in the *Shiji* include the first name, Er, and in the *Zhuangzi*, the first name of Dan. Both mean or imply "ear" or "rimless ears," indicating one with long ears. The reference has to do with the elderly possessing long ears, many years, and great wisdom.[23] Another indication of his extraordinary wisdom and unusual age is that immediately at birth, Lord Lao is able to walk and talk. Finally, he is identified as the savior of the world.

Birth and Childhood of Jesus in Luke

The passages in Luke that parallel the birth narrative of the *Huahu jing* are not all found in one chapter, but are scattered among the events of Jesus's conception, birth, and youth. Like Lord Lao, Jesus is divinely conceived (Luke 1:26–38), witnessed by nature by the animals in the stable (Luke 2:7) and by heaven (Luke 2:9–14), proclaimed the savior of the world (Luke 2:11), and recognized as having wisdom beyond his years (Luke 2:46–47).

Luke is often thought of as a work of history in a way the other gospels are not. However, it is not the intention of the author to record history, but to provide notes about the messiah for the believing community.[24] These notes are laid out logically and therefore read with a history book's order and richness. But having expectations of the gospel that one would attribute to modern history misunderstands the period in which Luke writes: the Period of the Church under Stress. The text on its own does not answer the historical question of "what really happened?" The events of the birth of Jesus are literary devices to indicate the uniqueness of the newborn child.[25] For example, Mary's virginity is never a matter of biological state. It is intended to be a statement about the wondrous person Jesus is. It is not Mariology but Christology.[26]

To begin, the conception is simply announced and accepted by Mary. There is no other explanation of how it took place than that. The narrative is placed in a historical context in 1:26, and it proclaims Jesus to be within the past history of Israel by placing him in the Davidic line (1:27; 32). In addition to the time of his birth, the place—Bethlehem, a town of David—is an affirmation of his Davidic heritage; it is the hometown of his Davidic father, Joseph.[27]

Jesus, by his divine birth, joins heaven and earth.[28] The divine being that is born is the savior of the world, not just a heavenly visitor. However, the child is not surrounded by thrones and comforts, but is close to nature in the manger, surrounded by the animals of the stable. Even the skies give witness through the heavenly host (Luke 2:9–14).

At the end of chapter 2 (Luke 2:41–52), Jesus, while a human boy, is shown to have remarkable abilities. His questions reveal his human intellect, and his answers reveal divine interpretation. Again, the divine child exceeds expectations, as he does later in his public ministry. His miracles and spiritual insight beg questions as to when and where he acquired such abilities. This passage answers that he acquired them from an early age,[29] and the reference to his Father points to his divine origins, as did the proclamation of Luke 1:35.

Divine Designation: An Examination of Titles

Luke	*Huahu jing*
Do not be afraid; for behold, I proclaim to you good news of great joy that will be for all the people. For today in the city of David a savior has been born for you who is Messiah and Lord. And this will be a sign for you: you will find an infant wrapped in swaddling clothes and lying in a manger. (2:10–12)	In heaven above, on the earth below, I alone am venerable. I shall reveal the highest law of the Dao. I shall save all things moving and growing, the entire host of living beings. I shall wander across the ten directions and reach to the dark prisons of the underworld. I shall lead all those not yet saved and all those lost in error to certain salvation.[30]

The authors of both Luke and the *Huahu jing* give images of events and characteristics of the descended deity to legitimate their claims that the child in each story will be different and will do something great. The Christian comparativist could read the *Huahu jing*'s claim that Lord Lao is the savior and discount him as a competitor to Jesus Christ, the unique savior of the world.

Another option is to acknowledge that the experience of a deity coming into the world is too fantastic for common words. The event is beyond our normal experience, so special words or literary devices are necessary to tell it.[31] A common device is the virgin birth story. Indeed, it is so ubiquitous that early missionaries concluded that Satan was planting these stories before them in order to mock them and undermine their efforts.[32]

Rather than being distracted by the particularities of the images, the reader is better served by considering more closely what these images are trying to convey. The language is drawing attention to the special identity of these people. But who is Jesus? Who is Lord Lao? And why are they here? The texts identify them as savior, lord, and in the case of Jesus, messiah.

Though Lord Lao and Jesus appear to be competing for the title of savior of the universe, such a competition may not be the case. A closer look at the key claims of the passages of the *Huahu jing* (Lord Lao as the bringer of salvation) and those cited in Luke 2:10–12 (Jesus as savior, lord, and messiah) brings into question whether Jesus and Lord Lao are competitors.

Title of Lord Lao

The idea of salvation as the end of earthly struggles was a radical shift in Chinese thought before the Han dynasty.[33] Up until that time, a Heavenly Mandate (*Tianming*) supported dynasties by empowering the sovereign to provide prosperity, security, and integrity. A dynasty arose when the ruler received a mandate (*ming*) from Heaven (*Tian*) and remained through the ruler cultivating his *de*, "virtue" or "power."[34] Upon wandering from the Dao and allowing his *de* to fade, the ruler would lose the Heavenly Mandate and watch his kingdom fall into chaos. Heaven would then bestow the mandate on the next dynasty, which would follow the next predictable fate of rise and fall.

In post-Han texts like the *Huahu jing*, Lord Lao brings harmony from chaos. He does so by making several appearances to rulers at times when they have wandered significantly. Upon following his divine teachings, the kingdom regains harmony with the Dao, prosperity returns, and Lord Lao ascends back to Heaven. In this way, Lord Lao brings salvation one episode at a time until the final kingdom of Great Peace (*Taiping*) blooms, and a perfect harmony with the Dao endures on earth. Examples of his appearances range from the god's revelations to Confucius during the Zhou Dynasty; to Emperors Wen, Wu, and Huan of the Han; Gan Ji of the Great Peace movements; Zhang Daoling of the Celestial Masters; and many others.[35]

The state of Great Peace is the ideal of Chinese society. Historically, this ideal is first sought in small, utopian communities; once attained there, cosmic harmony will resonate from that community out into the empire. Ultimately, the harmony will spread to include not only the human realm, but also harmony with Heaven and Earth. The Chinese saw the Tang Dynasty—commonly thought of as the Golden Age of Chinese culture—as the fulfillment of the state of Great Peace.[36]

Lord Lao's appearance on earth, acceptance of disciples, and movement to the west were, according to the *Huahu jing*, for the purpose of moving the cosmos toward the Great Peace promised to the first Celestial Master, Zhang Daoling, in 142 CE. These attributes—savior, advisor to monarchs, and divinity—are reflected in the many titles given to him in the *Huahu Jing*:

Highest Venerable Lord
Perfect Divine Wisdom
All-Highest Worthy
Teacher of Emperors and Kings
Great Officer
Great Immortal Worthy
Father of Gods and Peoples
Highest One of Nonaction
Great Compassionate and Benevolent One
Heavenly Worthy of Primordial Beginning[37]

These titles reflect his divine status and characteristics, such as source of perfect wisdom (Perfect Divine Wisdom) and all personalities (Father of Gods and Peoples). The final title, Heavenly Worthy of Primordial Beginning, identifies him as an exalted god from whom the world itself was formed in the first *kalpa*, known as Red Illumination, when he revealed sacred scriptures in heavenly script beyond any human tongue. The revelations were translated into human language by an assisting deity, the Lord of the Dao, and came into the possession of the Numinous Treasure School of Daoism. The scriptures themselves were the Numinous Treasure.[38]

Having titles and names, as well as a body, make the god accessible and human-like but still the tangible embodiment of the mysterious Dao. He can act in human affairs and help human history along toward fulfillment of Great Peace. As fantastic as this is, one must remember that the entire cosmos is the Dao, so Lord Lao is not a transcendent god who has touched down on Earth, but is the face of the Dao, a personality who resonates with the Dao so perfectly that he can be considered one and the same. Ordinary people are also the Dao, but in such dissonance that any comparison is nonsensical.

As an advisor to the king, the Lord Lao serves as one component of the king-sage binary in the human realm. The king has wandered from the Dao to such a great extent that he is driving the kingdom to destruction. In contrast, Lord Lao is the great counselor, hero, and savior of the kingdom. This binary appears most clearly in the *Huahu jing*'s story of the conversion of the barbarians in the west. The ignorant king cannot recognize Lord Lao as the divinity he is, and so, Lord Lao reveals his powers to the consequently humbled king. Not ready for the full revelation of the Dao, the king is instructed to discontinue his misguided behavior by following precepts revealed by the god. These precepts, the *Huahu jing* asserts, are the origins of Buddhism.[39]

The message is that the Dao is a part of humanity and involved in its affairs:

> [The Dao] supports good government and increases the ruler's benevolence; it lovingly helps those who believe and rescues them from harm. At the same time, it will not be mocked and ruthlessly puts down its enemies, reigning victorious even in the most desperate situations. The Dao, then, not only encompasses all aspects of the world when seen in cosmological perspective, it also mediates all movements and activities. Within the world of humanity, it also shows the power of good and stands for the civilizing, beneficent force that inspires rulers.[40]

Jesus as Savior, Lord, and Messiah

Luke 2:10–12 provides important titles that tell the reader who Jesus is: savior, messiah, and lord.[41] For convenience, lord appears before messiah below, although Luke gives them in the opposite order.

The first title, savior (*soter*), appears for the first time with reference to Jesus in Luke, and Luke is the only one of the synoptic gospels to use it (Luke 2:11; Acts 5:31; 13:23).[42] The title combines elements of the secular and the sacred.[43] Used often in the Greco-Roman world, "savior" referred to gods, philosophers, physicians, statesmen, kings, and emperors. For example, Julius Caesar was called "god manifest and common savior of human life" on an Ephesian inscription, and "savior" was applied to Caesar Augustus as well.[44]

The sacred element comes from Luke's use of the Septuagint, the Greek version of the Hebrew Scriptures. There, *soter* is used for the Hebrew *mosia*, "savior," to refer to both individuals whom God chooses for the deliverance of Israel (for example, the judges of Judges 3:9, 15) and to God as deliverer (1 Sam. 10:19; Isa. 45:15, 21). The title thus relates Jesus to God as referred to in Luke 1:47 and 69.

Influenced by both the secular and the sacred background, Christians used "savior" early on (for example, Paul's use of it for Jesus in Phil. 3:20). The message of this bivalent term is that Jesus is to bring peace to earth and heaven alike. Curiously, the term is used in the Period of the Church under Stress, but it is noticeably missing from the Period of Jesus.[45]

"The lord" ([*ho*] *kyrios*) or "lord" (*kyrios*) also has secular and sacred aspects. It is the most frequently used title for Jesus, even more so than "messiah" or *christos*. The secular aspect is similar to that of *soter* in the sense that it was used in reference to both gods and rulers as the source of power in the Greco-Roman world.[46]

Likewise, the sacred element is similar to that of "savior" in that Jesus and God (YHWH) are connected by this title. Some scholars have traced the early Christian use of *kyrios* for God to the Septuagint. Although pre-Lucan texts such as Mark and Q establish the use of *kyrios* for God among the Christian communities, *kyrios* only refers to God in Christian copies of the Septuagint dating from the fourth century on. In pre-Christian Greek translations of the Hebrew text, "God" was written in the Hebrew. Some evidence does point to a pre-Christian, Jewish practice in Palestine to speak of God as *adon*, "lord," or *mara* and *marya* in Aramaic. Using *kyrios* for Jesus would then put him on the same level as God—though Luke never directly identifies him with the Godhead, because he never refers to Jesus as *abba* or as *despota*, "sovereign Lord," a title exclusively used for the Godhead (Luke 2:29; Acts 4:24).[47]

By using *kyrios* for both Jesus and God, Luke is situating himself within an established tradition in the early church. By retrojecting *kyrios* into the birth narrative, Luke is claiming Jesus as a transcendent and as dominant over the nations.[48]

The third element, messiah or christ (*christos*), however, is entirely Jewish and wholly sacred. It comes from Palestinian Judaism and the Old Testament *masiah*, which the Septuagint translates as *christos*. English renders these as "anointed one." Although it is not used with the frequency of *kyrios* in Luke-Acts, its importance is clear from three usages: Jesus invoking the title in reference to himself (Luke 24:26), its coupling with the word for "name" such that it becomes part of Jesus's name, "Jesus Christ," and its designation for Jesus's followers as "Christians" (Acts 11:26; 26:28).[49]

The Old Testament uses *masiah* for kings. By Jesus's time, its meaning expanded to reflect an expected agent of God in the Davidic line for the restoration of Israel and for the establishment of God's kingdom. Perhaps because of its political implications, the title is not used frequently in the New Testament. Ironically, what solidified the title was Pilate's use of it for Jesus on the cross (Mark 15:26).[50]

What is unusual is how Luke places the term "messiah" in juxtaposition with the terms "savior" and "lord." Savior and lord were used widely in the Greek world with reference to imperial power, which throws a striking contrast to the Davidic messiah.[51] What is also unusual, and peculiar to Luke, is connection of the messiah with glory (the glory of the angels, references to Isaiah 40's proclamation of the glory of the Lord). Salvation and glory lead the reader to consider a kingly reign.[52] For Luke, "glory means kingly reign, a king who is also a servant. He delegates his kingdom, enters his glory by his death and resurrection, and rises to his throne."[53] So up to that time, scripture was taken to pre-figure the long awaited messiah, but Luke portrays Jesus as the king of Israel, due to the bivalence of the two terms savior and lord and to the meaning of messiah, which is specific to Israel.[54] Furthermore, although Luke mostly uses the title for Jesus during his ministry, he also uses it during the resurrection (Acts 2:32, 36) and in the announcement of his birth (Luke 2:11). Significantly, *christos* is also used to refer to the Jesus of the *parousia* in Acts 3:19–21, which is the only such reference in the New Testament.[55]

This messiah, Jesus, has come down with the intention of bringing the good news of his kingdom: a kingdom that had come in part during his own time, but is yet to come more fully in a new heaven and a new earth. He establishes the kingdom through his birth, ministry, death, and resurrection, and in his future second coming.

Other titles for Jesus in Luke-Acts are:

Son of God
Son of Man
Servant
Prophet
King (*basileus*)
Son of David

Leader
Holy One
Righteous One
Teacher
God (perhaps)[56]

Lord Lao and Jesus Christ Compared

While the narrative of the birth of the savior may travel across traditions in a general way, the titles are more specific to identifying *these* saviors. Both are identified as the individual with the power to save. The use of the *Huahu jing* in the Toba court debates places Lord Lao's saving activity in the political realm. Luke's use of titles that have both political and sacred applications—savior and lord—also render a politically charged message. Of course, for first-century Palestinian Jews, "messiah" was also a politically charged term with a use specific for the people of Israel. Therefore, messiah—although exclusive to the religion of the Jews—does not remain there. It breaks into the political realm. Likewise, one should not read the *Huahu jing* as identifying Lord Lao as exclusively an advisor to kings. Lord Lao, the embodiment of the Dao, demonstrates the power of the Dao running throughout the kingdom and cosmos.

The religious, metaphysical claim that the Daoists make for the superiority of their political philosophy is the power of the Dao. By having Lord Lao convert the Indians, the Daoists assert their triumph over Buddhism. In a less polemical way, the birth narrative of Luke makes similar universalist claims by placing the Jewish-specific title of messiah side-by-side with savior and lord—titles the Christian community now shares with the Greco-Roman world. Here, however, the Church under Stress uses the titles to assure those within the Christian community that God's saving plan of the Old Testament is fulfilled in the birth of Jesus, not to convince those outside the Christian community of Jesus's superiority. Moreover, the saving plan includes the Greco-Roman Gentiles.

The similarities of the political and universal claims of the birth narratives serve to heighten the tension in the concept of salvation. The ostensible challenge Lord Lao, in this birth narrative, brings to the uniqueness of Jesus Christ hinges on who is doing the saving; however, salvation means different things to each text. For the *Huahu jing* and Daoism, Lord Lao saves kingdoms from chaos, collapse, and general disharmony with the Dao. Because Lord Lao reveals through Daoism, the Toba should adopt the Daoist political philosophy. It is the higher and older source of wisdom over Buddhism. At best, Buddhism might only allow for a slower demise of the kingdom. Daoism alone can bring about the ideal of the Great Peace.

Salvation in Christianity emphasizes a healing of a cosmic wound, which occurred shortly after creation and separated humanity from its transcendent creator.[57] Christ's life, death, and resurrection achieve the healing of this wound. He has established the Kingdom of God, a Kingdom that will come more perfectly at his second coming at the end of time, the *parousia*. Thus, in the Christian view of history, Jesus Christ came once in the past and will come once and for all in the future. The second coming will be that of the apocalypse when the world will come to an end and will be replaced by "a new Heaven and a new Earth" (Revelation 21:1).

In contrast to this end, the Daoist world continues eternally with Lord Lao descending from above to re-tune kingdoms to the flow of the Dao. The Dao is never really separate from Earth. Its re-harmonizing ("saving") activity, through Lord Lao, is ongoing. Furthermore, as advisor to kings, Lord Lao, despite his exalted status, never replaces the king or directly fixes royal problems. Instead, the human king must accept and follow the advice of the sage to establish Great Peace. Lord Lao's saving activity works through the king who is responsible for carrying it out. Indeed, the ultimate purpose of the *Huahu jing* is to persuade the Toba rulers to do just that.

One cannot understand salvation without being aware of what one is being saved from and what one is being saved for. In the *Huahu jing*, Lord Lao saves from political disharmony for the Chinese ideal of the Great Peace. In Luke-Acts, Jesus saves from the separation from God for a sharing in God's divine life fully at the end of time. Lord Lao and Jesus Christ therefore are not competing for the same soteriological space.[58]

Perhaps more importantly, however, the Christian looking at Lord Lao's birth in the *Huahu jing* may be reminded that God's saving activity is not entirely an event of the past for the purpose of an otherworldly kingdom of the future. The observation highlights two points of Christian spirituality.

First, the saving activity of Christ is ongoing in *this* world. The Daoist worldview calls the Christian to appreciate the rich sacramental tradition that emphasizes the experience of God's grace through people, events, and the cosmos here and now. Indeed, long before the ink dried on Luke-Acts or any of the scriptures, God revealed through people and creation. The authors of the Bible continue this revelation by using the language of the natural world, the skies, agriculture, shepherding, and the like. Sacramental spirituality is world affirming; the world is the mediator of God's revelation.

Second, the king-sage binary calls attention to how harmony with the Dao comes through the work of the king; it does not happen on its own. Likewise, God, while active in history, does not overcome human freedom. The peace and justice of the Kingdom of God comes through human activity, and Christians should not presume upon the *parousia* and merely wait for justice. The *Huahu jing* serves to remind Christians that social justice and works of mercy are primarily the responsibility of human beings. The birth of Jesus Christ, his ministry, and resurrection are demonstrations of proper human activity, not substitutes for it.

In other words, people act in human history and in this sacred universe, into which God constantly enters. Christ's embodiment means that the world is actively involved in God's divinizing work. The entire cosmos is moving toward fulfillment—that is, an end—in God. Furthermore, people take part in that fulfillment. People's activities divinize the world.[59]

That said, the titles in the *Huahu jing* provoke attention to the politically charged titles for Christ in Luke's birth narrative. Examination of these titles and the function of Lord Lao may serve as a possible model for resolving the tensions between low and high Christologies. Human activities bring about a politics that serves the common good and works for justice, as a low Christology supports. In this way, one sees the application of Jesus as savior and lord in the Greco-Roman, political sense of sovereign and the Jewish sense of deliverer. When people act in a Jesus-like manner, they participate in establishing the Kingdom of God here and now.

At the same time, that activity shares in the divine life of Christ, the savior, lord, and messiah in the sacred dimensions of those terms. The relationship between politics now—represented by a low Christology—and salvation at the *parousia*—a high Christology—is analogous. Analogical language presents two instances that are not the same, but that hold a real relationship.[60] The low Christology of Jesus as political activist and the high Christology of Christ as God are referring to the one and the same Jesus Christ. One need not feel forced to prefer the sacred dimensions of Jesus's titles in Luke's birth narrative over the political or secular dimensions as if to do so would deny the divine nature of Christ. Lord Lao in the *Huahu jing* demonstrates such a possibility in Daoism. He is both advisor to kings and the personification of the Dao.

Conclusion

This experiment of reading the birth narratives of Lord Lao and Jesus Christ side-by-side has demonstrated three things. First, the Christian reader should not panic when faced with similarities that strike the nerve of Christian religious commitment. One need not ignore religious difference ("all religions are the same"), nor be dismissive of the other tradition ("your birth narrative is a fictional story, but mine is true"). The comparative method of close reading across traditions allows the reader to discover, or re-discover, insights from within his or her home tradition. Research can distance similarities that initially appear to challenge the uniqueness of Christ. Of particular importance is to note the differing contexts of each text. Aside from obvious distance of time, geography, and culture, the Daoist text is directed outwardly as a polemic for asserting religious triumph over its Buddhist rivals; the Christian text is addressed inwardly to a believing community to assure them of God's salvific plan. Given these differences along with the different systems of salvation, Lord Lao of the *Huahu jing* makes no threat to the uniqueness of Christ. The context and the function of the savior figures are vastly different in each case.

Second, with the help of Lord Lao, the Christian reader observes that Christ's birth signals the affirmation of the world and of the human responsibility to participate in and bring about its fulfillment. Salvation is not only something won by Jesus in the past, to be fulfilled in the future, but also an ongoing healing that involves human activity.

Third, Lord Lao calls our attention to the titles for Jesus in Luke's birth narrative. Lord Lao, as both politically active and divinely ultimate, provides a model for reconciling the supposed polarity between the secular and sacred dimensions of savior, lord, and messiah. Jesus is politically present when we participate in Christ-like political activity, just as he is present as the Second Person of the Trinity. Such a model eases the tension often perceived between low and high Christologies.

Notes

1. Livia Kohn, *The Taoist Experience* (Albany, N.Y.: SUNY Press, 1993), 72.
2. For a variety of approaches to divine embodiment, see the collection of essays in *Studies in Interreligious Dialogue* listed as Bede Benjamin Bidlack, et. al. "Divine Embodiment in a Comparative Perspective," *Studies in Interreligious Dialogue* 22.2 (2012): 133–91. My contribution in the journal is an anthropological approach rather than the Christological approach I take here. For a study of Lord Lao as the embodied Dao in relation to Jesus, the embodied God, see Kohn "Embodiment and Transcendence in Medieval Taoism."
3. Livia Kohn, "Embodiment and Transcendence in Medieval Taoism," in *The Chinese Face of Jesus Christ*, ed. Roman Malek, S.V.D. (Netherlands: Insitut Monmenta Seriva and China Zentrum Sankt Augustin, 2002).
4. Livia Kohn, *God of the Dao: Lord Lao in History and Myth* (Ann Arbor, Mich.: Center for Chinese Studies, The University of Michigan, 1998), 2. For a summary of Lord Lao's transformation, see Livia Kohn, "The Lao-Tzu Myth," in *Lao-Tzu and the Tao-Te-Ching*, ed. Liva Kohn and Michael LaFargue (Albany, N.Y.: SUNY Press, 1998), 41–62.
5. Livia Kohn, "The Northern Celestial Masters," in *Daoism Handbook*, ed. Livia Kohn (Leiden: E. Brill, 2000), 287.
6. Kohn, "The Northern Celestial Masters," 295.
7. Kohn, *God of the Dao*.
8. Kohn, "The Northern Celestial Masters," 295, 298–301.
9. Kohn, *God of the Dao*, 238.
10. However, it takes little historical criticism to notice that the story, at least, has its origins in Buddhism and not the other way around. Anachronism is not this chapter's concern.
11. Livia Kohn, "The Looks of Laozi," *Asian Folklore Studies* 55.2 (1996): 193–236.
12. Kohn, "The Northern Celestial Masters," 299.
13. Joseph A. Fitzmyer, *The Gospel According to Luke: Introduction, Translation, and Notes*, 1st ed., 2 vols, *The Anchor Bible* (Garden City, N.Y.: Doubleday, 1981), 53.
14. Raymond E. Brown, *An Introduction to the New Testament* (New York: Doubleday, 1997), 274.
15. Fitzmyer, *The Gospel According to Luke*, 182–83.
16. Brown, *An Introduction to the New Testament*, 272.
17. The Presentation in the Temple (Luke 2:21–40) has no parallel in the *Huahu jing*, so this discussion omits it. For the sake of brevity, the introduction to Jesus's parents finding him in the Temple when he was a boy (Luke 2:41–45) is also omitted.
18. Kohn, *The Taoist Experience*, 72.
19. Kohn, *God of the Dao*, 237–28.
20. Kohn, *God of the Dao*, 241.
21. Kohn, "Embodiment and Transcendence in Medieval Taoism," 82. See also Kohn, *God of the Dao*.
22. Laozi translates as "old child." The *Huahu jing* gives a literal interpretation of that.
23. Kohn, *God of the Dao*, 246.
24. Brown, *An Introduction to the New Testament*, 227.

25. Fitzmyer, *The Gospel According to Luke*, 335–36.
26. Fitzmyer, *The Gospel According to Luke*, 340–42.
27. Fitzmyer, *The Gospel According to Luke*, 393.
28. Brown, *An Introduction to the New Testament*, 229.
29. Brown, *An Introduction to the New Testament*, 234.
30. Kohn, *The Taoist Experience*, 72.
31. Fitzmyer, *The Gospel According to Luke*, 179. See also Francis X. Clooney, S.J., *Seeing through Texts: Doing Theology among the Srivaisnavas of South India* (Albany, N.Y.: SUNY Press, 1996), 266.
32. Joseph Campbell, *The Hero with a Thousand Faces* (New York: Pantheon Books, 1949), 309. The birth narrative in hero myths has been explored by both religious studies scholars, such as Campbell, as well as scholars of other disciplines, such as C. G. Jung. See C. G. Jung, "The Psychology of the Child Archetype," in *Essays on a Science of Mythology*, ed. C. G. Jung and Karl Kerényi (New York: Pantheon Books, 1950). For a summary of the scholarship in relation to Lord Lao, see Kohn, *God of the Dao*, 250–52; for the hero pattern and Jesus, see, for example, Alan Dundes, "The Hero Pattern and the Life of Jesus," in *In Quest of the Hero* (Princeton: Princeton University Press, 1990), 177–223.
33. This was such a radical shift that an outside influence cannot be ruled out. Kohn, *God of the Dao*, 308, note 22.
34. This is the same *de* as the famous *Daode jing*, *The Book of the Way and Virtue*.
35. Kohn, *God of the Dao*, 330.
36. The Tang Dynasty rulers traced their family name Li to Lord Lao, and sought to follow his divine teachings. See Kohn, *God of the Dao*, 330.
37. Kohn, *God of the Dao*, 249; Kohn, *The Taoist Experience*, 72–73.
38. Stephen R. Bokenkamp, with a contribution by Peter S. Nickerson, *Early Daoist Scriptures* (Berkeley: University of California Press, 1997), 376, 380–81.
39. Kohn, *God of the Dao*, 332.
40. Kohn, *God of the Dao*, 333.
41. The name "Jesus" means "God help!" but tradition understands it as "God saves." See Fitzmyer, *The Gospel According to Luke*, 347.
42. Fitzmyer, *The Gospel According to Luke*, 181.
43. Mark Coleridge, *The Birth of the Lukan Narrative: Narrative as Christology in Luke 1–2* (Sheffield: Sheffield Academic Press, 1993), 140.
44. Fitzmyer, *The Gospel According to Luke*, 204.
45. Fitzmyer, *The Gospel According to Luke*, 204.
46. Coleridge, *The Birth of the Lukan Narrative*, 141.
47. Fitzmyer, *The Gospel According to Luke*, 201–2.
48. Fitzmyer, *The Gospel According to Luke*, 203.
49. Fitzmyer, *The Gospel According to Luke*, 197.
50. Fitzmyer, *The Gospel According to Luke*, 197–98.
51. Coleridge, "The Birth of the Lukan Narrative," 141.
52. A. R. C. Leany, *A Commentary of the Gospel According to St. Luke* (London: Adam & Charles Black, 1966), 36.
53. Coleridge, *The Birth of the Lukan Narrative*, 140.

54. Leany, *A Commentary of the Gospel According to St. Luke*, 36.
55. Fitzmyer, *The Gospel According to Luke*, 198–200.
56. Fitzmyer, *The Gospel According to Luke*, 205–19.
57. "Salvation" comes from the Latin *salus*, meaning "to heal."
58. For an overview of the different problems proposed by religions of the world and their proposed solutions, see Stephen R. Prothero, *God Is Not One: The Eight Rival Religions That Run the World—and Why Their Differences Matter* (New York: HarperOne, 2010).
59. Of course, people's activities tear the world apart as well, but these reflections upon the birth narratives do not address that. For these observations, I am grateful to the work of Pierre Teilhard de Chardin and Thomas Berry.
60. On the relationship between participation, analogy, and politics, see David Grumett, "Metaphysics, Morality, and Politics," in *From Teilhard to Omega: Co-Creating an Unfinished Universe*, ed. Ilia Delio (Maryknoll, N.Y.: Orbis Books, 2014), 111–26.

11 Who Is the Suffering Servant?

A COMPARATIVE THEOLOGICAL
READING OF ISAIAH 53
AFTER THE SHOAH

Marianne Moyaert

The years after the Shoah saw a growing awareness of a connection between two thousand years of Christian anti-Judaism and certain Christological beliefs. Rosemary Radford Ruether expressed this cogently in her claim that "anti-Judaism is the left hand of Christology."[1] This chapter is a contribution to the construction of a Christology after the Shoah, based on a comparative theological reading of Isaiah 53 and its Jewish and Christian commentaries.

Isaiah 53 played an important role in Christianity's self-definition as it parted ways with Judaism, and it continued to have an impact far into the Middle Ages in theological-hermeneutical disputes between Jews and Christians. After the Shoah, in light of the suffering inflicted on the Jewish people in the name of Christ, the question "Who is then the suffering servant?" gains a new significance that challenges and criticizes the triumphalism of mainstream Christology. If it can be said that the suffering of Christ led to a problematic reinterpretation of God's covenant with Israel, this chapter argues that the suffering of Israel must now lead to a revaluation of the role of Isaiah 53 in Christology.

THE SUFFERING SERVANT (ISAIAH 52:13–53:12)
13 See, my servant shall prosper;
he shall be exalted and lifted up,
and shall be very high.
14 Just as there were many who were astonished at him
—so marred was his appearance, beyond human semblance,
and his form beyond that of mortals—
15 so he shall startle many nations;
kings shall shut their mouths because of him;

for that which had not been told them they shall see,
and that which they had not heard they shall contemplate.
53/1 Who has believed what we have heard?
And to whom has the arm of the LORD been revealed?
2 For he grew up before him like a young plant,
and like a root out of dry ground;
he had no form or majesty that we should look at him.
He was despised and rejected by others;
a man of suffering and acquainted with infirmity;
and as one from whom others hide their faces
he was despised, and we held him of no account.
4 Surely he has borne our infirmities
and carried our diseases;
yet we accounted him stricken,
struck down by God, and afflicted.
5 But he was wounded for our transgressions,
crushed for our iniquities;
upon him was the punishment that made us whole,
and by his bruises we are healed.
All we like sheep have gone astray;
we have all turned to our own way,
and the LORD has laid on him
the iniquity of us all.
7 He was oppressed, and he was afflicted,
yet he did not open his mouth;
like a lamb that is led to the slaughter,
and like a sheep that before its shearers is silent,
so he did not open his mouth.
8 By a perversion of justice he was taken away.
Who could have imagined his future?
For he was cut off from the land of the living,
stricken for the transgression of my people.
9 They made his grave with the wicked
and his tomb with the rich,
although he had done no violence,
and there was no deceit in his mouth.
10 Yet it was the will of the LORD to crush him with pain.
When you make his life an offering for sin,
he shall see his offspring, and shall prolong his days;

through him the will of the Lord shall prosper.
11 Out of his anguish he shall see light;
he shall find satisfaction through his knowledge.
The righteous one, my servant, shall make many righteous,
and he shall bear their iniquities.
12 Therefore I will allot him a portion with the great,
and he shall divide the spoil with the strong;
because he poured out himself to death,
and was numbered with the transgressors;
yet he bore the sin of many,
and made intercession for the transgressors.

The suffering servant refers to a figure that appears in four songs in the book of Isaiah.[2] These songs can probably be attributed to Deutero-Isaiah, the "second" Isaiah who appeared on the scene at the end of the Babylonian Exile (586–539 BCE) and wrote, according to critical exegesis, chapters 40–55. These songs sing a particularly difficult idea, namely, that of vicarious suffering. This is the idea that someone (who is he?) intervenes and takes the burden of the sins of the world on himself and thus brings redemption (53:4–6). He fulfills God's will with this vicarious suffering. The following elements seem particularly important if theologians are to speak of vicarious suffering.

The suffering servant is himself innocent and righteous (53:9). It seems that he can only act vicariously because he is righteous and because he himself has no guilt (53:11). It is also striking that he does not protest but quietly receives his afflictions. The passive language in this song stands out: he is "despised," "stricken," "struck down," "oppressed," "afflicted," and "led to slaughter." At the same time, however, it seems that the suffering servant does not simply submit to his lot but instead shoulders it and willingly assumes it. There is a play between passive and active language. Verse 4b states: "Surely he has borne our infirmities and carried our diseases." He bears the pain, suffering, sin, and sorrow of others—he assumes the yoke of others.

This suffering servant is rejected and humiliated; there is nothing that might lead one to think that he is beloved of God. Every form of glory or majesty is foreign to him (53:2–3); there is nothing attractive about him. This person is despised by "others" (the kings of the nations) but he is nonetheless loved by God. The special relationship between God and the servant is central in the idea of vicarious suffering.

He has not chosen his lot; rather, he has been elected and accepts his lot. God's will and the will of the suffering servant seem to be one. That is why a better future awaits the suffering servant. It is said about him: "See, my servant shall prosper; he shall be exalted and lifted up, and shall be very high" (53:1, cf. 53:12).

The Suffering Servant between Church and Synagogue

This prophetic text has been at the center of the conflict between synagogue and church right up to the present. This conflict concerns, to a certain extent, the "right" interpretation of the Jewish scriptures after the coming of Christ. The claim that Jesus was the suffering servant entails a fundamental reinterpretation of these writings that are now called the Old Testament by Christians.[3] The difficult relationship between Judaism and Christianity can truly be felt in interpretations of Isaiah 53: The Jew Jesus of Nazareth unites and divides Christians and Jews.

CHRISTIAN INTERPRETATIONS

In the prevailing Christian hermeneutic, Christ's life, suffering, and resurrection function as the hermeneutical key for understanding the Old Testament. The underlying idea is that the Old Testament must be read as prophecy about the coming of Jesus the Christ, understood as the Messiah. Although this hermeneutic can be criticized from a historical-critical perspective, it still receives a great deal of support in Christian faith communities where it is confirmed week after week in the liturgy of the Word.[4] Such preaching cultivates a kind of direct, uninterrupted, and continuous connection between "Old Testament prophecies" and the suffering, death, and resurrection of Jesus Christ. Christians *cannot*, it seems, understand the suffering servant in any other way than as a Messianic prediction of the coming of Jesus Christ, the Son of God (see, for example, Matt. 8:17, 12:18–21; Acts 8:30–33; Mark 15:28; Luke 22:37, 24:26, 24:46).

The almost seamless transition that is suggested between Isaiah 53:10–11 and Philippians 2:5–8 and Mark 10:42–45 is well known. The idea developed here is that through his obedience unto death, Jesus assumed the role of the suffering servant who gave his life as an atoning sacrifice. Christ's "vicarious suffering" receives a messianic, and thus salvific interpretation.[5] Central to this Christology is the idea that Jesus must be seen as a voluntary sacrifice for the salvation of those who believe he is the Savior sent from God. The fact that the prophecy of the suffering servant is read in its entirety on Good Friday contributes to the dramatics of this Christological interpretation.[6] Many Christians view Isaiah 53 as one of the clearest prophecies of Jesus the Messiah and find it difficult, from that point of view, to understand why their reading is rejected by Jews.[7]

JEWISH INTERPRETATIONS

Jewish commentaries interpret the text of Isaiah 53 in divergent ways. There is no unanimity on the question of who *the suffering servant* is. The Jewish commentaries are, for the most part, divided between individual and collective interpretations. According to the dominant interpretation, the figure of the suffering servant is understood in a collective sense: It is Israel, the beloved people of God, who has suffered and endured much under foreign heathen kings and nations.[8] Israel's destiny, to be a light in the world as the chosen people, is a heavy burden. The song of the suffering servant is a parable that describes Israel's collective experience of suffering. This collective reading accords with other passages in Isaiah (such as 41:8–9; 44:1; 44:21; 45:4; 48:20; 49:20) which, indeed, speak of Jacob/Israel as the suffering servant.

The innocence of Israel is important in this collective interpretation. The expectation that is cultivated here is that the foreign oppressors will open their eyes in the messianic end times and see that the suffering inflicted upon the Jews is not the result of Jewish sinfulness but of the oppressors' "trespasses" and "unrighteousness." This presents, as in the story of Job, an indictment against unjust suffering and especially against those who claim that whoever suffers must have sinned. In the end, these foreign nations will see that Israel always remained faithful to God and, conversely, that God has always remained faithful to Israel. The surprise will be unprecedented: "so he shall startle many nations; kings shall shut their mouths because of him; for that which had not been told them they shall see, and that which they had not heard they shall contemplate. Who has believed what we have heard?" (52:15); they will see how God "will lay bare his holy arm in the sight of all the nations, and all the ends of the earth will see the salvation of our God" (52:10). The suffering of the Jewish people has a "redeeming power" for all of humanity. This interpretation is not followed in the Christian tradition, and as a result, the theological meaning of Jewish suffering is denied in Christianity, while the suffering of Christ becomes the cornerstone of the Christian creed.

Next to the dominant collective readings, of the Jewish commentaries that see the suffering servant as an individual, most still do not imply a messianic interpretation. In some commentaries, the suffering servant is identified with the prophet Jeremiah, Hezekiah, or Isaiah himself. In 1 Enoch 71:14–17, a first-century CE Jewish composition, Enoch is given the title of Servant. Still, there are a few Jewish commentaries that *do* apply a messianic interpretation to the suffering servant, the most important being the Babylonian Talmud, where one can read in a discussion on the Messiah: "'The leper,' those of the house of Rabbi said: 'The sick one' is his name; for it is written: 'Surely he hath borne our griefs, and carried our sorrows: yet we did esteem him stricken with leprosy, smitten of God, and afflicted.'" Messianic interpretations of this kind circulated in the inter-testamental period, and the first Christians themselves (and possibly Jesus) interpreted and understood the death of Christ in that sense.[9]

The Jewish No and Christological Supersessionism

A central theme in the messianic hope of the Jews is that the messianic redemption and liberation happens in the here and now and is thus very much part of this world. Many Jews saw (and see) Jesus's death as a contraindication to the claim that he is the Messiah who would liberate Israel (Luke 24:21). It is possible that Jesus saw himself as the Messiah, but he was mistaken: He did not do what a messiah was expected to do—liberate Palestine from Roman oppression and restore the Davidic golden age.[10] For Jewish interpreters, the Christological reading of the suffering servant, which sees Jesus as the Messiah, is intuitively unacceptable. If Jesus is the redeemer, the savior sent by God, so they have wondered for centuries, why is the world still "unredeemed"? Jews—and they have every reason—do not share the Christian optimism of salvation. Martin Buber speaks in this context of an inability to accept Christ: "We know more deeply, more truly, that world history has not been turned upside down to its very foundations—that the world is not yet redeemed. We *sense* its unredeemedness."[11] From a Jewish perspective, Jesus is a false or failed messiah.[12]

The Christological claim, however, that Jesus *did fulfill* the messianic hope of Isaiah 53 led to ecclesiological triumphalism: The church superseded Israel as God's chosen people. The implication of this theology is that there is no longer any place for Israel in God's plan of salvation. Israel's role in the history of revelation and redemption has been written out of the world's script forever. This supersessionist theology very quickly assumed a prominent role in Christian thinking. It is thus not surprising that it formed an undisputed element for centuries of Christian doctrine in both the Western and Eastern churches. For two thousand years, Christianity cultivated an anti-Jewish polemic, traces of which can already be found in the gospels. These traces were continued by various church fathers and were impressed on the collective memory of Christian "civilization" via sermons, theological pamphlets, art, and popular culture.[13]

Although a distinction can be made (and should be made) between Christian anti-Judaism and Nazi anti-Semitism, as the Jewish document Dabru Emet (2002) also agrees, it is clear that the Nazi ideology could never have proliferated as it did at the heart of European civilization without the long history of Christian anti-Jewish views and anti-Jewish acts of violence that resulted.[14] It is quite simply the case that Christian anti-Judaism constituted the soil in which Nazism could take root and ultimately led to the destruction of two-thirds of European Jews. For Jews, the Christ figure expressed everything but the promise of salvation and rescue: It was much more a symbol for the suffering that was inflicted on them in his name. Many no longer want to hear his name, let alone that God is worshipped in his name.[15]

Christology after the Shoah

The shadow of Christian complicity in this genocide undermines the credibility of Christians who still speak about liberation, salvation, and redemption in the name of Christ. According to Harry Cargas, Christians should not underestimate the importance of the Shoah; this tragedy invokes a number of fundamental questions that touch the heart of the Christian tradition, in particular Christology.[16] The question of the identity of the suffering servant needs to be asked again. What can Isaiah 53 still mean in light of the Shoah? What can Christ's vicarious suffering mean when his followers have caused such immense suffering? Can Christians still claim with any shred of credibility to be disciples of the Christ who fulfilled the prophecy of the suffering servant, in light of the Shoah? We will need to revisit this text after the Shoah. However, before we can begin to examine this difficult contested text anew, we first need to try to get more of a handle on the complexity of comparative readings in a post-Holocaust setting. More precisely, this section will clarify how a comparative reading that does not take into account the location from which the comparative post-Holocaust theologian speaks risks ending, however unintentionally, in a *Christianization of the Holocaust, thus again causing suffering.*

Since the dramatic events of the Second World War, various Christian theologians have attempted not only to give meaning to the Shoah but also to reinterpret their Christology in light of Jewish suffering. Three things are striking. First, they often make use of the testimonies of Holocaust victims. They (seem to) listen to Jewish answers to their question: Where was God then? Second, many post-Holocaust Christian theologians fall back on the "figures, narratives, and symbols" they are familiar with to understand the Shoah. The cross and the suffering of Christ take a prominent place in this.[17] The "memories of Golgotha" are thus combined with the "memories of Auschwitz."[18] Third, Christology is undergoing a transformation in this process: The sacrificial theology, according to which Jesus assumed the role of the suffering servant who gave his life as a sin offering, is giving way to Christologies in which there is much more emphasis on God's suffering and God's empathy with those who suffer.[19] In that sense, not only is Auschwitz being read in the light of the cross, but conversely, the cross is also being reinterpreted in the shadow of Auschwitz. Is that precisely not what comparative theology represents—a rereading of one's own tradition in light of another? Nevertheless, I get an unpleasant feeling when I read this post-Holocaust theology. I would like to explore that unpleasant feeling more before returning to the song of the suffering servant. To this end, the next section examines the Christology of one of the most important post-Holocaust theologians, Jürgen Moltmann.

MOLTMANN'S CHRISTOLOGY

The German theologian Jürgen Moltmann developed a systematic theological answer to the Shoah. In his main work, *The Crucified God*, he rejects triumphalist interpretations of the cross and takes seriously the Jewish critique of Christian salvation optimism. It is not possible, in Moltmann's view, to formulate a Christology that does not take the Jewish suffering of the Shoah as its starting point. The famous passage from Elie Wiesel's witness to the Holocaust, *Night*, in which Wiesel testifies to the hanging of two men and a child, has a central place in Moltmann's theology of the cross.

> The two adults were no longer alive. Their tongues hung swollen, blue-tinged. But the third rope was still moving; being so light, the child was still alive....
>
> For more than half an hour he stayed there, struggling between life and death, dying in slow agony under our eyes. And we had to look him full in the face. He was still alive when I passed in front of him. His tongue was still red, his eyes were not yet glazed.
>
> Behind me, I heard the same man asking:
>
> "Where is God now?"
>
> And I heard a voice within me answer him:
>
> "Where is He? Here He is—He is hanging here on this gallows."
>
> That night the soup tasted of corpses.[20]

Moltmann's response to this passage is: "Any other answer would be blasphemy. There cannot be any other Christian answer to the question of torment."[21]

Moltmann is not only affected by Jewish suffering; he identifies with it. As a young German soldier during the Second World War—he was only 17—he was himself captured and also experienced the dehumanizing atmosphere of the prison. He remembers his despair: his prison experience was permeated by the absence of God. In the midst of misery, however, Moltmann had an experience of hope, which was his salvation. God found him in the midst of his suffering.[22] Moltmann comments on this passage and points out that human suffering is also God's suffering: God is with people in their pain and death.[23] Not only does God commiserate with people who suffer, but suffering is also in God himself. Suffering, Moltmann argues, concerns the deepest mystery of God, where God is confronted with Godself. To understand this requires a trinitarian framework in which the relation between Father and Son is central.

The crucified Son, Christ, cries out: "My God, my God, why have you forsaken me?" (Mark 15:34). This exclamation is one of agony, confusion, and outrage. Christ, the Son of God, thus experiences Godforsakenness: He experiences God's absence. But not only the Son suffered, but the Father suffered as well: He suffered the loss of his Son. Thus the suffering of the crucified is a tragedy that takes place in God and concerns the divine mystery itself. God suffers as the loving Father who mourns his son, and God suffers as the Son who is betrayed, beaten, and crucified.

The Son's experience of Godforsakenness is, moreover, nothing other than an identification with all people who have become the victim of violence inflicted on them by others. In other words, given that God suffers, God can never be a neutral unmoved mover. Through divine suffering, God is always with people who suffer; God knows their pain, suffers with them, and bears their suffering.

> Whoever suffers without reason always feels at first that he is forsaken by God and all good things. Whoever cries to God in this suffering, however, joins fundamentally in the death-cry of Jesus. . . . He cries with the abandoned Son to the Father, and the Spirit intercedes for him with groanings.[24]

To say that God himself hung on the gallows in Auschwitz implies that Auschwitz, just like the cross of Christ, is in God himself, and that Auschwitz is included in the pain of the Father and the surrender of the Son.

A profound hope can be heard here. After all, the cross is not the last word. Christ is risen, and Christians live out of hope: "God is not dead. Death is in God. . . . When he brings his history to completion (1 Cor. 15:28), his suffering will be transformed into joy, and thereby our suffering as well."[25] This does not, of course, in any way mean a justification of Auschwitz. It does offer the prospect of the completion of God's trinitarian history and of victory over the history of human suffering.[26]

In order to avoid a new form of Christian triumphalism, Moltmann also emphasizes that redemption has not yet been realized. In that sense, he gives a positive meaning to the Jewish "no" to Jesus: even more, Christology needs this rejection! The Jewish "no" reminds Christians of the "not yet" of the Kingdom of God. According to Moltmann:

> Jesus of Nazareth, the messiah who has come, is the suffering servant of God, who heals through his wounds and is victorious through his sufferings. He is not yet the Christ of the parousia, who comes in the glory of God and redeems the world, so that it becomes the kingdom. . . . The Christian "yes" to Jesus Christ is therefore not in itself finished and complete. It is open for the messianic future of Jesus. It is an eschatologically anticipatory and provisional "yes"—"maranatha. Amen, come Lord Jesus" (Rev. 22:20).[27]

The emphasis on the eschatological qualification, Moltmann also argues, can bring Jews and Christians together. Both Jews and Christians live in a waiting period: Both are hoping for the definitive coming/return of the Messiah, whom Christians believe will be Jesus Christ. Moltmann hopes that the Christian openness for the Jewish "no" can be met by a Jewish openness for the Christian "yes." He concludes his thoughts as follows: "Cannot Israel, in spite of its own observance of the Jewish No, view Christianity as the *praeparatio messianica* [preparation of the Messiah] of the nations, and thus recognize in it the way in which its own hope for the messiah is taken to the nations?"[28]

Moltmann's Theology of the Cross Challenged

Moltmann's theology of the cross is not without problems for several reasons. First, it is far from evident that he can simply compare the death of six million Jews and one and a half million Jewish children with the death of an obstreperous Jewish man living in first-century Palestine under the oppressive regime of the Romans.[29] This comparison is not "credible in the presence of the burning children."[30] Second, Moltmann's trinitarian theology turns Wiesel's testimony around and again ends in a Christological triumphalism, which differs from the former in that it is now a triumphalism that is cloaked as anti-triumphalism. In Moltmann's claim that "even Auschwitz is taken up into the grief of the Father, the surrender of the Son and the power of the Spirit,"[31] Jewish suffering is taken up via a kind of Hegelian schema into the cross of Christ.[32] Not only does that sound like triumphalism, it even sounds like blasphemy, according to A. Roy Eckhardt in his very sharp critique:

> For what would constitute a more dreadful example of this than the trinitariazation, the christianization of Auschwitz, of those poor souls who, had they been allowed the choice, would have in many instances *willingly*, rather than unwillingly, inhaled the gas and entered the flames rather than accede to any trinity of God. Such can be the quality of Jewish faithfulness to God.[33]

Third, one gets the impression that Moltmann does not hold on long enough to the experience of Godforsakenness as described by Wiesel and the deep despair that results. It is clear that the experience of Godforsakenness, as Christ also experienced it on the cross, is central to

Moltmann's theology: It is its starting point. But, because of the way in which the experience is taken up in a dialectic between Father and Son that opens up the prospect of redemption, I wonder if his *theologia crucis* takes sufficient account of the rupture of this experience. Moltmann's theological interpretation is too fast, does not hold on to the pain, does not let the rupture sufficiently penetrate. In his article on "The Church After Auschwitz," the political theologian Johan Metz quotes Wiesel, who has this to say about Christians after the Shoah: "Yesterday it went: 'Auschwitz? Never heard of it.' Today: 'Auschwitz. Oh yes, I already know about that.'"[34] What Wiesel wants to say here is not that Christians know everything about Auschwitz. Rather, he notes that they *already* succeeded in giving these dramatic events a place theologically and are able to interpret them. They have already found an answer to the questions the Shoah raises. As so often, systematization comes too quickly (an inclination found in much of Christian theology), resulting in a "forgetting" of the fragmentation—the fact that our concepts of God, the human being, and the world have been *shattered* by Auschwitz. Theologically speaking, one could say that the transition from Good Friday to Easter is still always presupposed in Moltmann, which allows the rupture of the lostness and uncertainty that is symbolized by Holy Saturday to be forgotten.[35] At no moment does Moltmann, with his eschatological perspective, seriously consider the possibility that the glorious Messiah is not Jesus Christ.

The Suffering Servant Revisited

Christians speak a great deal about the passion of Christ, and the cross is central in their Christology, but are they truly prepared to carry the cross? This question is the starting point for rereading the song of the suffering servant once again, this time through the eyes of the Jewish philosopher Emmanuel Levinas, who, rooted in Talmudic tradition, came to his own unique interpretation of the suffering servant after the Shoah.

In his works, Emmanuel Levinas is very reserved about the Shoah. He was wary of any form of exhibitionism. Nevertheless, it is clear that the events of the twentieth century, which also claimed his family (except for his wife and child), play a role in his thinking. His ethical philosophy seems to have been designed in response to forms of totalitarianism, such as Nazism, that stripped people of their dignity (alterity). The source of his thinking was not wonder, as it was for the Greeks, but the trauma, the injury, of inhumanity. The trauma of the war was one of dehumanization, a paralyzing chaos from which there was no escape. It was the total destruction that emerges from the radical denial of the fundamental dignity of the other. In the Final Solution, evil reached an extreme point. "They [the Jews] experienced a condition inferior to that of things, an experience of total passivity."[36]

Levinas connects the figure of the suffering servant with the persecutions of suffering that the Jews underwent during the Nazi regime. He writes: "Chapter 53 was drained of all meaning for them. Their suffering, common to them as to all the victims of the war, received its unique meaning from racial persecution which is absolute, since it paralyses by virtue of its very intention, any flight."[37] The situation of the Jews under the Nazi regime was "an experience of Passion" because of the radical nature of the persecution from which no escape was possible. Hitlerism nailed humanity to the fatality of its race: "The pathetic lot of being Jewish [became] a fatality. You [couldn't] escape it any more. The Jew [became] inescapably tied to his Judaism."[38] Even conversion to Christianity did not offer any escape. People were unable to see Jews as people; they saw only Jews, whom they viewed as inferior. They remained insensate to the ethical command *You shall not kill*.[39]

In Levinas's view, God identifies first with those who suffer. He humbles himself in a kenotic movement, understood as a "self-inflicted humiliation on the part of the Supreme Being, of a descent of the Creator to the level of the creature; that is to say, an absorption of the most active activity into the most passive passivity."[40] In biblical tradition, God sides with those who are "small," the poor, the widow, and the orphan. God's majesty shows itself in humility. But that is not all.

For Levinas, the image of a God who commiserates with those who suffer is not enough. A God who only commiserates allows evil to have the last word. Here, he criticizes Christianity, which, to his mind, embraces the idea of God's defenselessness. He says in a reaction to the Christian understanding of kenosis: "This powerless kenosis costs people much too much."[41] God calls us to responsibility, and it is precisely in the "responsible relation with the other" that we see the trace of God. The stranger, the widow, and the person living in poverty command us to responsibility. We hear the word of God in the appeal of the other who commands and implores:

I mean that the other person, in his nakedness, in his vulnerability, in his destitution, appeals to me. In a certain sense he forces me to become engaged, to place myself at the service of the other who hides behind that nakedness and the destitution of that face. And, at the same time, the appearance is a command. The face is what lends itself to murder and what resists it.[42]

In this appeal, I become aware of God as the idea of the Good: "God comes to mind when the naked and defenseless eyes of the neighbor commands and graces us to be responsible. It is a purely passive experience where the Infinite God overflows our consciousness with the Good. The Divine Word proclaims to our conscience, 'You shall not kill!'"[43]

Ethics as intimacy with God—that, Levinas argues, is typically Jewish. God becomes concrete, not through the incarnation but in the Torah, through the law, in ethics. Religion is inseparably bound up with ethics. It is in that sense that one must understand Levinas's statement that we need to love the Torah more than we love God. We can only serve God by serving our neighbor.

THE SUFFERING SERVANT

For Levinas, responsibility is the essential, primary, original, fundamental structure of subjectivity. Subjectivity, according to Levinas, can only be described in ethical terms. We are indebted in the sense that we all owe it to one another to accept responsibility for the other. Central in Levinas's ethics is the idea that the subject is always placed in the accusative. To be a *mensch* is to recognize that I am commanded to say *hineini: here I am*. In other words, the position of the subject, Levinas says, is entirely one of responsibility or service.[44]

According to Levinas, this responsibility for the other finds its origin in creation. This creational interconnectedness is the primal condition for the responsibility of the ethical relation. Because I am created by God, the other already concerns me. God is revealed through the face of the other and enjoins me to attend to the other unconditionally. I hear the voice of God in my neighbor. The other, begging me not to kill him, is in the trace of God and reveals to me my creatureliness. Creation precedes choice: As an ethical being I am a creature, and this createdness and thus responsibility precedes any choice. It is an obligation that affects the very structure of being human. Of course, it is always possible not to respond to the other, but to not respond to the other is what Levinas would call evil.

Levinas expresses the relationship with the other in terms of substitution, which is closely connected to the notion of responsibility. To his mind, it means to bring comfort by associating oneself with the weakness and finitude of the other. To carry the burden of the other; to bear the weight of his existence, while sacrificing one's egotistical interests and complacency. To put the other first. He connects this notion of substitution with the notion of election or chosenness:

> "We are each of us guilty with respect to all," says a character in Dostoevsky's *The Brothers Karamazov*, thereby expressing this "originary constitution" of the I or the unique, in a responsibility for the neighbor or the other, and the impossibility of escaping responsibility or of being replaced. This impossibility of escaping is not a servitude, but rather being chosen. Religions that have recourse to this term, chosenness, see it in the supreme dignity of the human.[45]

From here, Levinas makes a parallel with the suffering servant, who is sent by God, whose task he is fulfilling. Levinas's interpretation of Isaiah 53 should not be read as a particularly Jewish interpretation, which only concerns Israel. It is an interpretation with a universal claim. This particular biblical story tells us something about what it means to be human: this song can help us better reflect on the radical form of humanism that Levinas advocates.

> Our age certainly no longer needs to be convinced of the value of nonviolence. But it perhaps lacks a new reflection on passivity, and a certain weakness that is not cowardice, a certain patience that we must not preach to others, in which the ego [*le Moi*] must be held, one which cannot be treated in negative terms as though it were just the other side of finitude. Enough of Nietzscheanism, even when purged of its Hitlerian deformations! But who will dare to say such a thing. The humanism of the suffering servant—the History of Israel—invites us to create a new anthropology, and perhaps, by bringing about the end of Western triumphalism, a new history.[46]

The suffering servant embodies the responsibility to which *all* are called. The emphasis in this passage lies on the complete availability of the servant of God. In Levinas's interpretation, this song is about responsible subjectivity that, "persecuted by men and nevertheless incapable of shirking his task[,] is described in terms close to this chapter from Isaiah."⁴⁷ The position in which the "I" finds itself, Levinas argues, is entirely that of responsibility or service, as in Isaiah 53.⁴⁸ Just as in Christianity, he links the figure of the suffering servant to the Messiah, but unlike Christianity, the messianic expectation is once more open; it is not closed-off.

If Messianism still has any meaning, it is that *every* unique individual is called to devote herself to the other. The suffering servant as Messiah is then the person who is completely responsible for others and thus also assumes the errors and suffering of others on herself. The Messiah is the righteous human being who suffers, who, as the servant of God, takes the suffering of others on himself, who is concerned about the lot of others, who does not remain indifferent. But the call does not concern a single God-man but every single subject. Messianism is responsibility: One must, as a unique individual, dedicate oneself to the other, and to do so without any attendant promises. According to Levinas:

> The fact of not evading the burden imposed by the suffering of others defines ipseity itself. All persons are the Messiah. The Self (Moi) as Self, taking upon itself the whole world, is designated solely by this role. . . . Messianism is therefore not the certainty of the coming of a man who stops History. It is my power to bear the suffering of all. It is the moment when I recognize this power and my universal responsibility.⁴⁹

The Messiah, he once dared to say, does not come. If we do not devote ourselves to this world, then history will end badly.

Conclusion

In light of the tragedy of the Holocaust, Christian theology has an ethical responsibility to re-examine its Christology. Christians are being challenged to reflect anew on who they say Jesus is and what it means to be his disciples. After the Shoah, this reflection should be done in the proximity of Jewish others. The purpose is not to Judaize Christianity, but rather to formulate a Christology that ends a long Christian tradition of supersessionism. Christians are being challenged to reconsider their Christology in a way that is congruent with tradition while being conscious of the potential anti-Jewish power of their religious discourse.⁵⁰ A reading of the suffering servant through the eyes of Jewish commentaries not only brings to light the violent potential of classical Christology; it also yields new meanings and insights that may contribute to the formulation of a Christology *after the Shoah*.

Classical Christology revolves around the notion of vicarious suffering, the idea that Christ has taken the burden of human sins on himself and has thus brought reconciliation between God and humankind. Because we cannot liberate ourselves from our sinfulness, Jesus Christ, the suffering servant, took the lot of sinful humanity upon himself in order to reconcile humankind with God. The suffering, death, and resurrection of Christ, the Son of God, is a peace offering. Christ is seen as the complete, final, and perfect fulfillment of the Hebrew prophecies, in particular that of Isaiah 53. The church replaces Israel, which no longer has a role to play in God's plan of salvation. This Christological interpretation of the suffering servant gave way not only to a Christological exclusivism but also to an ecclesiological triumphalism. As Rosemary Radford Ruether explains, the church began to see itself as the Kingdom of God on earth until the Second Coming. This allowed the Church to ignore historical ambiguities, real suffering, and violence.[51]

Turning to Jewish commentaries on the suffering servant shows first of all that this text, like all literary and poetic texts, is open to multiple readings; its meaning cannot be exhausted by one (Christological) interpretation. At the very least, the Christian assumption that there is a kind of direct, uninterrupted, and continuous connection between "Old Testament prophecies" (such as Isaiah 53) and the suffering, death, and resurrection of Jesus Christ, must be nuanced.

Next, the collective reading of Jewish commentaries, which projects Israel in the role of the suffering servant, challenges Christian replacement theology. This Jewish reading places the church in the role of the "oppressors," who do not see that Israel is and remains God's beloved people. Isaiah 53 projects a future time in which these oppressors will finally see that the suffering endured by the Jews is not divine punishment. Read through Jewish eyes, one might even say that this song prophesies how the church, in the role of oppressor, would wrongly assume that God had fallen out of love with Israel and would wrongly attribute Israel's suffering to its presumed sinfulness. This prophecy holds up a mirror to the church's face, with even more significance after the Shoah. It challenges Christians to reflect on their role as perpetrators, certainly when it comes to oppression of the Jewish people. This is something Christian theologians still find difficult to recognize. Moltmann's theology of the cross, in which he connects Auschwitz with Golgotha in an effort to express solidarity with Jewish suffering, shows this difficulty. Comparisons are never innocent.

Though Christological solidarity is to be preferred over supersessionism, this talk of solidarity comes too quickly; it comes before Christians have thoroughly confronted their history and what it effected. In one movement, it is forgotten that Christians emphasized the discontinuity between Judaism and Christianity for centuries; it is forgotten that the Jewish people were held collectively responsible for centuries for the death of Christ; it is forgotten that Christians were more often perpetrators than victims.[52] The benefit of solidarity talk is that it allows Christians to overlook the fact that they have been complicit in Jewish suffering.

The Shoah, however, was not Christian suffering, and in the light of history it is also inappropriate to claim that it was, even indirectly. This recognition raises serious Christological questions and has forced us to ask the question once more, "Who is the suffering servant?" Joel Marcus remarks,

> when Isaiah speaks of the Lord's servant being despised and rejected by people, he is speaking of us [the Jewish people], who were branded as subhuman, not only by common opinion, but by law. When we hear him describe the way in which folk hid their faces from the Servant, we recall how we were turned away by our neighbors when we knocked at their doors and pleaded with them to hide us from the Gestapo, and how afterward, they claimed that they did not know what had happened to us. When he describes the Servant being led like a lamb to the slaughter, we recall our parents, our spouses, and our children, who filed so silently to the gas chambers, not daring to open their mouths.[53]

And if we (Christian theologians) then nevertheless very carefully compare the suffering of the Jewish people with the suffering of Christ, if we then nevertheless want to make a connection between Auschwitz and Golgotha, then we should also, as Christians, ask with whom we identify: with the suffering of Christ or with his sleeping disciples, who simply let this happen, despite Jesus's plea with them to stay awake during this night? Is it not the case that we (Jesus's disciples) slept then, during Jesus's fearful night on the Mount of Olives, and that we were again sleeping when his people asked for help during the Shoah?[54]

This connection between Christology and Christian irresponsibility has been brought to light by the Jewish philosopher Emmanuel Levinas. His reading of the suffering servant entails a fundamental critique of Christianity. One cannot get around the fact, he says, that "all those who participated in the Shoah had received Catholic or Protestant baptism in their infancy. However, this presented no obstacle to them!" Because of that, he claims, the Gospel has, in his view, been compromised forever.[55] Levinas is very clear: Christians are too inclined to place their lot in the hands of God in Christ, who will ultimately set everything right. As far as he is concerned, this is an immature form of faith. Christianity suffers from its forgetting of the other and the responsibility to which the subject is called. Redemption depends on us and not on a Messiah sent by God. The idea that someone else died for our sins is, according to Levinas, a dangerous idea, for it minimizes our personal responsibility. His religion is one without promise. God, he claims, is not in heaven.[56]

From a Levinasian perspective, Christians can recognize that we have focused too much on what Christ can do for us because of our faith in him, and that we have thought too little about what we must do if we are to be his disciples. Instead of focusing solely on this suffering, death, and resurrection, as is the case in classical atonement Christologies, Levinas's reading of the suffering servant urges Christians to refocus their attention to Christ's earthly life, where Jesus exemplified what radical responsibility for others entails. The whole world concerns him. He carries the burden of all humankind, not to discharge his followers from their responsibility in this world, but to show them the way forward. The suffering servant realizes the responsibility to which all are called here and now. The Christian narrative after the Shoah should not primarily be one of commiseration but one of collective guilt and a search for responsibility.

Notes

1. Rosemary Radford Ruether, "Anti-Judaism Is the Left Hand of Christology," *New Catholic World* 217 (1974): 12–17.
2. The other three songs are Isaiah 42:1–4, Isaiah 49:1–6, and Isaiah 50:4–11.
3. The term "Old Testament" is problematic in view of Jewish-Christian relations. It does not do justice to the self-understanding of Judaism as a living tradition and fits in a supercessionist framework. See Emmanuel Levinas, *Difficult Freedom: Essays on Judaism*, trans. Sean Hand (London: Athlone Press, 1990), 13.
4. Patricia K. Tull, "'Isaiah 'Twas Foretold It': Helping the Church Interpret the Prophets," in *Strange Fire: Reading the Bible after the Holocaust*, ed. Tod Linafelt (Sheffield: Sheffield Academic Press, 2000), 198.
5. Peter Stuhlmacher, "Isaiah 53 in the Gospels and Acts," in *The Suffering Servant*, ed. Bernd Janowski and Peter Stuhlmacher (Grand Rapids: William B. Eerdmans, 2004), 152.

6. Christian belief that the suffering servant texts are a prophecy of Jesus Christ is probably what led to their exclusion from the canon of prophetic readings publicly recited in the synagogue on Shabbat (*haftorot*), many of which are derived from Deutero-Isaiah. See David Neuhas, "The Suffering Servant," in *A Dictionary of Jewish-Christian Relations*, ed. Edward Kessler (Cambridge: Cambridge University Press, 2005), 412–13.
7. Mitch Glaser, "Introduction," in *The Gospel According to Isaiah 53: Encountering the Suffering Servant in Jewish and Christian Theology*, ed. Darrell. L. Bock and Mitch Glaser (Grand Rapids: Kregel, 2012), 21.
8. This interpretation can be found in *Midrash Rabbah* (Numbers XXIII.2), *Zohar* (Genesis and Leviticus), the Talmud (Brochos 5a), Rashi, Joseph Kara, Ibn Ezra, Joseph Kimhi, David Kimhi, and Nachmanides, among others.
9. Stuhlmacher, "Isaiah 53 in the Gospels and Acts," 161.
10. Michael Cook, "Evolving Jewish View of Jesus," in *Jesus through Jewish Eyes: Rabbis and Scholars Engage an Ancient Brother in a New Conversation*, ed. Beatrice Bruteau (Maryknoll: Orbis, 2001), 23.
11. Martin Buber, *Der Jude und sein Judentum: gesammelte Ausätze und Reden* (Colonia: Melzer, 1963), 562.
12. Byron L. Sherwin, "Who do you say that I am?" in *Jesus through Jewish Eyes*, ed. Beatrice Bruteau, 36.
13. Janrense Boonstra et al., *Antisemitism. A History Portrayed* (Amsterdam: Anne Frank Foundation, 1993).
14. Tikva Frymer-Kensky et al., *Dabru Emet: A Jewish Statement on Christians and Christianity*, National Jewish Scholars Project (2002), accessed June 13, 2014, www.icjs.org/what/njsp/dabruemet.html.
15. Beatrice Bruteau, "Preface," in *Jesus through Jewish Eyes*, ed. Beatrice Bruteau (Maryknoll: Orbis, 2001), viii.
16. Harry Cargas, *Reflections of a Post-Auschwitz Christian* (Detroit: Wayne State University Press, 1989).
17. James Edward Young, *Writing and Rewriting the Holocaust: Narrative and the Consequences of Interpretation* (Indianapolis: Indiana University Press, 1988).
18. Tania Oldenhage, "Reading the Cross at Auschwitz: Holocaust Memories and Passion Narratives," in *A Shadow of Glory: Reading the New Testament after the Holocaust*, ed. Tod Linafelt (New York: Routledge, 2002), 140.
19. The opposition of Christian post-Holocaust theologians to this interpretation of the cross resonates, for that matter, with the opposition of various Jewish thinkers to the concept of *holocaust*, which means "burnt offering."
20. Elie Weisel, *Night* (Bantam: Penguin Books, 1982), 75–76.
21. Jürgen Moltmann, *The Crucified God: The Cross of Christ as Foundation and Criticism of Christian Theology* (London: SCM, 1974), 273–74.
22. Jürgen Moltmann, *Experiences of God* (London: SCM, 1980), 9.
23. Jürgen Moltmann, "The Crucified God," *Theology Today* 32 (1974): 9–10.
24. Moltmann, "The Crucified God," 16–17.
25. Moltmann, "The Crucified God," 18.
26. L. Kenis, "God in Auschwitz: Enkele theologische bemerkingen bij het werk van Elie Wiesel," *Kultuurleven* 54 (1987): 440–52.

27. Jürgen Moltmann, *The Way of Jesus Christ: Christology in Messianic Dimensions* (Minneapolis: Fortress, 1993), 32–33.
28. Jürgen Moltmann, "Israel's No: Jews and Jesus in an Unredeemed World," *Christian Century* 107.32 (1990): 1024.
29. A. Roy Eckhardt, "Jürgen Moltmann, the Jewish People and the Holocaust," *Journal of the American Academy of Religion* 44 (1976): 687.
30. Irving Greenberg, "Cloud of Smoke, Pillar of Fire: Judaism, Christianity and Modernity after the Holocaust," in *Auschwitz: Beginning of a New Era? Reflections on the Holocaust*, ed. Eva Fleischner (New York: KTAV, 1977), 315.
31. Moltmann, *The Crucified God*, 278.
32. Graham B. Walker, Jr., *Elie Wiesel: A Challenge to Theology* (London: McFarland & Company, 1988), 163.
33. Eckhardt, "Jürgen Moltmann, the Jewish People and the Holocaust," 684.
34. Johann Baptist Metz, *A Passion for God: The Mystical-Political Dimension of Christianity*, trans. J. Matthew Ashley (New York: Paulist, 1998), 121.
35. Walter Brueggeman, "Reading from the Day 'in Between,'" in *A Shadow of Glory: Reading the New Testament after the Holocaust*, ed. Tod Linafelt (London: Routledge, 2002), 105–16.
36. Emmanuel Levinas, *Difficult Freedom: Essays on Judaism* (London: Athlone, 1990), 12.
37. Levinas, *Difficult Freedom*, 12.
38. Emmanuel Levinas, "L'inspiration religieuse de l'alliance," *Paix et droit* 8 (1935): 4.
39. There is a whole program behind that command, *You shall not kill*. After all, Levinas argues, there are various ways of killing a person. It does not necessarily have to be, he argues, by pulling a trigger. Indifference, under-appreciation, and exclusion kill as well. All these forms of violence, Levinas states, are characterized by the fact that they do not look those to whom they do violence in the eyes.
40. Emmanuel Levinas, *Entre Nous, Thinking-Of-The-Other*, trans. Michael B. Smith and Barbara Harshav (New York: Columbia University Press, 1998), 53–54, 46.
41. Levinas, "Judaism and Christianity after Franz Rosenzweig," in *Is It Righteous to Be? Interviews with Emmanuel Levinas*, ed. Jill Robbins (Stanford: Stanford University Press, 2001), 261.
42. France Guwy, "Houd van je naast, dat is wat je zelf bent. Gesprek met Emmanuel Levinas in 1985," in *De ander in ons: Emmanuel Levinas in gesprek: een inleiding in zijn denken*, ed. France Guwy (Amsterdam: Sun, 2008), 62.
43. Emmanuel Levinas, *Collected Philosophical Papers*, trans. Alphonso Lingis (Pittsburgh: Duquesne University Press, 1998), 55.
44. Emmanuel Levinas, *Het menselijk gelaat*, trans. A. Peperzak (Baarn: Ambo, 1969), 178–79.
45. Levinas, "Responsibility and Substitution," 229.
46. Levinas, *Difficult Freedom*, 117.
47. Catherine Chalier, "Le serviteur souffrant: Isaïe 52, 13–15; 53, 1–12," in *Mythe et philosophie: Les traditions bibliques* (Paris: Presses Universitaires de France, 2002), 154.
48. Levinas, *Het menselijk gelaat*, 179.
49. Levinas, *Difficult Freedom*, 89–90.

50. World Council of Churches, *Who do we say that we are?—Christian Identity in a Multireligious World* (Bussan: World Council of Churches, 2013), 1.
51. Rosemary Radford Ruether, *Faith and Fratricide: The Theological Roots of Anti-Semitism* (New York: Seabury Press, 1997), 247–48.
52. Bjorn Krondorfer, "Of Faith and Faces: Biblical Tests, Holocaust Testimony and German 'After Auschwitz' Theology," in *Strange Fire: Reading the Bible after the Holocaust* (Sheffield: Sheffield Academic Press, 2000), 86–105.
53. Joel Marcus, *Jesus and the Holocaust: Reflections on Suffering and Hope* (New York: Double Day, 1997), 28.
54. Here, I am inspired by Oldenhage, "Reading the Cross at Auschwitz," 150.
55. F. Guwy, *De ander in ons: Emmanuel Levinas in gesprek: een inleiding in zijn denken* (Amsterdam: Sun, 2008), 45.
56. Michael de Saint Cheron, *Conversations with Emmanuel Levinas, 1983–1994*, trans. Gary D. Mole (Pittsburgh: Duquesne University Press, 2010), 16.

12 Response: Christology in Comparative Perspective

Hugh Nicholson

The heart of Christian theology is Christology. Christology can be defined as theological reflection on the question of who Jesus was—and is—for Christians. The multiplicity of Christological titles in the New Testament—Messiah, Lord, savior, prophet, high priest, Son of God, and so on—all qualify each other and become reinterpreted in light of the Christ event. Together they express the centrality and sui generis nature—in short, the uniqueness—of Jesus for Christian faith. The New Testament evinces a process by which early Christians drew upon the available concepts and images, whether found in the biblical (Jewish) tradition or the surrounding Greco-Roman culture, to express what God has done in the person of Jesus. Contemporary Christology follows the same basic procedure in understanding what Jesus Christ means to men and women of faith today. That is, Christians today draw upon the conceptual and imagistic resources of today's interreligious culture, interpreting these in light of the gospel narrative, while at the same time reflecting, sometimes critically, on past Christological concepts. To the extent, then, that those resources can have extra-Christian origins, an interreligious or comparative dimension is integral to contemporary Christological reflection, as it was, in fact, in the formative period of Christianity.

Even while they each testify to this interreligious dimension of contemporary Christological reflection, however, the two essays presented here represent two fundamentally distinct ways of doing comparative theology. Bede Benjamin Bidlack's comparison of the Daoist birth narrative of Lord Lao to the Lukan infancy narrative brings together religious ideas that, for the most part, have yet to encounter each other historically. As his paper demonstrates, such juxtapositions can be used to challenge, in salutary ways, prevailing notions of Christian uniqueness. They also can be used strategically to reread familiar Christian texts in fresh and exciting ways. In contrast, Marianne Moyaert's effort to rethink the traditional Christian messianic interpretation of the suffering servant motif of Second Isaiah in light of Christian complicity in the Holocaust critically re-examines a Christological concept that is itself the product of a past interreligious encounter. Concepts like that of Jesus as the Messiah are not only products of the invariably conflictual and ethically problematic relations between two religious communities in their formative period. Such Christological concepts also sustain such relations as part of their ongoing history of effects. Recognizing the intimate link between certain core doctrines and relations of religious conflict demands a rethinking of those doctrines. Here, comparative theology represents one of the modes through which a tradition like Christianity comes to terms with the ambiguities of its past.

Jesus and Laozi

Bidlack's comparison of the birth narratives of the Gospel of Luke and the *Huahu jing* explores the theological discomfort provoked by the uncanny sense of familiarity that one sometimes experiences in the encounter with a foreign—that is to say, historically unrelated—religious idea. This discomfort is the subjective response to the challenge such ideas present to Christian claims of uniqueness and thus to prevailing notions of Christian identity. Historically, such encounters have usually provoked a negative reaction. The typical response has been a peremptory denigration of the foreign idea in question as a way of evading the challenge it presents. One thinks, for example, of medieval Christian polemical representations of Muhammad as a false prophet and imposter.

Bidlack sets up a comparison that, prima facie, challenges the Christian conception of Jesus Christ as the unique savior of the world. Like Christ, the Lord Lao is the embodiment of the highest reality, the Dao. He descends from Heaven to earth in order to restore the latter's lost harmony with the Dao. In his reflections on this comparison, Bidlack deliberately chooses to abide in the tension and discomfort that the juxtaposition produces. In this reflective space, he submits his two texts to careful and patient analysis. That is, he refuses to yield to the apologetic reflex arc that seeks to defuse the threat to Christian identity through a hasty assertion of Christian uniqueness. Bidlack's measured and thoughtful response to this particular challenge to Christian identity exemplifies the feature of comparative theology that, more than anything else, distinguishes it from traditional Christian apologetics. One could argue, in fact, that the very point of comparative theology is to create, by juxtaposing Christian concepts with challenging parallels from other traditions, opportunities to experience and abide in this kind of tension. As Moyaert described it at the Wake Forest conference, comparative theology "values asking questions above formulating definitive and final answers."

Bidlack's theological response to the challenge of the *Huahu jing* is threefold. The first aspect of that response stands in continuity with Christian apologetic tradition. The encounter with a text like the *Huahu jing* occasions a search for a more fine-grained articulation of the distinctiveness of Christianity. To be sure, Christ is not unique in the history of religions as a cosmic savior figure. And yet the Christian conception of salvation (salvation from separation from the divine life of God) is distinct from the Daoist (salvation from cosmic disharmony, epitomized in the political order). Ultimately, Lord Lao and Jesus Christ are not competitors because they are "not competing for the same soteriological space." Having distinguished the Christian and Daoist conceptions of salvation, Bidlack is able to conclude that "Lord Lao of the *Huahu jing* makes no threat to the uniqueness of Christ." Rereading Luke in light of the *Huahu jing* thus focuses attention on the distinctiveness of Christian salvation. Although an irenic sensibility pervades Bidlack's essay, his comparative reading of the *Huahu jing* and Luke can be compared to more overtly apologetical projects such as Henri de Lubac's Christian reading of Pure Land Buddhism or Rudolf Otto's well-known comparison of Meister Eckhart and the great Non-dualist Vedantin, Shankara. Both de Lubac and Otto base their respective Christian apologetics on what appear, prima facie, to be the closest of parallels, namely, the Pure Land doctrine of grace and its Christian counterpart, for the one, and Shankara's doctrine of the unity of Brahman and Eckhart's "mysticism of the ground," for the other. And yet both de Lubac and Otto go on to show that the similarity is more or less superficial; closer analysis reveals an essential difference between Christianity and the Hindu or Buddhist parallel in question.[1] Each of these apologetic projects implies an *a fortiori* argument for the uniqueness of Christianity: If an essential difference between Christianity and the non-Christian "other" can be discerned even in the most striking of parallels, how much more starkly will this difference appear when less striking parallels are considered. Unlike de Lubac or Otto, Bidlack refrains from making value judgments; he is content simply to reassure his Christian readers that the *Huahu jing*'s portrait of Lord Lao, despite its uncanny resemblance in certain respects to the Lukan Christological tradition, does not threaten the uniqueness of Christian salvation.

One reason Bidlack's comparison is refreshingly free of the strident apologetic tone of more typical demonstrations of Christian uniqueness is that it offsets this contrastive reading of the Chinese text with an appreciative one. Here we come to the second aspect of Bidlack's response: namely, the use of the *Huahu jing* to underscore aspects of the Christian salvation that might otherwise escape notice. Specifically, comparison with the Daoist text highlights the world-affirming, sacramental dimension of Christian salvation as well as the integral role played by human agents in the work of salvation. I might add that one ironic consequence of this use of comparison to highlight previously unnoticed features of the home tradition is that successful comparison, like the Indian tale of the cat who renders his service to the lion superfluous by catching the mouse that was the reason for his employment, appears superfluous after it has performed this function.[2] Readers may, in fact, no longer need the Daoist parallel once they have reclaimed what was already hidden within their own tradition.

Third and finally, reflecting on the Lukan Christological titles in light of the Daoist dynamic between king and sage draws attention to the integral relation between the temporal-political and eschatological-spiritual dimensions of Christ's saving activity. In this way, the Daoist parallel suggests a way of resolving the perennial tension between high and low Christologies—that is, between conceptions of Christ that emphasize his divinity and those that emphasize his humanity.

In contextualizing the *Huahu jing*, Bidlack draws attention to the text's polemical nature. The *Huahu jing*, as indicated by its title, exemplifies the so-called *huahu* theory, according to which the Buddha was nothing but a manifestation of Laozi,[3] and Buddhism was the doctrine that Laozi preached to the barbarians after his legendary departure to the Western Region.[4] The *huahu* myth was one of the means by which Buddhism was able to overcome China's suspicion of and generally low regard for foreign cultural imports. It was only thanks to such efforts to cast Buddhism as a version of indigenous teaching that this foreign teaching was eventually able to take root in classical Chinese culture.

Later on, as Bidlack notes, the *huahu* theory was put to more expressly polemical uses as Buddhists and Daoists competed for imperial favor.

The *Huahu jing* thus exemplifies a feature of religious texts and doctrines more generally that becomes especially problematic in the area of Christian-Jewish relations, namely, that these texts and traditions are, more often than not, constituted by polemics with rival communities.

Jesus as the Suffering Servant

Moyaert's paper shows just how problematic, both in terms of its apologetical origins and its history of effects—a history culminating in the Nazi genocide[5]—the Christian identification of Jesus with the suffering servant of Isaiah 53 really is. The Christological interpretation of Isaiah 53 is inextricably bound up in a long, troubled, and, for Christians, often shameful history of Christian-Jewish relations.

Moyaert sees a particular affinity between, on the one hand, the nature of comparative theology as a method of theological reflection designed to generate questions more than providing definitive answers and, on the other, a post-Auschwitz suspicion of definitive, rounded-off solutions to basic theological problems. In other words, the provisional method of comparative theology dovetails with a post-Auschwitz appreciation of the broken, fragmentary nature of our understanding of God, the world, and humanity.

The demand to acknowledge the radical and irrevocable challenge that the Holocaust presents to the assurances of the Christian faith forms the basis of Moyaert's sharp critique of Christological interpretations of the Holocaust like that of Jürgen Moltmann. In her critique of Moltmann's effort to relate the trauma of the Holocaust to the suffering of Christ, Moyaert tries to put a finger on the "unpleasant feeling" she gets when reading post-Holocaust Christian theology. Her critique of Moltmann's theology is that it "is too fast, does not hold on to the pain, does not let the rupture sufficiently penetrate." Moreover, Moltmann's eschatological antidote to the triumphalist implications of this identification of the suffering of God in the Crucifixion and the suffering of God in Auschwitz—namely, that both Christians and Jews are hoping for a definitive coming/return of the Messiah—constitutes an insidious form of "triumphalism that is cloaked as anti-triumphalism." In short, Moltmann's otherwise laudable attempt to find a Christian meaning to the Holocaust has the unintended effect of containing—and ultimately evading—the radical challenge this event poses to Christian faith. Moltmann's identification of the suffering of Christ with the suffering of the victims of the Holocaust, moreover, invokes a Christological reading of the suffering servant motif and to that extent fails, despite its sincere intentions, to break free of the long tradition of Christian supersessionism.

Moyaert contrasts the Christological interpretation of Isaiah 53 with both the Levinasian reading of the suffering servant as a symbol for the responsibility and openness that all human beings are called upon to have with respect to the other, as well as the Jewish commentarial tradition, which interprets Israel as the suffering servant while casting the Church in the role of the oppressor. A post-Holocaust Christian reading of Isaiah 53 combines both readings. For Moyaert, the text "challenges Christians to reflect on their role as perpetrators, certainly when it comes to the oppression of the Jewish people." A post-Holocaust reading of Isaiah 53 thus challenges the reflexive and ultimately self-flattering tendency on the part of Christians to identify with the suffering servant. This message, of course, can be extended. When read in light of the biblical principle that God sides with the powerless and dispossessed, the Isaiah text challenges the presumptions of any community, Christian or Jewish, that finds itself in a position of power, whether it be a triumphalist, established Church vis-à-vis dispersed Jewish communities or, dare I say it, today's Israeli state vis-à-vis defenseless Palestinian civilians living under military occupation.

A post-Holocaust Christian theology is forced to reckon with the possibility, pointedly expressed by Rosemary Radford Ruether in her thesis that "Anti-Judaism is the left hand of Christology," that the ambiguities of Christian identity formation go "all the way down," that even the Christological titles of the New Testament are the products of polemics between the followers of Jesus and other Jews.[6] In this connection, it is worth pointing out that the most fundamental Christological title, Jesus as the long expected Messiah, appears to have been inextricably intertwined with the Christian "proof from prophecy" by which late first- and second-century Christians sought to claim the biblical tradition against the objections of non-Christian Jews. With little evidence for a general messianic expectation in pre-Christian Jewish literature,[7] Luke's depiction of Jesus as the long-awaited Messiah foretold in the scriptures may be more a matter of late first-century Christian apologetics than actual history.[8] Returning to Bidlack's comparison, the Lukan infancy narrative may be as polemical as the *Huahu jing*.

Christological Maximalism

In light of the unsavory and indeed tragic legacy of Christian anti-Judaism, it might be tempting to imagine a Christology stripped of all polemical elements. To this end, one might seek a Christology based on a retrieval of the dramatic revelatory experiences of the first Christians, as suggested by the work of Larry Hurtado.[9] Or one might appeal to the venerable theory of the *lex orandi, lex credendi*, according to which orthodox Christology was enshrined in the practices of Christian worship before it found outward theological expression.[10] Such appeals to an "authentic" and generative Christian experience betray a commitment to the notion of an essence of Christianity unaffected by outside influence, along with its corollary that heresies are invariably the result of undue foreign influence.[11] And yet this notion that Christian identity is founded on an experience or a way of life that is self-generating and self-contained is dubious from both a historical and theoretical standpoint.[12] We must accept that what the Germans call an *Auseinandersetzung*—a setting-over-against-another—with rival belief systems, whether heretical or non-Christian, was, from the very outset, constitutive of the Christological concepts that have sustained Christian identity. This truth underlies Ruether's provocative thesis that anti-Judaism is the left hand of Christology, and it explains, in fact, why the latter is so disconcerting: If polemic is, in fact, constitutive of traditional Christological concepts, then anti-Judaism is not merely a contingent matter that can be painlessly excised from the body of orthodox Christian belief without affecting the latter.[13] In the remainder of this essay, I will expand on this thesis that inter-communal polemic played an integral role in the development of Christian understandings of Christ. To be more specific, I will argue that the dynamics of what I would call, borrowing a phrase from Raymond Brown, "Christological one-upmanship" drives Christology upward, from the synoptic notion of Jesus as the expected Messiah to the Johannine understanding of Jesus as the preexistent "Man from heaven," and, later, from the Logos theologies of the second and third centuries to the Nicene confession of the Son's consubstantiality with the Father. It would be impossible, of course, in the space permitted here to defend this thesis with the requisite historical detail and methodological justification. All I can do is to note the constitutive role of polemic in several key moments, three to be precise, of Christological development.

The first of these moments was the emergence, reflected in the later literary strata of John's Gospel, of the notion of Christ as a preexistent, heavenly figure. According to an established tradition of critical Johannine scholarship, the early strata of the Gospel text reflect tensions between the Johannine Christians and their parent synagogue. We are told, in fact, that the confession of Jesus as the Messiah was grounds for expulsion from the synagogue (Jn. 9:22; 12:42; 16:2). Later literary strata reflect tensions between the emergent Johannine community and other Christian groups that had also broken with the synagogue.[14] These intra-Christian tensions expressed themselves in terms of rival Christologies. According to J. Louis Martyn's influential analysis of Gospel's literary strata, the most recent strata evince a transition from what Martyn felicitously calls a "*heilsgeschichtlich* Christology from behind" to a "dualistic Christology from above."[15] In other words, in an act of Christological one-upmanship, the Johannine Christians affirmed Jesus's preexistence, heavenly origins, and oneness with God, a Christological understanding that goes beyond, yet while preserving, the messianic Christology of the group of what Raymond Brown dubs the "apostolic Christians" associated with the tradition of Peter and the twelve apostles.[16] On the level of narrative, the greater depth of Johannine Christology is reflected in the greater intimacy that the Beloved Disciple, the putative founder of the Johannine community, enjoys with Jesus in comparison with Peter.[17] As I have argued elsewhere, these dynamics of Christological one-upmanship, moreover, can be understood in terms of an important principle in social identity theory, namely, the tendency of factions engaged in hegemonic struggle to maximize the contrast with the relevant out-group—in the Johannine case, "the Jews" with their rejection of the messianic claims of Jesus.[18]

We see the same dynamics of Christological one-upmanship at work in another foundational Christological text, Justin Martyr's mid-second-century *Dialogue with Trypho*. Although preceded by the celebrated prologue of the Fourth Gospel by decades, Justin's Dialogue was arguably the single most important text in establishing the doctrine of Christ as the pre-existent Word or Logos of God as a defining tenet of Christian belief.[19] According to Daniel Boyarin's perceptive reading of this text, Justin is simultaneously engaged in two projects: first, to define Judaism by a rejection of the Logos of God as a second divine person; second, to define as heretics those Christians who, for whatever reason, do not accept the doctrine of the Logos.[20] The text ostensibly records Justin's attempt to persuade Trypho, his Jewish interlocutor, to convert to Christianity on the basis of a Christological reading of the Hebrew Bible. And yet, Justin's principal preoccupation may have been to establish hegemony over the various Christian groups of which there are numerous disparaging references in the *Dialogue*. Among these are, on the one hand, the Marcionites, who reject the authority of the Hebrew scriptures and thus Justin's "proof from prophesy," and, on the other, adoptionist and monarchian Christians who regard Justin's conception of the Christ/Logos as "a second God" (*deuteros theos*) to be tantamount to ditheism.[21] By making Trypho symbolize the alleged Jewish rejection of the Logos,[22] Justin rhetorically assimilates the latter group—that is, those Christians who recognize the authority of the Jewish scriptures but reject the theology of the Logos—to Jews like Trypho. Justin's defense of Logos theology as a touchstone of Christian identity represents an attempt, one that was to prove quite successful, to establish intra-Christian hegemony by maximizing the contrast with Christianity's archetypal other, Judaism.

The third polemically driven moment in Christological development I wish to highlight is the virtual elimination of subordinationism between the Son and the Father in the context of the so-called Arian controversy of the fourth century.[23] The controversy begins with a dispute between the Alexandrian priest Arius and his bishop, Alexander, over the generation of the Son. The dispute quickly spreads throughout much of the eastern part of the empire, and soon, in a development that would prove decisive for the future of Christianity, involves the emperor, Constantine. The polemics of Alexander and, later, his successor Athanasius against Arius's denial of the Son's coeternity with the Father embody a rhetoric of Christological maximalism: Arius's insistence on the ontological priority of the Father—which he no doubt regarded as a straightforward, indeed banal, inference from the concept of divine Sonship—denigrates the Son. For Alexander and Athanasius, Arius's claim is tantamount to a denial of Christ's divinity. This invidious characterization of Arius's theology allows Alexander and Athanasius to link Arius's Christology to the Jewish denial of Jesus's status as Messiah. Athanasius accuses the Arians of killing the Logos (inasmuch as they deny Christ's divinity), thereby reenacting the crucifixion at the hands (allegedly) of the Jews.[24] Once again, we see a Christian faction seeking to establish intra-Christian hegemony by maximizing the contrast with the Jewish outgroup. Interestingly enough, we see Eusebius of Caesarea, during what Sara Parvis calls "the lost years of the Arian Controversy," employ the same rhetoric of Christological maximalism against the modalist theology of Athanasius's one-time ally, Marcellus of Ancyra. Marcellus, a fierce opponent of Arius and likely one of the architects of Nicaea, condemned "Arianism" for its appeal to Origen's doctrine of three divine hypostases, a doctrine that Marcellus regarded as tantamount to tritheism.25 In response, Eusebius accuses Marcellus of denigrating the Son by denying him his own hypostasis.26 By denying a hypostatic distinction between God and God's Word, Marcellus is forced to distinguish between the pre-existent Word and the incarnate Son. And this distinction exposes him to Eusebius's admittedly unfair charge that he, like the Jews, makes Christ a "mere man." Thus we see theologians on both sides of the so-called Arian controversy rhetorically assimilating their adversaries to the Jews, the archetypal "enemies of Christ" (*christomachoi*).

The upward trajectory of Christology culminates in the confession that the Son is "of the substance (*ousia*)" of the Father. The claim was first affirmed in the Council of Nicaea in 325 and eventually formed the basis of the orthodox, one-substance, three-persons doctrine of the Trinity supposedly formulated in Constantinople in 381.27 It is remarkable that the doctrine of consubstantiality, with a dubious genealogy in Gnostic speculation and a disconcerting proximity to the modalist heresy associated with the early-third-century figure of Sabellius, was destined to become a touchstone of Christian orthodoxy. When one steps back and surveys the development of fourth-century Trinitarian theology as a whole, it would seem that the Church was driven by polemical considerations to accept a doctrine that most, at least initially, were quite reluctant to embrace. In his first-hand account of the proceedings at Nicaea, Athanasius tells us that the bishops reluctantly introduced the fateful term *homoousios* ("consubstantial") into the creed for no other reason than that it was a formulation that Arius and his hard-core supporters could not, under any circumstances, accept.28 Most of the bishops who, under considerable pressure from the emperor, ended up signing the creed remained uncomfortable with the term for the very same reasons as Arius. It is telling that nobody, not even those who, like Eustatius of Antioch and Marcellus, were most strenuously opposed to the subordinationist trajectory associated with Arius, defends the term in the decades immediately following the council.29 Even Athanasius does not defend the *homoousios* until the 350s, and then only because he is forced to respond to his adversaries, who had made the term the focus of their criticism of both Nicaea and the theological trajectory represented by Athanasius.[30] In the end, the doctrine of consubstantiality becomes an acceptable expression of Christian faith only when it is welded together with the doctrine of three divine persons or hypostases, a qualification that effectively purges the original Nicene confession of its Sabellian associations.[31] At any rate, it is scarcely imaginable how the orthodox Trinitarian and Christological doctrines, the quintessential Christian expressions of the mystery of God, could have achieved their present forms in the absence of the polemical processes that drove the Church, almost in spite of itself, to an acceptance of the doctrine of consubstantiality.

Conclusion

The foregoing sketch suggests that inter-communal polemic is theologically productive. To the extent that the tendency to exalt Christ can be traced back to the need on the part of early Christian communities to distinguish themselves from non-Christian Jewish ones, it becomes difficult to maintain the distinction between doctrine and its formulation that theologians commonly make in order to isolate a core of doctrinal conviction from the particular circumstances, including the inevitable social conflicts, that condition its expression.[32] This means that even the most sublime and edifying Christological concepts cannot be neatly dissociated from the often unsavory, and indeed unChristian, polemics that the Church Fathers waged against heretics, pagans, and Jews. For myself, as a Greek Orthodox Christian, nothing better exemplifies this ambiguity than the text of the beautiful Divine Liturgy, which was penned by the same man, John Chrysostom, who was responsible for some of the most noxious Anti-Judaic sermons in the history of Christianity.

While difficult, an acknowledgment of the inherent ambiguities of religious commitment, and Christology in particular, is salutary in at least two respects. First, it represents an important first step in the task of the post-Holocaust Christian theologian as eloquently presented in Moyaert's essay, namely: to accept responsibility for the injuries inflicted on others as part of Christianity's historical process of identity formation. Second, by abandoning the quixotic effort to identify an essence of Christian identity untouched by the ambiguities of religious commitment, this acknowledgment of ambiguity frees Christians to address the more productive question of how, given the inevitability of theological *Auseinandersetzungen*, one can remove the specific conditions for the denigration of others. While efforts to differentiate one's community from others may, in fact, be inevitable, the tendency to vilify and denigrate the cultural-religious other is not. So while it is true that the relational processes by which Christians maintain their sense of identity today are continuous with those by which Christians staked out a distinctive sense of identity in Christianity's formative period, there is one obvious difference. Christians today relate to others, including Jews, as members of an established and recognized tradition. That is, Christian communities today do not belong, as they did initially, to an emergent movement struggling to pull itself over the threshold of recognition and thereby establish itself in being. It is important to remember that the harsh rhetoric found in many New Testament and other early Christian writings not only reflects the experience of a fledgling movement struggling to attain legitimacy in the ancient world. It also reflects their (eventual) rejection by a Jewish mainstream that the broader culture recognized, if grudgingly, as the custodians of a venerable tradition deserving respect. Thus the Christian discursive practices that have functioned to foster a contempt for the Jews are ultimately rooted in the fear, however exaggerated or unfounded, that the Church would never succeed in winning recognition, respect, and legitimacy so long as the Jews, with the prestige of their sacred traditions, continued to maintain a robust cultural presence.[33] The subsequent history of Christianity in the West exemplifies what can happen when a once embattled community carries this fear, born from its formative experience and enshrined in its founding narratives, images, and symbols, into a new situation in which it finds itself in a position of cultural dominance. Christians have long been in a position, of course, in which they can afford to extend to various religious others recognition and respect. Christian comparative theology, as demonstrated in both Bidlack and Moyaert's essays, exemplifies the kind of interreligious magnanimity of which Christianity at its best is capable. One can only hope that, with time, the understandable reserve and apprehension with which Jews, Muslims, and others greet Christian overtures in light of the history of European anti-Semitism at home and colonialism abroad, will give way to fully reciprocal interreligious reflection and dialogue.

Notes

1. On de Lubac, see Jan Van Bragt, "Buddhism—Jodo Shinshû—Christianity: Does Jodo Shinshu form a bridge between Buddhism and Christianity?" *Japanese Religions* 18:1 (1993): 50–51; cf. Henri de Lubac, *Amida* (Paris: Editions du Seuil, 1955), 268. For Otto, see Hugh Nicholson, *Comparative Theology and the Problem of Religious Rivalry* (Oxford: Oxford University Press, 2011), 110–11; Rudolf Otto, *Mysticism East and West*, trans. Bertha L. Bracey and Richenda C. Payne (New York: Collier Books, 1962), esp. "Part B"; cf. also, Otto, *India's Religion of Grace and Christianity Compared and Contrasted*, trans. Frank Hugh Foster (New York: Macmillan, 1930).
2. Paul Roscoe, "The Comparative Method," in *The Blackwell Companion to the Study of Religion*, ed. Robert Segal (Blackwell, 2006), 39.
3. Eric Zürcher, *The Buddhist Conquest of China* (Leiden: Brill, 2007), 37–38.
4. Zürcher, *Buddhist Conquest*, 290–320.
5. Moyaert is careful to distinguish between Christian anti-Judaism and Nazi anti-Semitism. As Gregory Baum argues, the former indirectly contributed to the latter by fostering "an abiding contempt among Christians for Jews and all things Jewish" that "was fundamental in Hitler's choice of the Jews as a scapegoat." See Baum, Introduction to *Faith and Fratricide* by Rosemary Radford Ruether (New York: Seabury, 1974), 7.
6. See Baum, "Introduction," 5; 11–13.
7. William Scott Green, "Introduction: Messiah in Judaism: Rethinking the Question," in *Judaisms and Their Messiahs at the Turn of the Christian Era*, ed. Jacob Neusner, William Scott Green, and Ernest S. Frerichs (Cambridge: Cambridge University Press, 1987), 8; J. H. Charlesworth, "From Messianology to Christology: Problems and Prospects," in *The Messiah*, ed. J. H. Charlesworth (Minneapolis: Fortress Press, 1992), 5; Andrew Chester, "Jewish Messianic Explanations and Mediatorial Figures in Pauline Christology," in *Paulus und das antike Judentum*, ed. Martin Hengel and Ulrich Heckel (Tübingen: Mohr-Siebeck, 1991), 41.
8. Charlesworth, "From Messianology to Christology: Problems and Prospects," 4–6; 34.
9. Larry W. Hurtado, "Religious Experience and Religious Innovation in the New Testament," *The Journal of Religion* 80:2 (2000): 183–205, esp. 204; Larry W. Hurtado, *Lord Jesus Christ* (Grand Rapids, Mich.: William B. Eerdmans, 2003), 64–74. See also C. D. F. Moule, *The Origin of Christology* (Cambridge: Cambridge University Press, 1977), 135: "[T]he characterizations of Christ in the New Testament are better accounted for as springing from contact with Jesus himself than as springing from contact with extraneous sources."
10. See, for example, Maurice Wiles, *The Making of Christian Doctrine* (Cambridge: Cambridge University Press, 1967), 62–93. For thoughtful critique, see Rebecca Lyman, "*Lex orandi*: Heresy, Orthodoxy, and Popular Religion," in *The Making and Remaking of Christian Doctrine*, ed. Sarah Coakley and David Palin (Oxford: Clarendon Press, 1993), 131–41.
11. Helmut Koester, "GNWMAI DIAFOROI: The Origin and Nature of Diversification in the History of Early Christianity," *Harvard Theological Review* 58 (1965): 280. Hurtado's effort to trace the belief in Christ's divinity to early Christian "Christ devotion"

can perhaps be regarded as an extended rebuttal of Wilhelm Bousset's thesis regarding the Hellenistic origins of the belief in Christ's divinity. Hurtado acknowledges the influence of the latter's classic *Kyrios Christos* (1913) on his own work. See Hurtado, *Lord Jesus Christ*, xiii; 13–15.

12. For a historical argument, see, for example, Koester, "GNWMAI DIAFOROI: The Origin and Nature of Diversification in the History of Early Christianity," *Harvard Theological Review* 58 (1965): 280: "Christianity in all its diversified appearances is a thoroughly syncretistic religion including its so-called orthodox developments." For a theoretical argument, see Kathryn Tanner, *Theories of Culture* (Minneapolis: Fortress Press, 1997).

13. Once again, see Baum, Introduction to *Faith and Fratricide* by Rosemary Radford Ruether (New York: Seabury, 1974), 5–6; 13–14.

14. J. Louis Martyn, "Glimpses into the History of the Johannine Community," in *The Gospel of John in Christian History* (New York: Paulist Press, 1978), 107–21.

15. Martyn, "Glimpses into the History of the Johannine Community," in *Gospel of John*, 113; 106.

16. Raymond Brown, *The Community of the Beloved Disciple* (New York: Paulist Press, 1979), 81–88.

17. See John 13:23–26; 18:15–16; 19:26–27; Brown, *The Community of the Beloved Disciple*, 82–83.

18. Hugh Nicholson, "Social Identity Processes in the Development of Maximally Counterintuitive Theological Concepts: Consubstantiality and No-Self," *Journal of the American Academy of Religion* 82:3 (2014): 741–53.

19. Justin does not seem to have drawn directly on John for his Logos theology. See Thomas H. Tobin, SJ, "Logos," in *The Anchor Bible Dictionary*, Vol. 4, ed. David Noel Freedman et al., 348–56 (New York: Doubleday, 1992), 355–56.

20. Daniel Boyarin, *Border Lines* (Philadelphia: University of Pennsylvania Press, 2004), 37–40.

21. Boyarin, *Border Lines*, 38, 92.

22. Boyarin, *Border Lines*, argues that such a rejection was *not* a defining feature of "Judaism" at the time Justin wrote (28–29, 30–31, 90, 92, 112).

23. As R. P. C. Hanson points out in *The Search for the Christian Doctrine of God* (Grand Rapids, Mich.: Baker Academic, 2005), xvii–xviii, the label is a misnomer in two respects. First, it falsely suggests that Arius was a more important and influential theologian than he actually was; in reality, Arius was important only for a historically brief period between 318 and 325. Second, it suggests that this single issue was disputed throughout the period, when in fact there were many discrete subjects of controversy.

24. Athanasius, *Orationes contra arianos* I.8, Nicene and Post-Nicene Fathers II.4, 310.

25. Arius's less radical opponents like Alexander based their criticism on the former's subordinationism, not on his appeal to the doctrine of multiple divine hypostases. See Manlio Simonetti, *La Crisi Ariana nel IV Secolo* (Rome: Augustinium, 1975), 68, 75, 95.

26. Colm Luibhéid, *Eusebius of Caesarea and the Arian Crisis* (Dublin: Irish Academic Press, 1981), 91, 93. Eusebius of Caesarea, *De eccl. theol.* 1.1 (Erich Klostermann, ed., *Eusebius Werke, Bd. 4: Gegen Markell, Über die kirchliche Theologie, Die Fragmente*

Markells [Berlin: Akademie Verlag, 1972], 63); *De eccl. theol* 2.11 (Klostermann, *Eusebius Werke*, 113).

27. Technically and historically this is not entirely correct. See Joseph T. Lienhard, "*Ousia* and *Hypostasis*: The Cappadocian Settlement and the Theology of the 'One Hypostasis,'" in *The Trinity*, ed. Stephen T. Davis, Daniel Kendall, and Gerald O'Collins (New York: Oxford University Press, 1999), 100.
28. Athanasius, *De decretis* 19–20 (Hans-Georg Optiz, ed. *Urkunden zur Geschichte des arianischen Streites*, vol. II/1 of *Athanasius Werke* [Berlin and Leipzig, 1934–35], 15–17).
29. Simonetti, *La Crisi Ariana nel IV Secolo*, 93.
30. Lewis Ayres, *Nicaea and Its Legacy* (New York: Oxford University Press, 2004), 133–40; Hanson, *The Search for the Christian Doctrine of God*, 329.
31. Michel René Barnes, "The Fourth Century as Trinitarian Canon," in *Christian Origins: Theology, Rhetoric, and Community*, ed. Lewis Ayres and Gareth Jones (New York: Routledge 1998), 62.
32. See George A. Lindbeck, *The Nature of Doctrine* (Philadelphia: Westminster Press, 1984), 92.
33. Here we see the central symbolic importance of the destruction of the Jerusalem Temple in early Christian ideology. And, recognizing this, we can understand the consternation caused by the Emperor Julian's plan to rebuild the Temple. See Robert L. Wilken, *John Chrysostom and the Jews* (Berkeley: University of California Press, 1983), 128–30.

PART V
Soteriology

13 The Way(s) of Salvation

THE FUNCTION OF THE LAW
IN JOHN CALVIN
AND ABU HAMID AL-GHAZALI

Joshua Ralston

The majority of Christian soteriologies written in context of religious diversity have focused on the possibility of salvation for those who are not Christian. Traditionally, these theologies of religious diversity have been divided into three major paradigms: exclusivism, inclusivism, and pluralism. *Exclusivism* maintains that salvation is given only through Christ to those that explicitly embrace faith, the Church, and/or Christianity. The assertion that there is no salvation apart from the church serves as a classical articulation of this position. The second category, *inclusivism*, recognizes the unsurpassed saving power of Christ and Christianity but also recognizes that truth is present in other religions, thereby affirming the possibility of salvation in Christ apart from explicit confession. *Pluralism*, which has been championed by theologians such as John Hick and Paul Knitter, emphasizes the equality and saving possibility of each religious way of life.

In recent years, Christian theologians have grown increasingly uncomfortable with this three-fold categorization. Thinkers from across the theological spectrum, such as Gavin D'Costa, Wolfhart Pannenberg, and Jeannine Hill Fletcher, have challenged Hick's paradigm as artificial, inattentive to the diversity within religions, and reliant on a modern epistemology.[1] One of the more creative critics of the pluralist model is the comparative theologian S. Mark Heim. In *Salvations: Truth and Difference in Religion*, Heim suggests the possibility of affirming the validity of distinct religious ends that accompany different religious ways of life. He critiques the pluralist view for failing to give attention to the particularity of each religion and the competing visions of life, practice, and "salvation." Other religious communities have distinct views of humanity's and the cosmos's ultimate end. Nirvana and the beatific vision cannot simply be equated. To claim, as certain proponents of the pluralistic position do, that all religions ultimately lead to salvation, God, or the Real is to avoid the challenges raised by religious diversity and different traditions' distinct views of the world's *telos* and the nature of the divine. Moreover, the practices and disciplines that form persons in their traditions are themselves shaped by the religion's vision of their ultimate end. The fasting and feasting of Ramadan and the pressing of one's forehead to the ground five times daily in prayer are all part of the "technologies of self" that intend to create Muslims—those who submit to God's will.

This chapter builds on Heim's comparative methodology by considering the way(s) that divine law functions on the road to salvation, rather than focusing on the possibility of salvation for Muslims or the differing religious ends of Christians and Muslims. The use of the term "way(s)" is meant to highlight both early Christian habits of identifying themselves and their movement as the Way and to highlight the primary meaning of the term *shariʻa*. *Shariʻa*, which is often translated as Islamic Law, has a much broader connotation than what is often understood by the term "law." The word shares the same Arabic root letters of *sh-r-ʻ* with the words for road and path. For most Muslims, *shariʻa* is less about legal requirements enforced by a judge or the state and more a way, road, or path to a flourishing life. More specifically, this essay juxtaposes the Protestant reformer John Calvin's theology of the law with the Sunni reviver Abu Hamid al-Ghazali's by considering how each depicts the function, gifts, and limits of divine law in the human movement toward God.

A comparative approach between Christianity and Islam enters into a delicate and historically fraught terrain, one that has often been marked by polemic and rivalry. These traditions' history of partly overlapping scriptures and shared yet diverging views of God raise serious questions about how far comparative theology might actually go in addressing areas of acute theological disagreement. As Josef von Ess notes, "On the whole, taken in relation to Christianity, Islam did not treat new problems; it treated the same problems differently."[2] At the outset, it is important to note the differences in how Calvin and Ghazali understand the way of salvation.

In terms of the substance of religious faith, Calvin's and Ghazali's divergent views reflect wide swaths of their respective traditions of Protestant Christianity and Sunni Islam. According to Calvin, salvation is a gift of divine grace secured by the atoning death of Jesus and received by faith through the power of the Holy Spirit. For Ghazali, confession of the revelation of the Qur'an, the unity of God, and the prophethood of Muhammad are the sure foundation of religion and necessary components of any movement toward salvation. Both understand damnation to be the likely eternal destination for those who do not embrace the religion revealed by God.[3] Historically, both Calvin and Ghazali knew of the other religious community and considered it to be in grave error.

Within the subcategory of Christian thought termed "justification," then, a comparative theological conversation between these two thinkers stalls before it begins. And yet, it is the wager of this chapter that if we shift the discussion away from questions about the content of faith and toward the themes of law and its role in human growth toward God (what Christian theologians often term sanctification or the Christian life), we may find possibilities for mutual enrichment. For it is here that Calvin and Ghazali both struggle to articulate a coherent account of the law's gifts and its limitations in the human movement toward God. Furthermore, by shifting the conversation from the specific question of which central confession is true to a study of the path or way toward holiness, we might reframe confrontational understandings of law in Christian-Muslim dialogue (and indirectly Christian-Jewish dialogue).

Two factors, however, mitigate against comparative understandings of law. First, for many non-Muslims, *shari'a* is largely associated with theocratic government, limits on personal freedom, punishments of amputation, and patriarchy. Tariq Ramadan notes how "in the West, the idea of *shari'a* calls up all the darkest images of Islam."[4] These negative stereotypes of *shari'a*, coupled with its use in the fundamentalism and violence of organizations like Boko Haram and al-Shabaab and the governments of Sudan and Saudi Arabia, hinder a broader engagement with the place of *shari'a* in Muslim thought and practice.

Second, in the history of Christian discourse, the law has often been placed in a starkly oppositional relationship to love, grace, and/or the gospel. Salvation is understood to be the gracious gift of a loving God and not an achievement earned by appeasing a juridical Master. While there is much to commend in these views, such understandings have had the unfortunate byproduct of denigrating Judaism and by extension Islam. Within the common history of anti-Jewish rhetoric, Christianity is often described as a religion of grace or love, while Islam and Judaism are depicted as religions of works or law. This too-neat dichotomy, which has roots in New Testament arguments, has the unfortunate effect of misconstruing both Jewish and Islamic conceptions of the compassionate One who gives *Torah* and/or *shariʻa* for the sake of human flourishing. While there are important distinctions between Christianity, Judaism, and Islam over the nature of salvation, the centrality of law, and the form of divine mercy, neither Judaism nor Islam understands human obedience to the law to be the sole means of securing God's mercy. For all three traditions, divine forgiveness, mercy, and love are the free acts of a good God—or at least this is what a comparative theological conversation between Calvin and Ghazali might surface. Before turning to that comparative study, however, it will be beneficial to survey the ambiguous place of the law in the New Testament and the complicated legacy these texts have bequeathed to Christian traditions.

The Ambiguous Place of the Law in the New Testament

Christian ambivalence about the law, and its role in salvation and moral pedagogy, is rooted in the New Testament's often-conflicting depiction of the law. Take the case of the biblical depictions of Jesus of Nazareth's relationship to the law. On the one hand, he is portrayed as upholding the centrality of the Torah. Famously, Jesus proclaims in the Sermon on the Mount, "Do not think that I have come to abolish the law and the prophets; I have come not to abolish but to fulfill. For truly I tell you, until heaven and earth pass away, not one letter, not one stroke of a letter, will pass from the law until all is accomplished" (Matt. 5:17–18). The Sermon on the Mount is often read as an intensification of the mosaic law, demanding that outward conformity of action be accompanied by internal purity of motivation (cf. Luke 16:14–18; Mark 10:1–12 and 17–31; and John 7:14–24).

At the same time, Jesus's ministry regularly bumps up against certain practices and interpretations of religious law in first-century Judaism. His willingness to enter into table fellowship with tax collectors and sinners (for example, Matt. 9:9–13, Mark 2:13–17, Luke 15:1–2), his healing on the Sabbath (for example, Matt. 12:9–14, Mark 1:21–28, Luke 6:6–11, John 5:1–18), his attitude toward certain purity laws (Mark 7:1–22), and most dramatically, the cleansing of the Temple (Matt. 21:12–17, Mark 11:15–19, Luke 19:45–48, John 2:13–25) all garner critique from some of the religious authorities. And yet Jesus never pits these actions over and against the divine law itself. He argues instead that he is in conformity with it, while the religious authorities "abandon the commandment of God and hold to human tradition" (Mark 7:8). Even with this critique of tradition in place, Jesus is rarely described as overturning central aspects of Jewish law such as dietary rules, circumcision, and festival celebrations—the very aspects of the Torah that the later Christian community deemed optional and/or revisable. Jesus's actions against particular traditions of the law are justified as being in conformity with the law in so far as they uphold the central demands of love of God and love of neighbor. For Jesus, like other rabbis in the first century, it is love of God and neighbor on which all the laws and prophets hang, and this love is the criterion by which ritual practices are to be judged (Matt. 22:40).

The various accounts of the early Christian communities' relationship to the law after the death, resurrection, and ascension of Jesus are more complicated. The Acts of the Apostles initially depicts the early community in Jerusalem as following in Jesus' specific approach of abiding by the Torah and participating in the life of early Judaism, including its legal components. However, as the gospel begins to spread beyond Jerusalem, Judea, and Samaria, the question of the relationship between Torah observance and membership in the new community becomes an issue of considerable debate. Chapters 9 and 10, with Paul's conversion, Peter's vision, and the conversion of Cornelius and his family, are the turning point. After Gentiles hear the good news and receive the Spirit (Acts 10:34–48), a debate erupts about whether or not circumcision and adherence to dietary laws are a necessary part of the Christian way. Eventually, the Council of Jerusalem (Acts 15) decided that it was unnecessary for either salvation or membership in the community of faith either to be circumcised or to keep the law of Moses (although James remains adamant that certain dietary restrictions remain in place).

Paul, especially in his letters to the churches in Galatia and Rome, offers the most comprehensive theological account of the role of the law in the economy of salvation. In Galatians, he vehemently argues against those who wish to (re)introduce adherence to Torah, exemplified by circumcision, as a necessary component of salvation for Gentiles. Against such a view, Paul contends that human beings are free from the law because God's justification of humanity is accomplished "not by the works of the law but through faith in (or of) Jesus Christ" (Gal. 2:16). Salvation is given by the Spirit and not through the works of the law or the flesh. The law, according to Paul, is incapable of making human beings righteous. Thus, to rely on the "works of the law" is to subject oneself to the curse of the law, a curse that Jesus Christ has already redeemed us from (Gal. 3:10–14). This is not to say the law plays no part in God's saving action. On the contrary, Paul is adamant that the law does not contradict the promises of God; it reveals sin and transgression and serves as a necessary disciplinarian before the coming of Christ. After the saving action of God in Christ, believers are no longer in need of such discipline and are thus freed from the law and made to live by the Spirit. Interestingly, Paul goes on to say that the freeing work of the Spirit results in a life lived for the other, not in antinomian avoidance of law: the "whole law" is summed up in love of neighbor (Gal. 5:14), and "bearing one another's burdens" fulfills "the law of Christ" (Gal. 6:2). Paul's description of the Christian life of freedom as one that fulfills the purpose and meaning of the law is consistent with Jesus's identification of the heart of the law with love of neighbor.

Debates about law are not limited to the Pauline corpus. The epistle of James is often read as something of a counterbalance to Paul's perspective on the law and faith. Like Paul, James holds a rigorous standard of obedience to the law, claiming that transgressing any one law makes one guilty of violating the whole law (James 2:10–13). However, James's response is not to emphasize the need for faith alone. Instead, the letter continually demands that people "be doers of the word, and not merely hearers" (James 1:22); he is also adamant that "faith by itself, if it has no works, is dead" (James 2:17). James is concerned, much like Paul in his letters to the church at Corinth (1 Cor. 8), that freedom from the law has become an occasion for laxity (James 1:25), and for James, like Jesus and Paul, the law centers on love of neighbor and care for the other (James 2:1–8, 4:7, 5:1–6).

The connection between commandments and love is nowhere more clearly expressed than in 1 John. Love is defined as obedience to the way of Jesus (1 John 2:1–6). According to John, the command to love one another is not a "new commandment, but an old commandment that you have had from the beginning" (1 John 2:7). The ancient law of God is summed up not in *Halakhah* (Jewish religious law), but in the command to abide in the love of God and neighbor. For John, the Christian life does not leave the law of Israel and the will of God behind, but lives it more perfectly: "And this is his commandment, that we should believe in the name of his Son Jesus Christ and love one another, just as he has commanded us.... And by this we know that he abides in us, by the Spirit that he has given us" (1 John 3:23–24). The spirit of God that dwells within Christians empowers them to love God and one another and thus to fulfill the commandments of God. For John, love and obedience are mutually reinforcing realities (1 John 5:1–5). To love is to obey and to obey is to love.

Viewed together, these texts paint a complex, diverse, and somewhat ambiguous picture of the law. On the one hand, salvation and membership in the community of Christ do not depend on obedience to the law but on God's grace given in and through Christ and the Spirit. On the other hand, the authors of the various gospels and epistles go to great pains to insist that the law is "holy and just and good" (Rom. 7:12). These biblical ambiguities have given rise to a number of theological schemas that aim to make sense of both the law's gifts and its limitations in the economy of salvation. Justin Martyr's dialogue with the Jewish thinker Trypho, Augustine's polemical attack on the Pelagians, Martin Luther's distinction between the law and the Gospel, the canons of the Council of Trent, and John Wesley's order of salvation are all attempts to grapple with this scriptural legacy.

John Calvin—The Law as Tutor and Guide

For John Calvin, the French refugee turned Geneva reformer, the law was a central preoccupation of this life and thought. He initially studied to be a lawyer and, in fact, was never formally trained as a priest or theologian. His first early version of the *Institutes of Christian Religion* (1536) is largely organized around the Ten Commandments, which indicates his attempt to integrate his appreciation of the law within his commitment to Luther's argument that salvation is through faith alone. Law, for Calvin, is first and foremost a theological and communal concept: "I understand by the word 'law' not only the Ten Commandments, which set forth a godly and righteous rule of living, but the form of religion handed down by God through Moses. And Moses was not made a lawgiver to wipe out the blessing promised to the race of Abraham."[5] Serene Jones argues that "stated this way, the law does not look primarily like a set of abstractly asserted standards for measuring right behavior but more like an exquisite, acclaimed portrait that presents to us a vision of the godly life."[6] What role does this "exquisite, acclaimed portrait" play in Calvin's pedagogy toward piety? How does the law function to draw the human person into true wisdom and thus to salvation?

Locating Calvin's discussion of the law within the broader movements of the 1559 edition of *The Institutes of Christian Religion* can aid us here. Calvin's main treatise on the law is situated within Book II's discussion of "The Knowledge of God as the Redeemer." Calvin does not treat the law in his study of the knowledge of God as Creator (Book I) but in his exegesis of God's revelation and action to save humanity (Books II and III). For Calvin, the law is thus primarily a soteriological and not a moral issue. Within Book II, Calvin's discussion of law follows after his account of human sin, the insufficiency of human works, the bondage of the will, and the need for redemption in Christ. For Calvin, the law interrupts human sin to draw sinners toward divine blessings. Law is a means for revealing the need for divine redemption; it is not the means for acquiring, let alone achieving, grace. Grace is made known through the law, and in some ways externally given in the law, but the full reception of grace awaits Calvin's discussion of justification, sanctification, adoption, and atonement in Book III.

To make sense of the diverse functions of the law in God's saving action, Calvin argues, in a similar fashion to Martin Luther, that the law has distinct uses. According to the Reformation schema, the *first use of the law* is theological (*usus theologicus*): The law displays God's righteousness, reveals sin, and thereby shows forth humanity's desperate need for God's grace. Calvin compares the law to a mirror in which "we contemplate our weakness, then the iniquity arising from this, and finally the curse coming from both."[7] For fallen human beings, there is "one sole means of recovering salvation": Jesus Christ.[8] Human works, even in obedience to the law, are impotent to save. The *second use of the law* is political (*usus politicus*): The law restrains evildoers, enforces external righteousness, and offers a space for public life together. According to this view, after the Fall, human existence is marred by sin and the power of the devil. The world requires a means for restraining evil, controlling civil unrest, and resisting the devil. God provides such protective intervention in the form of the temporal authorities and legal threats.

While Calvin is adamant that one of the chief functions of the law is to expose sin and drive human beings toward God, his language for the way that the law accomplishes this is not exclusively negative. In fact, Calvin goes on to argue that there is a *third use of the law* (*usus didaticus*):

> The third and principal use, which pertains more closely to the proper purpose of the law, finds its place among believers in whose hearts the Spirit of God already lives and reigns. For even though they have the law

written and engraved upon their hearts by the finger of God, that is, have been so moved and quickened through the directing of the Spirit that they long to obey God, they still profit by the law in two ways.[9]

In contrast to Luther's argument that the law's primary function is accusatory, Calvin argues that the law is meant to be first and foremost a guide or tutor. While he does insist that the law accuses, condemns, and destroys the sinner, Calvin also employs language that highlights the law's blessing and the subsequent desire and longing that such blessing elicits in sinners: "These maxims—far from abusing the law—are of greatest value in more clearly commending God's beneficence. Thus it is clear that by our wickedness and depravity we are prevented from enjoying the blessed life set openly before us by the law."[10] Like Moses's vision of the Promised Land from Mount Horeb, the law entices us toward the promise, even as it exposes our inability to realize the promises of God through our own works. When such longing is met in Christ's work, the graciousness of God becomes all the more astonishing: "Thereby the grace of God, which nourishes us without the support of the law, becomes sweeter, and his mercy, which bestows that grace upon us, becomes more lovely. From this we learn that he never tires in repeatedly benefiting us and in heaping new gifts upon us."[11] The law shows forth the divine blessing of God and in so doing both condemns human sin and elicits human longing.

For Calvin, the law should ultimately be received as a good gift of God. The principal intention of the law is to provide a guide for a life well lived, not to condemn humanity. Once Christ and the Sprit secure our justification, the law becomes a rule for a life lived in accordance with God's will. The law offers guidance on God's will for humanity and also encourages obedience to God's will. It charts a path toward holiness:

> We ought not to be frightened away from the law or to shun its instruction merely because it requires a much stricter moral purity than we shall reach while we bear about with us the prison house of our body. For the law is not now acting toward us as a rigorous enforcement officer who is not satisfied unless the requirements are met. But in this perfection to which it exhorts us, the law points out the goal toward which throughout life we are to strive.[12]

Calvin consistently argues that the law's third use is a genuine gift of God and a life-giving guide that draws us toward flourishing. And yet this view of the law's use stands in considerable tension with Calvin's understanding of the first and second uses of the law. While Calvin emphasizes the law's blessings and beauty, he also does not shrink from describing it is as supremely frightening. The law is always a gift, but it can be a terrible one. As such, it is unclear how Calvin reconciles these different stages in the law's use. There are open questions about how a community or individual that first encounters the law as a terrible accuser can later view it as a loving and beautiful guide. Certainly, Calvin attributes such a shift to the Holy Spirit, but it is challenging to understand how the same demand from which the Christian was once free is now morally beneficial to their maturation in holiness. When the law is first and extensively described as either a shameful accuser or a source of works righteousness, it is difficult to then demand these same, or similar, practices be reintroduced into the Christian life. Calvin's inability to reconcile the first and third uses of the law might go some way to explaining the legacy of puritanism and legalism that has often marked the Reformed tradition. Too often in traditions that trace aspects of their heritage to Calvin, the third use of the law has actually been applied in shame ridden and legalistic ways akin to the first and second uses.

Part of the reason for this difficulty is that Calvin's theology stands within a long line of Christian accounts of the law that depend on a number of strong divisions: faith and works, gospel and law, and interior and exterior. The former is the depicted as genuine, trustworthy, and vital aspect of life, while the latter is either a divine concession to human sin or a symbol of a more spiritually important internal reality. Once the internal reality of faith is appropriated properly, the external and bodily practices can be discarded. This way of thinking is illustrated in Paul's discussion of Abraham and circumcision in Romans 4. Paul offers something of a midrashic reinterpretation of the promises and covenant with Abraham, so that exterior acts of circumcision are understood to be mere signs of his internal faith. It is faith that justifies and makes righteous, not the external act of circumcision. He not only interprets external acts as signifying an internal disposition, but also replaces the external restraints. External practices of law like circumcision, ritual purity, and dietary prohibitions become elective and thus fall away for many Christians. While this freedom from legalism is a vital aspect of the Christian vision of life, it also creates an ambivalent relationship with bodies, law, and human practices.

Is there a more coherent way to recognize the law's beauty and also its limitations than Calvin's schema of the law's three uses? A model that neither denigrates the body and external acts nor relies on shame? To find such a depiction, we might turn outside of the Christian tradition and consider the law and its limitation in the thought of the great reviver (*mujaddid*) of Islam, Abu Hamid al-Ghazali.

Ghazali: Breathing Life into the Law

Ghazali's *Revival of the Religious Sciences* (*Ihya' 'ulum al-din*) thoroughly reimagines the religious, legal, and theological practices of his day.[13] His text, like Calvin's, aims to breathe life into the religious learning of a community grown complacent.[14] Ghazali was convinced that the religious sciences of law (*fiqh*), philosophy (*falasafa*), and theology (*kalam*) that dominated the Islamic world of the eleventh century had become unduly focused on worldly concerns and thus needed to be redirected toward God, or what he dubbed the sciences of the hereafter. This comprehensive program of the *Revival* is divided into four quarters: 1) acts of worship, 2) acts of daily life, 3) qualities leading to destruction, and 4) qualities leading to salvation. Within this fourfold division, each quarter further breaks down into ten books that cover specific issues pertinent to the broader category. For instance, in the first quarter, he addresses issues such as purity and prayer; in the second, he discusses themes related to eating and marriage; in the third, he considers the perils of the tongue and condemns pride; finally, in the fourth, he moves from repentance through hope and trust to love and remembrance of death.

Ghazali's organization of the *Revival* playfully mimics or riffs on the traditional manuals of *fiqh* (jurisprudence) and *usul al-fiqh* (legal theory). The classical manuals of law were often organized in a fourfold structure that moved from considerations of worship to issues of daily life and then on to questions of trade and criminal punishment. Similar to Judaism and its practice of *Halakhah*, Islamic understandings of law cover a much wider range of subject matter than Western Christians are accustomed to associating with the term law. Questions of what to eat, what to wear, how to break fast, how to raise children, and who should have the first right of refusal on sales, are all part of *shari'a*. Still, *shari'a* is not first and foremost a set of legal rulings, but a way of life. In its only explicit use of the word *shari'a*, the Qur'an says, "Then we put you on the clear way (*shari'a*) of our commandment, so follow it and do not follow the inclinations of those who do not know" (45:18). For Muslims, law is a guide for a life lived in obedience to God and with respect for neighbor, one that covers all aspects of human interaction from prayer to property rights. *Shari'a* is a central component of Islamic identity, thought and practice. The practice of *fiqh* by the *'ulema* (religious and legal scholars) is an attempt to discern through reference to the Qur'an, hadiths, custom, and analogical thinking the proper legal demands of God for a particular situation.

By framing the *Revival* in this apparently jurisprudential manner, Ghazali initiates a reform of the way that the law was understood and practiced in his day. In particular, he seeks to correct the *'ulema*'s undue focus on worldly matters and reorient legal and ritual practice to its ultimate end, which is felicity or life with God in the hereafter. As he writes in his introduction, he wants to challenge those religious leaders who had become satisfied "with the husk of knowledge rather than the flesh of the fruit."[15] Moreover, Ghazali suspects that his jurisprudential framing might ensnare unsuspecting students and bring them into an understanding of *shari'a* that is refracted through the eschatological end of human beings: "And since he who dresses as the beloved will also be beloved, I am not off in deeming that the modeling of this book after books of jurisprudence will prove to be a clever move in creating interest in it."[16]

The staging of the *Revival* also indicates something of Ghazali's understanding of the place or use of the law within the person's pilgrimage toward God. By locating discussion of ritual observances and daily customs, issues traditionally related to *shari'a* and *fiqh* within what he calls the study of the sciences of the world, Ghazali dislodges law from the center of the religious sciences. In its place, he fashions a framework for moving through the entirety of human existence so as to purify the heart and meld knowledge and practice (*'ulm wa 'amal*). And yet, for Ghazali, progressing beyond the law never entails the abandonment of law and practice: "Human beings, then, are beckoned beyond the external dictates of the law. And yet for Ghazali going beyond law does not entail the abandonment of law. There is a progression in the chapters from the humblest duties to the highest pinnacles of insight. Each topic is a step in a slow ascent, each new theme depends upon the themes that precedes it. At the same time, however, nothing is superseded or supplanted."[17]

To accomplish this legal-spiritual pedagogy, Ghazali couples traditional *fiqh* exposition with attention to spiritual practices, particularly those drawn from the examples of Muhammad, the prophet's companions, and Sufi exemplars. Part of Ghazali's ongoing influence in the Islamic world is often traced to the *Revival's* integration of legal Sunni orthodoxy and Sufi mysticism. This combination of legal prescription and interior re-orientation is evident not only in the broader macro-structure of the work, but also in Ghazali's analysis of each aspect of Quarter 1's study of worship. Throughout he pairs reflection on the outward or legal obligations of ablution, prayer, fasting, and pilgrimage with a consistent focus on the proper interior disposition necessary for each act. For instance, in his reflections on prayer in Quarter 1, Book 4, he offers extended legal opinions on the various intricacies and commands regarding the daily prayer. This includes specific legal rulings about how one comports the body during prayer, from the space between one's feet, to the distance of one's gaze, to the proper movements of bowing and prostration.

This exploration of the legal requirements of prayers is a traditional part of *fiqh* and is considered the central entry point into *shari'a*. Prayer, and not rulings on property or prescribed punishment, is actually the most consistent and vital part of *shari'a*.[18] Here, Ghazali inserts within his legal opinions a lengthy treatment on the interior aspect of prayer. The exterior act must be accompanied by an interior disposition, or the obligatory act is of little spiritual value:

> The object is not utterance by means of the letters because it is simply utterance, but because it is beneficial utterance, and it becomes beneficial utterance only whenever it expresses what is in the mind, and it becomes such an expression only by the presence of the heart. Thus, what request is there in the saying, "Guide us into the Straight Road!" (Qur'an, i. 5), when the heart is unmindful and when one does not intend that it should be an intercession and a supplication? For what hardship is there in moving the tongue with it, along with unmindfulness, especially after it has become customary?

While Ghazali notes the priority of the interior life and the proper disposition of the heart, nowhere does he render external embodied legal actions to be unnecessary: "Al-Ghazali insists throughout the *Revival* that following the law and performing ritual acts correctly is an indispensable foundation of the Science of the Hereafter . . . ritual duties never become superfluous as one progresses along the path."[19] What Ghazali adds, then, is a deeper appreciation of the way that the law's obligation might create the type of posture conducive to growth in knowledge, trust, and purity of heart. The law is limited, and yet the law is never disconnected from divine mercy. It is, in fact, a site of mercy and growth toward God: "What God loves above all, is his Law (*sharia*). God's love, far from dispensing men from obeying the prescriptions of His Law, puts them in a position to observe these even more scrupulously and more profoundly."[20] To draw from the Psalmists, the law revives the soul. It does this, not through some crude Christian stereotype about human effort or works apart from divine mercy, but by properly positioning human beings to discern and live in light of God, who is the Merciful One (*al-Rahman*), the Compassionate One (*al-Raheem*).[21]

By the time the reader, or better the pilgrim, arrives in Quarter 4 of the *Revival*, she has been prepared to engage in the deeper mysteries of Islamic piety—what Ghazali inventively names the science of the hereafter. As in his earlier discussions of worship, Ghazali divides his accounts of fear, trust, faith, and love into various stages within the movement toward God. For instance, in his discussion of fear and hope in Book 33, Ghazali depicts the proper and improper reasons for fear of and hope in God. Like Calvin, he thinks that fear of God can be a motivating or correcting factor in the pursuit of piety. However, nowhere is Ghazali's theology of fear connected to the terror of law. Fear arises from either recognition of human sin or recognition of the majesty and mystery of God. These two forms of fear are not of equal merit, as one should move from preoccupation with self to worship of God: "And this accords with the division of those who fear into the person who fears his disobedience and sin, and the one who fears God in Person, because of His attributes and majesty and characteristics which, without a doubt, compel awe."[22] Proper fear is a result of God's wholly otherness and not a fixation on the self and its limitations. To progress in piety, we must move from fear grounded in our failings to a fear based on God's majesty: "If the disobedient person 'knew' God as he ought to 'know' Him, he would fear God and would not fear his disobedience."[23] This fear of God should not be mischaracterized as grounded in a vision of God as juridical taskmaster, but rather within Islamic understandings of God's absolute uniqueness. God induces holy awe or fear, not because God is unforgiving, but because God is *al-'Aziz* (the most majestic).

While fear of God can drive us toward the hereafter, it is not the primary vehicle for transformation. Hope and love prove to be truer engines for growth than fear: "Know that action on account of hope is of a higher order than action on account of fear, because the creatures who are nearest to God are those who love Him most, and love dominates hope."[24] Fear then moves toward trust and love, which "is the final goal among the stages and the supreme summit of the journey."[25] The way to love of God, however, must pass through ascetical, legal, and mystical practice, so that the human emotion of love can be properly oriented toward God. This is partly achieved through the legal practices of ablution and prayer, the framing of worldly practices of eating and drinking, and the relationship of moderation that marks financial exchange, which all become part and parcel of the proper pilgrimage toward God. Love, then, is not set up in opposition to law because love is expressed in and through obedience to the law: "It is the duty of every lover of God that he should love what God loves and hate what God hates."[26] Law is not love of God, but it is not other than love of God.[27]

Love of God, then, produces particular fruits or virtues. These fruits are laid out before the pilgrim by the law, but they are not experienced except through a lifelong journey of practice in accordance with the law coupled with an interior disposition of spiritual growth: "When love for God is established and one's purposes are immersed in divine love, it becomes then clear that it is love which brings contentment in the deeds of the Beloved."[28] In contrast to Calvin's claims about the conditional blessings of the law, Mona Siddiqui has argued that Ghazali understands "both love and law to be central tenets of Islam and being a Muslim. He does not see any conditionality in the prior fulfillment of the law, but rather sees observing of the law as the sublime way to show love for God..."[29] Ghazali, then, understands the law as something akin to Calvin's vision of the third use of the law. "Love must necessarily come first and only then, in its aftermath, does he who loves obey."[30] It is a useful tutor, a guide, a lure, but it is not the end in and of itself. Only God is our final home.

Conclusion

This comparative engagement on the place and function of the law in the thought of John Calvin and Abu Hamid al-Ghazali suggests possibilities for reframing Christian theological discussions on the human journey toward redemption. Often such theologies, at least in Protestant theology, have depended on dichotomies between law and grace, and the exterior actions and interior realities. Much of this legacy can be traced to the genuine insights of the Apostle Paul, Augustine of Hippo, and Martin Luther, particularly their attempt to highlight the absolute graciousness of God and the fact that all we have depends on the mercy and generosity of God. And yet to make these arguments about grace, they construct divisions, unintentionally or not, that denigrated the law, Judaism, or Islam.

While Calvin's account of the third use of the law sought to wrestle free of these negative renderings by highlighting the gift and goodness of the Law, his schema is not entirely consistent. He succeeds in highlighting that the basic problem of human life is not found in the law itself, but in our propensity to misuse the law for our own prestige, merit, and gain. And yet one aspect of Calvin's "solution" to this predicament of human works is to employ Luther's ideas of the first and second use of the law and thereby make adherence to divine law a source of shame and accusation. By making the law first a judge and accuser, the law becomes a source of enmity. When Calvin then returns to his discussion of the law after justification and the impartation of the Spirit, one is left with the sense that the law is not actually a good gift. If law was once unnecessary for salvation beyond accusation and shame, why does it suddenly regain importance in the Christian life? If I need not act before, why must I act now? Certainly, there is a need to be disabused of false comfort about one's own righteousness and thereby to move deeper in spiritual practice and piety, but might this be accomplished through an alternative imaginary than that employed by Calvin? We need a better account of the way that sanctification or growth in piety depends on law and grace, the body and the heart, works and faith—all of which find their source in the irrevocable gift of God.

In Ghazali, we discover an alternative model of the relationship between law and mercy, interior motive and exterior act. Ghazali recognizes the central importance of purity of heart, faith, and intention in the pursuit into love of God, but such a move toward love does not replace acts of ritual enactment or legal prescriptions. The law remains a genuine gift and its practice is necessary—not because mere repetition of exterior and bodily acts alone can purify the heart—but because it is in and through these activities that we move toward higher goals of spiritual life. Yes, we must draw distinctions, such as those between knowledge and practices, this world and the next, the body and the heart; but none of these distinctions in Ghazali is marked by the strict dualism that comes to dominate some of Calvin's thought. The heart takes priority over the body, love over law, the next world over this world; but the concerns of the body, the law, and this world are never denigrated of their import in quite the same way as in Calvin's thought. The law can and does become insufficient, especially when its application is primarily concerned with excessive personal achievement or religious policing, but its limitations are not overcome by abandoning it but by breathing vitality into it.

When the Divine Spirit breathes life into the law, it ceases to be either legalism or a curse but becomes again what it always was, a gift. Christians, particularly Protestants, might reconsider the way they depict the giving of the law at Sinai. Instead of primarily interpreting the law as a prologue or sign of future grace, we might instead consider how the law is only given after the previous act of God freeing the Israelites from slavery in Egypt. The law is not primarily a standard that must be met in order to merit God's blessings, but a gift given because of God's prior mercy. Of course, the law remains limited, capable of human manipulation and fossilization, and it cannot enact the fullness of divine life. For both Calvin and Ghazali there is a keen recognition that the religious authorities often abuse the law by making it tool of social control rather than a guide to the hereafter. Such human abuses, however, need not result in the antinomianism that has often plagued Christian thinking. For Christian theology, then, we might think of Jesus and the Spirit as reviving or breathing life into the law—or the divine way of life—and not as replacing or making irrelevant divine commands. As such, we receive the law as a gift to guide, shape, and form us as people marked by love and not as a set of external restraints or legal hoops that merit divine approval. Law is thus a form of the gospel through which God graciously addresses us.[31]

Finally, this examination of the divine way(s) of salvation in Calvin and Ghazali might disabuse us of drawing too strict divisions between Christianity as a religion of grace and Islam and Judaism as religions of law. This comparative theological approach to dismantling stereotypical renderings of law and grace does not mean that Calvin and Ghazali are simply saying the same things about God and salvation, albeit in different cultural-religious terms *à la* pluralism. Calvin and Ghazali map distinct ways of salvation, and the paths they chart converge and diverge along the way. For one, Christianity lacks the type of comprehensive law that is central to the life and practice of Jews and Muslims. Moreover, Christianity alone points to a single event, that of Jesus, that secures or establishes God's mercy. It is through God alone that we are saved, not the human work of adhering to the law. Making this classically Christian claim need not depend on the disparaging of *shari'a* or *Halakhah*, for both Muslims and Jews recognize that law is a sign of divine mercy, patience, and love. Now Calvin and Ghazali remain distinct in their understandings of how mercy is mediated to human beings and of the condition from which human beings need saving—original sin or ignorance—but these other differences are obscured when the focus of exchange is dominated by the Christian divisions between law and grace.

Notes

1. See for instance, Gavin D'Costa, ed., *Christian Uniqueness Reconsidered: The Myth of a Pluralistic Theology of Religions* (Maryknoll, N.Y.: Orbis Press, 1990); Wolfhart Pannenberg, "Religious Pluralism and Conflicting Truth Claims: The Problem of a Theology of the World Religions," in *Christian Uniqueness Reconsidered*, ed. Gavin D'Costa (Maryknoll, N.Y.: Orbis, 1990), 96–116; and Jeannine Hill Fletcher, *Monopoly on Salvation?: A Feminist Approach to Religious Pluralism* (Edinburgh, UK: T&T Clark, 2005).
2. Josef Van Ess, *The Flowering of Muslim Theology*, trans. Jane Marie Todd (Cambridge: Harvard University Press, 2006), 15.
3. For more on this, see Jan Slop, "Calvin on the Turks," in *Christian-Muslim Encounters*, ed. Yvonne Haddad and Wadi Z. Haddad (Gainesville: University of Florida Press, 1995), 126–42; and Muhammad Hassan Khalil, *Islam and the Fate of Others* (New York: Oxford University Press, 2012), especially Chapter 1.
4. Tariq Ramadan, *Western Muslims and the Future of Islam* (New York: Oxford University Press, 2004), 31.
5. John Calvin, *Institutes of Christian Religion*, ed. John T. McNeill and Ford Lewis Battles, 2 vols. (Philadelphia, Pa.: Westminster Press, 1960), II.7.1.
6. Serene Jones, "Glorious Creation, Beautiful Law," in *Feminist and Womanist Essays in Reformed Dogmatics*, ed. Amy Plantiga Pauw and Serene Jones (Louisville: Westminster John Knox Press, 2006), 33.
7. Calvin, *Institutes*, II.7.6.
8. Calvin, *Institutes*, III.11.1.
9. Calvin, *Institutes*, II.7.12.
10. Calvin, *Institutes*, II.7.7.
11. Calvin, *Institutes*, II.7.7.
12. Calvin, *Institutes*, II.7.13.
13. Currently this major work of Islamic thought has yet to be completely translated from Arabic into English. While individual books have been translated, a complete translation is forthcoming with Fons Vitate in 2016–2018. When available, I will cite existing English translation with some alterations in the translation; otherwise, all translations are mine and taken from the ten-volume edition of *Ihya' 'ulum al-din* (Jeddah: Dar al-Minhaj, 2011), with page numbers corresponding to this edition.

14. *Ihya'* is variously translated as revival or resuscitation because the root word involves connections to reviving and life.
15. Ghazali, *Revival of the Religious Sciences (Ihya' 'ulum al-din)*, Introduction, Vol. 1, 10.
16. Ghazali, *Ihya' 'ulum al-din*, Introduction, Vol. 1, 15.
17. Eric Ormsby, *Ghazali: The Revival of Islam* (Oxford: Oneworld Publications, 2007), 118.
18. As Wael Hallaq, one of the foremost scholars of *Shari'*a, writes, "these performative works are constructivist, in that they are constituted and created by the believers as devotional acts for the purpose of fulfilling a covenant with God ... Their priority in the overall corpus of the law is reflected in their universal placement at the beginning of legal treatises, a long standing tradition of arranging legal subject-matter that no jurist has ever violated. But the placement was not merely an emblem of symbolic importance and priority; rather, it had a function which made this ritualistic group a logical and functional antecedent. The function was subliminal as well as psychological, laying as it did the foundations for achieving willing obedience to the law that was to follow, that is, the law regulating human affairs." Wael Hallaq, *Shari'a: Theory, Practice, Transformation* (Cambridge: Cambridge University Press, 2009) 225–26.
19. Kenneth Garden, *The First Islamic Reviver: Abu Hamid al-Ghazali and His Revival of the Religious Sciences* (Oxford: Oxford University Press, 2014), 81.
20. Remi Brague, *The Law of God: A Philosophical History of an Idea*, trans. Lydia G. Cochrane (Chicago: University of Chicago Press, 2007), 184.
21. These names of God are the most common and regular of those invoked by Muslims, coming as they do at the beginning of all but one *Sura* (chapter) of the Qur'an.
22. Ghazali, *Ihya'*, 4:33, Exposition on Fear and Hope. Translation taken from William McKane, *al-Ghazali's Book on Fear and Hope* (Leiden: Brill, 1962), 34.
23. Ghazali, *Ihya'*, 4:33, Exposition on Fear and Hope, 35.
24. Ghazali, *Ihya'*, 4:33, Exposition on Fear and Hope, 7.
25. Ghazali, *Ihya'*, 4:36, Exposition on Love, Longing, and Attachment. Translation from Eric Ormsby, *Love, Longing, Intimacy and Contentment* (Cambridge: Islamic Texts Society, 2011), 2.
26. Ghazali, *Ihya'*, 4:36, Love and Attachment, 171,
27. This way of phrasing the relationship is indebted to al-Ash'ari's conception of the relationships of the divine attributes to God's unity, where he claims that knowledge, power, speech, and so on are both not God and not other than God.
28. Ghazali, *Ihya'*, 4:36, Love and Attachment, 154.
29. Mona Siddiqui, *Christians, Muslims, and Jesus* (New Haven: Yale University Press, 2013), 205.
30. Ghazali, *Ihya'*, 4:36, Love and Attachment, 5.
31. This way of framing the relationship between the gospel and law is indebted to Karl Barth. See Karl Barth, *Church Dogmatics* II.2, trans. G. W. Bromiley and T. F. Torrance (Edinburgh: T&T Clark, 1957).

14 Sleeper, Awake

CONSIDERING THE
SOTERIOLOGICAL PROMISE
OF POPULAR SPIRITUAL GURUS

Sharon V. Betcher

In her novel *A Tale for the Time Being*, author and Zen Buddhist priest Ruth Ozeki sets before the reader—in the figure of a young Japanese girl, raised by her grandmother, a Buddhist nun—the question of how we live as "a time being," as a floating speck of stardust in cosmic vastness: "Our human body appears and disappears moment by moment..., and this ceaseless arising and passing away is what we experience as time and being... In even a fraction of a second, we have the opportunity to... turn the course of our action either toward the attainment of truth or away from it.... [W]e must understand how quickly time flows by if we are to wake up and truly live our lives."[1] Wakefulness, Ozeki reminds us—the theme resounding off the Pauline epistle, i.e., "Wake up, sleeper," (Eph. 5:14) and its reverberation through the Advent season—is the first condition of the spiritual path: How do we stay awake to the nature of time and self or, in the social venue, to the trivialization of life by cultural and subjective power plays? How do we save, not waste, life? This question of how to live awake and aware situates before us the theological venue called soteriology.

Spiritual practices are, in the contemporary West, often taken up as tools for navigating trauma—whether the psychic pain of despair, depression, or cultural dislocation. While Ozeki positions her story in the wake of the 2011 earthquake and tsunami that wracked Japan, the advent of the Anthropocene epoch more generally ratchets up the poignancy of the soteriological question: How do we live as and for a time being, while now keeping company with nearly immortal hyperobjects like plutonium 239, cesium, and climate change? Human ineptitude in living within ecosystems, and its blowback for the younger generations, exacerbates the apprehension of the venture of life itself. Further, within modern capitalism, everyone becomes an entrepreneur of the self, and the self—as its own natural resource, packaged, branded, and repackaged—becomes that which we offer at the marketplace. That intense objectification of and productive relation to the self generates excruciating self-consciousness: "The self becomes the site for one frantic achievement after another, rather than life experienced as sacred, entrusted gift."[2]

Psychic pain—loosely registered as depression or chronic anxiety—is rampant. As one of the millennial generation in Vancouver put it to her audience, explaining her entrance into a Hindu-inspired Meditation Movement (HIMM), "I just wanted a giant eraser for the pain." In such scenarios, "religious identity—perhaps the most fundamental of all identities," can seem to "offer the consolations of an identity embedded in sacred, transcendent life-worlds that are ultimately intractable to the power of rationality alone."[3]

In North America, questions of how to live as a time being, in pain and saturated by anxiety, are asked and answered against the backdrop of a materialist cosmology cut loose of heaven, in the open (if media/ted) public, amidst the final break with social kin and communal determinations of identity, and by the mixing and melding of what had been presumed to be geographically, ethnically distinct religious paths. Think of this as the full scale democratizing of spirituality, set in motion in the West when Luther taught peasants to interpret biblical texts for themselves in the sixteenth century. "Humans are no more born into their identities, but in compulsive and obligatory self-determination," sociologist Zygmunt Bauman summarily notes.[4] This equally applies to one's spiritual path: Each of us must, even in the religious arena, pick up a personal craft kit. As multifaith campus chaplain K. P. Hong puts it, religious identity is today "inevitably a promiscuous, selective reconstruction from an array of possibilities that work to provide meaning and purpose."[5] And, he continues, "However much the idea is discounted by those skeptical of the vagaries of spiritual consumerism, religious hybridity may serve as strategic response to sociopolitical challenges, cultural dislocation and existential uncertainty."[6]

In this vein, this chapter engages one of the popular gurus of the "spiritual, but not religious" agora—namely, Deepak Chopra. Chopra—by measure of his book sales, teaching seminars, and presence in the media and celebrity circles—exceeds the reach of traditional religious communities in North America. He is in the business of offering salvation to populations loosed from scripture and community. Like Eckhart

Tolle, another of the popular gurus, Chopra has recognized that numerous Westerners have an aversion to "belief," which treats God, it is contended, as an externality to the cosmos, safeguarded by propositional truths authoritatively preached, and owed intellectual consent. "Spirituality," Chopra insists, "is supposed to . . . give you the experience of unbounded freedom. All organized religions do exactly the opposite. They're judgmental . . . . Every religion is fear-based."[7] As not a few sociologists of religion have pointed out, North American culture has long tended to favor experience or, more precisely, inner ecstasy, while downplaying the philosophical aspect of spiritual practice.[8] Chopra recognizes this yearning for direct, affective communion with the force of life, with Spirit, in a way that retains scientific credulity.

Trained in Western medicine, Chopra left his U.S.-based endocrinology practice in the 1980s, though he had been distraught already in medical school about the Western problematization of disease rather than the promotion of health. At this juncture, he studied under Maharishi Mahesh Yogi, the founder of Transcendental Meditation (TM). At the invitation of Maharishi, Chopra initially developed the Ayurvedic or ancient medicinal side of TM. Today, he is an entrepreneur at the edge of alternative medicine and the West's craving for eastern spirituality. He operates the chain of Chopra Life Centers, and he has authored over fifty books, a number of which have dominated the *New York Times*' bestseller lists. This chapter discusses his earliest text, *Quantum Healing* (1989), which was followed by his *Ageless Body, Timeless Mind* (1993), and then his more recent *How to Know God* (2000) and *God: A Story of Revelation* (2012).[9] With a popular image that borrows upon the tradition of guru, media star, and model minority,[10] Chopra leverages the post-1960s energies for self-realization through self-help, the on-going exploration of Hindu-Inspired Meditation Movements (HIMM), and the American subterranean spirituality of New Thought and Positive Thinking.[11]

Because Chopra has claimed that "whatever I've written, you can find in one of the Upanishads,"[12] his work can be read as falling into the lineage of Advaita Vedanta. The work of Anantanand Rambachan, *The Advaita Worldview*, will serve as the guide to the philosophical elaboration of that tradition in this essay. One of six orthodox schools of Hindu thought, Advaita Vedanta describes a philosophical commitment to "nondual" reality. Nonduality refers to three key axes of a tradition—the nonduality of self and non-self, of self and other (or subject and object), and of self and the ultimate. This latter axis, sometimes referred to as the nonduality of the conditioned and the Unconditioned, affirms that existence abides in the hold of Brahman or Spirit.

In the Advaita tradition, the transient character of life tempers all goals: "The basic problem of human beings . . . is that the experience of the finite and the satisfaction of desires for wealth and pleasure leave us wanting. . . . It is dissatisfaction with the finite and the desire to be free from sorrow that brings one to the door of a teacher."[13] Rambachan consequently begins, like the Mundaka Upanishad, with questions such as those asked above: "Why were we born? By what do we live? On what are we established?"[14] For Chopra, consistent with his tradition, to know the world correctly—cosmology, that is—constitutes soteriology.

I work comparatively with a Christian theology of Spirit—itself to be distinguished from "the Holy Spirit" as the third person of the Trinity. Religions in the ancient Mediterranean basin were stewed together by the Roman Empire in the mash-up of which Christianity, itself a hybrid, emerged. Spirit was, at that juncture, the assumed and unarticulated basis from which developed systematic theology and, specifically, Christology.[15] Christianity's most ancient baptismal vow was itself set in nondual language: "In Christ there is neither Jew nor Greek, slave nor free, male and female" (Gal. 3:28). Spirit theology, the critical base for the emergent authority of women in Christian tradition as well as the Diggers of the English Reformation, has been among the most radical political potencies brewing in Christian traditions. And Spirit—a metaphor of the holy never owned by one religious tradition—moves facilely within the contemporary "spiritual, but not religious" and secular Christian milieu.

G. W. F. Hegel's *Philosophy of Spirit* was itself ventilated by reading Hindu philosophy in Europe, as the aeration of Hinduism was a significant spark mobilizing the Enlightenment. And even amid critiques of Hegel's "Spirit" having served as the motor of modern progress, powering over and plowing under difference, Christian theology seems yet again to be drawn back to the "theopoetics" of Spirit. Spirit returns to the lips of Christians where the distinction between God and world has been positively ruined, especially in ecotheologies. This theology of Spirit will here be positioned by reading Catherine Keller's *On the Mystery: Discerning Divinity in Process* (2008). Keller, like Chopra, is also conversant with contemporary science.

This comparative exercise sounds things out not from a historical distance, but "in the air" of the contemporary, where these theologies swirl and dance around each other. Each of these theological forms—Chopra's science of consciousness (his *jnana* yoga or "knowledge" yoga), which is set within a quantum worldview, and the Christian, philosophically inclined, and scientifically engaged theopoetics of Spirit—shares a commitment to rousing the desire for life after years of mechanistic materialism. Their mutual attraction, as well as the contemporary ability to live among multiple metaphysical proposals with irresolvably "partial faiths,"[16] may suggest a developmental interplay not easily flushed open by this comparative exercise.

Manifest Destiny

Chopra sets out a spiritual practice that explores human belonging to the universe, proposing a path of waking up from the stupor of materialist reductionism to salvific consciousness by living in a spiritual modality. "*Atman* (true self) is Brahman (Spirit)": this basic dogma—that the spiritual nature of self participates in the immortal, in the infinite—constitutes the resident heart of Advaita Vedanta pulsing in Chopra's cosmological proposal. "In this scheme," he writes, "traditional belief gets reversed." He explains, "The virtual domain"—by which he refers to quantum theory's hypothesis of a pre-physical vacuum dimension that he identifies with Spirit or Brahman—"is our source rather than our destination after death."[17] Melding Advaita Vedanta with quantum theory, Chopra embeds the human in an inspired cosmos, waking Westerners from the deadness of the Cartesian dualism that still grips us, a sluggishness turned cynical as the Enlightenment sheered the heavens. And "in place of the old dualism" that kept one's interior, spiritual life as secret as the crypt of heaven to which it hoped to depart, we can, Chopra promises, restore the integrity of spiritual life by thinking of it now as taking place in the quantum soup of the cosmos.[18] "Everyone can have the direct experience of divinity"[19] and yet keep a scientific perspective. And we, who have lost heaven and the immortality of the soul, can relearn, Chopra promises, "the physiology of immortality."[20] To know God, to awake to our own divine nature and recognize it as one with the divine nature of the cosmos, constitutes salvation.

WHERE SPIRIT BECOMES FLESH

Chopra is, in his own way, committed to thinking that "spirit matters"—as Keller puts it.[21] He conflates the unitive experience of meditative bliss with the field metaphor from speculative physics, which designates for Chopra the realm of Spirit, to name the quantum point of origin as "the unified field." The creation story from the Rig Veda, one of Hinduism's ancient sacred texts, "tells us," he asserts, "that God can only be found in a virtual state, where all energy is stored before creation."[22] Chopra, in other words, theologizes that juncture where, as quantum theory proposes, space-time emerges at the quantum dimension. In this three-tiered "reality sandwich,"[23] "God [as] pure potential"[24] occupies a realm outside the material world; and God and human consciousness meet via meditative practice in the "transition zone."[25]

Vedic science constitutes, in turn, "a medicine of consciousness... [used to] pierce the body's matter."[26] Meditation is the medicinal-spiritual technology that unites us with the "unified field," the purported force field of cosmic intelligence from which the world was created: "There is no more beautiful experience than when the world expands beyond its accustomed limits..., when reality takes on splendor. The Veda calls such an experience *ananda* or bliss."[27] Meditation, Chopra contends, drops us into a plenum of cosmic potentialities or the zone of quantum virtuality, where "invisible, immortal, uncreated spirit [becomes] flesh."[28]

BECOMING AGELESS BODY, TIMELESS MIND

Chopra assumes that the meditative experience of unified consciousness reaches into the reality at the heart of the universe and that it names a force of physics, Spirit, with which we can interact through meditation. God, another name for that plenum of virtual potentialities, Chopra explains, "exists to unfold anything and everything."[29] If Vedanta speaks of the goal of manifesting one's divine nature, the spiritual aspect that has never been born nor will ever die, Chopra's ayurvedic and scientific interests carry this quickly into assertions regarding "quantum biology." Meeting God in the transition zone through meditative practice, one may manifest one's own destiny, thereby reversing aging and managing immunity from bacteria and disease. Because unfamiliarity with sciences of consciousness and one's own sudden reactive grasp on materialism can leave a Western reader incredulous, one might think of "manifesting" as like the practice of an artist, situated before a blank canvas, recognizing what may be resident there.

For Chopra, consciousness—a typical translation of *atman* or "self," which Rambachan translates as "awareness" to avoid old ruts of mind-matter dualism[30]—constitutes the truest form of the world and of personhood, namely, Spirit. He writes, "Awareness is the same thing as spirit."[31] Again, meditation constitutes a practice of realizing the underlying essence of all conjoined with Spirit. And yet Chopra's hybridization of the term "consciousness" with the underlying Western habit of consciousness, established during our materialist phase, seems to say something more than that. Chopra, working suggestively around the basic Advaita teaching that "*atman* (self) is Brahman (Spirit)," imputes a strong or causal relevance to that teaching: "We are not onlookers peering into the unified field ... We are the unified field."[32] Chopra thereby concludes that "one becomes manifestly all-knowing."[33] Insomuch as quantum theory proposes that "the observer participates in that which she observes,"[34] and since, on Chopra's reading, "quantum reduces the physical to illusion," Chopra concludes that "the physical world, including our bodies, is a response of the observer."[35]

In this way, Chopra insinuates that the somatic potential of mindfulness practice could recuperate "ageless body, timeless mind"—that it could, as one locates self in Spirit at the quantum level, reverse aging or heal disease.[36] "Ageless body, timeless mind" is, in fact, a possible rendering of *atman*, of self as Spirit, in Vedanta philosophy.[37] But Chopra asserts that perfect health—a self "that is free from disease, that never feels pain, that cannot age or die"—is a state found in every person.[38] That quantum potential and its comparable physical manifestation of health is something every person can choose for her/himself. "Ill health is ... due to our own 'mistake of the intellect,'" Maharishi taught. Disease erupts where we have forgotten "the underlying unity ... By failing to understand our true nature, we become estranged from the ultimate source of universal consciousness and we fall ill."[39] Illness, Chopra comparably asserts, constitutes but a disturbance in perfect Mind. *Avidya*, or ignorance of our true self, is the cause of bondage (ill health). This can be cured by mind with and through the technologies of consciousness that constitute TM.[40]

Suffering is here reset as a salvific concern for self-realization as divine Spirit, or for the "time being" to see itself as a locus for experiencing God. Maharishi's undergirding sentiment, carried now by Chopra, is a straightforward teaching of Advaita Vedanta: Ignorance implies "misunderstanding the nature of the self that is immediately available and manifesting unceasingly as self-existent awareness."[41] Rambachan speaks comparably of the fundamental problem of human sorrow, fear, and anxiety, which is amended by meditative practice (including philosophical reflection) that "protects from despair."[42] And yet, Chopra—contrary to Rambachan, who explains that "ignorance does not imply that suffering is nonexistent"[43]—asserts a strong, causal or determinative, connection that makes illness an issue of an unskillful mind or false consciousness.

PRACTICING SPIRITUAL INTELLIGENCE

In *Quantum Healing*, Chopra's soteriological project begins by waking the reader to ways of knowing the body other than those legitimated by the Western bio-medical sciences. "Ayurveda," he writes, "does not treat the body as a lump of matter but as a web of sutras"—dense strings of intelligence or wisdom, which form the ligatures of the subtle body-self.[44] Chopra, interpretively moving with the sensibilities that "*atman* is Brahman," explains that "Each of us inhabits a reality lying beyond all change. Deep inside us, unknown to the five senses, is an innermost core of being, a field of non-change . . . The seer . . . is immune to any form of change. This seer is the spirit, the expression of eternal being."[45] Chopra here gives a fairly straightforward explication of the nature of Brahman, consistent with Rambachan.[46] Meditation, Chopra then proposes, allows us to interact with those somatic sutras in such a way as to be able "to change the very patterns that design the body" as well as "wipe mistakes off the blueprint . . . and destroy any disease—cancer, diabetes, coronary heart disease."[47]

Thinking between string theory, which assumes the universe's elementary particles to be something like the oscillating strings of a musical instrument, and the proposal that there is a field of cosmic intelligence, a force field like gravity, from which the cosmos foams forth, Chopra continues: "Intelligence is the purest form of existence." [48] Intelligence, viewed as an overlay of the somatic sutras upon the basic nature of the universe, "is more important than the actual matter of the body," he informs us.[49]

Assuming the ethos of harmony to be inherently natural, Chopra teaches that Spirit—this field of intelligence, or mesh of ley lines, that is never really separate from Earth—provides ethical orientation. "Participants trust that upon attaining enlightenment," explains Lola Williamson, based on her research into HIMMs, "they will experience a shift from feeling limited and separate to feeling unlimited and united with all things.... From this expanded awareness, they assume that all thoughts and actions will be spontaneously right and in accordance with the laws of nature"[50]—that they will learn to flock like birds attentive to their magnetic migrational songlines. Ethical responsibility appears resolved by becoming awake because meditative consciousness is assumed to unify. Indeed, *maya*, the delusional bondage into which life can fall, names for Chopra "the illusion of boundaries, the creation of a mind that has lost the cosmic perspective ... the invisible field that is the origin of the universe."[51]

Prodigal Universe, a Christian Spirit Theology

Chopra reads Advaita Vedanta to promise that abundance is our natural state.[52] Christian cosmology can well respect Chopra's vision of the prodigal or gratuitous nature of the world, but it manifests that somewhat distinctly. In Christian vicinities, this generative squandering begins with Spirit's immanental gracing of finitude as distinct from Chopra's quantum escalator into the deeps of virtual potentiality: The Gospel of John hymns the creation of the material world as generated when God's desire overflows. Hegelian philosophy, reading with the Gospel of John, celebrates Spirit emptying itself into the material world. According to Dalit theologian Moses P. P. Penumaka, when comparing Luther, Hegel's theological ancestor, and Shankara, the ninth-century philosopher of Advaita Vedanta, "This constitutes a kind of metaphysical reversal. What an Advaita philosopher might dub *maya* or non-reality now becomes valorized, ... because ultimate reality absorbs it."[53] Consequently, finite existence can be lived as privilege—even if Christians, whether stupefied with fear or having had desire become trivial and grasping amidst consumerism, fall asleep on this point. Rambachan himself has been critical of Vedanta in this regard, insisting that, while the teachings can be philosophically interpreted to support compassionate, inclusive, and just community, as Christianity forwards based on God's unreserved residence with the finite world, "this will not occur ... until the Advaita tradition positively asserts the value of the world and human existence within it."[54]

Likewise, Christianity has insisted on the immanental embedding of Love as salvifically constitutive for each of us as "time beings." Peter Abelard, a twelfth-century theologian, spoke of Jesus as a manifestation of God's love, who awakens a corresponding love in the hearts of humanity. This awakening of love constitutes salvation for the Christian as a way of affectively tending life so as to save—not waste—this planetary experiment. "Saving is the opposite not of damning but of wasting," Keller writes. She shares with Chopra as with Rambachan the worry that "the human experiment has long been at risk of wasting itself."[55] Soteriology within a Christian theological perspective insists that "Spirit matters" by investing itself within the finite, physical constitution of space-time and communities in their contexts.

In Christian theology of Spirit, religious consciousness does not meditatively tap into the Infinite (as it does for Chopra), but is faithful to the finite. It cannot be said to be of a different order or essence of being than flesh. "Our entire capacity to discern is creaturely," Keller writes. "To discern divinity is not," she then concludes, "to see or hear something separable from the creation," but is rather to hold in mind, as would God, the multiplicity of creation.[56] Spirit or "Christ" serves as a projection that settles upon our enemies as our neighbor beings, a recognition that these others are *homoousian* or "of the same nature" of God, so that we can move through riptides of disgust, fear, and pain in order to love. For Christians, to know God warms the affections so as to love one's neighbor as oneself.

Roused by divine passion, the Christian practice of nonduality—practiced as a way to overcome the exclusions created among humans (Gal. 3.28), in which God's transcendent character is itself emptied into immanence so as to value the finite world—is set in motion socially: "Privatistic and exclusivistic modes of existence are set aside as are distinctions based in mastery, power, position, sex, and wealth."[57] To speak of God as Spirit and God as Love suggestively insinuates, phenomenologically discernible in each moment, "a mobile animating spatiality" flush with empathy. God as Love "propositions us to and from a bottomless well of compassion" at the heart of the Universe, Keller poetically proposes.[58] Jesus—whether considered a historical individual or a figural Torah meant to be practiced—awakens the passions—mercy, forgiveness, generosity, hospitality. Hanging onto Jesus is no more the point of this theology of Spirit than it was for Mary in the Easter garden. Rather, we are trained into the physics of love such that twentieth-century theologian and paleontologist Teilhard de Chardin could summarily speak—with all hopefulness—of Christianity as "a phylum of love" planted around the planet. The end result of spirituality, asserted Alfred North Whitehead, an early twentieth-century philosopher and child of an Anglican rectory, is world loyalty. Yet for all its conversation with science and philosophy, Spirit theology speaks "theopoetics more than theoscience"[59]—a point to which the comparative analysis will return.

Comparative Theology Situated

"You are here to enable the divine purpose of the universe to unfold. That is how important you are!"[60] The words are those of Eckhart Tolle, but Chopra would most concertedly agree. The estimation of human mortality and of humanity's relation to the universe could hardly appear more starkly than between these two theologies of Spirit—between Chopra's speculative quantum cosmology implicitly promising immortal worth, if also human health and abundance, and this Christian constructive theopoetic vision that values finitude in and for itself, encouraging humans to think less of themselves by renouncing anthropocentric arrogance in relation to the planet and embracing humility in relation to human knowledge and ethical reach. Whereas Christianity's theology of Spirit admits transience and vulnerability, weaving across the Earth a physics of love, Chopra's ensconces the human as pivotal for unfolding the cosmos—although most of his address is made to the individual human. What, then, might Christian soteriology learn from this dialogue with Chopra on the relation between Spirit and the finite?

KNOWING GOD

We suffer a spiritual malaise, Chopra insinuates. We do not know how to affectively engage the gripping cynicism, even nihilism, that may be an outcropping of the loss of world teleology. If psychic pain—depression, anxiety, melancholy, all of which may name spiritual malaise—is driving religious seekers, this is a significant insight. Human life today takes place, as philosopher Claire Colebrook observes, without transcendental orientation: "because modern capitalism no longer has an explicit center or foundation ... 'man' [sic] becomes a private being, who no longer subjects [her/]himself to anything Other than the pure fact that there must be law, rather than a specified subjection to a transcendent power."[61] Persons may be more or less resilient when living into this new cultural construction without orientation or obligations. But one wonders, given the reach for spiritual technologies such as HIMMs, if the disorientation that many feel in the wake of that loss of the transcendent can be healed or tended in any way but by the developmental path of spiritual technologies.

If Advaita Vedanta speaks of "liberation from bondage," meaning release from the karmic cycle of rebirth, even the Maharishi bemoaned the fact that Americans preferred "'relief from stress to relief from bondage.'"[62] If that touches upon the context of reception for Chopra's teaching, then the identification of "*atman* is Brahman" may generate what psychologist John Bowlby spoke of as a "secure base"—a sense of being "well held," sheltered, and accepted; of an inner peace and stability that absolves the existential pain of nihilism. This core psychic capacity, built up from receiving empathic attention, allows us to enter the world as trustworthy.[63]

Chopra narrates the resonance between cosmology and healthy psyche as follows. In a Vedantic vein, he contends that knowing God saves us because knowing the true Self unites us with Brahman. Redress of suffering within Chopra's corpus takes two forms: As already considered, the promise of "ageless body, timeless mind" derives from his application of quantum theory to ayurvedic medicine and transcendental meditation; his more psycho-philosophical redress of despair is taken up in *How to Know God*. There Chopra, now moving into suggestive applications of neuroscience, asserts that "the brain is hardwired to know God." "To match [the brain], there is a God of pure being, one who doesn't think but just is.... The brain can directly contact 'the light,' [that is, Spirit,] a form of pure awareness that feels joyful and blessed."[64] Consequently, "instead of God being a... projection, he [*sic*] turns out to be the only thing that is real."[65] And prayer, Chopra insists, proves that "there is a reachable place beyond material reality," because prayer has been scientifically proven to have efficacy in healing.[66] In such ways, Chopra proclaims as veridical the experiential knowledge that "*atman* is Brahman," and "Brahman is Spirit."

This secure base—whether generated through Chopra's embedding of the human in the deep field of cosmic Spirit or Christian liturgical sensibilities of "the face of God shining upon us" (Num. 6:25)—is not to be ignored as a psychological undergirding for persons cut loose from familial, religious, institutional, career, and social structures. If this secure base is part of what Chopra offers, it suits the mobile individuality of North American sociality. While one hears already her biting critique, Barbara Ehrenreich, too, recognizes the situation that makes these versions of the salvific path attractive: "Positive thinking promised ["end of career-ers"] a sense of control in a world where the cheese was always moving. They may have had less and less power to chart their own futures, but they had been given a worldview—a belief system— almost a religion—that claimed they were in fact infinitely powerful, if only they could master their own minds."[67]

Because "the body" has become the cultural linchpin in Western economic and consumer culture, Chopra's promise seems all the more enticing: Bliss names the "body's own awakening," an oceanic feeling of well-being.[68] Chopra favorably cites Maharishi to say that "'the boundaries of the individual life . . . extend far beyond [somatic, domestic, and terrestrial] spheres to the limitless horizon of unbounded cosmic life.'"[69] Self as connected with quantum potential—that is, with Spirit, as Chopra insists—could seemingly capacitate and enable the maneuverability of the body outside of the increasing biopolitical and economic entrepreneurial demands on the Western body-mind complex. And yet, a caution may be in order.

The collapse of notions of eternal life and the transcendental elsewhere has resulted in the turn toward thinking life within cultural notions of well-being: "Salvation has become linked to our existence as corporeal, somatic individuals . . . The body itself has become sacred . . . And health, not truth, has become the central [cultural] value."[70] The intensification of medical knowledge about the body has led to a situation in which we live ever already "in prognosis," in an anxious vortex of worry that, given its centripetal pull and the importance of health to our viability as economic agents of our own somatic resource, makes us voracious consumers of health care and technologies of mood management. Neoliberal policy—and Chopra follows these well-trenched tracks—responsibilizes individuals toward the health of the body, which has become diagnosed at mindnumbing micro-intensities. Chopra's way of analytically locating problems, like illness, within the deep structures of a personality, amended by bliss, all too easily joins itself to neoliberal responsibilization. Philosophical understanding becomes social policy that puts the onus of health and happiness on individuals. Given "the narcissistic captivation" of the body "in terms of the viability of our own sensory-motor apparatus" within contemporary neoliberal policy,[71] we should be aware that even spiritual practices can be used to generate social conformity and normativity,[72] especially where salvation is summed up in the hope but for health and happiness.

Chopra provides a medicine for psychic pain, but his is an individuated medicine in terms of diagnosis, technology, and resolve. Whereas Chopra imagines that detachment through meditative contentment allows a person to engage social obligation insofar as s/he is at peace with her/himself, persons can become (as Williamson reports of HIMMs) "so wary of 'stress'"—or negativity, in popular parlance—"they do not contribute enough to society."[73] While it has been a commonplace within Christian Platonism as with Chopra to assume that spirituality yields tranquility, harmony, serenity, and therefore peace (as if these were always godly virtues), such an assumption forecloses the capacity to tend entanglements and elides the stamina needed for interpreting social pain. If there is to be the public practice of justice, suffering will first need to be heard into political speech; and suffering often first comes into articulation within vocal ranges from the groan to the blues to anger and protest. Vijay Prashad's socio-political history of orientalist desire (which essentializes differences between Asian and European ways of being), notes the ways in which spiritual practitioners such as Chopra are "used as a weapon" within the racial politics of the United States.[74] These practitioners either offer an ancient "transcendental piety," modeled by the good, achieving brown immigrant, or, more forthrightly, they serve to legitimate the "spiritual posture" of bliss as political detachment, even when anything but detachment is demanded in the face of economic injustice. In this way Chopra's practice may constitute a tool in socio-political repression.

Christian theologians have argued that salvation, the passionate touch of the holy called "grace," generates a spaciousness of "freedom for" the other (Luther) within the moral and material demands of human and ecological facets of community. "Com/passion," writes Keller, "holds open a solidaristic space. It widens the context of our relationships. It fosters a persistence beyond the hope of the moment."[75] Liberative freedom becomes availability to the neighbor, who may require of us the postponement of our own desires. The requisite generosity, justice, and forbearance may also require knowledge of the ways of fear and the capacity to carry pain. Love as com/passion, Keller explains, wakes desire amidst duty to the neighbor, awakes, then, the spirit of justice—the structure of "com" or shared "passion." In other words, Christianity has insisted upon not just the well-being of an individual, but the communal nature of salvation. In "the kin[g]dom of God," of love as justice, or in the gracious spaciousness of an individual life become alert to our interdependent context, "spirit enfolds me, across painful difference, in a shared world."[76]

Like Chopra's Advaita Vedantic teaching, Christianity has also recognized and analytically engaged existential anxiety, which seems exacerbated as a social condition prompting religious seekers today.[77] Ancient patristic literature, more attuned to guilt, fear, melancholia, acedia, and the like, hymned the "sweet exchange" by which Christ carried the loneliness, alienation, guilt, and angst of the human, so that the human could breathe freely.[78] When Sounds of Blackness sings, "He [sic] took away all my pain, and gave me Love," one is reminded of how much this remains a contemporary soteriological contribution.[79]

But Christianity has no contemporary modality to make this personally practicable as we loose persons into socio-relational cosmopolitanism free of obligatory bonds, but also without direction amidst the marketplace of spiritualities. Christianity long ago displaced the monastic arts of the self, at least in Protestant venues. Further, Christianity's philosophical trajectory has often been severed from the twine of activism and devotion, which affectively shape one's availability for neighbor love. Protestant Christianity's "logorrhea" has suffocated its own traditions of singing and ritual aesthetics. Consequently, amidst the exhaustion of mechanistic materialism and the daily media-inflation of the volleys of political ideologies, assessing the path of liberation by means that grant a reprieve from the flood of words and beliefs—hence by meditation, chant, yoga—cannot be understated.

THEOPOETICS OR THEOSCIENCE

By theologizing that juncture where space-time disappears at the quantum dimension, and by assuming that God is certainly immaterial, Chopra seemingly invites a repristination of Cartesian dualism, even while disavowing it. His spiritual technology reinserts a practical dualism by psychically valuing and identifying with a purportedly superior, higher form of matter, while detaching from the transient base. To be sure, Vedanta thereby cultivates an appreciative non-attachment—letting go of the struggle with life, stepping back into the potential of the present, and living without resistance. This move resembles something of a Sabbath reserve, refusing to meddle in the orders of being. And yet, as practitioners of the tradition themselves recognize, it can also create something of a "spiritual bypass," whereby one uses spirituality to ignore obligation and the demands of interdependence.

Despite Spirit being constitutive of the world, Chopra's worldview grants no spiritual kinship to the non-human. From a Christian perspective this pivotal internal dualism and value hierarchy between the infinite and the finite, which Christians have carried in classical systematic theological streams, insinuates, we now recognize, tehomaphobia—a fear of chaos, of the turbulence of being—at the heart of the tradition. Keller, like Chopra, speaks of our co-creative participation in a world ever becoming; but creativity, she underscores—and here she has in mind the emergent systems of chaos-complexity theory as well as the creaturely and the bacterial menagerie—is "not solely human."[80] To take place as a time being within the cosmic symphony implies not only the work of the young human creatives, but receptive prehension of the cosmos, whereby we together weave "the genesis collective."[81] Although quantum theory does propose an open-ended system that is responsive—even in non-local ways—to our presence, this hardly takes place without the embodied mass of beings. Tucked into the quantum vacuum, Chopra admits no sense of risk, as is incurred when self-organizing complexity reaches new levels. His notion of creativity does not recognize the precipitous edge of chaos where life is often most fecund. Nor does Chopra's proposed practice appear responsive to the fragility of finitude.

Chopra, in an effort to value human life and its conscious contribution and in order to overcome materialist reductionism, rescues Spirit writ large. Western Christianity has been tempted likewise, situated before the sheer suchness of the material world, to distill from life an essence, to infinitize Spirit. The West consequently turned the world into an experience museum, wringing the "spirit" out of everything: We continue to swill its sediments for a transcendental high, an adrenaline fix, whether on bucket lists, through tourism, or even at today's religious consumer market. The mundane cannot bear the demand for the intensity of experience that those of us often addicted to ecstasy of a transcendental sort expect of it; releasing transcendentalism can then itself become a spiritual practice of humility and respect for difference. "Spirit" has worked as a transitional object, whereby some now find themselves affectively awake to the suchness of existence, but exuberantly unknowing (learning again to release their grasp on God, to think with, while not circumscribing, the incomprehensible), hoping thereby to learn not to over-reach the constitution of elemental and finite life.

Further, a Westerner tempered by the philosopher Immanuel Kant, who cautioned humanity not to assume its phenomenological experience to be self-identical with the movement of the universe, has more difficulty with Chopra's science of mind. Kantian philosophical humility has been redoubled with poststructuralist analysis, which refuses teleological purpose to the universe as a whole because the universe is not "one," but something more like a "bubble multiverse." For a person conditioned by Western Enlightenment and poststructuralist philosophy, with spiritual dispositions such as humility of knowledge enfolded therein, there is not a trajectory or purpose to be deciphered within the universe of events. Likewise, creativity—such as that involved in evolution—seems to move through chaotic restlessness, not harmony.

Of course this is precisely what Chopra analytically incises as problematic in the Western worldview—this severing of the artery of Spirit, which for him is situated in consciousness, from the flow of the universe itself. Such a severance would challenge the most basic dogma of Advaita, that we are of that Spirit which manifests the cosmos. The question of how a "time being" lives with rigorous faithfulness and devotion—without the move to capture and unify the pluriverse under the name God or Spirit—constitutes something of the quake in religious being into which Chopra has offered his positivist science. In that quake zone, Christian process theology refuses to create an equivalency between physics and the sacred (as is Chopra's wont) by speaking in analogy and metaphor of that which can never be wholly known. It thereby preserves a measure of the incomprehensible and situates the relationship of Spirit and world—and, therefore, the possibility of love—at the heart of existence.

If "Spirit" might serve as a transitional object, whereby we focus on God so as to learn to love the mundane, these two religious technologies (Chopra's Advaita Vedanta and a Christian theology of Spirit) may not be as diametrically opposed as they appear in theory; they may rather be but an epistemological blink of an eye apart. An idealism of Spirit, like that of Chopra, can offer something of a dangerous God's eye view that anesthetizes one to negativity and entanglement; the Kantian caution carried in Christian theopoetics of Spirit can discipline idealism's tendency to presume to get outside human interpretive constructs. The anxiety of being loosed as a singularity without the gravity of obligation might be quieted by being made to feel embedded in the purpose of the cosmos—as Chopra's system proposes. But in an age of needing to live finitude and limit and obligation as much as needing bliss or "being well held," a theopoetics of Spirit attendant to finitude and limit and transience can discipline what Chopra sees as Spirit's limitless pure potentialities.

PRACTICE, PRACTICE

In his earliest work Chopra argued,

> meditation is not simply another kind of thinking or introspection ... It is actually a way to slide to a new pitch. The process of transcending, or "going beyond," detaches the mind from its fixed level and allows it to exist ... without any level at all. It simply experiences silence, devoid of thoughts, emotions, drives, wishes, fears, or anything at all. Afterward, when the mind returns to its usual ... level of consciousness, it has acquired a little freedom to move.[82]

Given the speed of modern urbanism and its challenge to the reactive amygdala, one can appreciate the freedom generated by meditation. Christianity may be well advised to reconstruct its own monastic arts of the self in conversation with the tradition of Advaita Vedanta.

With the Kantian critique of immortality as an egoistic project of the self, what has slipped away from Western thought has been the notion of soul. "Soul" might be the better comparative term—not now as an immortal substance, but as a psycho-social muscle of corporeal generosity, forbearance, and forgiveness through which to engage the practicable work of keeping faith with the world. Twentieth-century reconstructions of Christian theology, like the social gospel and liberation theology, brought social systems into soteriological reflection. No person living within the purview of socio-political repression would underestimate the importance of how it feels to be unshackled from definitions not one's own; and Chopra's expression of Advaita Vedanta does bring this to bear. But conversely, no person in political struggle would conclude these sensibilities were all there is to the spiritual journey. Admittedly, the balance between the socio-political and the intersubjective character (soul, if you will)—which comes to light in Chopra, among other popular gurus—has not always been well tended by Christian theology, despite claims that "the essence of this community [of faith] is a unique, transfigured intersubjectivity, distinguishable from all other forms of human love and friendship," and wherein "privatistic and exclusivistic modes of existence are set aside as are distinctions based on mastery, power, position, sex and wealth."[83]

For Christianity's Spirit theology, knowing God becomes a way of staying with the world, of rousing passion for life—a psychically demanding, even overwhelming proposal. Mortality is not easy to bear for oneself or for one's loved ones. If Christology might be remembered and reconfigured as a practice of bearing pain with each other, then how does one develop the psycho-social muscle for that?[84] Christianity has had problems articulating itself within the popular movements of body-centered wisdom. As it transitions toward "a more Asian type"[85] amidst the cultural preference for a looser weave of associative relations (something distinct from "belonging"), Christians can learn from the practicable body wisdom of Advaita Vedanta.

Rest in Openness

Spirit, theologian Jürgen Moltmann suggested, named a kind of hidden roominess to life, a way of experiencing life without constricted breath, as wide-open room for living.[86] Whether sitting in meditation or observing Sabbath, religions have ways of pulling us back to rest in openness without judgment, a practice that in turn conditions the epistemological disposition and activities of "a time being." Christianity stories this openness, leaning on its Jewish heritage, as being brought out of slavery—out of "Egypt" (the Hebrew word for Egypt, *mitzrayim*, means "confines, constrictions, narrow places")—hence, out of anguish, distress, worry.

The Christian liturgical season of Advent names the time devoted to learning the attention necessary to "wake up" to this boundless freedom. For Chopra, "waking up" implies directly experiencing God as "pure potential, ... [who] exists to unfold anything and everything."[87] This chapter has suggested that this repose, solipsistic in nature, all too easily can become "transcendentalized," whether as human exceptionalism or, socially, as quietism or a comfortable economic enclosure of health and well-being. Wakefulness shapes and conditions; it is a disposition one carries into the interdependent entanglement of existence. Restful openness—as Rambachan makes clear in his articulation of Advaita Vedanta—is not a goal in itself but contributes toward living. Restful openness allows one to stay with all that aches and groans until heard into speech. As Advent in/of the Anthropocene arrives on the doorsteps of our daily world, such meditative technologies as are comparatively encountered here may be among those that will enable our endurance, our resilience—effectively, saving us.

Notes

1. Ruth Ozeki, *A Tale for the Time Being* (New York: Viking/Penguin, 2013), 324, 408.
2. K. P. Hong, "Religious Hybrids: A New Interpretation," in *College and University Chaplaincy in the 21st Century: A Multifaith Look at the Practice of Ministry on Campuses across America*, ed. Lucy A Forster-Smith (Woodstock, N.Y.: Skylight Paths Publishing, 2013), 241.
3. Hong, "Religious Hybrids," 243.
4. Zygmunt Bauman, *Liquid Modernity* (Malden, Mass: Polity Press, 2000), 32.
5. Hong, "Religious Hybrids," 226.
6. Hong, "Religious Hybrids," 228.
7. Deepak Chopra, cited in Brad Gooch, *Godtalk: Travels in Spiritual America* (New York: Alfred A. Knopf, 2002), 72.
8. Lola Williamson, *Transcendent in America: Hindu-Inspired Meditation Movements as New Religion* (New York: New York University Press, 2010), xi, 21–22.
9. Deepak Chopra, *Ageless Body, Timeless Mind: The Quantum Alternative to Growing Old* (New York: Three Rivers Press, 2010); *God: A Story of Revelation* (New York: HarperOne, 2012); *How to Know God: The Soul's Journey into the Mystery of Mysteries* (New York: Harmony Books, 2000); *Quantum Healing: Exploring the Frontiers of Mind/Body Medicine* (New York: Bantam Books, 1990).
10. Vijay Prashad, *The Karma of Brown Folk* (Minneapolis: University of Minnesota Press, 2000), 7.
11. Jane Naomi Iwamura, *Virtual Orientalism: Asian Religions and American Popular Culture* (Oxford: Oxford University Press, 2011), 110.
12. Chopra as cited in Gooch, *Godtalk*, 136.
13. Rambachan, *The Advaita Worldview: God, World, and Humanity* (Albany: SUNY Press, 2006), 17, 31.
14. Rambachan, *The Advaita Worldview*, 31.
15. Philip Rosato, S.J., "Spirit Christology," *Theological Studies* 38 (1977): 425.
16. John McClure, *Partial Faiths: Postsecular Fiction in the Age of Pynchon and Morrison* (Athens: University of Georgia, 2007).
17. Chopra, *How to Know God*, 205.
18. Chopra, *How to Know God*, 205.
19. Chopra, *How to Know God*, book jacket.
20. Chopra, *Ageless Body*, 6.
21. Catherine Keller, *On the Mystery: Discerning Divinity in Process* (Minneapolis: Augsburg Press, 2008), 56.
22. Chopra, *How to Know God*, 31.
23. Chopra, *How to Know God*, 4.
24. Chopra, *God: A Story of Revelation*, 110.
25. Chopra, *How to Know God*, 4.

26. Chopra, *Quantum Healing*, 5.
27. Chopra, *Quantum Healing*, 235.
28. Chopra, *How to Know God*, 177.
29. Chopra, *Ageless Body*, 110.
30. Rambachan, *The Advaita Worldview*, 36.
31. Chopra cited in Gooch, *Godtalk*, 73.
32. Chopra, *Quantum Healing*, 217.
33. Chopra, *How to Know God*, 105.
34. Keller, *On the Mystery*, 23.
35. Chopra, *Ageless Body*, 108, 5.
36. Chopra, *Ageless Body*, 5.
37. Gooch, *Godtalk*, 78.
38. Chopra, *Quantum Healing*, 123.
39. Cynthia Ann Humes, "Maharishi Ayur-Veda: Perfect Health through Enlightened Marketing in America," in *Modern and Global Ayurveda: Pluralism and Paradigms*, ed. Dagmar Wujasktyk et al. (New York: SUNY Press, 2013), 315.
40. Within the field of quantum studies, "quantum biology" remains, even almost 30 years after Chopra's first proposals, but speculative: "Even those of us who make a career of studying these [quantum] effects," writes Vlatko Vedral, "have yet to assimilate what they are telling us about the workings of nature." Vlatko Vedral, "Living in a Quantum World," *Scientific American* (June 2011): 40.
41. Rambachan, *The Advaita Worldview*, 53.
42. Rambachan, *The Advaita Worldview*, 10, 17.
43. Rambachan, *The Advaita Worldview*, 100.
44. Chopra, *Quantum Healing*, 251.
45. Chopra, *Ageless Body*, 7.
46. Rambachan, *The Advaita Worldview*, 48.
47. Chopra, *Quantum Healing*, 2.
48. Chopra, *Quantum Healing*, 181, referencing Bohm's implicate order.
49. Chopra, *Quantum Healing*, 45.
50. Williamson, *Transcendent in America*, 9.
51. Chopra, *Quantum Healing*, 219.
52. Deepak Chopra, "The Reality of Abundance-Day 1 Meditation," from his 21 Day Meditation Challenge, "Creating Abundance," YouTube video 3:13, https://www.youtube.com/watch?v=Yq4k2gc0-j4. Also see Prashad, *Karma of Brown Folk*, 64.
53. Moses P. P. Penumaka, "Luther and Shankara: Two Ways of Salvation in the Indian Context," *Dialog* 45, no. 3 (2006): 260.
54. Rambachan, *The Advaita Worldview*, 111.
55. Keller, *On the Mystery*, 64.
56. Keller, *On the Mystery*, 63–64.
57. Peter C. Hodgson and Robert C. Williams, "The Church," in *Christian Theology: An Introduction to Its Traditions and Tasks*, ed. Peter C. Hodgson and Robert H. King, (Minneapolis: Fortress Press, 1994), 259.
58. Keller, *On the Mystery*, 32.
59. Keller, *On the Mystery*, 50.

60. Eckhart Tolle, *The Power of Now: A Guide to Spiritual Enlightenment* (Vancouver: Namaste Publishing, 2004), epigraph.
61. Claire Colebrook, *Deleuze and the Meaning of Life* (London: Continuum, 2010), 15.
62. Maharishi Mahesh Yogi, cited in Humes, "Maharishi Ayur-Veda," 313.
63. John Bowlby, *Attachment and Loss*, Vol. II: *Separation* (Basic Books, Inc., 1973), 182.
64. Chopra, *How to Know God*, 7–10.
65. Chopra, *How to Know God*, 2.
66. Chopra, *How to Know God*, 17.
67. Barbara Ehrenreich, *Bright-Sided: How Positive Thinking Is Undermining America* (New York: Picador, 2009), 122.
68. Chopra, *Quantum Healing*, 236, cf. 239.
69. Chopra, *Quantum Healing*, 218.
70. Nicolas Rose, "Normality and Pathology in a Biological Age," *Outlines: Critical Practice Studies* 1 (2001): 22.
71. Colebrook, *Deleuze and the Meaning of Life*, 42
72. Trent H. Hamann, "Neoliberalism, Governmentality, and Ethics," *Foucault Studies* 6 (2009): 37–59.
73. Williamson, *Transcendent in America*, 233.
74. Prashad, *The Karma of Brown Folk*, 2–3, 9.
75. Keller, *On the Mystery*, 114.
76. Keller, *On the Mystery*, 114.
77. See, for example, Paul Tillich's *The Courage to Be* (New Haven, Conn.: Yale University Press, 1952).
78. The concept of the "sweet exchange" is based on 2 Cor. 5:21 ("For our sake he became sin who knew no sin, so that we might become the righteousness of God"). The communication of attributes (*communicatio idiomatum*) is first posed in the *Epistle to Diognetus*, circa 130 CE: "O sweet exchange... O benefits surpassing all expectation! that the wickedness of many should be hid in a single righteous One, and that the righteousness of One should justify many transgressors!" (Chapter IX), http://www.earlychristianwritings.com/text/diognetus-roberts.html.
79. Sounds of Blackness, *Africa to America: the Journey of the Drum*, Perspective Records, compact disc, 1994.
80. Keller, *On the Mystery*, 59.
81. Keller, *On the Mystery*, 47.
82. Chopra, *Quantum Healing*, 192.
83. Hodgson and Williams, "The Church," 259.
84. Sharon V. Betcher, "Breathing through the Pain: Engaging the Cross as *Tonglen*, Taking to the Streets as Mendicants," chap. 3 in *Spirit and the Obligation of Social Flesh: A Secular Theology for the Global City* (New York: Fordham University Press, 2014).
85. Harvey Cox, "The Myth of the Twentieth Century: The Rise and Fall of 'Secularization,'" in *The Twentieth Century: A Theological Overview*, ed. Gregory Baum (Maryknoll, N.Y.: Orbis, 1999), 135–143.
86. Jürgen Moltmann, *The Spirit of Life* (Minneapolis: Fortress Press, 1992), 43.
87. Chopra, *Ageless Body*, 110.

15 Salvation in the After-Living

REFLECTIONS ON SALVATION
WITH JOSHUA RALSTON
AND SHARON BETCHER

Shelly Rambo

Leafing through introductory textbooks in Christian systematic theology, you will find discussions of salvation located in multiple places—under the topics of Christology (the nature and work of Christ), the "other" religions, and eschatology, the study of last or final things. Insofar as these primers orient elementary readers into knowledge of Christian faith, they set out the major points for theological discussion and debate. Eschatology often becomes the major landing point for discussions of salvation because the question of salvation is often framed in terms of ultimate ends. Under the doctrine of eschatology, soteriological discussions will circle around Jesus's saying, "I am the way, the truth, and the life," the eternal destiny of Christian believers, the fate of the cosmos, views about the afterlife—heaven, hell, and judgment, and universal salvation. In many strains of Christianity, salvation can be summarized in the question, "Are you saved?" to be followed by the question of destiny: "Do you know where you are going when you die?" While the discourse about salvation, found under eschatology, is speculative in nature (forecasting the future), these two questions target a kind of bottom-line apologetic approach. To be "saved" means to have certainty about your end, to have comfort in knowing that you will be with God, that you will be united with loved ones, and that all things will come to a good ending. This question of salvation projects into a future, evoking dread and hope, anxiety and comfort. There is affective weight to this question of ends, as one's personal destiny rests in the balance. Salvation, in Christian theology, is a very high stakes enterprise.

Given the claims that Christianity makes about Jesus as the Christ, and the account of ultimate ends, the challenge for comparative theology is apparent. Soteriology often represents the impasse to fruitful comparative dialogue. Comparative theology has turned attention away from an exclusive discussion of ends in its attempt to open up what has been a very soteriologically-driven study, as least from the perspective of Christian theology. When Christian theologians set out to address the question of the religious 'other,' the focus was on salvation. In fact, one of the distinguishing marks of comparative theology is that it has tried to move beyond the soteriological conundrum to open up a different basis for the study.[1]

Both Ralston and Betcher direct the conversation about salvation away from ends and thus detour from some of the major topics in the introductory textbooks. Instead of death and ends, they focus attention on life and means. Both authors approach salvation in terms of transformation, and the discourse of "ends" is refocused on the process of formation *in* faith. Ralston rightly notes that Christian theological engagement with other religions has centered on the question of the "possibility of salvation" for those outside of Christianity. There, salvation was identified as an end point, and the fate of Christian believers the central focus. Both authors speak about the path and process of salvation, focusing on the formation and transformation of the believer within this life. Thus, salvation is about a broader orientation to the life of faith. And the question becomes, then, how the religions orient believers in this path. In Betcher's iteration, she is interested in how the contemporary spiritual guru, Deepak Chopra, orients "seculars" in the path of self-fulfillment. Ralston refocuses attention on the use of the law in the transformation of the believer in both Islam and Christianity.

This turn to the *life* of faith to talk about salvation moves Christian theology into productive comparative territory. Directing attention to the spiritual path also reclaims an aspect of salvation that was lost in modern Christian thought when divisions between "spirituality" and "theology" were established. The arena of spirituality was concerned with formation and the arena of theology with matters of ultimate ends. The language of the Spirit and spirituality infuses these essays, and it offsets the exclusively Christological nature of soteriology. Conceiving of the work of the Spirit as salvific has been a challenge for Christian theology, and Ralston and Betcher counteract this by offering pneumatologically inflected insights.[2]

Highlighting major contributions of each author, this chapter will return to the question of "ends" because much of the on-the-ground engagement between the religions is still driven by the questions in the primers. While comparative theological engagements point to a constructive future and greater religious understanding and appreciation, the rise of religious fundamentalism tells another story, one about animosity between the religions. In many cases, violence between the religions is driven by soteriological visions of ends. The work of comparative theology has the potential to contribute to the work of interreligious peace building, and yet, in order to do so, it must return to questions of soteriological ends.

The Path of Salvation

The salvation question has been omnipresent in the Christian framing of the dialogue about the religions and is the "elephant in the room" in the three-fold categorization that Joshua Ralston names in the opening of his essay. Here, Ralston takes up the comparativist challenge of addressing salvation *otherwise*. He shifts focus from thinking about the "possibility of salvation" in other religions to the "way(s) that divine law functions on the road to salvation." By looking at two major thinkers within Christianity and Islam, Ralston moves *cautiously* in hopes of finding points of "mutual enrichment." If both traditions look at the *use* of the law, something else might emerge.

Each of the monotheistic religions positions its followers in relationship to divine law. They differ, however, in the function of the law in the life of the believer and the religious community. Beginning with reflections on the law in the Christian tradition, Ralston acknowledges the "ambiguous place of the law in the New Testament and the complicated legacy these texts have bequeathed to Christian traditions." While Ralston is working comparatively between Christianity and Islam, he interjects important commentary on the fraught relationship between Christianity and Judaism concerning divine law. He points briefly to the legacy of the law in the Christian scriptures, which does not provide a definitive word about the law; in its transmission, however, Christian theologians have "construct[ed] divisions, unintentionally or not, that denigrated the law, Judaism, or Islam." His aim, in reexamining one Christian theologian, John Calvin, is to diagnose this slippage in the function of the law within Christianity.

He focuses on John Calvin's third use of the law. This points to an inner use of the law in which the Spirit operates as guide and tutor, inscribing the laws into believers' hearts. This guiding function is consistent with Calvin's understanding of the Spirit and the process of sanctification. The Spirit inscribes the law on the believer's heart and guides believers into the process of faith. The question remains, then, of the relationship between this inner inscription and the external function of the law. Ralston finds potential in Calvin's third use of the law to move beyond the problematic division between grace and law.

Al-Ghazali, in his reforms, aims to counter complacency by re-orienting believers to the law in relationship to their daily pilgrimage (combining legal prescription and interior re-orientation). And Ghazali, Ralston suggests, provides a model, via Islam, for a more positive understanding of the law's function. Ghazali emphasizes the believer's process of preparation and the development of an interior life. Both Calvin and Ghazali are interested in the constructive formation of believers and provide discussions of the *practice* and *function* of the law in the life of faith. Both provide a more full-orbed understanding of how the law orients believers to God. And yet, the law's interior function is much more developed in Ghazali than in Calvin.

In reading the two together, Ralston aims to dispel the problematic associations of the law with legalism within both religions, and also points to a new interpretation of the law within Calvin as a way of rethinking the tensions between Christianity and Judaism. And yet, in Ghazali, the law is a gift in a way that Calvin's third use cannot fully affirm. There is something about the interaction between interior and exterior in Ghazali's work that Ralston thinks is important and can potentially provide a corrective to the ways in which Calvin's notions of law fail to move beyond division, even if the third use of the law points there.

Fear plays a role in the exercise of the law for both Calvin and Ghazali. But fear is functioning quite differently in the two thinkers, and this becomes important in Ralston's comparison between the two. Ghazali identifies fear as an important part of the transformation process. "Like Calvin," Ralston notes, "he [Ghazali] thinks that fear of God can be a motivating or correcting factor in the pursuit of piety." However, God's "conditional blessing" of the believer is the specter that haunts the spiritual path in Calvin's thought. In application, Ralston notes, there is often little distinction between the third use and the other two in Calvinist theology. Ralston insinuates that the proper appropriation between the internal and external is difficult to achieve. If there is fear that God's inscription may be written *lightly/tentatively* on the believer's heart, then it is difficult to see the external acts of the law as expressions of a "secure base" (using Betcher's language). If there is any cause for instability, the external expressions will always be seeking security and confirmation. Ralston demonstrates symmetry between internal and external in Ghazali's discussions of the law but Ralston implies that the symmetry may only be achieved if the believer experiences the secure love of God. Thus, for the believer in Islam, fear operates without the combination of "terror" and "conditional blessing." In the Christian process of transformation as set out by Calvin, fear is present and thus linked to the question of the nature of God and salvific "ends."

This raises the question of whether salvation in Calvin's thought is inevitably driven by ultimate ends. If the blessing of God is conditional, then the process of faith will be directed to securing one's end. The obsession with ends in the Christian discourse about religions may be a manifestation of an obsession with ends built into Christian theology at a fundamental level.

Sharon Betcher situates her discussion of salvation within the context of peril. Clips of neo-liberal politics, global economic fragility, and exploitation of the earth's natural resources flash throughout Betcher's reading of "time being." She presents a reading of our current moment. The central challenge, as she presents it, is to stay awake to these realities and to face them head-on. Spirituality must be cultivated in order to be resilient in a world in which existence is threatened from all sides. Spiritual technologies arise within this perilous context, but the life of faith is presented in Betcher as a full-throttle engagement with *everything*. The believer is not separated from the unbeliever in her essay, because the question posed to all Anthropocenes is whether we possess spiritual resilience and courage to live. Religious traditions provide ways of orienting persons, but the object of faith is more incidental in Betcher's discussion. She is less focused on particular assertions of belief and, instead, is interested in spiritual attunement and fortitude.

Betcher acknowledges the appeal of the popular spiritual guru Deepak Chopra, and explores his proposed path for living in the midst of peril. She does probing exegetical work with Chopra, showing his interpretive moves from the Vedic texts for a Western audience. Betcher provides a more texted and textured sense of how Advaita Vedanta translates into the territory of popular spirituality. Reading Chopra between Hindu scholar Anantanand Rambachan and Christian theology, she intends to provide a corrective on what Chopra offers the "cultured despisers,"[3] but she does so without disparaging his project. In fact, there is a subtle indictment of Christian theologies for not taking seriously the need for spiritual technologies.

What promise, what salvation, does he offer? As Betcher presents it, Chopra promises the following: freedom from organized religion, alternatives to religious "belief," consistency with scientific mindset, intensity, and depth. Working in relationship to Advaita Vedanta, Chopra places the Anthropocene in a particular relationship with the Infinite. Betcher outlines several dimensions of Chopra's vision, yet it is deeply troubling to her on several counts.[4] She is concerned that salvation is linked to cultural notions of wellbeing, namely that physical perfection and health become the ends toward which the spiritual path is directed. In this vein, the quest for truth is now replaced with the quest for health. Wedded with a western medical model, this spiritual path becomes indistinguishable from normative models of beauty and health promulgated in a capitalistic marketplace. It is the prosperity gospel in which wealth can be calculated in terms of medical success. The goal is to escape the limitations of finitude. This is not "awakening" but, instead, finding routes around the peril.

While she is critical of aspects of Chopra's project, she says that his path to self-fulfillment recognizes the importance of a "secure base" (drawing from psychologist John Bowlby, originator of "attachment theory") upon which to interpret "time being." Betcher is not critical of Chopra's move to respond to the spiritual hunger; if anything, she is critical of Christian traditions for not responding to it. Chopra is correct in his diagnosis, according to Betcher: "We suffer a spiritual malaise . . . We do not know how to affectively engage the gripping cynicism, even nihilism, that may be an outcropping of the loss of world teleology." The challenge that she sets out for Christian theologians is to affectively attend to life, to keep faithful to the world, even in its threatened state.

This diagnosis returns us to Ralston's assessment of Calvin and Ghazali, triggering the question: how well does Christian theology address negative affect and shape positive affect? Betcher affirms that we need spiritual technologies to develop the courage it takes to live in the world as time beings, but she is concerned about the individuated and market-driven technologies associated with Chopra. The Christian theological vision that Betcher points to requires the communal development of "psycho-social muscles." The spiritual muscles that we need to develop must be communal and socio-politically attuned. With this in mind, John Calvin's third use of the law might require a "follow-up" manual to the proclamation that the law is inscribed on one's heart. "Wakefulness," Betcher says, "shapes and conditions." How do you strengthen this heart muscle? How might that inscription take hold and weave a constitution that cannot just withstand peril but transform it?

Both authors present the Hindu and Islamic comparative partners as attentive to the development of the disposition needed to live, to sustain, and to endure—either in the life of faith or in contemporary society. In Christian theology, the doctrines of justification and sanctification present a vision of the work of Christ and Spirit in the life of the believer. Often the work of the Spirit is eclipsed, and yet Ralston and Betcher counteract this, appealing primarily to the Spirit. Betcher introduces the Spirit as corporate and corporeal. In her appeal to the Spirit, she challenges Chopra's Infinitizing Spirit, but also Christian theological tendencies to detach the Spirit from flesh.[5] Ralston notes that the third use of the law depends on the Spirit's work in the believer's heart. Ralston draws upon Calvin's image of the inscripted heart; God writes on the heart of the believer. The Spirit quickens, moves, and directs this heart. Ralston asks if we need an alternative imaginary to think about this use of the law: "We need a better account of the way that sanctification or growth in piety depends on law and grace, the body and the heart, works and faith—all of which find their source in the irrevocable gift of God." But perhaps the imagery needs to be extended rather than replaced. Pairing this with Betcher's pneumatology, we can ask: How does this heart come to the surface of the skin? How might empathy, compassion, and gratitude flow from such hearts? Betcher brings this heart to the surface, asking us to wear this heart on our fleshy sleeve.

Salvation in the Afterlife

They are huddled together in a room, afraid to go out. The doors are locked. It is unclear how long they have been there together, but it is the safest place they could think of to go. They are still grieving, concerned about the future, and they are unable to see beyond the ending that was his death. And suddenly, he appears to them out of nowhere. The first word he speaks to them is "Peace." This is a snapshot from the gospel account of Jesus's post-resurrection appearance to his disciples, narrated in the Gospel of John, interpretively inflected with the peril of the post-crucifixion context. This gospel is distinct for placing the accounts of Pentecost and resurrection together, meaning that the giving and receiving of the Holy Spirit is intermingled with the accounts of Jesus's resurrection appearances. It is a compelling scene in that Jesus addresses the affective state of the disciples before anything else, and it is in this context that he gives them the gift of the Holy Spirit. This creates new synergy between them, and they begin to express themselves differently. The first admonition is followed by instructions about forgiveness, linking peace to the challenging imperative about the nature of their life together. Before his death, he had promised that a Spirit (*parakletos*) would guide them into the afterlife, and that they would carry forward his teachings with the assistance of this advocate-spirit. But this is the *present* "afterlife," in which they will come to know the world differently now given his departure. It is Spirit-filled territory. But it is also the territory in which things are difficult to discern, in which Jesus's presence with them is unclear. Things are tentative.

In much Christian theology, the resurrection accounts are strongly linked to salvific ends and to what we could identify as Christian triumphalism. These narratives are secured and securing, and the tentative aspects are removed in interpretation. These post-resurrection scenes are read for the "bottom-line" claims they make about Jesus as the Christ. Thus, the event of the resurrection becomes the site for claiming the truth of Christian faith. The encounters with the disciples are important insofar as they come to recognize the miracle of his resurrection. Risen from the dead, he proves that he is not only man, but God. This is very consistent with John Calvin's commentary on the resurrection, in that Thomas's affirmation, "My Lord and my God," according to Calvin, clearly refutes Arius's heresy about the nature of Christ.[6] Thomas becomes the voice of Christian orthodoxy, and the interpretation of John 20 is folded into truth claims, claims that constitute the soteriological impasse to which Ralston refers.

In these narratives of Jesus's return-resurrection, the focus can quickly turn away from the sensory and affective aspects of the encounters and away from the "corporate" and "corporeal" pneumatology present there. These scenes are catapulted into the future—the vision of the resurrected Jesus is transported to the heavenly realm in which the Christ sits on the throne in a reconstituted paradise. And yet the Pentecost/resurrection scene directly speaks to the affective formation of a community still struggling with death and loss. In these accounts, the Spirit is a central actor in the process of forming a new community. Jesus returns to the disciples and continues to teach them. Interestingly, his identity as teacher falls away in interpretations of the resurrection accounts. Now the glorified Christ, the ordinariness of his movements with them and his continued teachings are supernaturalized, as if the glory of the afterlife has already carried him away.

To conceive of him as a teacher in this present afterlife, however, is important; he returns to teach them a way amidst endings. These post-resurrection accounts feature his affective re-orientation of the disciples, attuning them to the sensory and turning them to each other. While eschatology speaks about ultimate ends, it can also make room for the multiple ends and endings.[7] From these gospel accounts, we can begin to construct an alternative eschatology.

Trauma studies expanded the vocabulary of endings, opening up a space in which to think about how Christian theology might reengage the imagery of the afterlife to different "ends." The concept of the afterlife has taken on new meaning with the rise of trauma studies. An early essay by Jacques Derrida, "Living On," provided an extensive reflection on the word survival (*sur-vivre*). Resonating with post-Holocaust sensibilities, his play on the word (living after/living beyond/overliving) emphasized a thin and porous line between death and life. There is something of death that remains in life, that carries on, despite an ending.[8] What does it mean to survive, to witness, to live beyond a violent event that was intended to be a final end? The end narrated here is not a literal death, but, instead, a form of death-in-life in which persons must reconstitute their sense of the world and their connection to it. The terminology of the "new normal" signifies the recalibration of life in the aftermath of violence. But it is important to think about how eschatology, a study of ends, could also enter into re-conceptualizing life "after" or after-life. The visions at the end of each of the Christian gospels can teach us about endings.

Brain studies as a route into interpreting trauma has become a thriving area of research—Bessel van der Kolk, Alexander McFarlane, and Babette Rothschild are just a few who describe the impact of trauma on the brain. Neurobiological studies in trauma indicate that traumatic events impact us in such a way that our frontal lobe, the part of our brain responsible for high-level cognitive functioning, shuts down.[9] Given the impact and force of traumatic events, adaptive systems shut down. What has emerged is a significant shift in identifying the locus of the shutdown. Trauma lodges in our limbic system, the "alarm bell" of the brain that registers the emotions and sensations of the experience. Once sensations are registered in the limbic system, they transfer to the frontal lobe in order to be categorized and stored. The challenge is to re-engage this part of the brain, and experts in this area propose that conventional forms of talk therapy might be "talking past" the trauma rather than working with it. Insofar as the frontal lobe is the primary target of therapeutic work, trauma cannot be healed. By contrast, somatic therapies aim at the limbic system and work to restore a person's capacity to regulate affect. Unless the affective center—fight/flight—is attended to, the path to healing is obstructed. Working with affect regulation is critical to treatments focused in this direction.

Given the prevalence of the post-traumatic and the apocalyptic, I want to highlight the importance of this for *eschatology*. The doctrine of the last things is a doctrine that evokes fear. If we paired affects with each of the doctrines, fear and anxiety would accompany eschatology. Theologian Richard Mouw writes that while eschatology might be seen as the most speculative doctrine, he identifies it as the most pastorally pressing one.[10] The discourse about ends is about human ends, both individual and cosmic. The prospect of endings, whether a final end or more episodic endings, stirs powerful affects. The doctrine, pastorally conceived, works between fear and security, anxiety and comfort. Eschatological images of endings and the afterlife (heaven, hell, judgment, the saved, and the damned) are jarring. These images are not just concepts but, rather, have visceral effects, as they work on the level of image and imagination, rather than word and logic. Although many recognize it as a discourse that evokes fear, and certainly preaching on ends has demonstrated fear-inducing rhetoric, somatic studies of trauma turn us anew to the affective dimension of eschatology.

This is where the brain studies may prove provocative, not just for psychotherapy but for theology. The critique is that clinicians are misdirected in aiming at the frontal lobe to address trauma when the site of trauma is elsewhere—the limbic system. Perhaps theologians, as well, are aiming at the wrong part of the brain in the doctrine of eschatology. Eschatology, while charging the limbic system, has often become the discourse in which certainty, reason, and confirmation have been most asserted (most dogmatic). What if teachings about eschatology were re-directed to focus on the formation of the limbic system? In this sense, the doctrine will teach us strategies for living as "time beings." Eschatology, as a speculative doctrine, places us in uncertain territory.

We cannot know the end for certain. If it is true that fear, anxiety, and its counter-affects comfort and assurance are the affects that orient us to ends, perhaps Christian theologies of ends can provide orienting practices in the midst of uncertainties.

Interestingly, John Calvin thought that the doctrine of predestination, as he developed it, was a comforting doctrine. It resounded with this message: Your destiny is in God's hands. You do not know the end, but God knows it. If believers rested in the fact that God is in control of all things, they would be set free to live without concern for their ends. He tried to assure believers by appealing to the notion of God's benevolence and sovereignty. The logic may work, but the affect moves in a different way. Despite Calvin's intentions, this doctrine about the believer's destiny set followers on a path to secure salvation. Rather than resting in the assurance of God's benevolence toward us (Calvin's definition of faith), they sought to secure signs of their salvation. The irony is that the doctrine precipitated anxiety rather than alleviating it. The anxious theologian transmits the doctrine despite his cognitive intentions to do otherwise.[11] As Calvin's ideas were conveyed to subsequent generations, should its recipients be faulted for misinterpreting his doctrinal intent, or should Calvin be faulted for his ignorance about the full-orbed and holistic effects of his teachings on his followers? Ralston notes the challenge of interpreting the law as gift if God's blessing is "conditional." Thus, the nature of God is key here. The believer is told to trust unconditionally, and yet there is affective wisdom in refusing to trust under conditional circumstances. Calvin thus fails to grasp the affective dynamics of faith. Unless a believer affectively experiences love and trust, the third use of the law will revert to the other two uses. This is what Betcher is describing when she invokes the secure base.

Medieval theologian Julian of Norwich is known for the statement, "All will be well."[12] But she is also potentially misread here, as the statement can be deployed as a way of covering over terrible realities. It can operate as a "giant eraser for pain." And yet Julian's context prompted her to write amidst endings. Around her, things were threatened, falling apart, and coming undone due to illness, wars, and ecclesial corruption. The assertion, "All will be well" was not a declaration about ultimate ends, but about living in the midst of peril. Writing before Calvin, Julian presents a very compelling picture of God's sovereignty. God cares and love can be witnessed in the smallest things, such as the hazelnut. And yet Julian struggled to make sense of the Holy Church's account of God punishing persons for their sins. Did this teaching compromise the nature of God and the goodness of God's creation? she asked. If we think of Julian as interpreting theology from ends, from her deathbed, we can place this alongside the classic conversations about death and resurrection, most notably Macrina's teachings to Gregory about death and resurrection in *On the Soul and Resurrection*.[13] The perilous contexts for discussing a theology of ends may not be incidental but, in fact, be a model for eschatological reflection; perhaps it cannot be done from "commanding heights" but must be situated in the midst of endings.[14] We are reminded, then, that Julian's eschatological statement, "All will be well," is deployed within the context of a world coming undone. What concerns Julian is that the Church teachings about God's nature—mercy and justice—produce the kind of conditionality that Ralston narrates in the theology of John Calvin. They provide an insecure base for the believer. Her extensive working out of the question of whether humans are blameworthy for sin cuts directly to the question of God's nature but also is situated within a context of societal instability. The theological assertion that God is Love is, for Julian, the secure base—the saving knowledge—that grounds her as she faces a myriad of endings. It is not a cognitive assertion alone. Julian displays affective wisdom about how Church teachings will be received. If the conditionality is introduced, the insecure attachment, as psychologists call it, will be established.[15]

Soteriology has always been a high-stakes doctrine in Christian thought because of the peril of endings. With images of sinners dangling over the fiery pits of hell and cosmic courtrooms of judgment, it is not difficult to imagine how these images can operate internally, motivating actions and determining choices. These operations often take place at an unconscious level. Yet, in many sectors of Christianity, these images of the afterlife are rarely discussed. The images of heaven, hell, angels, and demons are associated with conservative forms of religion and fundamentalism. Because of disdain for how they are employed (against the religious "other"), many progressive Christians step away from the eschatological imagery altogether. Operationally, this dimension of eschatology is absent from the theological framework. One of the consequences is that the images, and the imaginary, are not activated at all. And yet these images are operating nonetheless, not only within circles of religious extremism but in the popular imagination—post-apocalyptic, cybernetic, dystopic visions of the world collapsing and recreating.

Eschatology runs a great risk in inciting fear and anxiety, but it can also be a prism through which to address fear and anxiety. If eschatology is the arena in Christian theology that teaches about ends, about last things, perhaps it should be identified as the arena of Christian thought that guides and instructs its students in how to live in the midst of uncertainty about endings—operating like boot camp for affect like resilience, courage, and perseverance. The Spirit guides and strengthens believers in the life of faith—to "keep faith with the world," as Betcher casts it. This is consonant with Betcher and Catherine Keller, her major Christian interlocutor in the essay. But moving one step beyond this: What if Christian eschatology was conceived as the limbic arena of theology, with the vision of the disciples huddled in the Upper Room as a narrative guide. Afraid to engage the myriad of realities outside the door, the disciples are in lock-down. Jesus appears in their midst, addressing their fear. The world as they know it is gone, he forecasted in his final words to them. And if we carry this into another post-resurrection account, the famous doubting Thomas account, we can think of Jesus, again, as the teacher, returning to teach his disciples how to tend to wounds. Look, he says. See the wounds. Touch them.

The arena of salvation is suddenly remapped in terms of endings, but it is a different configuration of eschatology. Eyes are turned to this newly constituted community, rising up, "awakening," in new relationship to the world around them, even as the grief of the previous world is still palpable. This theology of the afterlife provides an inroad to addressing critical questions: How do communities reconstitute in the aftermath of tragedy, loss, and endings? How might Christian theology circumvent the deployment of religious violence—working an alternative eschatological vision?

Comparative Aesthetics in the Afterlife (of Violence)

While comparative theologians carefully attend to the resonance between religious traditions, displaying a mode of engagement that is noncombative and constructive, this work is done amidst the rise of religious fundamentalisms and violence enacted in the name of God and often justified on the basis of soteriological ends. Apocalyptic visions encircle us. Psychoanalyst and cultural theorist Charles B. Strozer notes that the rise of the apocalyptic is not relegated to a few fanatics but has permeated the culture more widely, creating an ethos of "endism." Fear and anxiety about endings constitute the air that we breathe. Betcher narrates this well. The vision of a group huddled together with the doors locked could easily translate into a vision of apocalyptic dis-ease. Thus, it is important for comparative theologians to return to the questions that mark traditional soteriology—ultimate ends, exclusive claims to salvation.[16] It will be important to reengage the imagery of endings, and to re-approach soteriological ends, while also expanding attention to the path and process of salvation, as offered here. The invitation here is to reoccupy the imagery, to reclaim the discourse of the afterlife in Christian theology for the sake of "working through" fear.

The format for Christian theological engagement with religious "others" was often focused on dialogue. It was a discourse shaped in the era of ecumenical councils, in which religious representatives were selected to meet together to discuss critical points of difference and conflict. The model of engagement, dialogue, is directed at the frontal lobe. And yet the conversations about salvific ends were charging the limbic system. Just as neurobiological researchers are claiming that talk therapy is aiming at the wrong part of the brain in trauma healing, comparative theologians are pointing to the limits of cognitive modes of interreligious engagement. Scholars such as Michelle Voss Roberts and Francis X. Clooney are forefunners in the aesthetic dimensions of comparative theology, which examines modes of religious knowing that extend beyond cognition and reason into the realm of emotions.[17] Their work attends to aspects of religious traditions that were not previously considered within theologies of religious pluralism. They emphasize practices and performance above profession, taking seriously the full-orbed bodily engagement in matters of faith. In this sense, comparative theologians are bringing the fruits of spirituality and spiritual practices into a discourse that has been heavily focused on addressing competing religious claims via the exercise of reason.

The turn to aesthetics by comparative theologians is fruitful for re-envisioning on-the-ground religious engagement in a world charged by religious violence. I want to offer, here, a glimpse into comparative aesthetics enacted within the context of religious violence.

Christian theologians engaged in theologies of religious pluralism have been committed to interreligious understanding for a variety of reasons. But peacemaking is often an underlying goal. Religious differences can lead to violence, and the work to bring faith leaders together is often precipitated by situational violence. In a dialogue with Francis X.

Clooney, Paul Knitter expressed concerns about whether comparative theologians were skirting the central responsibilities of theology. Knitter, a leading figure in theologies of religious pluralism, worked in a mode of theological engagement across religions that gathered theologians from the various traditions around religious claims (truth claims) that represented key places of theological difference. Comparative theologians have changed the mode of engagement and, in Knitter's assessment, stepped away from the important work of reconciling these claims. Have the comparative theologians stepped away from the theological table? Yes and no, Clooney argues. What emerges in the conversation is the implication by Knitter that aesthetics is divorced from the center of theology and that aesthetics fails to move the religions. And yet it is precisely in the engagement with aesthetics that these comparative theologians locate the power of religion to move persons.

Art, music, dance, and poetry convey affective ways of knowing that can actually cross religious differences in a way that dialogue, as a mode of theology, cannot. They can move believers within religious traditions into greater devotion, but could potentially cut across the polemics of truth-claims. For example, in examining religious plurality within the traditionally Hindu devotional dance practices of Indian classical dance, Katherine Zubko notes the positionality of bodied experience to allow for truth-claims to co-exist or be more fluid depending on context. As she demonstrates through her case studies, the dancing body becomes an "epistemological site that enacts lived religious praxis that both cultivates particular religious identities and allows for fluidity outside of what appears as more rigidly and neatly drawn lines of belief systems."[18]

Thus, the contributions of comparative theologians to peace-building work should not be underestimated. They offer new modes of "revivifying" the primary questions of theology.[19] Similarly, the arena of religion and conflict transformation has also taken an aesthetic turn; scholars such as John Paul Lederach and Mary Elizabeth Moore have also emphasized the importance of aesthetics as a mode of peacebuilding.[20] Similar to the trauma researchers, they insist that you cannot talk your way to reconciliation and healing. The challenge is not to reason your way out of the situation but, instead, to reshape the moral imagination. People need to envision the future differently than the violent present; thus, the work of shaping imagination is eschatological work. Engaging in aesthetic practices works different muscles, strengthening heart and head for the work of transformation. What will save religions from killing each other, or deter the use of religious claims in perpetrating violence? To enact an alternative eschatology will involve developing capacities to imagine a world beyond the end of violence, to build a cosmic community in the traumatic aftermath.

Septemmy Lakawa is a missiologist and theologian teaching at Jakarta Theological Seminary in Indonesia.[21] Following a particular instance of Muslim-perpetrated violence within the Christian community of Duma in 2000, Lakawa set out to interpret the operative theology of the community in the aftermath.[22] Visions of the attackers setting fire to the church building as worshippers scrambled to escape were live within the testimonies of Christians living in the village; those inside watched the walls crumble from the mortar and smoke filling the sanctuary. While practices of hospitality between religious groups predated the incident, the violence forced the Christian community to reconstitute its life together, now that its collective self-understanding was "intertwined with its experience of communal violence."[23] According to Lakawa, the Christian community had to imagine new ways of living.[24] In this "new normal," it became important to assist the community in re-approaching the religious symbols that were no longer innocent. In her context, the Christian Bible, a sustaining resource in the life of faith, was also used as an instrument of harm, deployed against the religious other. The violence went both ways: The Dokulamo mosque was attacked by the Dumas during the violence. The "afterlife" involved reengaging the texts and symbols, recognizing their instrumentalization in religious violence and reclaiming their meaning. The symbols could not be traded in, but they would need to be re-approached, given their history.

Small acts of hospitality began to reemerge between Muslims and Christians within the community, from the gift of bamboo from the Dokulamos to build the Christian church, to practices of exchanging rice. The everyday practices of providing food and shelter were a way of reclaiming the violent scape. Lakawa was curious about how the community narrated the aftermath and how they drew upon aspects of Christian faith to work across lines of religious division, practicing what she calls "risky hospitality."[25] One of the questions undergirding her research is: What *forms* of faith enable the community to open to a different future and to imagine the world differently?[26] What builds these spiritual muscles?

Based on her research, Lakawa began to rethink the preparation of Christian leaders within her context. She began to incorporate the practice of prayer-dance into her teaching and into workshops within local churches. These collective movements, both freeform and structured, were Lakawa's way of weaving her knowledge of trauma into her interreligious work. Her creation of the prayer-dance as a collective movement through grief, anger, and despair, and into celebration, praise, and hope was grounded in the premise that embodied spiritual practices provide ways of working out the trauma. For many of the Christian leaders, the collective movement had the effect of helping them to reclaim the physical space, which, in many cases, had been the sites of violence. The visceral images of bullet-holes and carnage do not go away, unless they are counter-acted. The active movement provided a sense of agency that had been lost. The postures empowered.

In a fascinating reworking of her own field of study, missiology, Lakawa provides a route for her communities to reimagine and re-embody a future. While scholars were writing about religious difference and interreligious dialogue, Lakawa found that the context of the traumatic aftermath radically transformed the mode of study. The aftermath changed everything, and, in this case, "everything" also meant many of the assumptions central to her field of study. Aesthetics is not linear, she claims, and neither is the process of grief. The timeline for healing does not point forward; it is, instead, a tangled process in which the central challenge is to keep one's balance in the midst of the fluctuation. It is a dancing eschatology, employed against the violence wielded by another operation of soteriological ends.

Conclusion

Lakawa is teaching her community to live in the afterlife. For many who experience extreme violence, time is marked differently, often by the "before" and "after" of violence. Many of the spiritual teachers within the religious traditions identify the passions and emotions as the site of intense conflict; orienting oneself to them requires careful attention and discipline. Turning to the affective dimensions of the doctrines requires drawing more heavily on the insights of spirituality and therefore refusing the false divisions between theology and spirituality. This affective work is often exercised within a community, and, in some cases, it cannot be practiced alone. Comparative theologians widen the scope of community, urging us to think across religious traditions—to learn *how* to hear different tongues.

The most succinct and familiar claim of Christian faith—"Jesus saves"—fills billboards on American highways. This statement has come to represent a certain kind of Christianity and its claim to soteriological ends. It is often filled with certainty and definitive claims about the fate of unbelievers. There is little room for questions about the way, about the process of faith. Ralston and Betcher, attentive to comparative concerns, redirect us. Theologies of religions have tried to find ways of contending with these root claims, but a dimension of this has gone unattended: the ways in which these claims work on an affective and somatic level. Unless these are addressed, openness to the religious "other" cannot take place. When the resurrected Christ returns to the disciples following his death, he targets the fear, first speaking peace into their midst. This saving vision redirects eschatology to envision ways in the midst of fear, to witnessing to violent ends and recreating community in the midst of lockdown. This vision gives rise to another billboard message that springs up, inscribed on our hearts and in our actions, a claim to practice our way into . . . "Perfect love casts out fear" (1 John 4:18).

Notes

1. James L. Fredericks, *Faith among Faiths: Christianity and the Other Religions* (Mahwah N.J.: Paulist Press, 1999). See especially Chapter 8, "After Pluralism: Doing Theology Comparatively," 162–80.
2. For a helpful overview of the development of pneumatology in the Christian tradition, see Veli-Matti Karkkainen, *Pneumatology: The Holy Spirit in Ecumenical, International, and Contextual Perspective* (Grand Rapids, Mich.: Baker Academic Press, 2002). For a more comprehensive overview, see Yves Congar, *I Believe in the Holy Spirit*, 3 vols. Milestones in Catholic Theology series (New York: Crossroads Publishing, 1997).
3. Friedrich Schleiermacher, often referred to as the father of systematic theology, identified his audience as the "cultured despisers," those who would be critical of religion and understand themselves as standing outside of it. Friedrich Schleiermacher, *On Religion: Speeches to Its Cultured Despisers (Cambridge Texts in the History of Philosophy)* (Cambridge: Cambridge University Press, 1994).
4. These phrases reflect problematic outcomes of Chopra's thought, according to Betcher: "repristination of Cartesian dualism," "suits the mobile individuality of North American sociality," and "ageless body, timeless mind."
5. Betcher: "In Christian theology of Spirit, religious consciousness does not meditatively tap into the Infinite (as it does for Chopra), but is faithful to the finite. It cannot be said to be of a different order or essence of being than flesh."
6. See John Calvin's commentary on John 20:28. John Calvin, *Calvin's New Testament Commentary*, John 11–21, Vol. 5 (Grand Rapids, Mich.: William B. Eerdmans, 1995).

7. Charles B. Strozier provides a provocative diagnosis of contemporary culture, influenced by the rise of nuclear arms and, more recently, the events of September 11. He suggests that what he calls "endism" is within all of us, positioning us in a particular way to events of violence. Modifying his diagnosis, I suggest that we are exercising a fear of living without identifiable endings. Charles B. Strozier, *Apocalypse: On the Psychology of Fundamentalism in America* (Boston: Beacon, 1994); *Until the Fires Stopped Burning: 9/11 and New York City in the Words and Experiences of Survivors and Witnesses* (New York: Columbia University Press, 2011).
8. Jacques Derrida, "Living On," *Deconstruction and Criticism*, ed. Harold Bloom (New York: Continuum, 1980), 62–142. Also Derrida, "Rams: Uninterrupted Dialogue—Between Two Infinities, The Poem," Chapter 5 in *Sovereignties in Question: The Poetics of Paul Celan* (New York: Fordham University Press, 2005), 135–63.
9. David Emerson and Elizabeth Hopper write, "The cutting edge of trauma treatment today involves alternative and integrative intervention strategies that move beyond traditional verbal therapies." David Emerson and Elizabeth Hopper, *Overcoming Trauma through Yoga: Reclaiming Your Body* (Berkeley: North Atlantic Books, 2011). 17; Bessel van der Kolk, *The Body Keeps the Score: Brain, Mind, and Body in the Healing of Trauma* (New York: Viking Adult, 2014).
10. Richard J. Mouw, "Where Are We Going? Eschatology," in *Essentials in Christian Theology*, ed. William C. Placher (Louisville, Ky.: Westminster John Knox Press, 2003), 335–47. He writes, "Indeed, it is difficult to think of a branch of academic theology that has more direct relevance to the lives of ordinary believers than eschatology" (337).
11. William J. Bouwsma presents Calvin as an anxious theologian, arguing that his anxiety is key to interpreting his theology. William J. Bouwsma, *John Calvin: A Sixteenth-Century Portrait* (Oxford: Oxford University Press, 1987). See also: William Bouwsma, "John Calvin's Anxiety," in *Proceedings of the American Philosophical Society* 128, no. 3 (1984): 252–56.
12. Julian of Norwich. *Julian of Norwich: Showings* (Classics of Western Spirituality), trans. Edmund Colledge and James Walsh (Mahwah, N.J.: Paulist Press, 1977). See the Long Text, Chapter 32.
13. Gregory of Nyssa, *On the Soul and Resurrection* (Crestwood, N.Y.: St. Vladimir's Seminary Press, 1993).
14. Willie Jennings, *The Christian Imagination: Theology and the Origins of Race* (New Haven, Conn.: Yale University Press, 2010).
15. John Bowlby, *A Secure Base: Clinical Applications of Attachment Theory* (London: Taylor and Francis, 2005); Susan Goldberg, Roy Muir, and John Kerr, *Attachment Theory: Social, Developmental, and Clinical Perspectives* (Hillsdale, N.J.: Analytic Press, 2000); Laurence Heller and Aline Lapierre, *Healing Developmental Trauma: How Early Trauma Affects Self-Regulation, Self-Image, and the Capacity for Relationship* (Berkeley. Calif.: North Atlantic Books, 2012).
16. Exchange between Paul Knitter and Francis X. Clooney, Luce Summer Seminars, American Academy of Religion, November 16, 2012.
17. Michelle Voss Roberts, *Tastes of the Divine: Hindu and Christian Theologies of Emotion* (New York: Fordham University Press, 2014); Francis X. Clooney, *His Hiding Place Is Darkness: A Hindu-Catholic Theopoetics of Divine Absence* (Stanford, Calif.:

Stanford University Press, 2013). See also Katherine C. Zubko, *Dancing Bodies of Devotion: Fluid Gestures in Bharata Natyam* (Lanham, Md.: Lexington Books, 2014). Zubko does not identify as a theologian, but her work contributes to demonstrating how embodied experience in interreligious aesthetic encounters bypasses many of the walls of verbal dialogue.

18. Zubko, *Dancing Bodies of Devotion*, 4.
19. The language of revivifying is connected to the doctrine of sanctification, which is understood within Christian theology to focus on the work of the Holy Spirit in the life of the believer. The process of a believer growing into the new identity conferred on her by Christ (justification) is often referred to as "vivification."
20. John Paul Lederach, *The Moral Imagination: The Art and Soul of Building Peace* (Oxford: Oxford University Press, 2005); Mary Elizabeth Moore, *Teaching as a Sacramental Act* (Cleveland, Ohio: Pilgrim Press, 2004).
21. Septemmy Eucharistia Lakawa, *Risky Hospitality: Mission in the Aftermath of Religious Communal Violence in Indonesia*, Ph.D. diss., Boston University School of Theology, 2011. She writes: "This study underscores the importance of linking trauma, healing, and the Holy Spirit in further studies on mission and religious pluralism in the aftermath of religious communal violence" (xxi).
22. I am drawing a distinction here between operative and professed theology. Operative theology refers to the theology demonstrated in the practices of a community and can be witnessed at work in the particular situation, as opposed to the stated and formal theology recognized by a community.
23. Lakawa, *Risky Hospitality*, 92–93.
24. Lakawa, *Risky Hospitality*, writes, "The community's choice to return to the village and to rebuild its life there, its continuing efforts to reconnect with its Muslim neighbors, and its annual ritual on June 19, all embed the sense of sacredness in the community's daily life" (233).
25. Risky hospitality, as a model, "is an appropriate response to the Indonesian challenge of religious plurality, which is embedded in the Christian-Muslim relationship in the aftermath of religious communal violence" (Lakawa, *Risky Hospitality*, 3).
26. Religion scholar Marc Gopin targets a similar question in *Bridges Across an Impossible Divide: The Inner Lives of Arab and Jewish Peacebuilders* (Oxford: Oxford University Press, 2013). Working in areas of intractable conflict, Gopin became increasingly aware of the role of trauma in conflict work and the impact of trauma on peacebuilders. While much of international conflict work focuses on policy and dialogue, Gopin turned attention to the inner lives of peacebuilders. What form—and force—of spirituality can sustain people *in the midst of* conflicts when they witness multiple upheavals but are unable to see an end to the violence?

CONTRIBUTORS

SHARON V. BETCHER is an independent scholar, writer, crip philosopher, and farmer living on Whidbey Island, Washington. She is the author of two academic texts, *Spirit and the Politics of Disablement* (Fortress, 2007) and *Spirit and the Obligation of Social Flesh: A Secular Theology for Global Cities* (Fordham University Press, 2014) as well as chapters within many anthologies. Her theo-philosophical work engages the critical lenses of ecological, postcolonial, gender, and disability studies theory.

BEDE BENJAMIN BIDLACK is an Assistant Professor of Theology at Saint Anselm College in Manchester, New Hampshire. He publishes in the areas of comparative theology, Daoist studies, theological anthropology, interreligious dialogue, and philosophy. He is the author of *In Good Company: The Body and Divinization in the Thought of Pierre Teilhard de Chardin, SJ and Daoist Xiao Yingsou* (Brill, 2015).

WENDY FARLEY is a theologian at San Francisco Theological Seminary whose teaching and research interests include women theologians, religious dialogue, classical texts, contemporary ethical issues, and contemplative practices. Her recent books include *Gathering Those Driven Away: A Theology of Incarnation* (Westminster John Knox, 2011) and *The Thirst of God* (Westminster John Knox, 2015), which argues for the contemporary relevance of three medieval women contemplatives.

HOLLY HILLGARDNER is Assistant Professor of Religious Studies at Bethany College in Bethany, West Virginia, where she teaches a wide range of courses in religious studies and philosophy. Her academic interests include comparative theology, feminist theology, mysticism, and transformative pedagogies. Her forthcoming book is entitled *Longing and Letting Go: Hindu and Christian Practices of Passionate Non-Attachment* (Oxford University Press, 2016).

AMIR HUSSAIN is Professor of Theological Studies at Loyola Marymount University in Los Angeles, where he teaches about Islam and world religions. From 2011 to 2015, Hussain was the editor of the *Journal of the American Academy of Religion*. He is the coeditor for the fourth editions of *World Religions: Western Traditions*, and *World Religions: Eastern Traditions* (Oxford University Press, 2014) and the third edition of *A Concise Introduction to World Religions* (Oxford University Press, 2015). He also authored an introduction to Islam: *Oil and Water: Two Faiths, One God* (Copper House, 2006).

KRISTIN BEISE KIBLINGER is Associate Professor of Religious Studies and Director of the International and Global Studies Program at Winthrop University in South Carolina. Her recent work includes "Comparative Theology as Repeating with a Difference: Deconstruction, Yogacara Buddhism, and our Conditioned Condition" in *Harvard Theological Review* and a chapter in *Twenty-First Century Theologies of Religions: Retrospection and New Frontiers* (Rodopi, 2016).

JEFFERY D. LONG is Professor of Religion and Asian Studies at Elizabethtown College in Elizabethtown, Pennsylvania. He is the author of *A Vision for Hinduism: Beyond Hindu Nationalism* (Tauris, 2007), *Jainism: An Introduction* (Tauris, 2009), the *Historical Dictionary of Hinduism* (Scarecrow Press, 2011), and the forthcoming *Indian Philosophy: An Introduction*, along with a companion reader of primary sources. He is an active member of the Hindu community in North America.

MARIANNE MOYAERT is a Professor at the Free University of Amsterdam (VU Amsterdam), where she holds the Fenna Diemer Lindeboom Chair in Comparative Theology and the Hermeneutics of Interreligious Dialogue. She has recently authored *In Response to the Religious Other: Ricoeur and the Fragility of Interreligious Encounters* (Lexington, 2014) and edited (with Joris Geldhof) *Interreligious Dialogue and Ritual Participation: Boundaries, Transgressions and Innovations* (Bloomsbury, 2015). Her research focuses on the hermeneutical, ethical, and theological presuppositions of interreligious dialogue.

HUGH NICHOLSON is Associate Professor of Theology at Loyola University Chicago. His first book, *Comparative Theology and the Problem of Religious Rivalry* (Oxford University Press, 2011), theorizes the field of comparative theology and attempts to reconcile the ideal of religious tolerance with a recognition of the extent to which religious identity is constructed by mobilizing religious difference. His most recent book project is *The Spirit of Contradiction in Christianity and Buddhism* (Oxford University Press, 2016).

ELAINE PADILLA is Assistant Professor of Constructive Theology at New York Theological Seminary. Her theological analysis constructively interweaves current philosophical discourse with Christianity, Latin American and Latino/a religious thought, mysticism, ecology, and gender. She is the author of *Divine Enjoyment: A Theology of Passion and Exuberance* (Fordham University Press, 2015) and coeditor of a three-volume project with Peter C. Phan, *Theology and Migration in World Christianity* (Palgrave Macmillan, 2013–15).

JOSHUA RALSTON is Lecturer in Muslim-Christian Relations at the School of Divinity, University of Edinburgh. He was a coeditor, with Susanna Snyder and Agnes Brazal, of *Church in the Age of Global Migration: A Moving Body* (Palgrave Macmillan, 2016). His forthcoming monograph, *Law and the Rule of God*, leverages political theology and comparative theology to engage longstanding debates over the place and function of law, both public and divine, in Muslim-Christian relations.

SHELLY RAMBO is Associate Professor of Theology at Boston University School of Theology. Her research and teaching interests focus on religious responses to suffering, trauma, and violence. She is the author of *Spirit and Trauma: A Theology of Remaining* (Westminster John Knox, 2010) and *Resurrecting Wounds: Living in the Afterlife of Trauma* (Baylor University Press, forthcoming 2017), which explores the significance of resurrection wounds within the Christian tradition and as it meets contemporary expressions of post-traumatic life in the broader culture.

KLAUS VON STOSCH studied Catholic Theology, Philosophy, and Economics in Bonn (Germany) and Fribourg (Switzerland). He completed his Ph.D. on Wittgenstein in 2001 and his habilitation on the Divine Action Debate in 2005, both in Catholic Theology. He is now professor of Systematic Theology and head of the Center for Comparative Theology and Cultural Studies at the University of Paderborn, Germany.

JON PAUL SYDNOR is Associate Professor of Theology and Religious Studies at Emmanuel College in Boston, where he teaches world religions, interreligious relations, and science and religion. He writes in the areas of comparative theology and theology of religions and is the author of *Ramanuja and Schleiermacher: Toward a Constructive Comparative Theology* (Pickwick, 2011). Sydnor is theologian-in-residence at Grace Community Boston, an emergent, progressive Christian gathering pastored by his wife, Reverend Abigail A. Henrich.

TRACY SAYUKI TIEMEIER is Associate Professor of Theological Studies at Loyola Marymount University in Los Angeles. She is the author of numerous articles on comparative theology, interreligious dialogue, and their intersections with gender and culture. She has also edited a volume entitled *Interreligious Friendship after Nostra Aetate* (Palgrave Macmillan, 2015) with James L. Fredericks. Tiemeier is co-chair of the Los Angeles Hindu-Catholic Dialogue.

MICHELLE VOSS ROBERTS is Associate Professor of Theology at Wake Forest University School of Divinity. She is the author of *Dualities: A Theology of Difference* (Westminster John Knox, 2010) and *Tastes of the Divine: Hindu and Christian Theologies of Emotion* (Fordham University Press, 2014), which received the American Academy of Religion's Award for Excellence in the Study of Religion. Her current book project, *Body Parts: A Theological Anthropology* (Fortress Press), explores the image of God in humanity via conversation with Kashmir Saivism.

INDEX

Abraham, 69, 70, 264
aesthetics, 96–98, 102, 103, 128, 130, 143*n*3, 158, 288; in comparative theology, 308–11, 312
agency, 136, 141, 178–80, 184*n*16, 312. *See also* power
al-Ghazali, Abu Hamid 256, 257, 265–69, 270–72, 299, 301
analogy, 32, 50, 211
anatman, 25, 33–34
Anselm, 9
anti-Judaism, 216, 222, 231, 243, 244, 248, 250*n*5, 257, 270; and John Chrysostom, 248
anti-Semitism, 222, 249, 250*n*5
apocalyptic, 305–9
apologetics, 239–43, 296
Arian controversy, 246–48, 303
asceticism, 138, 151, 158, 170*n*47, 179–80, 182, 187–88
Athanasius, 246–48
atman, 278–81, 285
Atmarupananda, Swami, 119
atonement, 219, 232, 234, 256
Attar, 93–95, 99, 128
Augustine, 28, 135, 143*n*3, 144*n*12, 149, 261, 270
Aurobindo, 115
Auschwitz, 223, 225, 227, 232, 242
avidya, 114, 116, 131, 280
ayurveda, 276, 279, 281, 285

Barth, Karl, 29, 273*n*31
Bauman, Zygmunt, 275

beauty, 128–30; divine, 95–98; and terror, 95–98
Bentley, Jerry, 187
Berdyaev, Nicolas, 144*n*12
Bhagavad Gita, 110, 116, 117
birth narrative, 196–97, 199–203, 207, 209, 212, 238, 239, 243
bliss, 278–79, 286, 287, 291
Block, Rory, 126
Blumenthal, David, 128
body, 151, 159, 162, 181–83, 286; denigration of, 265, 270–71; and health, 279–81, 310
Boko Haram, 136, 257
Bouwsma, William J., 314*n*11
Bowlby, John, 285, 301
Bracken, Joseph A., 48
Brahman, 109, 110, 118, 123; as Spirit, 278, 280, 281, 285
Brahmo Samaj, 112
bridal imagery, 153–54, 175, 182
Burkhart, Louise M., 60
Butler Bass, Diana, 1
Benedict XVI (pope), 175–76

Calvin, John, 135, 256, 261–65, 269–72, 298–303, 306, 307
Caputo, John D., 66–84
Cargas, Harry, 222
categories, 7, 12–13
Chopra, Deepak, 275–92, 296, 300–2
Christology, 202, 219–20, 238, 248, 303; and Judaism, 216, 221, 222–27, 231–34, 242;

Christology (cont.)
   high and low, 211–12, 241; Logos, 245–46; maximalism, 244–47
Cilappatikaram, 176–80, 181, 183, 186
Clooney, Francis X., 3, 6, 7, 8, 9, 103n2, 104n3, 108, 309–10
Coakley, Sarah, 182
Colebrook, Claire, 284
colonialism, 49–50, 62, 82, 196, 249. *See also* imperialism
comparative religion, 5
comparative theology, 2–6, 23–24, 108–9, 173–74, 185, 239, 240, 249, 308–13; and constructive theology, 3–6, 9–10, 16, 24, 42, 109, 142, 150, 216; method, 8–15, 31, 41–42, 126–27, 256; and pastoral theology, 24, 42, 89, 305; and similarity, 195–96, 212; and theology of religious pluralism, 5, 255–56, 296–98, 309–10; and truth, 75–76, 89, 310
compassion, 117, 119, 128, 131–32, 141, 143, 202
complaint: theodicy as, 93–94, 101
conditioning, 67–71, 74, 75–79, 81–83, 277
Connolly, William E., 65n38
construction, 74, 82, 137, 142
contemplation, 131–32, 138
Cornille, Catherine, 17
courtly love, 153–56, 189
creation, 47, 56–57, 59–61, 62, 115, 128, 143n3, 279. *See also* differentiation
cross, 100–1, 223–27, 232

Dao, 197, 201, 209, 239
darkness, 53–54, 57–61, 78–79. *See also* Tezcatlipoca
D'Costa, Gavin, 255
deconstruction, 68, 74, 76–77, 81
Derrida, Jacques, 63n9, 68, 304
desire, 150–51, 157, 158, 162, 164, 167, 182. *See also* love
detachment, 287
Dhand, Arti, 178
dialogue, 5, 126–27, 309–10
difference, 31, 33, 37–38, 40–41, 77, 163
differentiation, 51, 57, 58, 59–61, 82, 82. *See also* creation
diversity: religious. *See* pluralism: religious

divine embodiment, 196, 197, 205–6, 213n1, 239
Dostoevsky, Fyodor, 92, 128, 230
dualism, 30, 72, 114, 288–89. *See also* two-worlds doctrine
Dunne, John, 17
dynasty: Han, 197, 204; Tang, 205, 214n36; Wei, 196–98, 209–10; Zhou, 198, 201, 204

Eckhardt, A. Roy, 226
Eckhart, Meister, 144n10, 240
Ehrenreich, Barbara, 285
emptiness. *See sunyata*
eros: as desire, 151, 188; as love, 99; as communion with God, 150, 151, 158–60, 165, 166. *See also* love
eschatology, 108, 123, 134–35, 225–26, 266, 296, 304, 305, 307, 308, 310
Ess, Josef von, 256
ethics, 114, 137, 227–31, 282
evil, 89, 107, 109, 113, 126, 127, 139, 230; gratuitous, 91; moral, 113, 116, 121; natural, 113, 116; and separation, 114–15; source of, 114, 116
exclusivism, 3, 232, 255

faith, 98, 155; faithful infidelity, 76; noble unfaith, 150, 153–56
Farley, Wendy, 167n7
Fatima, 96–97
fear: of God, 268–69, 299–300; and anxiety, 308–9. *See also* terror
feminism, 82, 173
Feuerbach, Ludwig, 74, 85n38
finitude, 42, 67, 230, 274, 282–84, 289–92. *See also* conditioning
fins amour. See courtly love
fiqh, 265–67. *See also* law
Florentine Codex, 47, 49–52, 55, 60, 82
Francis (pope), 180–81, 187
Fredericks, James, 2, 5
Fredriksen, Paula, 7
free will, 90, 92, 99, 101–2, 108, 122, 128, 133, 135–38, 140
freedom, 40, 47, 121, 133, 135–38, 140, 211
fundamentalism, 257, 298, 307–8

gender, 172–74, 179, 188; and bodily power, 181–83; complementarity, 174, 175–76, 180–83, 188; and ritual power, 181–83; and virtue, 176–83
gnosticism, 24, 34, 247
God: as call, 68, 69, 72, 75, 78; as event, 70, 71, 74, 75, 79; and jealousy, 99, 103, 129; as love, 31, 95, 282–83, 307; as sacred mystery, 50, 54, 58–62, 78; suffering of, 224–25; weakness of, 70, 75, 84
Godforsakenness, 224–27
Gopin, Marc, 315*n*26
Gregory of Nyssa, 140, 144*nn*7,12, 307
Griffin, David Ray, 107–9, 120–22, 133, 135
Gschwandtner, Christiana M., 66, 78

Hadewijch, 150–56, 160–61, 163–67
Hallaq, Wael, 273*n*18
Hanson, R. P. C., 251*n*23
Hardy, Friedhelm, 158
Hasker, William, 90, 91
Hegel, Georg Wilhelm Friedrich, 42, 115, 226, 277, 282
hegemony, 6–8, 50, 76–78, 109, 167, 245, 246
Heim, S. Mark, 255
Hick, John, 4, 107–9, 119–20, 122, 133, 135, 143*n*3, 255
Hill Fletcher, Jeannine, 255
Hindu-Inspired Meditation Movements, 275, 276, 281, 284, 287
Holocaust. *See* Shoah
Hong, K. P., 275
hope, 40, 108, 122, 224, 225, 268–69
Huahu jing, 196–200, 203, 204, 211, 212, 239–42, 243
Hurtado, Larry, 244, 250*n*11
hybridity: religious, 13, 171, 275, 277

ignorance, 133. *See also avidya*
image of God, 28, 31, 34–35, 39, 137, 141, 173
immanence, 67, 71, 201
imperialism, 76–77, 113, 142, 208. *See also* colonialism; hegemony
impermanence, 26, 39, 73, 81. *See also* finitude

inclusivism, 3, 50, 255
interdependence, 30, 37, 39–41, 42, 71–74, 80, 81, 82, 163, 288–89, 292
Interfaith Youth Core, 1
Irenaeus, 133, 143*n*6
Isaiah, 216, 218, 221, 239, 242
Ishvara, 109, 123
Israel, 220, 222, 243

James (Epistle of), 259, 260
Jantzen, Grace, 134
Jesus, 199, 238, 240, 282–83, 296, 302–4, 308; in Islam, 101, 186, 187; and the law, 258–60, 271; as lord, 204, 207–9; as Messiah, 204, 207–9, 219, 221, 231, 234, 238, 243–45; titles of, 202–3, 206–12
jinn, 188
Job, 93, 102, 103, 128, 142, 220
John (Gospel of), 138, 245, 282, 302
John Paul II (pope), 174–75, 186–87
Jones, Serene, 261
Julian of Norwich, 144*nn*7,10, 306–7
justification, 257, 259, 302
Justin Martyr, 245–46, 261

Kaṇṇaki, 176–80, 181
Kant, Immanuel, 91, 93, 94, 101, 290–91
karma, 176, 178, 179, 180
Karma Yoga, 116–19
Kavunti, 176–77, 179–80, 182
Keats, John, 133, 135
Keenan, John, 19*n*16
Keller, Catherine, 48, 277, 278, 283, 287, 289, 308
Kermani, Navid, 90–103, 126, 127–30, 135, 140–143
Knitter, Paul, 4, 255, 310
Kreiner, Armin, 90
Krishna, 123, 157–61, 164

LaCugna, Catherine Mowry, 39
Lakawa, Septemmy, 311–12
lament, 58, 93–94, 128
Laozi. *See* Lord Lao
Latour, Bruno, 74

law, 256–58, 296, 298–300; and John Calvin, 261–65; and grace, 262, 269–71, 299; as guide/tutor, 262–64, 266, 271; natural, 90–92, 102, 136; in New Testament, 258–61
Lederach, John Paul, 310
Leiber, Jerry, 47
León-Portilla, Miguel, 52, 54
Levinas, Emmanuel, 77, 137, 138, 140, 227–31, 233–34, 243
Lewis, Bernard, 97
Lord Lao, 196–98, 201–6, 209–12, 239–41
love: for neighbor, 229, 259–60, 266, 287–88; God's, 98, 99, 129, 130, 133, 258, 268–69; God as, 31, 95, 282–83, 307; as longing, 149–52, 155–67; as *Minne*, 153–56
Lubac, Henri de, 240
Luke (Gospel of), 198–200, 202–3, 206–8, 238, 239, 241, 243
Luther, Martin, 261–63, 270, 275, 282, 287

McDougall, Joy Ann, 37
Macrina, 307
Maffie, James, 52, 65*n*38
Maharishi Mahesh Yogi, 276, 280, 285, 286
Marcos, Sylvia, 62, 64*n*20
Mary Magdalene, 180–81, 283
Mary, 69–70, 171, 174–76, 180–83; in Islam, 186–87; as mother, 174–75, 182. *See also* virginity
materialism, 71, 73, 80, 120, 275, 279, 289
meditation, 278–79, 281, 287, 291, 292
Menocal, María Rosa, 189
mercy, 102, 258, 268, 272
Messiah: in Christianity, 199–204, 206–9, 211, 212, 219–20, 225–27, 234; in Islam, 187; in Judaism, 208, 209, 220–21, 226, 231
Metz, John, 227
Minne. *See* love: as *Minne*
Mirabai, 150–52, 157–67
Moltmann, Jürgen, 27–28, 31–32, 38–39, 83, 223–27, 232, 242–43, 292
Moore, Mary Elizabeth, 310
Mouw, Richard, 305
Muhammad, 96–97, 257, 267

mysticism, 94–95, 100, 102, 153–55

Nagarjuna, 25–27, 28, 30, 31, 33, 80, 83
nature, 201, 203, 211
Nazism, 222, 228, 242
negative theology, 84*n*5, 153
neoliberalism, 286, 300
nepantla, 47, 51, 59–61, 81
Neville, Robert Cummings, 6, 7
Newman, Barbara, 153, 168*nn*11,12
Nezahualcóyotl, 54, 61
Nicene Creed, 46, 58, 244, 247–48
Nicholson, Hugh, 6
nirvana, 26, 255
non-attachment, 152, 164, 165, 167; critique of, 288; passionate, 151, 153, 156, 158, 166
non-dualism, 30, 33, 102–3, 111–12, 119, 279, 283
non-violence, 140, 144*n*7, 230
no-self. *See anatman*

obedience, 261, 266, 269
omnibenevolence, 108, 122
ontotheology, 70–71, 79
operative theology, 311, 315*n*22
oppression, 94, 95, 96, 102, 128, 220, 221
optimism: Christian, 221, 223; cosmic: 120–22, 132
orientalism, 287
Otto, Rudolf, 240
Ozeki, Ruth, 274

Panikkar, Raimon, 5
Pannenberg, Wolfhart, 255
parousia, 199, 208, 210, 211, 225. *See also* eschatology
passions, 136–37, 144*nn*12,13, 288
patriarchy, 139, 140, 142
Paul, 27, 259–60, 264, 270, 274
peace: building, 298, 302–3, 309–13; Great Peace, 204–5, 210–11
Pechilis, Karen, 157
Penumaka, Moses P. P., 282
perichoresis, 38, 39
phenomenology, 69, 75, 79, 80
pluralism, 119–120, 255–56. *See also* Hick, John

pluralism: religious, 112, 271, 309–10; as context for theology, 1–2, 8–15, 150–51, 238, 244, 248–49, 277–78; theology of, 5, 6, 77, 255–56, 309, 313
pneumatology, 296, 302, 303
polemics, 197, 209, 212, 222, 239–48, 256, 310
postmodernism, 66, 74, 78
power, 3, 40, 176, 243, 274, 283, 286, 292; as domination, 130, 139–41
practices: spiritual, 124n6, 129, 131–34, 183, 244, 256, 264, 274, 288, 291–92, 309–12. *See also* asceticism
Prashad, Vijay, 287
pratitya-samutpada, 25–26. *See also* interdependence
privilege, 36
process theology, 48, 56, 80, 107, 122, 133, 290
protest: against God, 93–95, 102, 128, 141; against violent theology, 142

quantum theory, 280, 284, 285, 288–89, 294n40
Qur'an, 102, 128, 185–89; and aesthetics, 96–98; as speech of God, 93–94

Rabi'a al-'Adawiyah of Basra, 188
Rahner, Karl, 29, 46–48, 55, 103
Ramadan, Tariq, 257
Ramakrishna, 107–9, 112, 113, 116, 117, 124n6, 131
Rambachan, Anantanand, 276, 277, 279–83, 292, 300–1
relationality, 29–31, 33, 35–36, 53, 71, 150, 166; interreligious, 42
responsibility, 62, 70, 80, 211, 228–31, 234; divine, 94, 121–22, 130; responsibilization, 286
resurrection, 302–4, 307–8
Revival of the Religious Sciences, 265–69
Ricoeur, Paul, 51, 130
Rig Veda, 279
Rilke, Rainer Maria, 143n5
risk, 24, 36, 42, 49–51, 57, 70–71, 77–79, 91, 289, 311
Roman Catholic Church, 171–73, 180–83, 186
Ruether, Rosemary Radford, 216, 232, 243–44

Sagahún, 49, 52
salvation, 210, 212, 220, 240, 255–61, 270, 271, 275, 278, 286, 287, 296–301, 308. *See also* theology of religious pluralism
samsara, 26, 30, 123
Sanatana Dharma, 111
sanctification, 257, 270–71, 299, 302, 315n19
Sarada Devi, 119, 124n13
sati, 184n16
savior, 202–6; Jesus as, 206–9, 238–39
Schleiermacher, Friedrich, 133, 144n7, 313n3
science, 276, 277, 279, 281, 284, 301
Second World War, 223–24
self, 150, 160–66, 274–75, 276, 286, 291. See also *atman*
self-disclosure: divine, 46, 47, 56, 58
service, 117–19, 229
sexism, 171–74, 183; and heteronormativity, 182, 183. *See also* gender
Shankara, 111, 240, 282
shari'a, 256, 257, 265–69, 272
Sherma, Rita, 10
Shiji, 198, 201
Shoah, 216, 222–23, 227, 231–34, 239, 242–43, 248, 304
Shulman, David Dean, 157
Siddiqui, Mona, 269
sin, 114, 173, 232, 262, 264, 268, 272
Smith, Wilfred Cantwell, 190
social justice, 130, 181, 211, 291
solidarity, 95, 102, 128, 167, 287
soteriology, 210, 255, 262, 274, 281, 283, 284, 291, 296, 307, 309, 312
soul, 33–37, 291
Sounds of Blackness, 288
Spector, Phil, 47
Spirit, 259, 260, 270, 271, 277–78, 282–84, 286, 289–92, 296, 302, 308; and Brahman, 278, 280, 281, 285; Holy Spirit, 27, 41, 257, 264, 299, 303; and Tezcalipoca, 56
"spiritual but not religious," 275, 277
Stosch, Klaus von, 8
string theory, 281
Strozer, Charles B., 308, 314n7

suffering, 91–95, 101, 107–9, 113–19, 126, 127, 131, 132, 139, 141, 220, 224–25, 280, 287; as transformative, 107, 120–21, 133–34; vicarious, 218, 219, 222, 232
Suffering Servant, 216–18, 222, 227–34, 239; Christian interpretations, 219–20, 242–43; Jewish interpretations, 220–21, 232–33
Sufism, 99, 124n6, 188, 267
sunyata, 25–27, 28, 29, 31, 33, 37, 38, 42, 80, 81, 83
supercessionism. *See* triumphalism
svabhava, 26, 33, 36, 39, 42, 81
systematic theology, 2, 3, 11, 13–14, 223, 227, 277, 296

Teilhard de Chardin, Pierre, 215n59, 283
teotl, 47–48, 52, 53, 64n12; teotlizing, 47, 51, 59–61, 81
Teresa of Avila, 137–38, 144n10
terror, 95, 97, 99, 128–30
Tezcatlipoca, 47, 53–56, 60–61
Thatamanil, John J., 19n27
theodicy: and free will, 89–91; practical, 93–94, 101–2
theological anthropology, 139, 152, 173–74, 182, 189
theological education, 1, 2, 4, 11–12, 311–12
theology of perhaps, 71, 78, 84
theology of religious pluralism, 5, 6, 77, 255–56, 309, 313; and comparative theology, 296–98, 309–10
theopoetics, 81, 278, 284, 288–91
Thompson, Richard, 189
Tolle, Eckhart, 275–76, 284
Tracy, David, 3
transcendence, 54, 57, 71, 120, 201, 207, 284, 286–87, 292; through meditation, 276
transformation, 107, 296. *See also* suffering
trauma, 242, 274, 304–5, 309, 310

Trinity, 41, 56, 224, 226, 247–48; social, 27–28, 30–33, 40, 83
triumphalism: Christian, 12, 221–22, 223, 226, 231–33, 234n3, 242–43
two-worlds doctrine, 71, 72–73, 80

Umar, 96–97
uniqueness: of Christ, 196, 203, 209, 212, 238–41
Upanishads, 110, 114–15, 276, 277

Vedanta, 107, 110–13, 115, 118, 122, 123, 127, 131–35, 138, 141, 240, 279; Advaita, 276–78, 280, 282, 285, 288, 290–92, 300–1
Vidyasagar, Ishwar Chandra, 116
violence, 131, 139, 140, 236n39; religious, 309, 311–12; sexual, 129–31, 140, 171
viraha-bhakti, 150, 157–65
virginity, 174–75, 182; and chastity, 176–80; virgin birth, 201–3
virtue, 176–83, 204, 269
Vivekananda, 107–9, 111, 113–15, 117–19, 122, 131, 134
Voss Roberts, Michelle, 309
Vrajaprana, Pravrajika, 114

wakefulness, 274, 282, 292, 301–2, 308
Ward, Keith, 5
Whitehead, Alfred North, 383
Wiesel, Elie, 128, 224, 226–27
Wildman, Wesley, 7
Williamson, Lola, 281, 287
women's ordination, 181–83
world: as moral gymnasium, 118–19, 123, 126, 132–34; salvation within, 210–12, 221, 231

Zubko, Katherine, 310

COMPARATIVE THEOLOGY: THINKING ACROSS TRADITIONS

Loye Ashton and John Thatamanil, *Series Editors*

Hyo-Dong Lee, ***Spirit, Qi, and the Multitude: A Comparative Theology for the Democracy of Creation***

Michelle Voss Roberts, ***Tastes of the Divine: Hindu and Christian Theologies of Emotion***

Michelle Voss Roberts, ed., ***Comparing Faithfully: Insights for Systematic Theological Reflection***

www.ingramcontent.com/pod-product-compliance
Lightning Source LLC
Chambersburg PA
CBHW030433300426
44112CB00009B/985